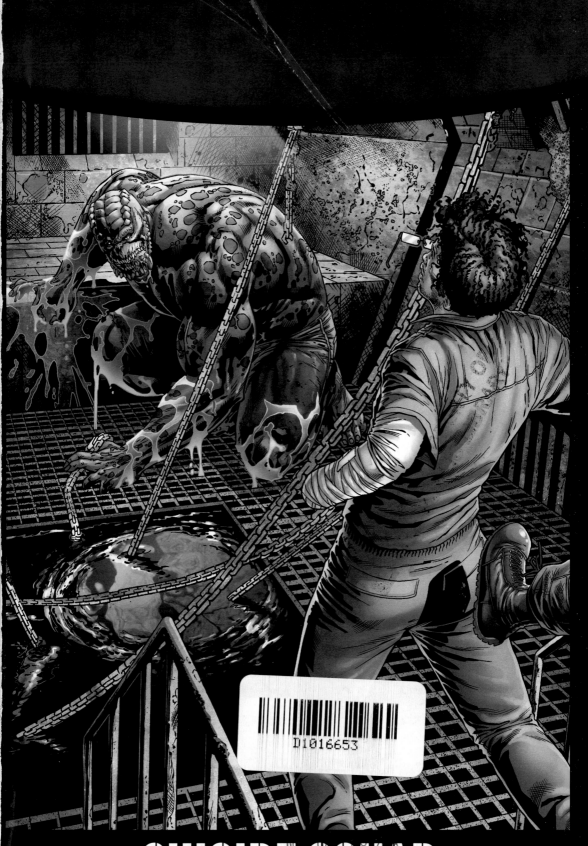

SUICIDE SQUAD

VOL.7 DRAIN THE SWAMP

D1016653

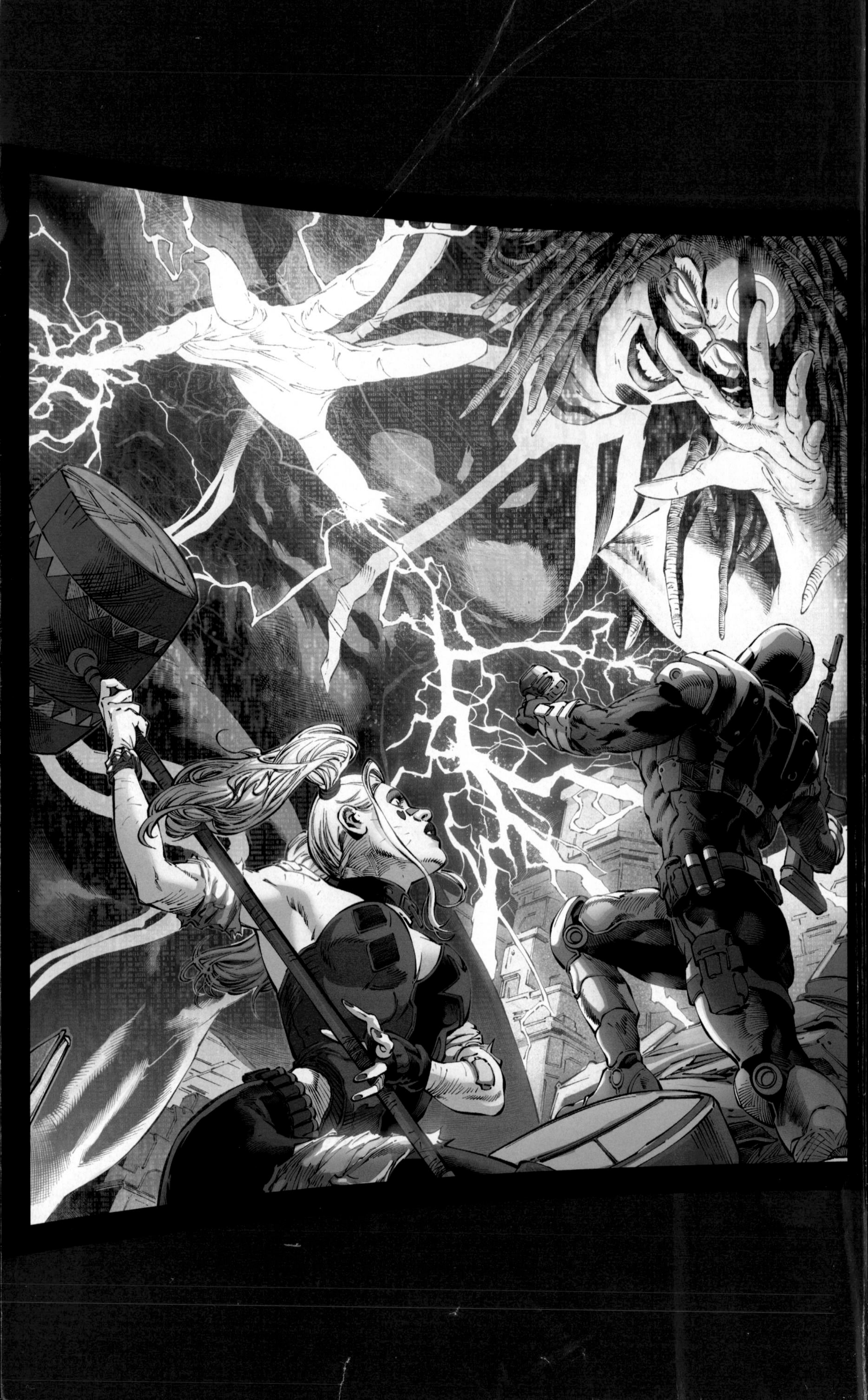

SUICIDE SQUAD
VOL.7 DRAIN THE SWAMP

ROB WILLIAMS * SI SPURRIER
writers

EDUARDO PANSICA * FERNANDO PASARIN * TOM DERENICK
NEIL EDWARDS * JACK HERBERT * JOSE LUIS
pencillers

JULIO FERREIRA * OCLAIR ALBERT * TOM DERENICK * NEIL EDWARDS
JACK HERBERT * SEAN PARSONS * JORDI TARRAGONA
inkers

ADRIANO LUCAS * BLOND
ULISES ARREOLA * HI-FI
colorists

PAT BROSSEAU
letterer

EDDY BARROWS, EBER FERREIRA and **ADRIANO LUCAS**
collection cover artists

HACK created by **ROB WILLIAMS** and **JIM LEE**
SUPERMAN created by **JERRY SIEGEL** and **JOE SHUSTER**
By special arrangement with the Jerry Siegel family

MIKE COTTON Editor – Original Series
DAVE WIELGOSZ ALEX ANTONE Associate Editors – Original Series ✳ **ANDREW MARINO** Assistant Editor – Original Series
JEB WOODARD Group Editor – Collected Editions ✳ **ALEX GALER** Editor – Collected Edition
STEVE COOK Design Director – Books ✳ **MEGEN BELLERSEN** – Publication Design

BOB HARRAS Senior VP – Editor-in-Chief, DC Comics ✳ **PAT McCALLUM** Executive Editor, DC Comics

DAN DiDIO Publisher ✳ **JIM LEE** Publisher & Chief Creative Officer
AMIT DESAI Executive VP – Business & Marketing Strategy, Direct to Consumer & Global Franchise Management
BOBBIE CHASE VP & Executive Editor, Young Reader & Talent Development ✳ **MARK CHIARELLO** Senior VP – Art, Design & Collected Editions
JOHN CUNNINGHAM Senior VP – Sales & Trade Marketing ✳ **BRIAR DARDEN** VP – Business Affairs
ANNE DePIES Senior VP – Business Strategy, Finance & Administration ✳ **DON FALLETTI** VP – Manufacturing Operations
LAWRENCE GANEM VP – Editorial Administration & Talent Relations ✳ **ALISON GILL** Senior VP – Manufacturing & Operations
JASON GREENBERG VP – Business Strategy & Finance ✳ **HANK KANALZ** Senior VP – Editorial Strategy & Administration ✳ **JAY KOGAN** Senior VP – Legal Affairs
NICK J. NAPOLITANO VP – Manufacturing Administration ✳ **LISETTE OSTERLOH** – Digital Marketing & Events ✳ **EDDIE SCANNELL** VP – Consumer Marketing
COURTNEY SIMMONS Senior VP – Publicity & Communications ✳ **JIM (SKI) SOKOLOWSKI** VP – Comic Book Specialty Sales & Trade Marketing
NANCY SPEARS VP – Mass, Book, Digital Sales & Trade Marketing ✳ **MICHELE R. WELLS** VP – Content Strategy

SUICIDE SQUAD VOL. 7: DRAIN THE SWAMP

Published by DC Comics. Compilation and all new material Copyright © 2018 DC Comics. All Rights Reserved.
Originally published in single magazine form in SUICIDE SQUAD 33-40. Copyright © 2018 DC Comics. All Rights Reserved.
All characters, their distinctive likenesses and related elements featured in this publication are trademarks of DC Comics.
The stories, characters and incidents featured in this publication are entirely fictional.
DC Comics does not read or accept unsolicited submissions of ideas, stories or artwork.

DC Comics, 2900 West Alameda Ave., Burbank, CA 91505
Printed by LSC Communications, Kendallville, IN, USA. 9/14/18. First Printing.
ISBN: 978-1-4012-8474-9

Library of Congress Cataloging-in-Publication Data is available.

PEFC Certified

Printed on paper from
sustainably managed
forests, controlled
sources

PEFC/29-31-337   www.pefc.org

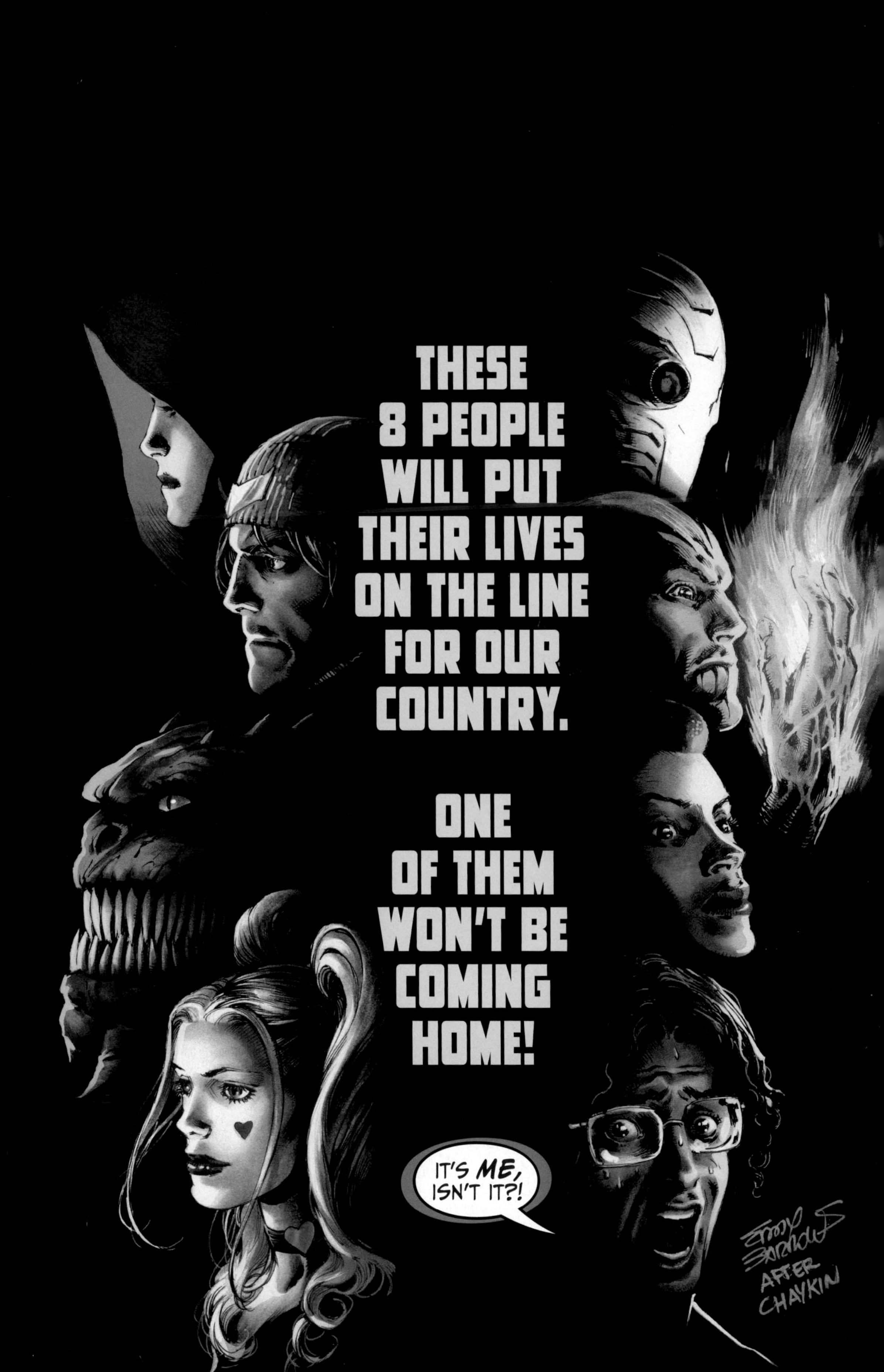
THESE 8 PEOPLE WILL PUT THEIR LIVES ON THE LINE FOR OUR COUNTRY.
ONE OF THEM WON'T BE COMING HOME!
IT'S ME, ISN'T IT?!
AFTER CHAYKIN

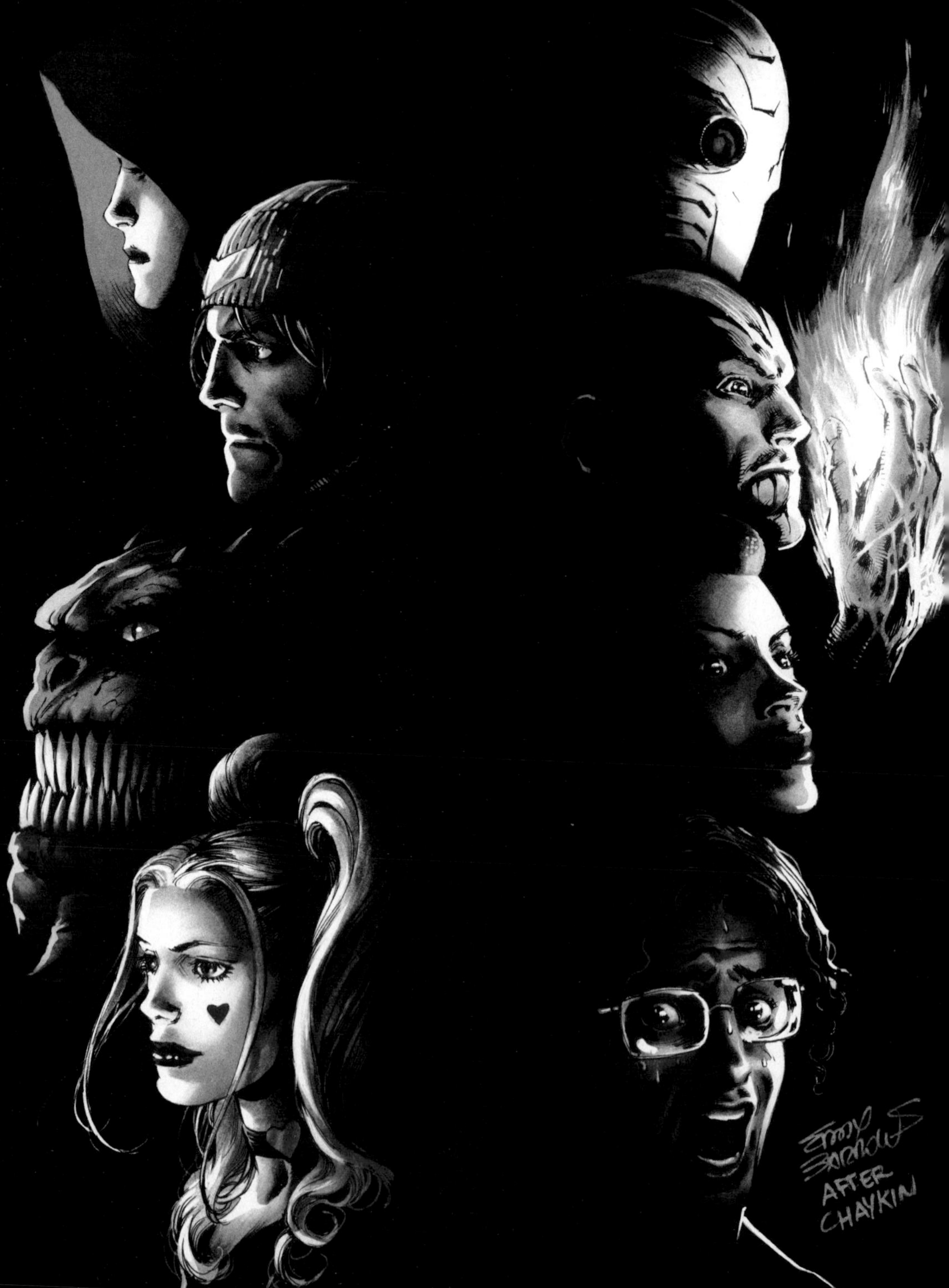
AFTER
CHAYKIN

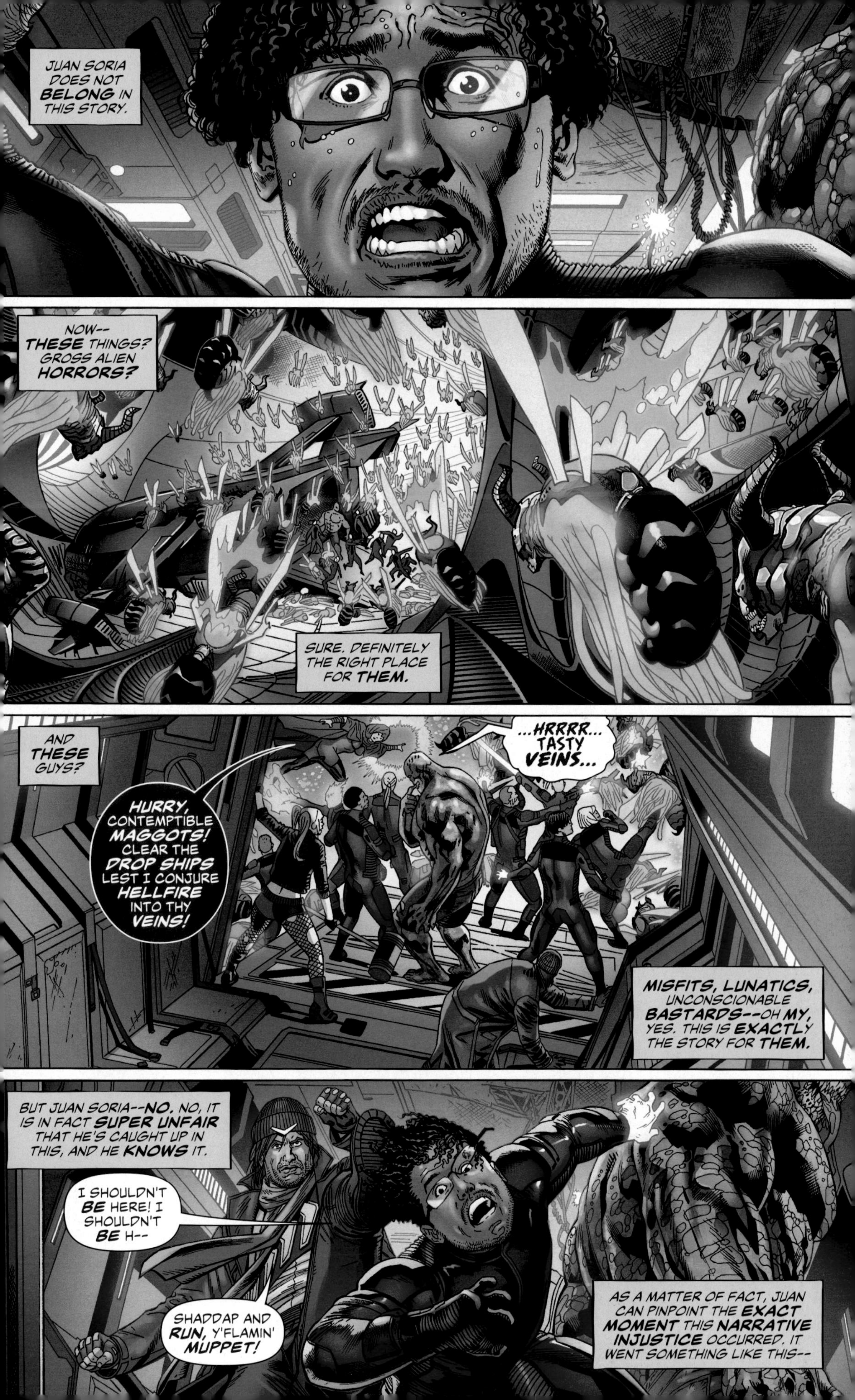
JUAN SORIA DOES NOT BELONG IN THIS STORY.
NOW-- THESE THINGS? GROSS ALIEN HORRORS?
SURE. DEFINITELY THE RIGHT PLACE FOR THEM.
AND THESE GUYS?
...HRRRR... TASTY VEINS...
HURRY, CONTEMPTIBLE MAGGOTS! CLEAR THE DROP SHIPS LEST I CONJURE HELLFIRE INTO THY VEINS!
MISFITS, LUNATICS, UNCONSCIONABLE BASTARDS--OH MY, YES. THIS IS EXACTLY THE STORY FOR THEM.
BUT JUAN SORIA--NO. NO, IT IS IN FACT SUPER UNFAIR THAT HE'S CAUGHT UP IN THIS, AND HE KNOWS IT.
I SHOULDN'T BE HERE! I SHOULDN'T BE H--
SHADDAP AND RUN, Y'FLAMIN' MUPPET!
AS A MATTER OF FACT, JUAN CAN PINPOINT THE EXACT MOMENT THIS NARRATIVE INJUSTICE OCCURRED. IT WENT SOMETHING LIKE THIS--

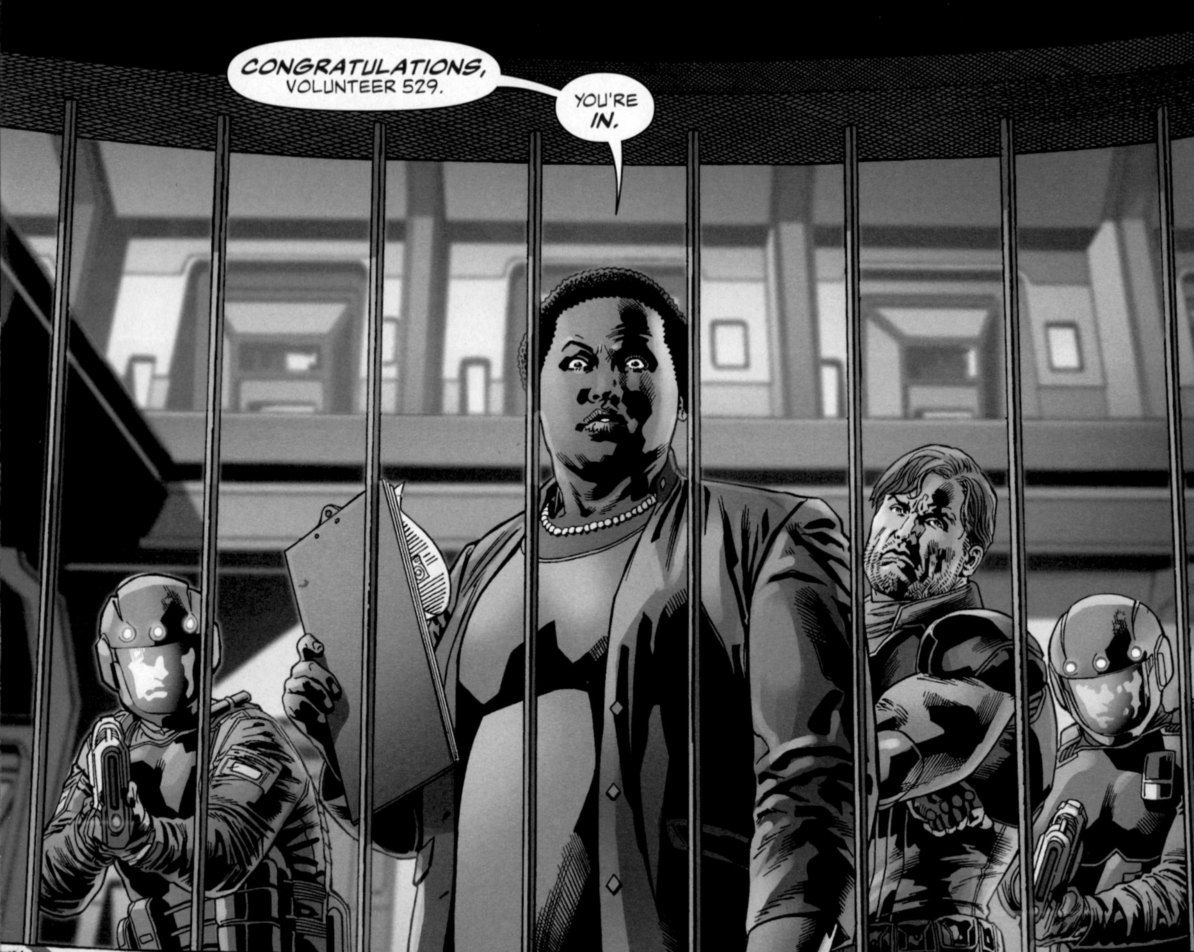
CONGRATULATIONS, VOLUNTEER 529.
YOU'RE IN.

THE CHOSEN ONE

SI SPURRIER WRITER FERNANDO PASARIN PENCILLER
OCLAIR ALBERT INKER BLOND COLORS PAT BROSSEAU LETTERING
EDDY BARROWS, EBER FERREIRA & ADRIANO LUCAS COVER
DAVE WIELGOSZ ASST. EDITOR ALEX ANTONE ASSOCIATE EDITOR
BRIAN CUNNINGHAM GROUP EDITOR

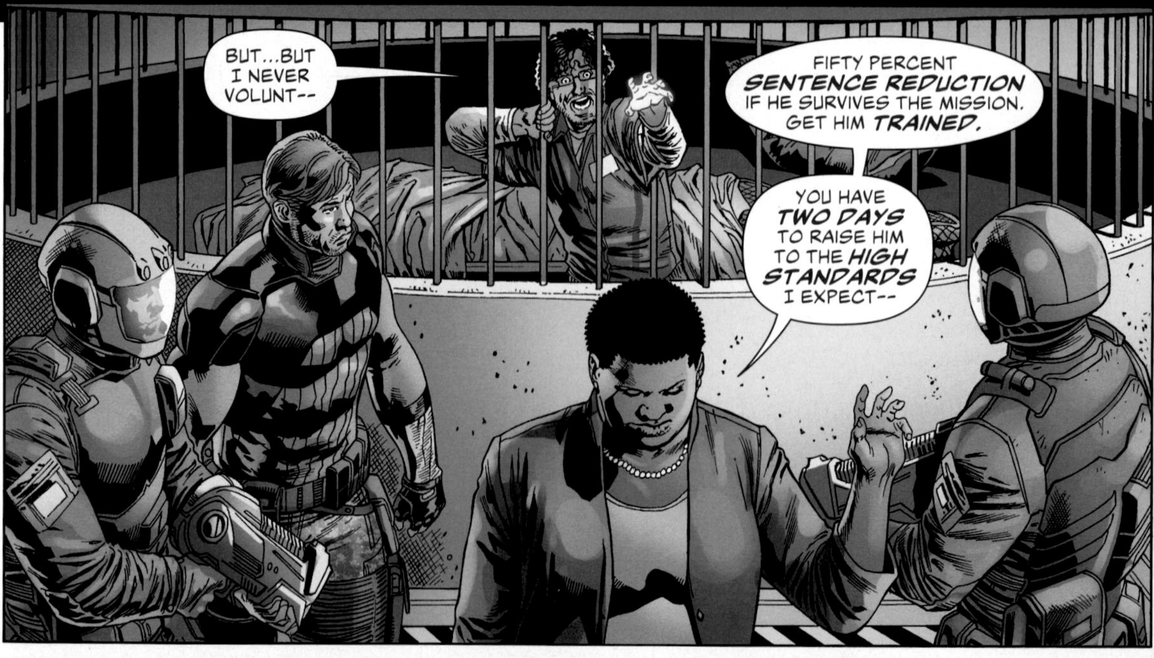
BUT...BUT I NEVER VOLUNT--
FIFTY PERCENT SENTENCE REDUCTION IF HE SURVIVES THE MISSION. GET HIM TRAINED.
YOU HAVE TWO DAYS TO RAISE HIM TO THE HIGH STANDARDS I EXPECT--

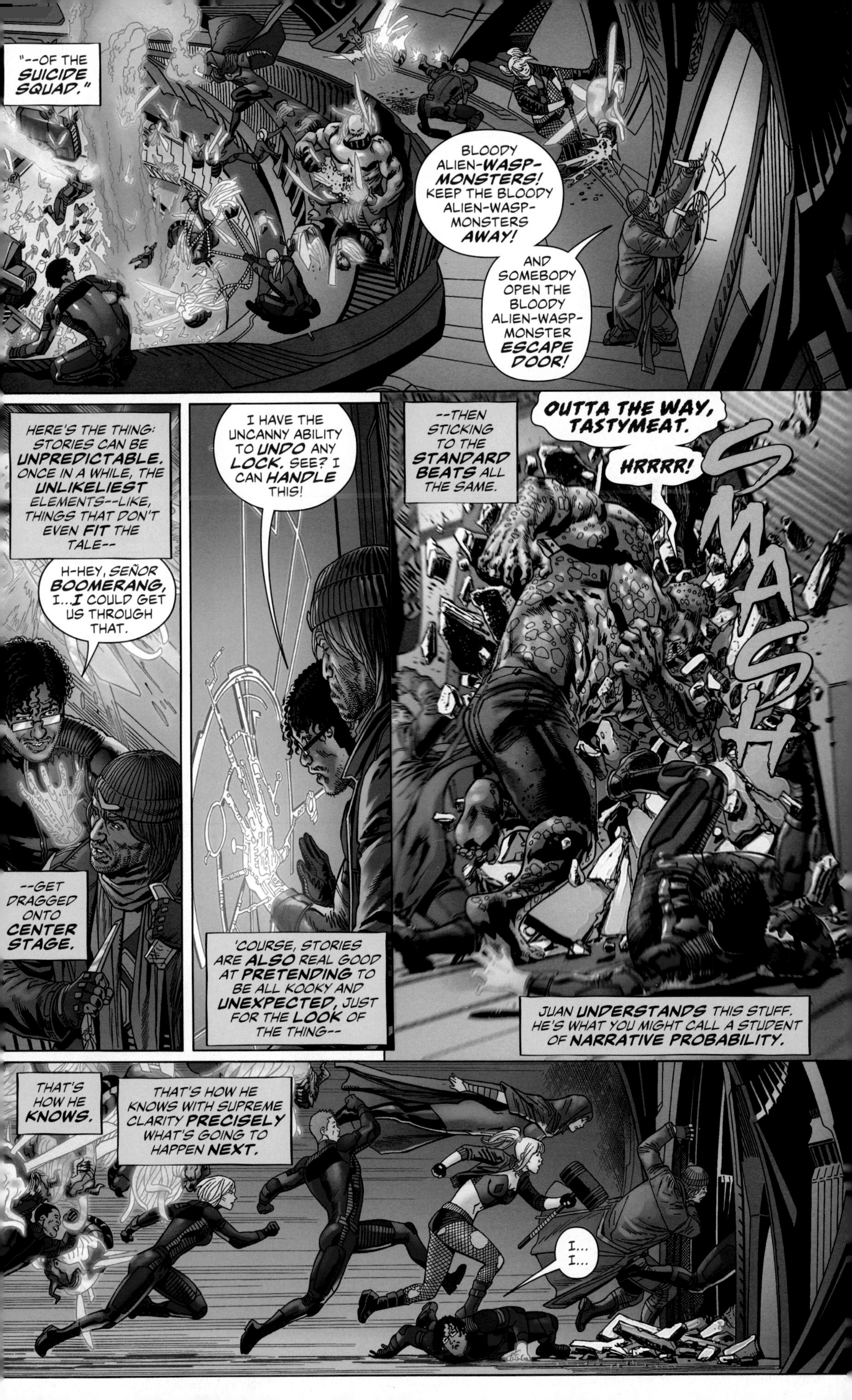
"--OF THE SUICIDE SQUAD."
BLOODY ALIEN-WASP-MONSTERS! KEEP THE BLOODY ALIEN-WASP-MONSTERS AWAY!
AND SOMEBODY OPEN THE BLOODY ALIEN-WASP-MONSTER ESCAPE DOOR!
HERE'S THE THING: STORIES CAN BE UNPREDICTABLE. ONCE IN A WHILE, THE UNLIKELIEST ELEMENTS--LIKE, THINGS THAT DON'T EVEN FIT THE TALE--
H-HEY, SEÑOR BOOMERANG, I...I COULD GET US THROUGH THAT.
--GET DRAGGED ONTO CENTER STAGE.
I HAVE THE UNCANNY ABILITY TO UNDO ANY LOCK. SEE? I CAN HANDLE THIS!
'COURSE, STORIES ARE ALSO REAL GOOD AT PRETENDING TO BE ALL KOOKY AND UNEXPECTED, JUST FOR THE LOOK OF THE THING--
--THEN STICKING TO THE STANDARD BEATS ALL THE SAME.
OUTTA THE WAY, TASTYMEAT.
HRRRR!
SMASH
JUAN UNDERSTANDS THIS STUFF. HE'S WHAT YOU MIGHT CALL A STUDENT OF NARRATIVE PROBABILITY.
THAT'S HOW HE KNOWS.
THAT'S HOW HE KNOWS WITH SUPREME CLARITY PRECISELY WHAT'S GOING TO HAPPEN NEXT.
I... I...

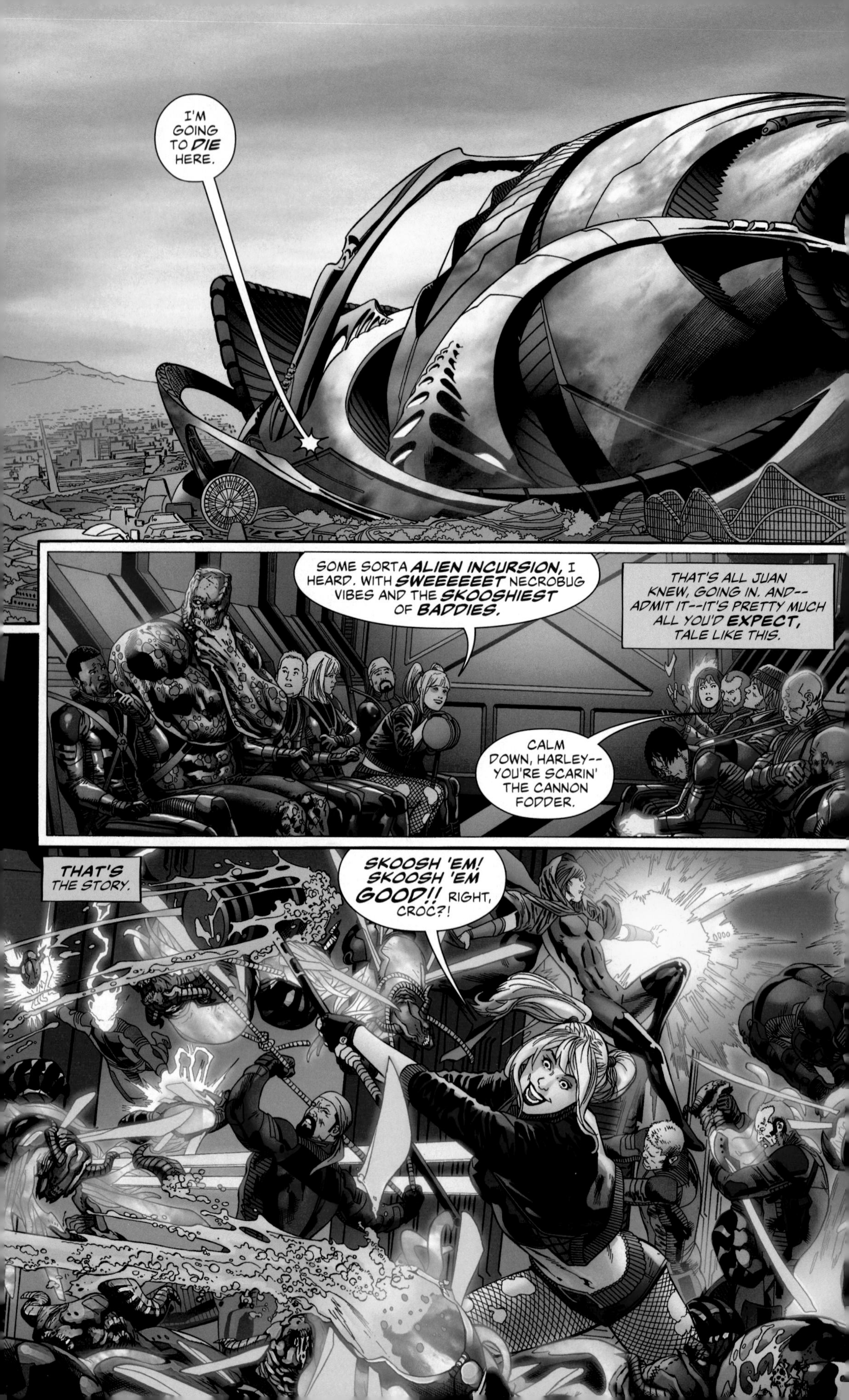
I'M GOING TO DIE HERE.
SOME SORTA ALIEN INCURSION, I HEARD. WITH SWEEEEEET NECROBUG VIBES AND THE SKOOSHIEST OF BADDIES.
THAT'S ALL JUAN KNEW, GOING IN. AND--ADMIT IT--IT'S PRETTY MUCH ALL YOU'D EXPECT, TALE LIKE THIS.
CALM DOWN, HARLEY--YOU'RE SCARIN' THE CANNON FODDER.
THAT'S THE STORY.
SKOOSH 'EM! SKOOSH 'EM GOOD!! RIGHT, CROC?!

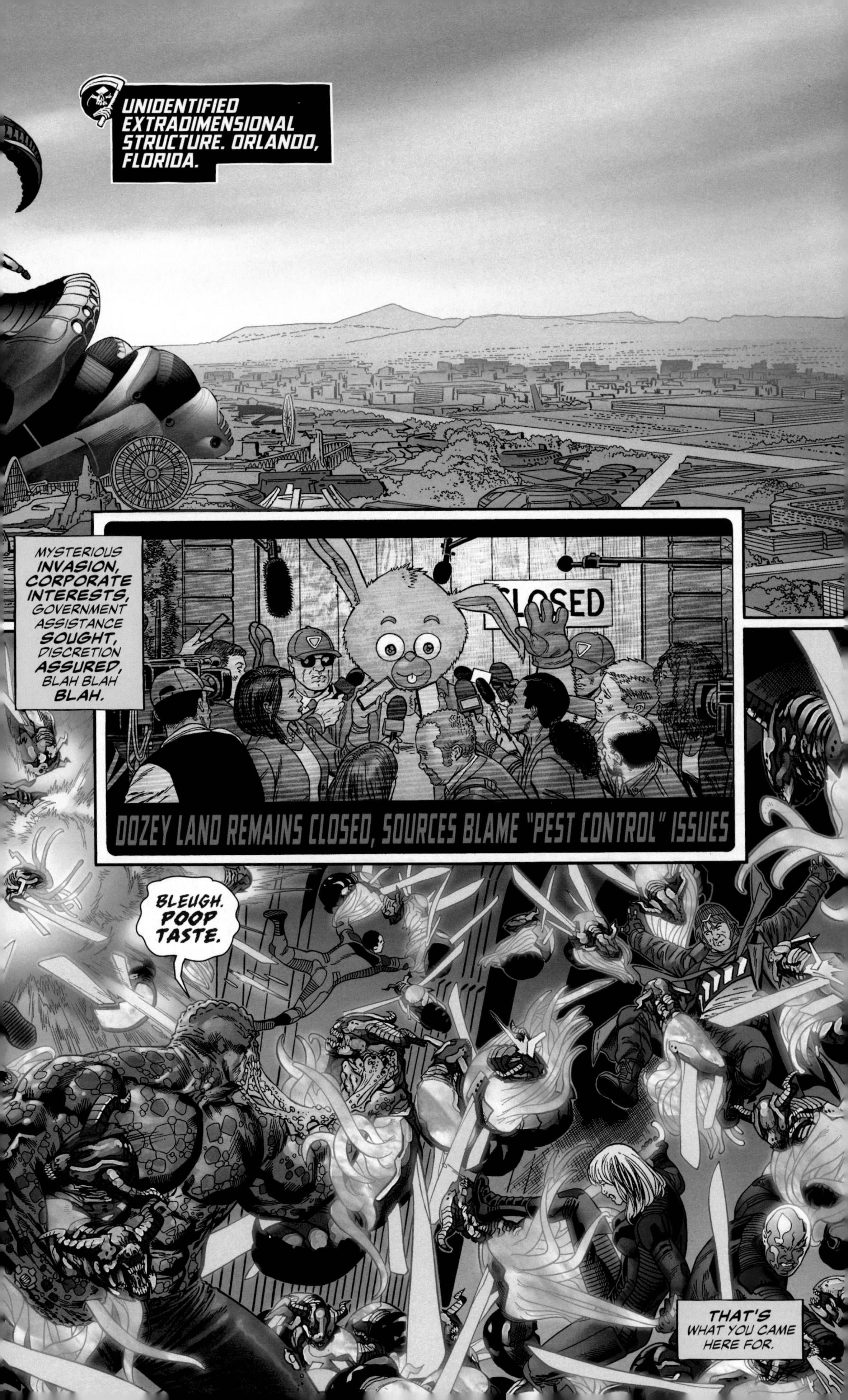
UNIDENTIFIED EXTRADIMENSIONAL STRUCTURE. ORLANDO, FLORIDA.
MYSTERIOUS INVASION, CORPORATE INTERESTS, GOVERNMENT ASSISTANCE SOUGHT, DISCRETION ASSURED, BLAH BLAH BLAH.
CLOSED
DOZEY LAND REMAINS CLOSED, SOURCES BLAME "PEST CONTROL" ISSUES
BLEUGH. POOP TASTE.
THAT'S WHAT YOU CAME HERE FOR.

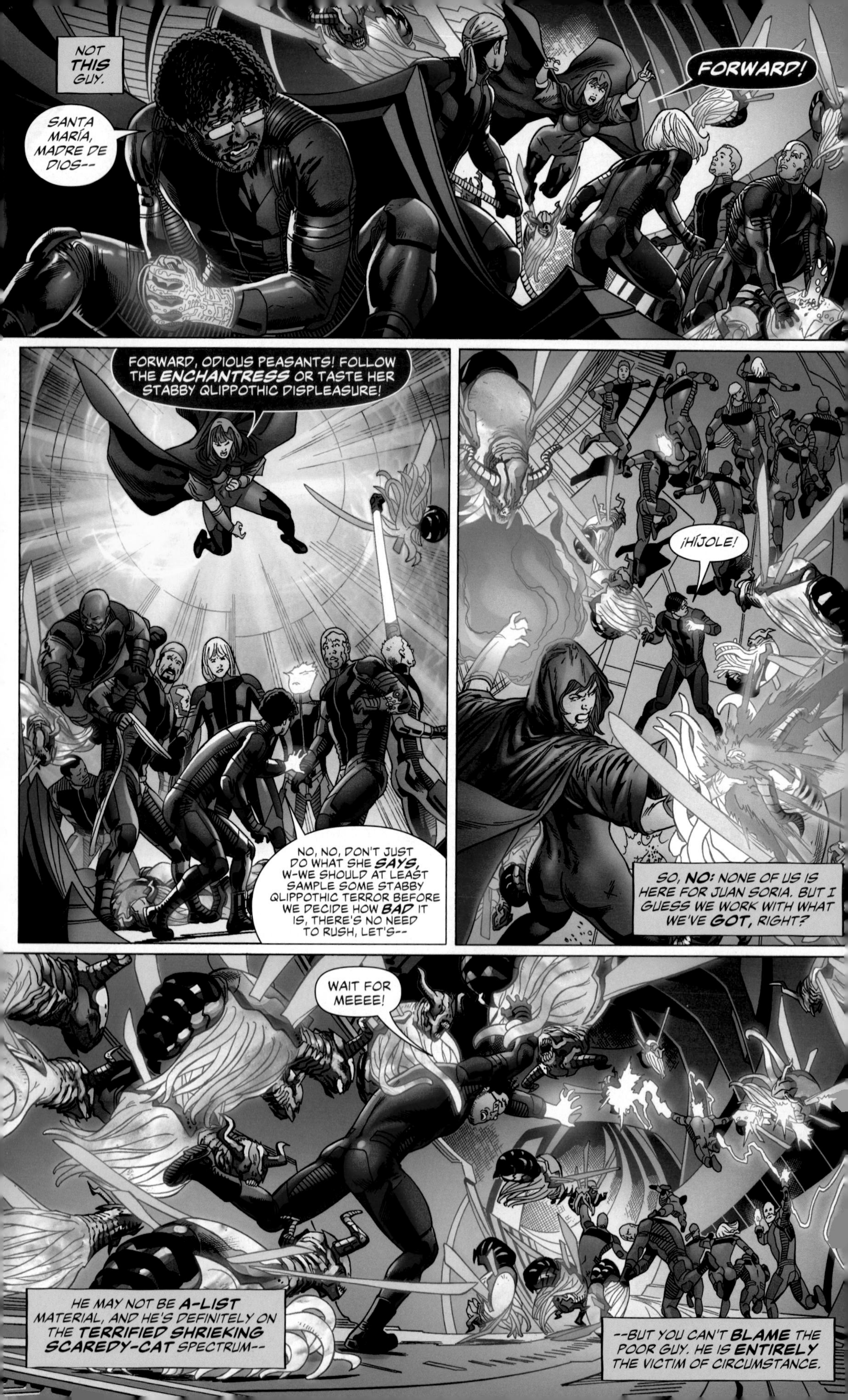

NOT THIS GUY.
SANTA MARÍA, MADRE DE DIOS--
FORWARD!
FORWARD, ODIOUS PEASANTS! FOLLOW THE ENCHANTRESS OR TASTE HER STABBY QLIPPOTHIC DISPLEASURE!
NO, NO, DON'T JUST DO WHAT SHE SAYS, W-WE SHOULD AT LEAST SAMPLE SOME STABBY QLIPPOTHIC TERROR BEFORE WE DECIDE HOW BAD IT IS, THERE'S NO NEED TO RUSH, LET'S--
¡HÍJOLE!
SO, NO: NONE OF US IS HERE FOR JUAN SORIA. BUT I GUESS WE WORK WITH WHAT WE'VE GOT, RIGHT?
WAIT FOR MEEEE!
HE MAY NOT BE A-LIST MATERIAL, AND HE'S DEFINITELY ON THE TERRIFIED SHRIEKING SCAREDY-CAT SPECTRUM--
--BUT YOU CAN'T BLAME THE POOR GUY. HE IS ENTIRELY THE VICTIM OF CIRCUMSTANCE.

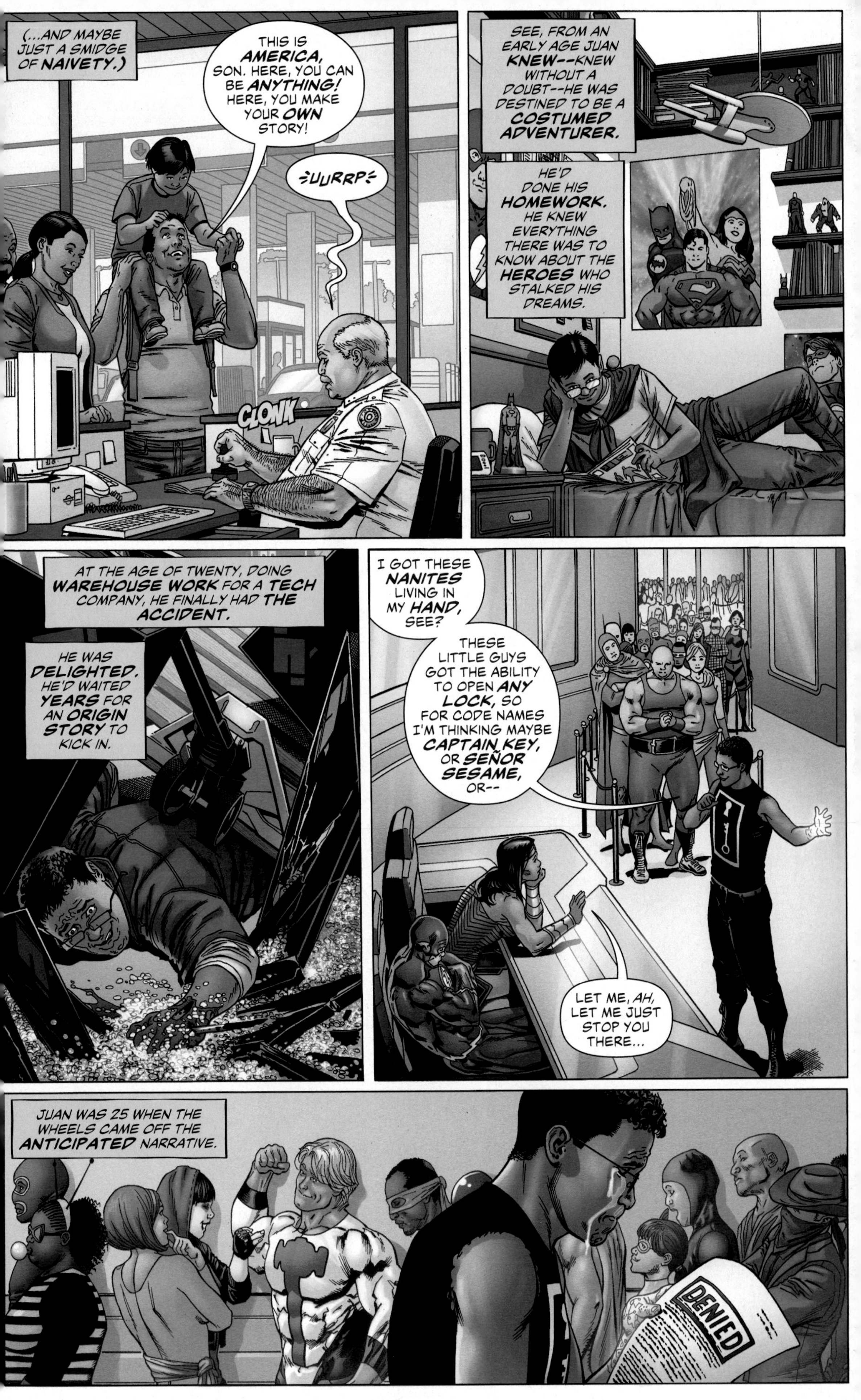
(...AND MAYBE JUST A SMIDGE OF NAIVETY.)
THIS IS AMERICA, SON. HERE, YOU CAN BE ANYTHING! HERE, YOU MAKE YOUR OWN STORY!
UURRP
CLONK
SEE, FROM AN EARLY AGE JUAN KNEW--KNEW WITHOUT A DOUBT--HE WAS DESTINED TO BE A COSTUMED ADVENTURER.
HE'D DONE HIS HOMEWORK. HE KNEW EVERYTHING THERE WAS TO KNOW ABOUT THE HEROES WHO STALKED HIS DREAMS.
AT THE AGE OF TWENTY, DOING WAREHOUSE WORK FOR A TECH COMPANY, HE FINALLY HAD THE ACCIDENT.
HE WAS DELIGHTED. HE'D WAITED YEARS FOR AN ORIGIN STORY TO KICK IN.
I GOT THESE NANITES LIVING IN MY HAND, SEE?
THESE LITTLE GUYS GOT THE ABILITY TO OPEN ANY LOCK, SO FOR CODE NAMES I'M THINKING MAYBE CAPTAIN KEY, OR SEÑOR SESAME, OR--
LET ME, AH, LET ME JUST STOP YOU THERE...
JUAN WAS 25 WHEN THE WHEELS CAME OFF THE ANTICIPATED NARRATIVE.
DENIED

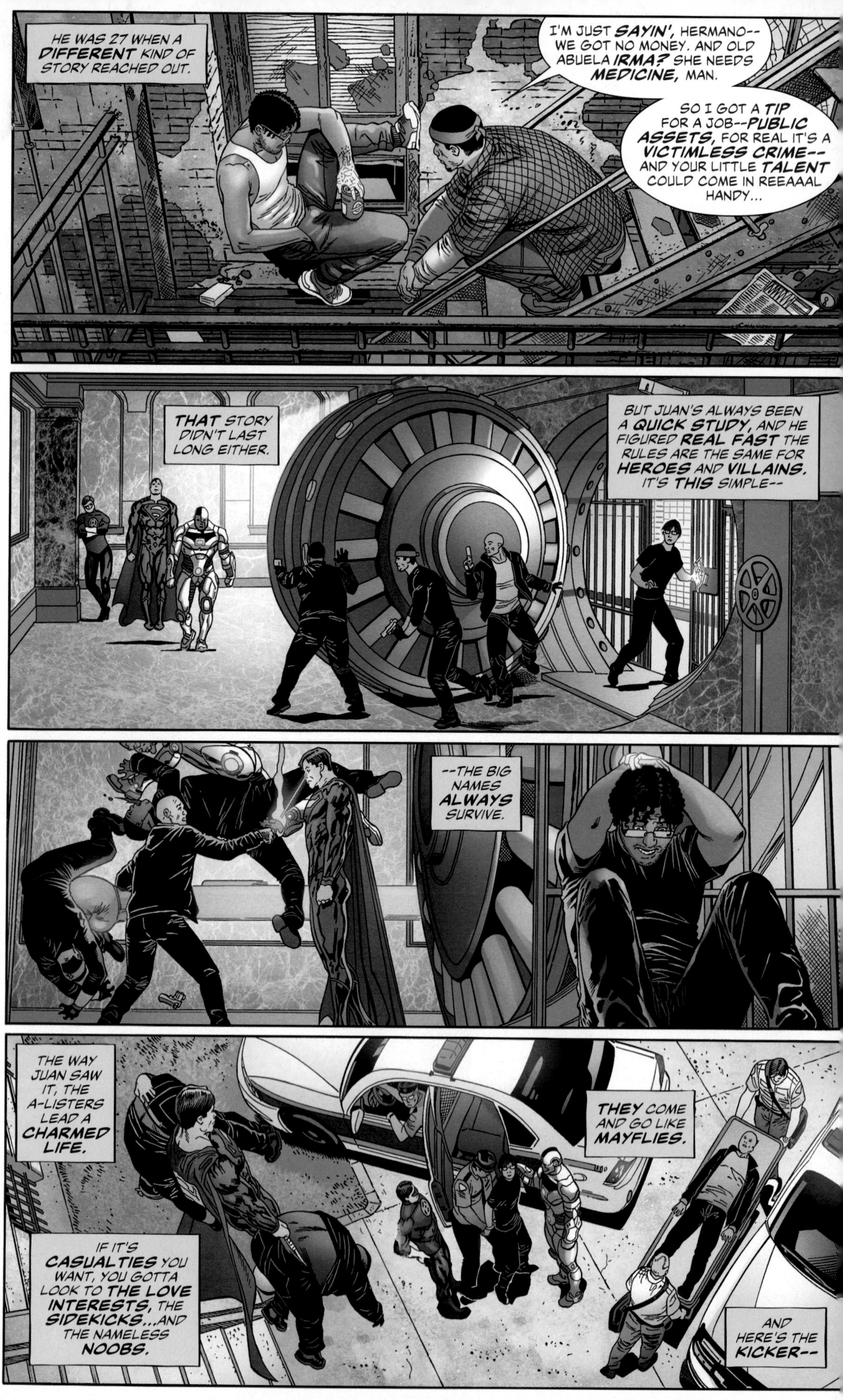

HE WAS 27 WHEN A DIFFERENT KIND OF STORY REACHED OUT.
I'M JUST SAYIN', HERMANO--WE GOT NO MONEY. AND OLD ABUELA IRMA? SHE NEEDS MEDICINE, MAN.
SO I GOT A TIP FOR A JOB--PUBLIC ASSETS, FOR REAL IT'S A VICTIMLESS CRIME--AND YOUR LITTLE TALENT COULD COME IN REEAAAL HANDY...
THAT STORY DIDN'T LAST LONG EITHER.
BUT JUAN'S ALWAYS BEEN A QUICK STUDY, AND HE FIGURED REAL FAST THE RULES ARE THE SAME FOR HEROES AND VILLAINS. IT'S THIS SIMPLE--
--THE BIG NAMES ALWAYS SURVIVE.
THE WAY JUAN SAW IT, THE A-LISTERS LEAD A CHARMED LIFE.
THEY COME AND GO LIKE MAYFLIES.
IF IT'S CASUALTIES YOU WANT, YOU GOTTA LOOK TO THE LOVE INTERESTS, THE SIDEKICKS...AND THE NAMELESS NOOBS.
AND HERE'S THE KICKER--

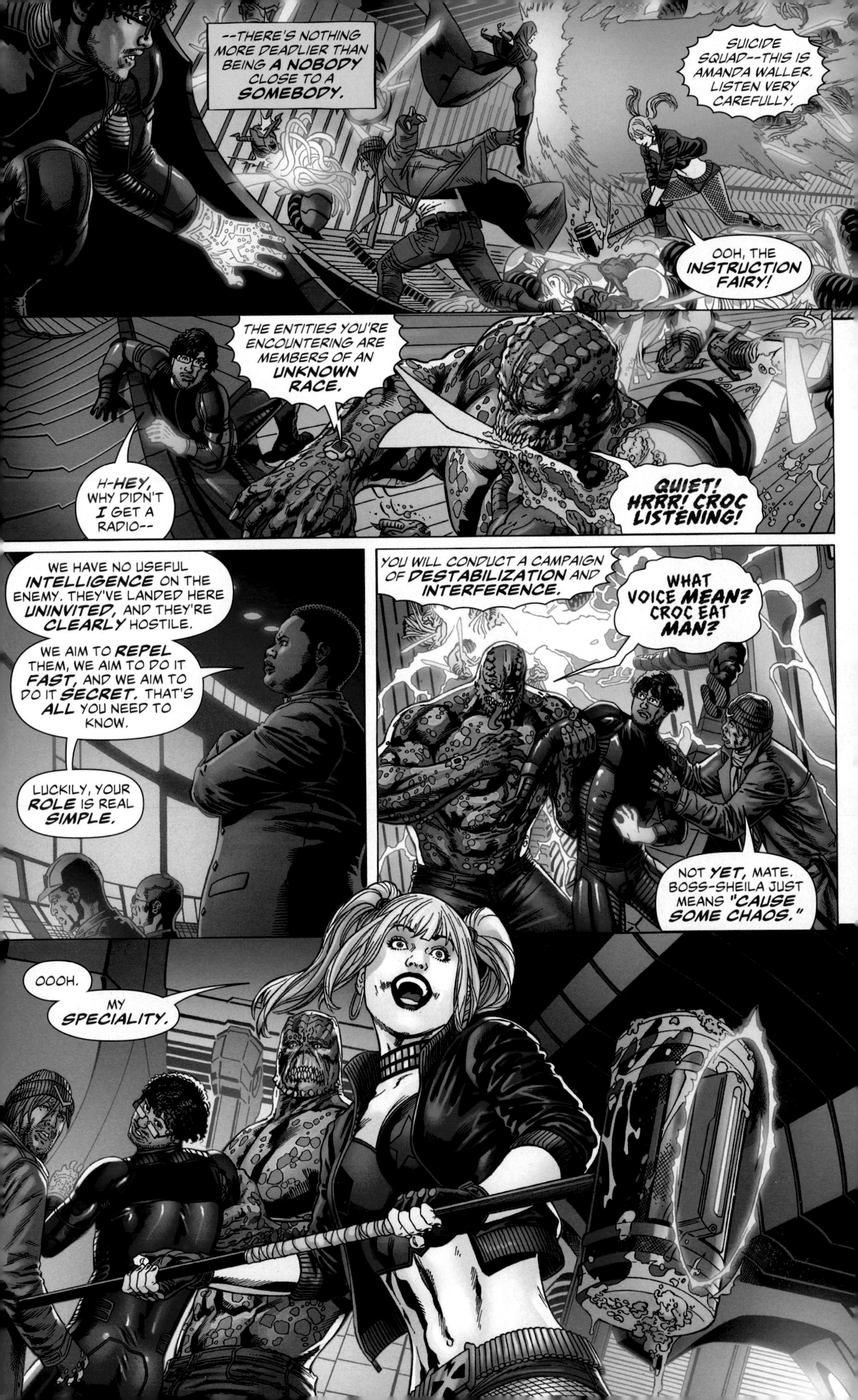

--THERE'S NOTHING MORE DEADLIER THAN BEING A NOBODY CLOSE TO A SOMEBODY.
SUICIDE SQUAD--THIS IS AMANDA WALLER. LISTEN VERY CAREFULLY.
OOH, THE INSTRUCTION FAIRY!
THE ENTITIES YOU'RE ENCOUNTERING ARE MEMBERS OF AN UNKNOWN RACE.
H-HEY, WHY DIDN'T I GET A RADIO--
QUIET! HRRR! CROC LISTENING!
WE HAVE NO USEFUL INTELLIGENCE ON THE ENEMY. THEY'VE LANDED HERE UNINVITED, AND THEY'RE CLEARLY HOSTILE.
WE AIM TO REPEL THEM, WE AIM TO DO IT FAST, AND WE AIM TO DO IT SECRET. THAT'S ALL YOU NEED TO KNOW.
LUCKILY, YOUR ROLE IS REAL SIMPLE.
YOU WILL CONDUCT A CAMPAIGN OF DESTABILIZATION AND INTERFERENCE.
WHAT VOICE MEAN? CROC EAT MAN?
NOT YET, MATE. BOSS-SHEILA JUST MEANS "CAUSE SOME CHAOS."
OOOH.
MY SPECIALITY.

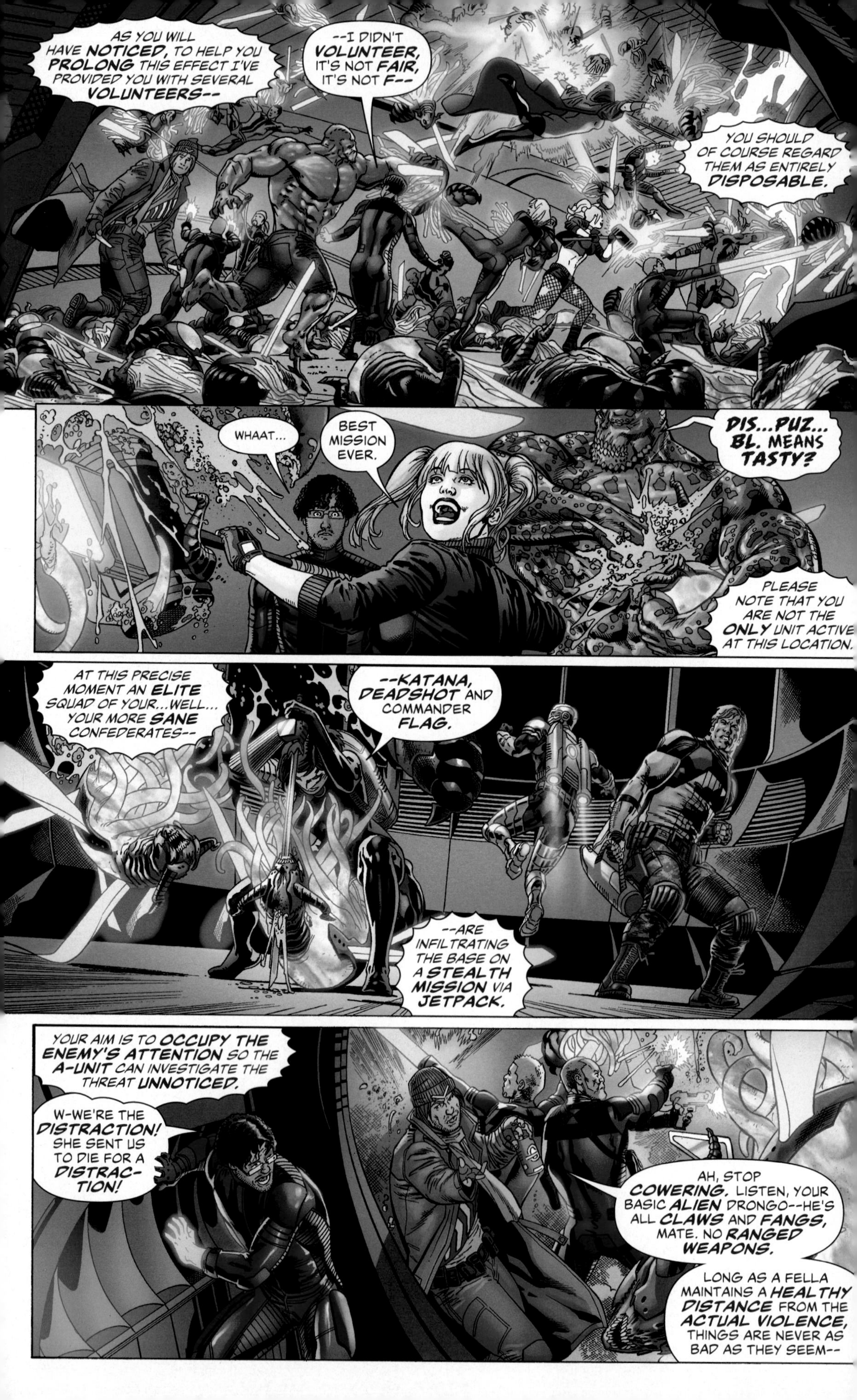
AS YOU WILL HAVE NOTICED, TO HELP YOU PROLONG THIS EFFECT I'VE PROVIDED YOU WITH SEVERAL VOLUNTEERS--
--I DIDN'T VOLUNTEER, IT'S NOT FAIR, IT'S NOT F--
YOU SHOULD OF COURSE REGARD THEM AS ENTIRELY DISPOSABLE.
WHAAT...
BEST MISSION EVER.
DIS...PUZ... BL. MEANS TASTY?
PLEASE NOTE THAT YOU ARE NOT THE ONLY UNIT ACTIVE AT THIS LOCATION.
AT THIS PRECISE MOMENT AN ELITE SQUAD OF YOUR...WELL... YOUR MORE SANE CONFEDERATES--
--KATANA, DEADSHOT AND COMMANDER FLAG.
--ARE INFILTRATING THE BASE ON A STEALTH MISSION VIA JETPACK.
YOUR AIM IS TO OCCUPY THE ENEMY'S ATTENTION SO THE A-UNIT CAN INVESTIGATE THE THREAT UNNOTICED.
W-WE'RE THE DISTRACTION! SHE SENT US TO DIE FOR A DISTRAC- TION!
AH, STOP COWERING. LISTEN, YOUR BASIC ALIEN DRONGO--HE'S ALL CLAWS AND FANGS, MATE. NO RANGED WEAPONS.
LONG AS A FELLA MAINTAINS A HEALTHY DISTANCE FROM THE ACTUAL VIOLENCE, THINGS ARE NEVER AS BAD AS THEY SEEM--

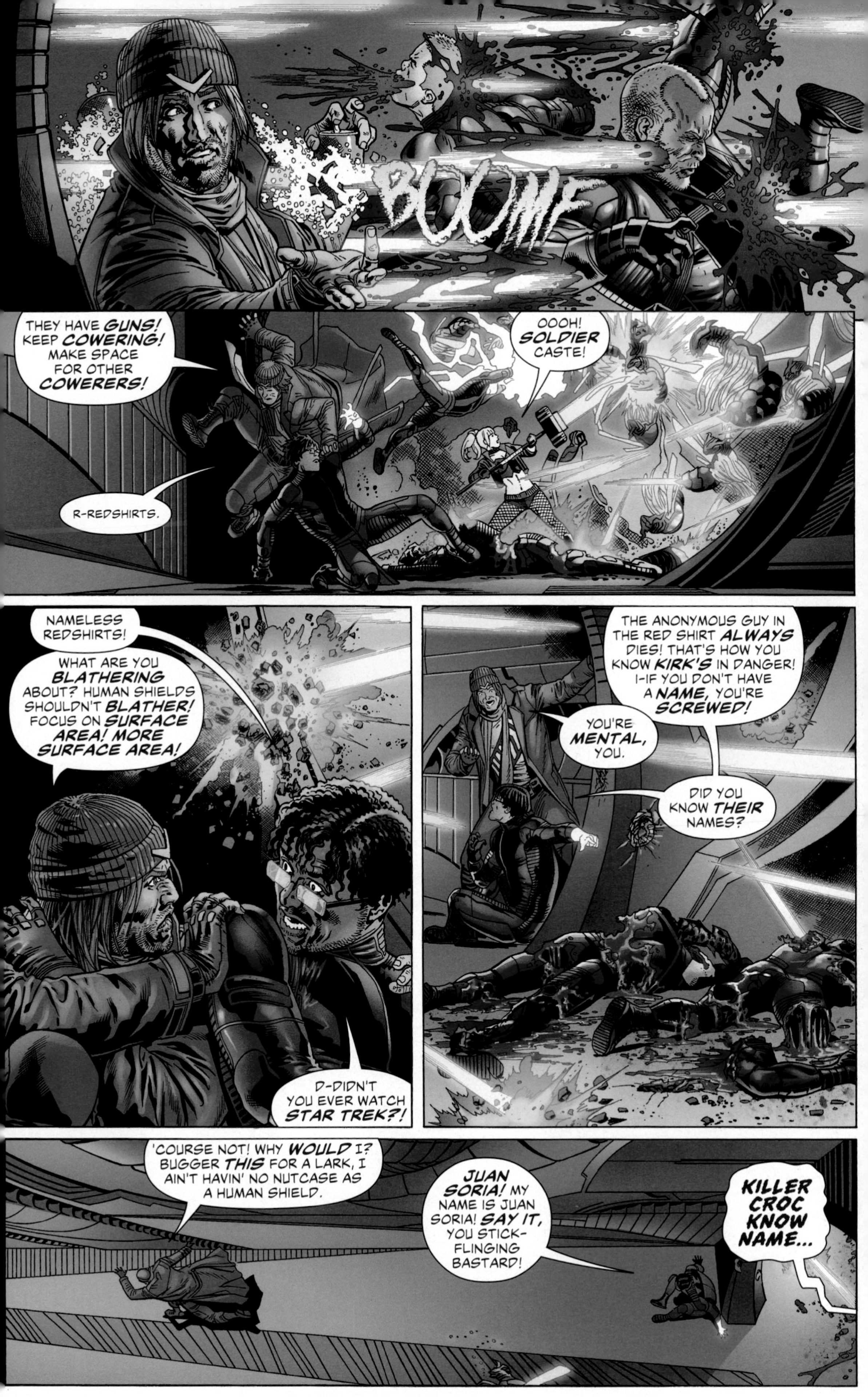
BOOMF
THEY HAVE GUNS! KEEP COWERING! MAKE SPACE FOR OTHER COWERERS!
OOOH! SOLDIER CASTE!
R-REDSHIRTS.
NAMELESS REDSHIRTS!
WHAT ARE YOU BLATHERING ABOUT? HUMAN SHIELDS SHOULDN'T BLATHER! FOCUS ON SURFACE AREA! MORE SURFACE AREA!
D-DIDN'T YOU EVER WATCH STAR TREK?!
THE ANONYMOUS GUY IN THE RED SHIRT ALWAYS DIES! THAT'S HOW YOU KNOW KIRK'S IN DANGER! I-IF YOU DON'T HAVE A NAME, YOU'RE SCREWED!
YOU'RE MENTAL, YOU.
DID YOU KNOW THEIR NAMES?
'COURSE NOT! WHY WOULD I? BUGGER THIS FOR A LARK, I AIN'T HAVIN' NO NUTCASE AS A HUMAN SHIELD.
JUAN SORIA! MY NAME IS JUAN SORIA! SAY IT, YOU STICK-FLINGING BASTARD!
KILLER CROC KNOW NAME...

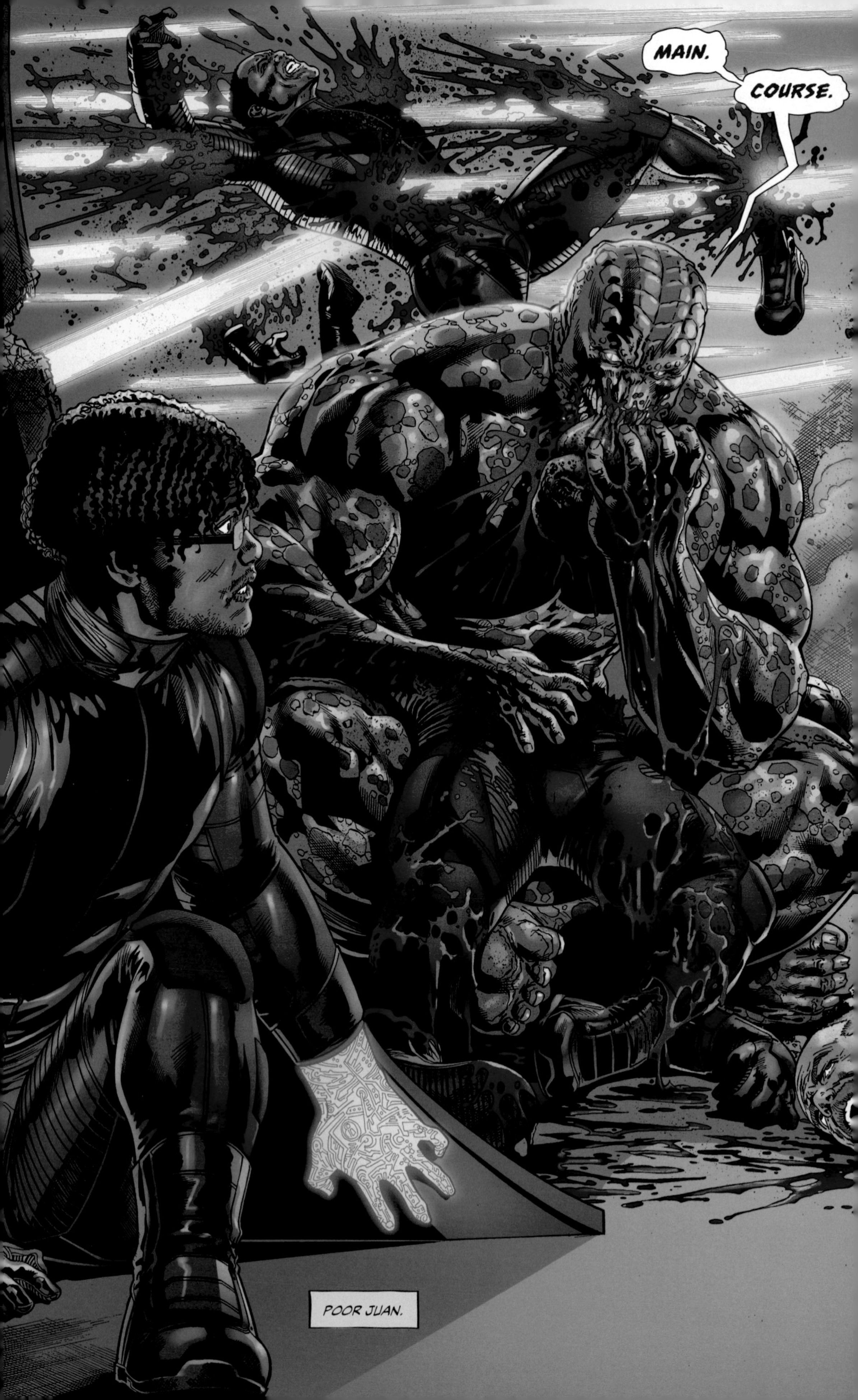
MAIN.
COURSE.
POOR JUAN.

TRUTH IS, HE'D BEEN **EXPECTING** SOMETHING LIKE THIS SINCE HE ARRIVED AT **BELLE REV.**

TH-THIS IS A PRISON FOR **SUPER-VILLAINS!** M-MY POWER SET'S GARBAGE! I DON'T **BELONG** HERE!

YOU GOT THE MEANS TO OPEN ANY **LOCK,** JUDGE SAYS YOU'RE SUPPOSED TO BE **BEHIND** ONE.

REQUIRES SOME **SPECIALIST ARRANGEMENTS,** PAL.

THAT'S NOT A **CELL!** THAT'S A **HOLE!** YOU CAN'T PUT ME IN **THERE!**

TURNS OUT LIVING IN A HOLE HAS A WAY OF **FOCUSING** ONE'S **ATTENTION.**

JUAN SUDDENLY HAD A WHOLE LOTTA TIME TO PONDER THE COMINGS AND GOINGS OF **VILLAINS.**

HEY, YOU GUYS? H-HOW ABOUT THAT **JAIL FOOD**-- PRETTY **GROSS,** RIGHT? HAHA!

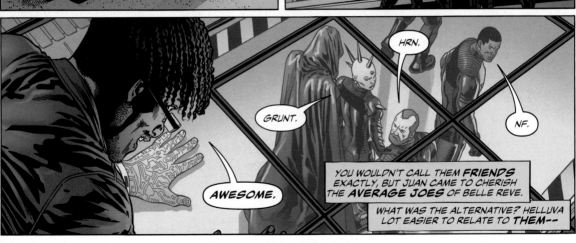

HRN.

GRUNT.

NF.

AWESOME.

YOU WOULDN'T CALL THEM **FRIENDS** EXACTLY, BUT JUAN CAME TO CHERISH THE **AVERAGE JOES** OF BELLE REVE.

WHAT WAS THE ALTERNATIVE? HELLUVA LOT EASIER TO RELATE TO **THEM**--

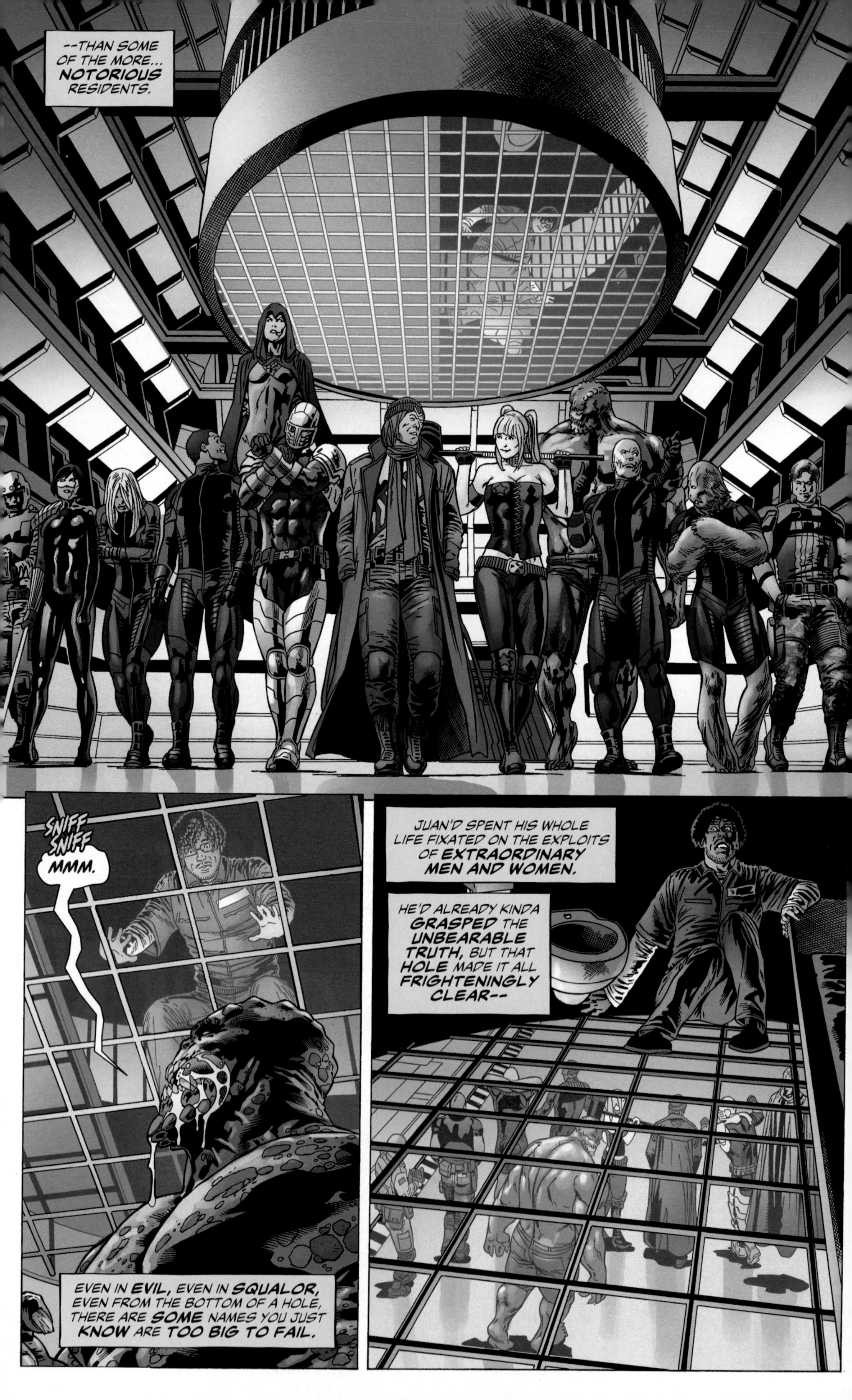
--THAN SOME OF THE MORE... NOTORIOUS RESIDENTS.
SNIFF SNIFF
MMM.
EVEN IN EVIL, EVEN IN SQUALOR, EVEN FROM THE BOTTOM OF A HOLE, THERE ARE SOME NAMES YOU JUST KNOW ARE TOO BIG TO FAIL.
JUAN'D SPENT HIS WHOLE LIFE FIXATED ON THE EXPLOITS OF EXTRAORDINARY MEN AND WOMEN.
HE'D ALREADY KINDA GRASPED THE UNBEARABLE TRUTH, BUT THAT HOLE MADE IT ALL FRIGHTENINGLY CLEAR--

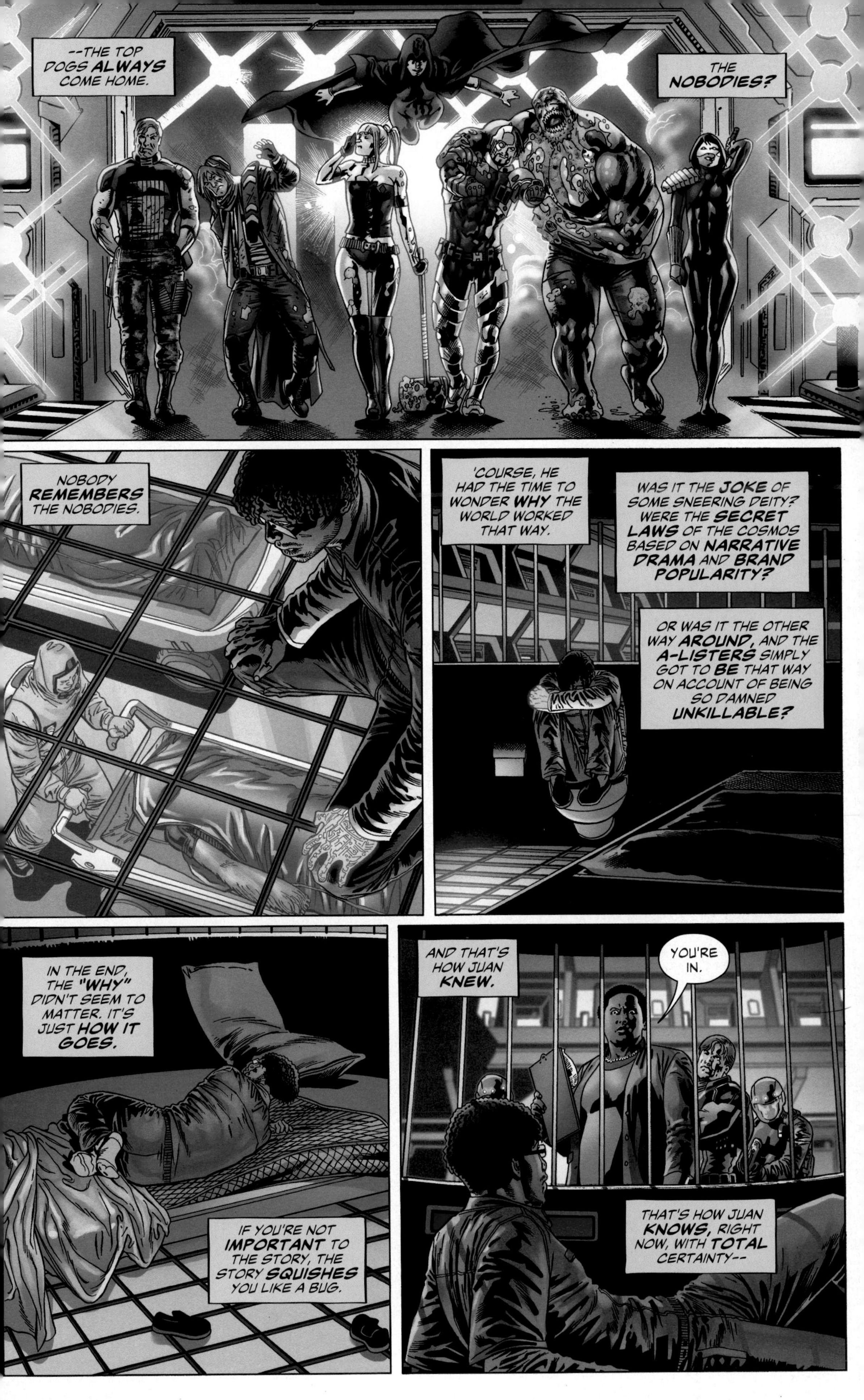
--THE TOP DOGS ALWAYS COME HOME.
THE NOBODIES?
NOBODY REMEMBERS THE NOBODIES.
'COURSE, HE HAD THE TIME TO WONDER WHY THE WORLD WORKED THAT WAY.
WAS IT THE JOKE OF SOME SNEERING DEITY? WERE THE SECRET LAWS OF THE COSMOS BASED ON NARRATIVE DRAMA AND BRAND POPULARITY?
OR WAS IT THE OTHER WAY AROUND, AND THE A-LISTERS SIMPLY GOT TO BE THAT WAY ON ACCOUNT OF BEING SO DAMNED UNKILLABLE?
IN THE END, THE "WHY" DIDN'T SEEM TO MATTER. IT'S JUST HOW IT GOES.
IF YOU'RE NOT IMPORTANT TO THE STORY, THE STORY SQUISHES YOU LIKE A BUG.
AND THAT'S HOW JUAN KNEW.
YOU'RE IN.
THAT'S HOW JUAN KNOWS, RIGHT NOW, WITH TOTAL CERTAINTY--

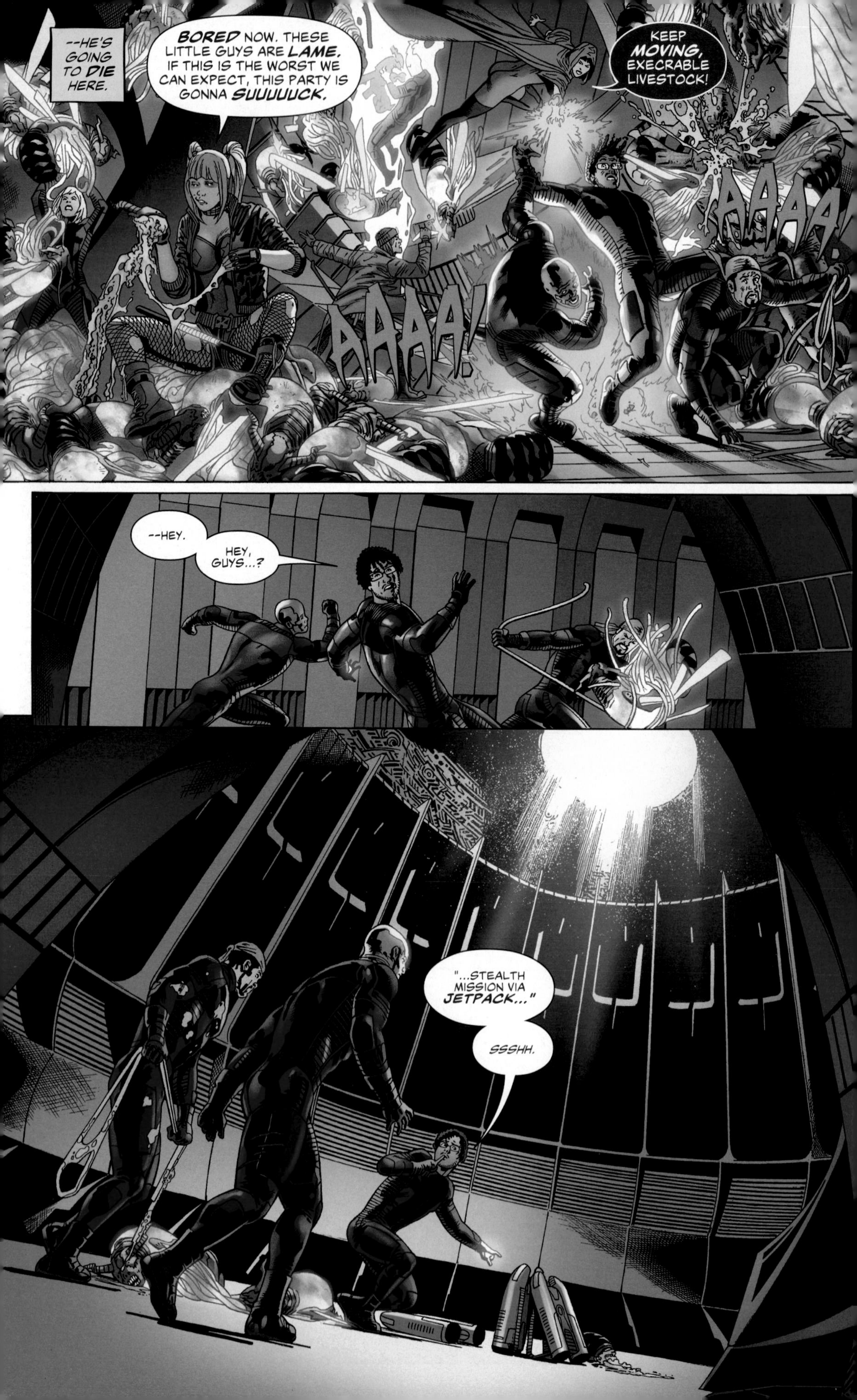
--HE'S GOING TO DIE HERE.
BORED NOW. THESE LITTLE GUYS ARE LAME. IF THIS IS THE WORST WE CAN EXPECT, THIS PARTY IS GONNA SUUUUUCK.
KEEP MOVING, EXECRABLE LIVESTOCK!
AAAA!
AAAA!
--HEY.
HEY, GUYS...?
"...STEALTH MISSION VIA JETPACK..."
SSSHH.

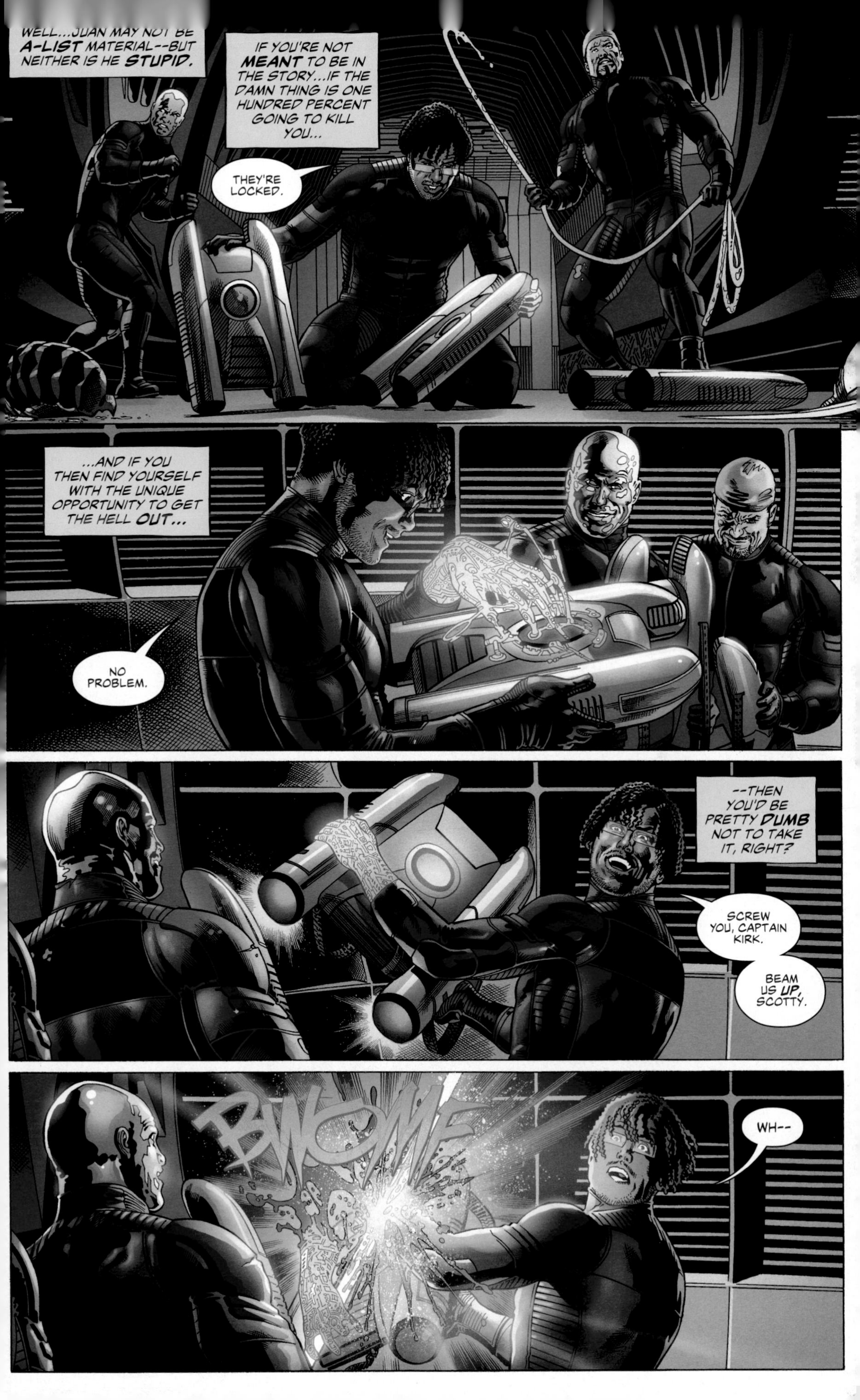
WELL...JUAN MAY NOT BE A-LIST MATERIAL--BUT NEITHER IS HE STUPID.
IF YOU'RE NOT MEANT TO BE IN THE STORY...IF THE DAMN THING IS ONE HUNDRED PERCENT GOING TO KILL YOU...
THEY'RE LOCKED.
...AND IF YOU THEN FIND YOURSELF WITH THE UNIQUE OPPORTUNITY TO GET THE HELL OUT...
NO PROBLEM.
--THEN YOU'D BE PRETTY DUMB NOT TO TAKE IT, RIGHT?
SCREW YOU, CAPTAIN KIRK.
BEAM US UP, SCOTTY.
BWOMF
WH--

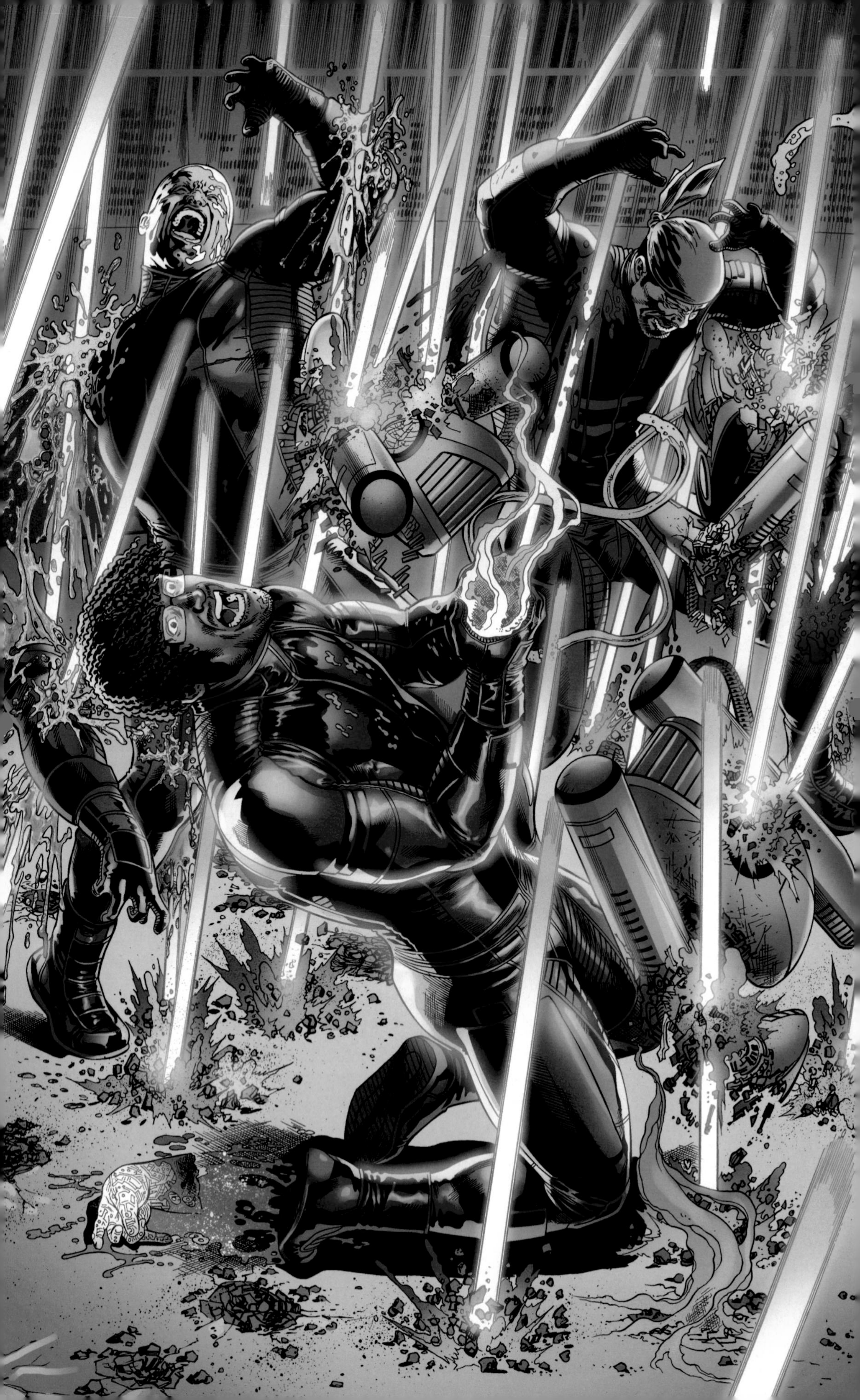

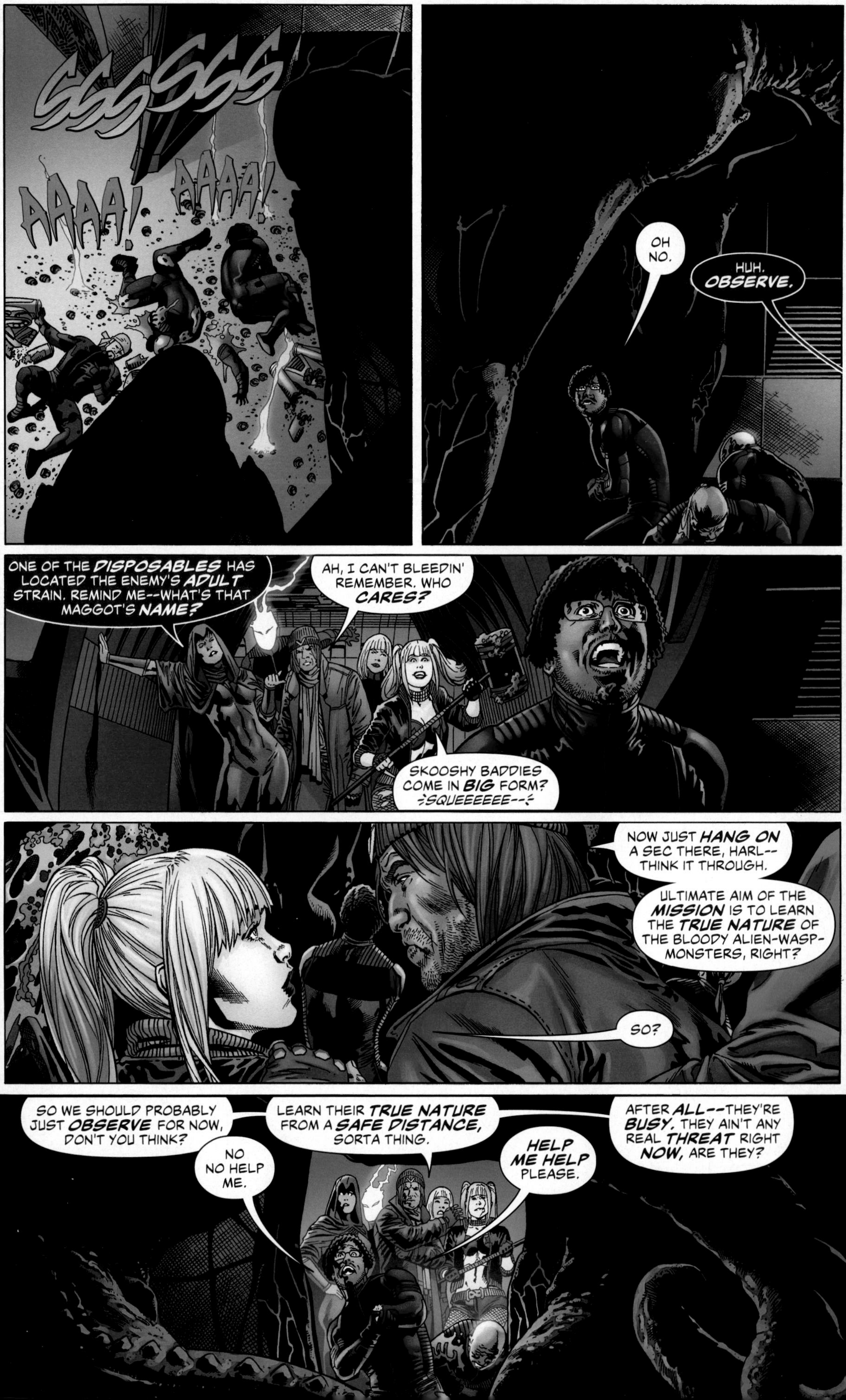
SSSSSS
AAAA!
AAAA!
OH NO.
HUH. OBSERVE.
ONE OF THE DISPOSABLES HAS LOCATED THE ENEMY'S ADULT STRAIN. REMIND ME--WHAT'S THAT MAGGOT'S NAME?
AH, I CAN'T BLEEDIN' REMEMBER. WHO CARES?
SKOOSHY BADDIES COME IN BIG FORM? SQUEEEEEEE--
NOW JUST HANG ON A SEC THERE, HARL--THINK IT THROUGH.
ULTIMATE AIM OF THE MISSION IS TO LEARN THE TRUE NATURE OF THE BLOODY ALIEN-WASP-MONSTERS, RIGHT?
SO?
SO WE SHOULD PROBABLY JUST OBSERVE FOR NOW, DON'T YOU THINK?
LEARN THEIR TRUE NATURE FROM A SAFE DISTANCE, SORTA THING.
AFTER ALL--THEY'RE BUSY. THEY AIN'T ANY REAL THREAT RIGHT NOW, ARE THEY?
NO NO HELP ME.
HELP ME HELP PLEASE.

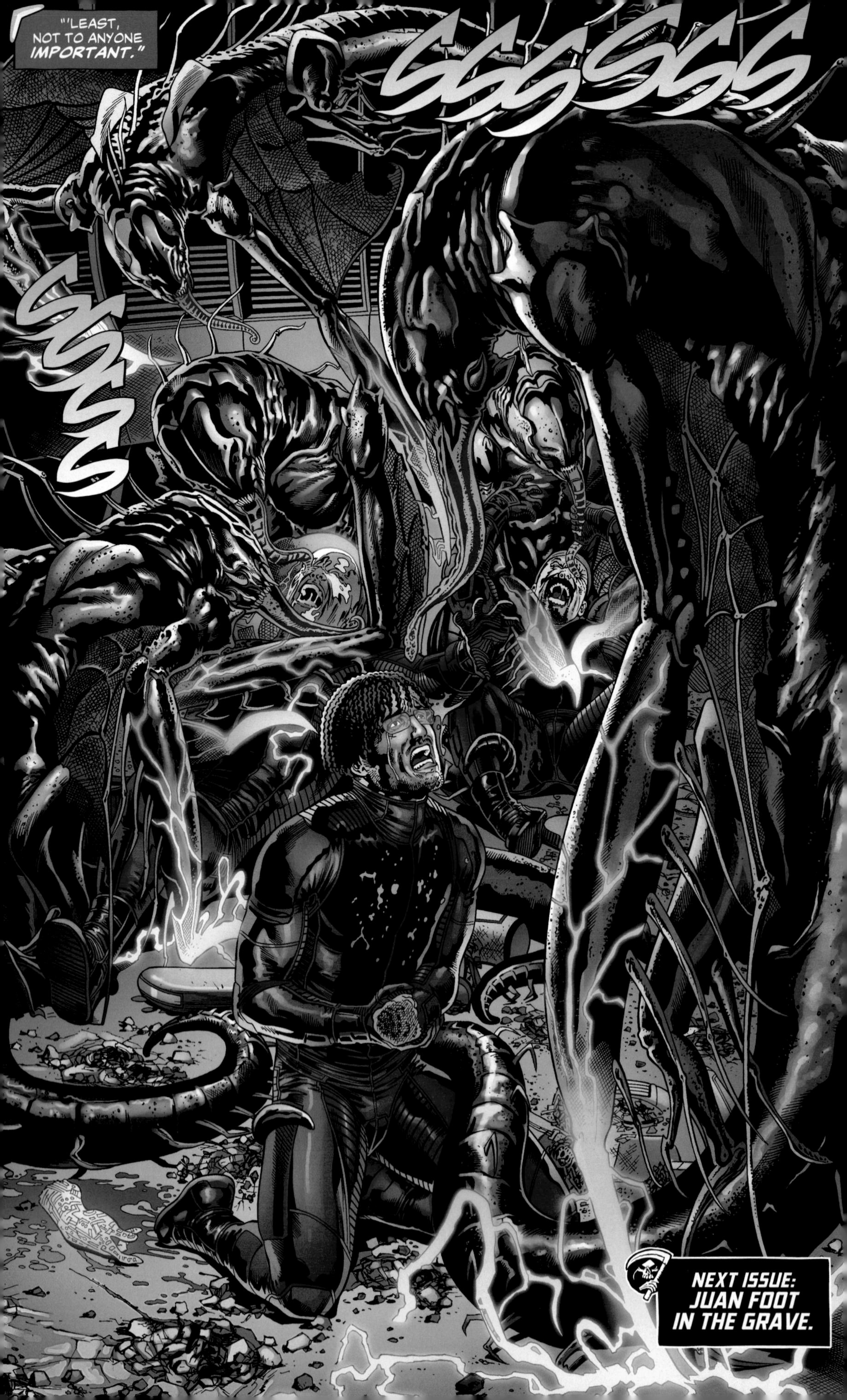
"'LEAST, NOT TO ANYONE IMPORTANT."
GGGGGG
GGGGG
NEXT ISSUE: JUAN FOOT IN THE GRAVE.

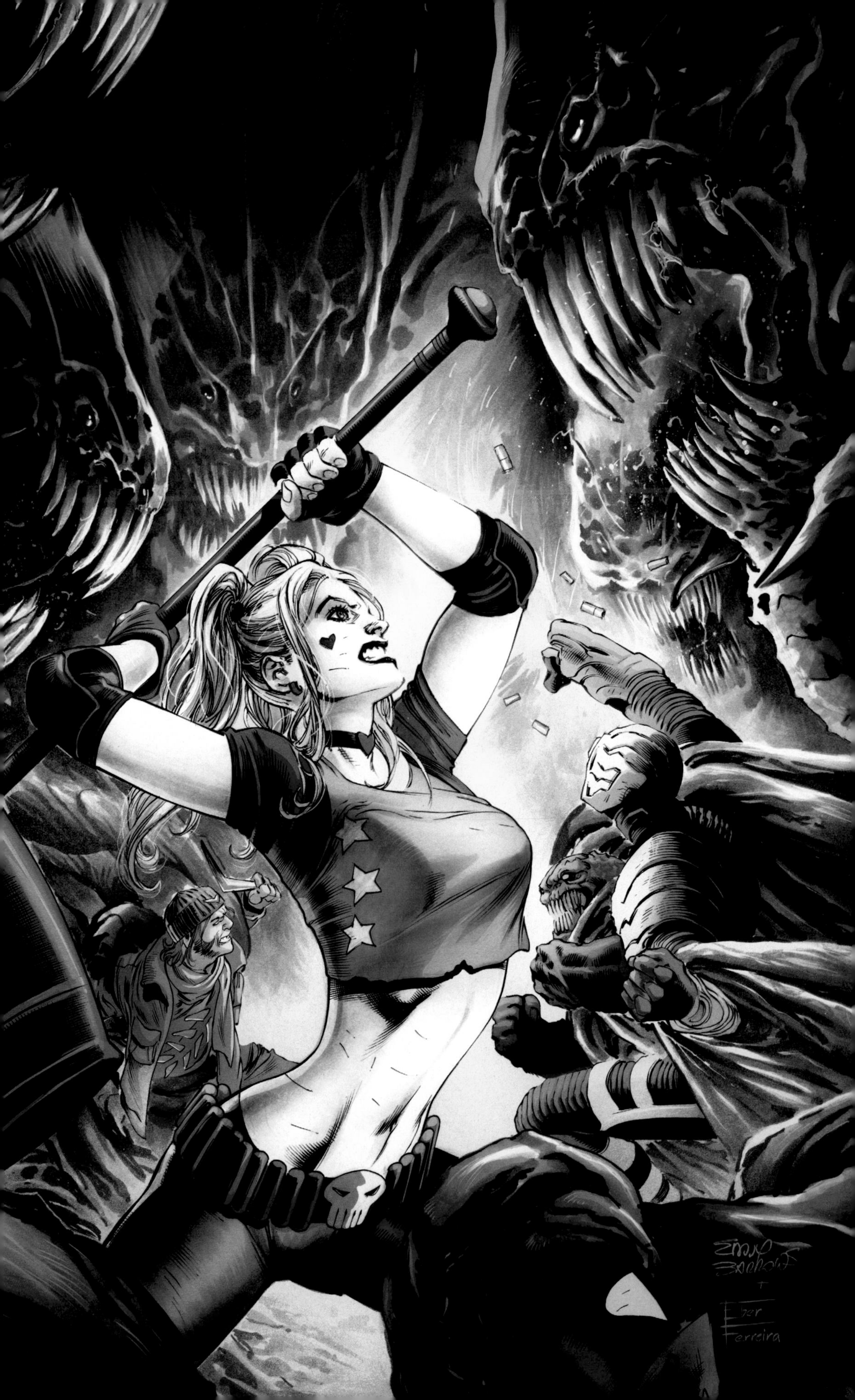
Eber
Ferreira

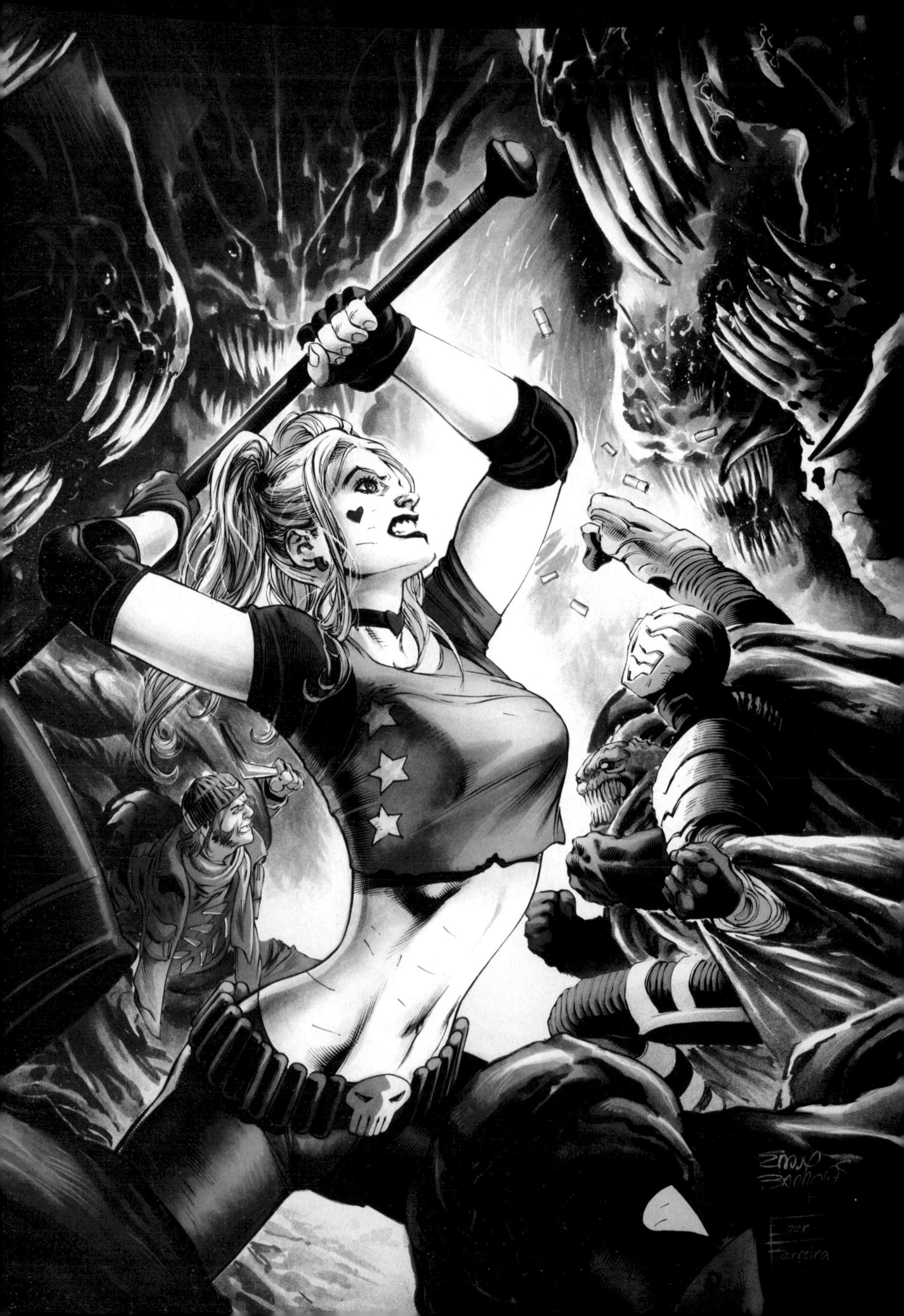

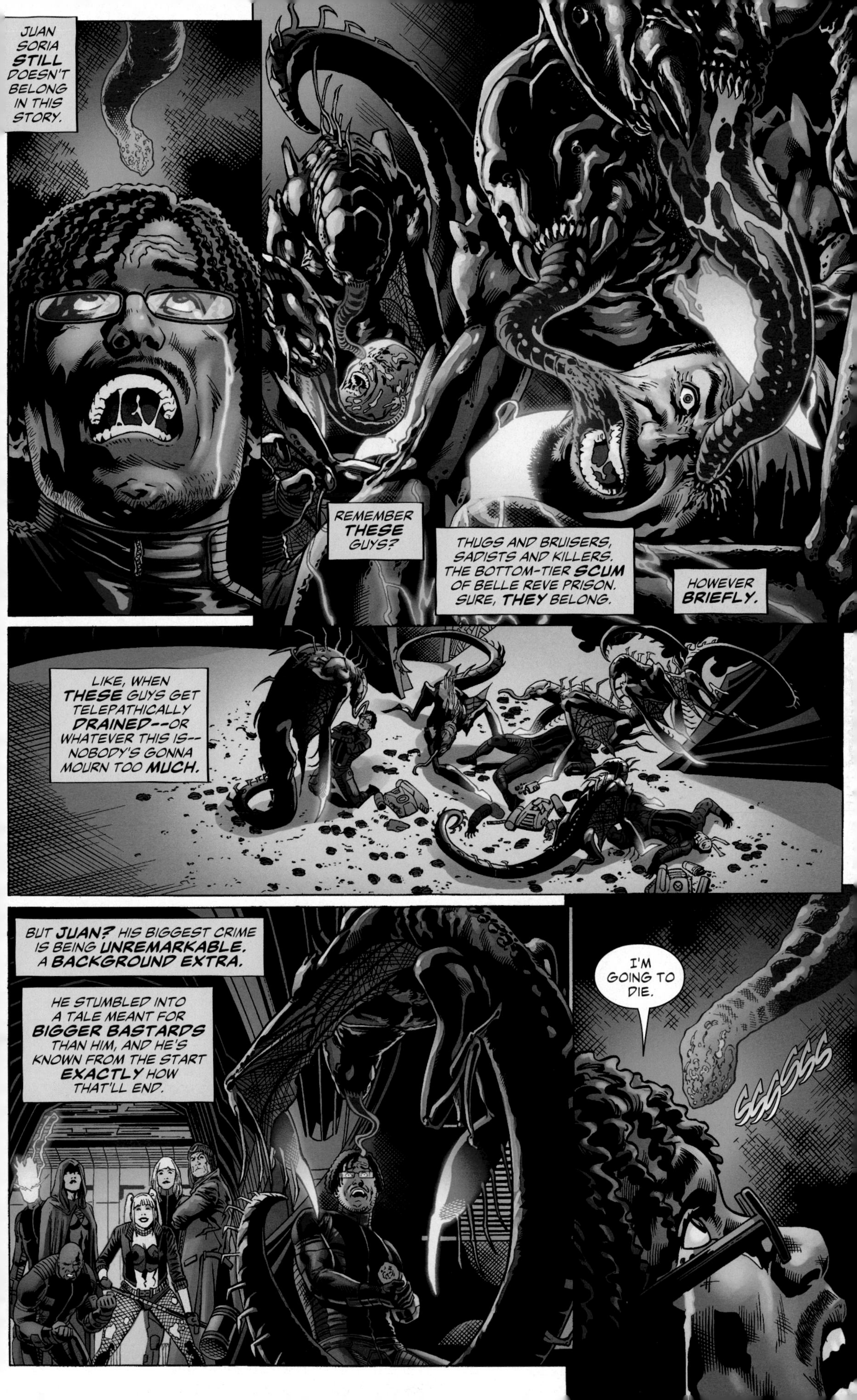

JUAN SORIA STILL DOESN'T BELONG IN THIS STORY.
REMEMBER THESE GUYS?
THUGS AND BRUISERS, SADISTS AND KILLERS. THE BOTTOM-TIER SCUM OF BELLE REVE PRISON. SURE, THEY BELONG.
HOWEVER BRIEFLY.
LIKE, WHEN THESE GUYS GET TELEPATHICALLY DRAINED--OR WHATEVER THIS IS--NOBODY'S GONNA MOURN TOO MUCH.
BUT JUAN? HIS BIGGEST CRIME IS BEING UNREMARKABLE. A BACKGROUND EXTRA.
HE STUMBLED INTO A TALE MEANT FOR BIGGER BASTARDS THAN HIM, AND HE'S KNOWN FROM THE START EXACTLY HOW THAT'LL END.
I'M GOING TO DIE.
SSSSSS

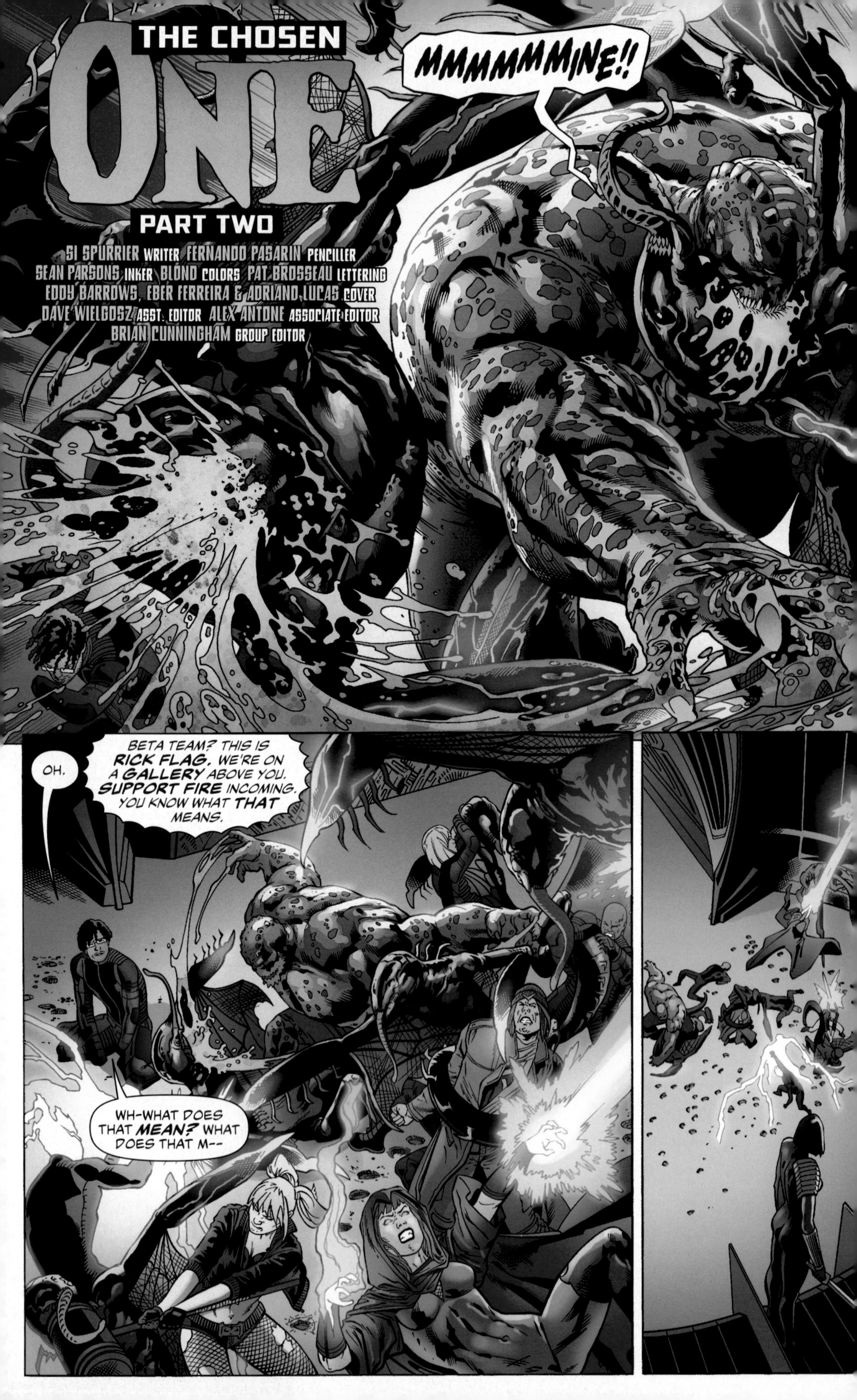
THE CHOSEN
ONE
PART TWO
SI SPURRIER WRITER FERNANDO PASARIN PENCILLER
SEAN PARSONS INKER BLOND COLORS PAT BROSSEAU LETTERING
EDDY BARROWS, EBER FERREIRA & ADRIANO LUCAS COVER
DAVE WIELGOSZ ASST. EDITOR ALEX ANTONE ASSOCIATE EDITOR
BRIAN CUNNINGHAM GROUP EDITOR
MMMMMMINE!!
OH.
BETA TEAM? THIS IS RICK FLAG. WE'RE ON A GALLERY ABOVE YOU. SUPPORT FIRE INCOMING. YOU KNOW WHAT THAT MEANS.
WH-WHAT DOES THAT MEAN? WHAT DOES THAT M--

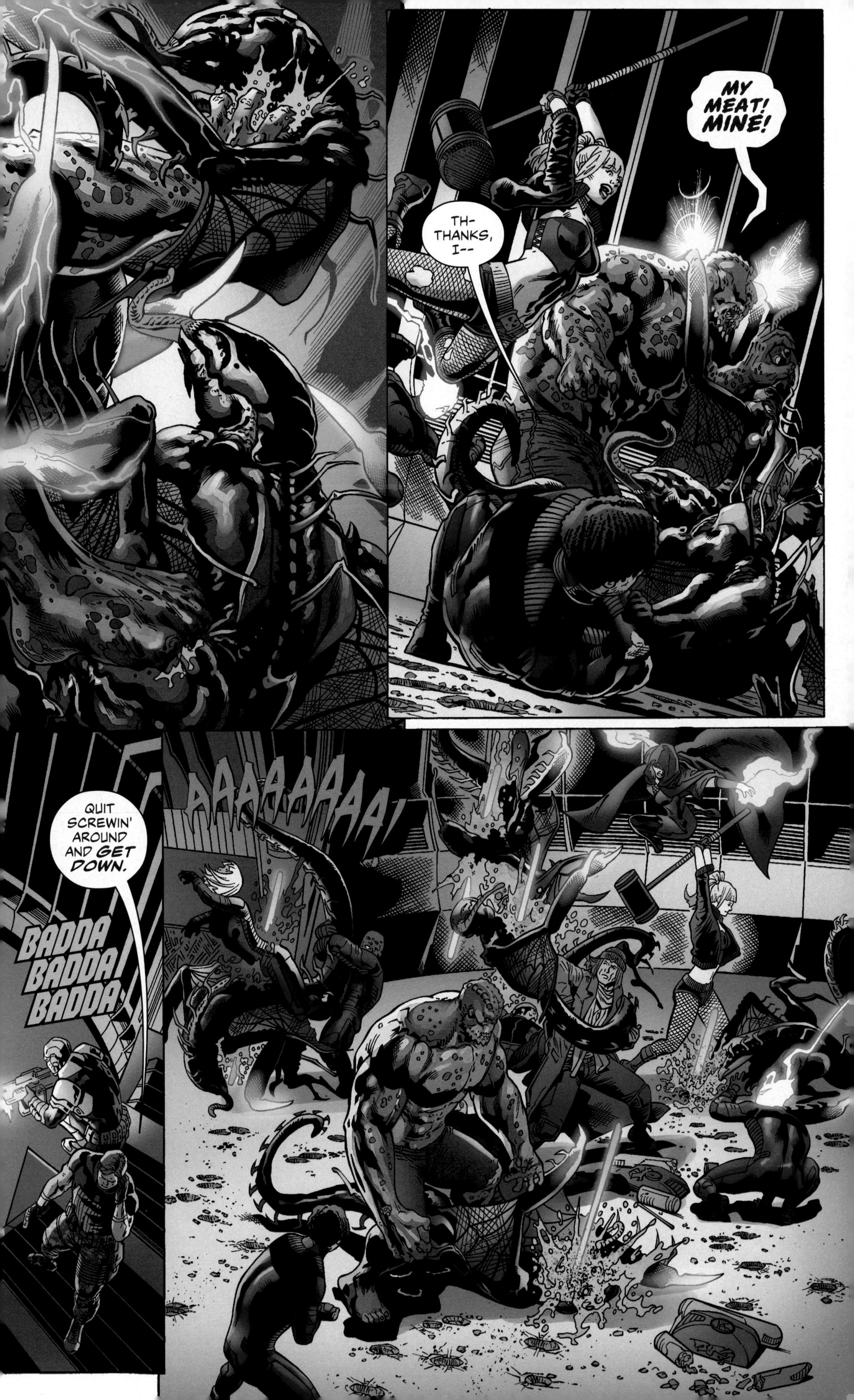
MY MEAT! MINE!
TH- THANKS, I--
QUIT SCREWIN' AROUND AND GET DOWN.
AAAAAAAAA!
BADDA BADDA BADDA

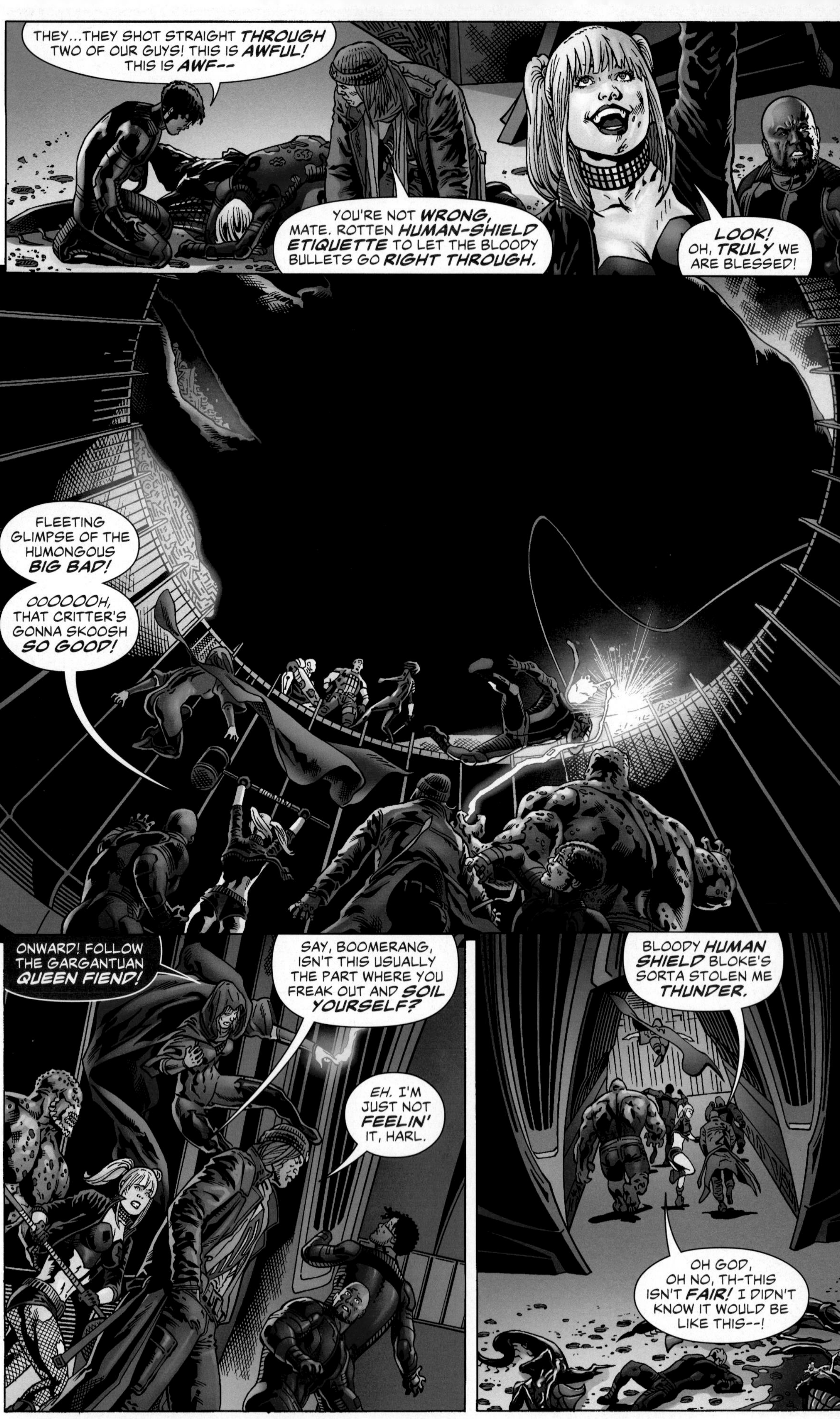
THEY...THEY SHOT STRAIGHT THROUGH TWO OF OUR GUYS! THIS IS AWFUL! THIS IS AWF--
YOU'RE NOT WRONG, MATE. ROTTEN HUMAN-SHIELD ETIQUETTE TO LET THE BLOODY BULLETS GO RIGHT THROUGH.
LOOK! OH, TRULY WE ARE BLESSED!
FLEETING GLIMPSE OF THE HUMONGOUS BIG BAD!
OOOOOOH, THAT CRITTER'S GONNA SKOOSH SO GOOD!
ONWARD! FOLLOW THE GARGANTUAN QUEEN FIEND!
SAY, BOOMERANG, ISN'T THIS USUALLY THE PART WHERE YOU FREAK OUT AND SOIL YOURSELF?
EH. I'M JUST NOT FEELIN' IT, HARL.
BLOODY HUMAN SHIELD BLOKE'S SORTA STOLEN ME THUNDER.
OH GOD, OH NO, TH-THIS ISN'T FAIR! I DIDN'T KNOW IT WOULD BE LIKE THIS--!

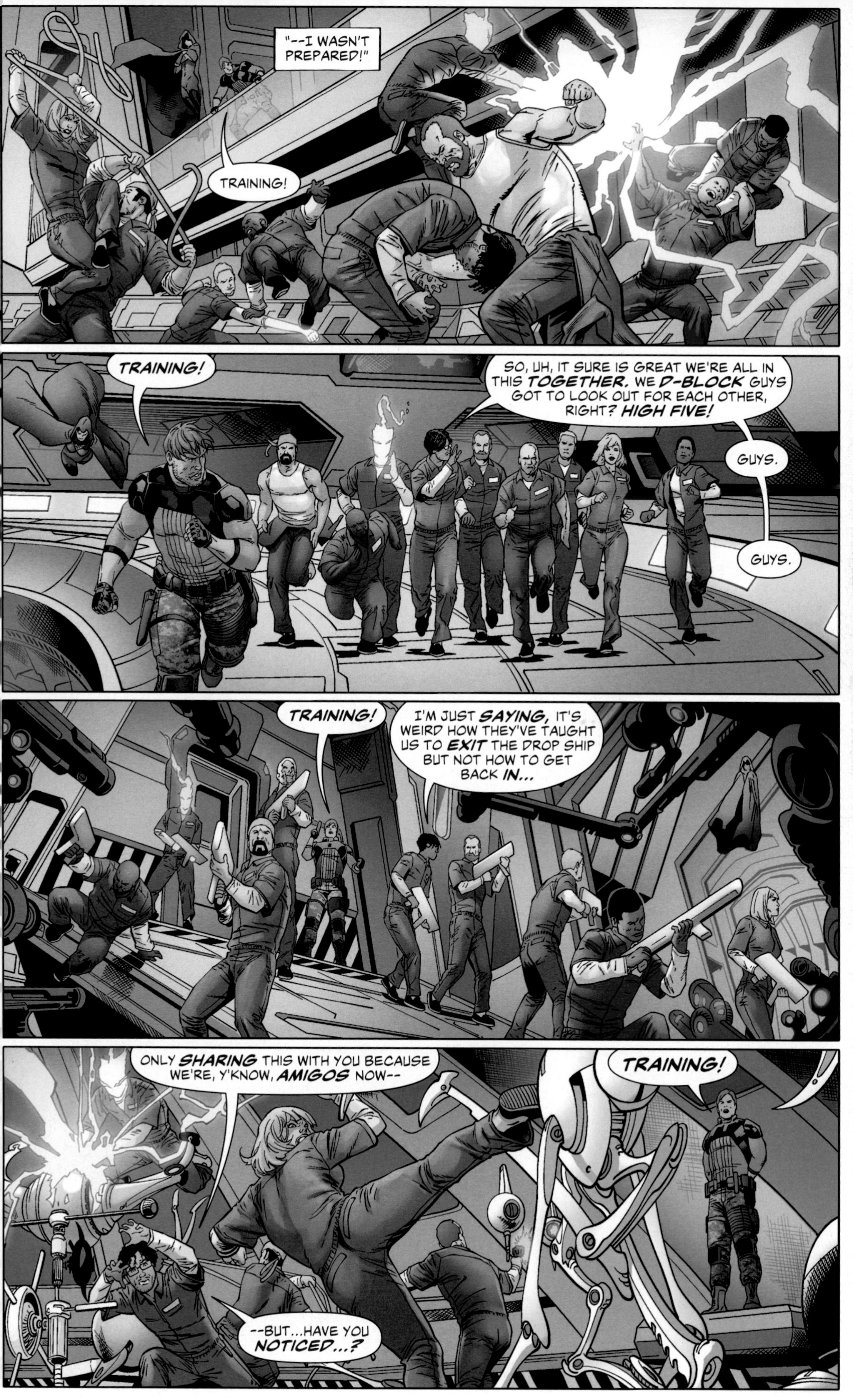
"--I WASN'T PREPARED!"
TRAINING!
TRAINING!
SO, UH, IT SURE IS GREAT WE'RE ALL IN THIS TOGETHER. WE D-BLOCK GUYS GOT TO LOOK OUT FOR EACH OTHER, RIGHT? HIGH FIVE!
GUYS.
GUYS.
TRAINING!
I'M JUST SAYING, IT'S WEIRD HOW THEY'VE TAUGHT US TO EXIT THE DROP SHIP BUT NOT HOW TO GET BACK IN...
ONLY SHARING THIS WITH YOU BECAUSE WE'RE, Y'KNOW, AMIGOS NOW--
TRAINING!
--BUT...HAVE YOU NOTICED...?

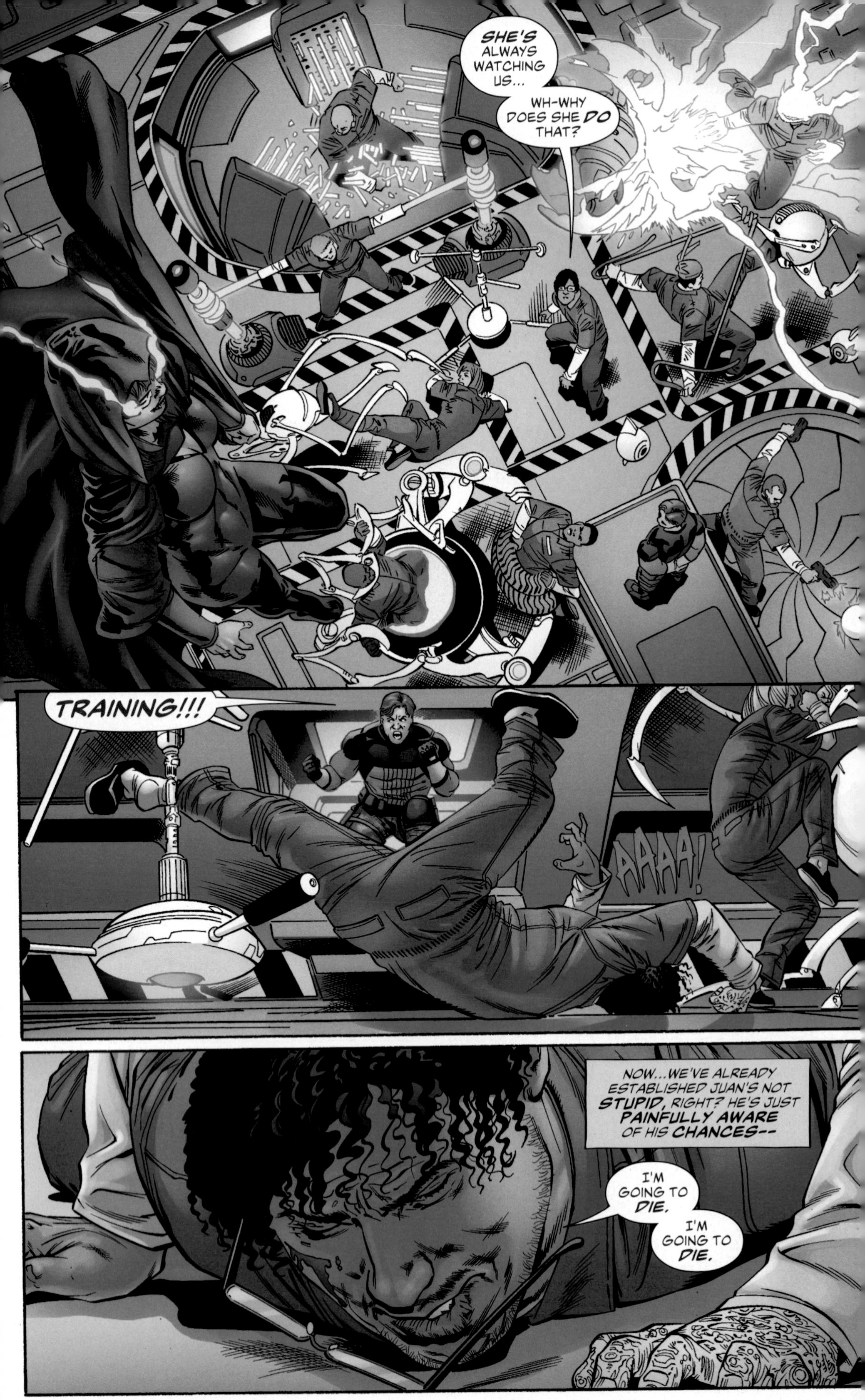
SHE'S ALWAYS WATCHING US...
WH-WHY DOES SHE DO THAT?
TRAINING!!!
AAAA!
NOW...WE'VE ALREADY ESTABLISHED JUAN'S NOT STUPID, RIGHT? HE'S JUST PAINFULLY AWARE OF HIS CHANCES--
I'M GOING TO DIE.
I'M GOING TO DIE.

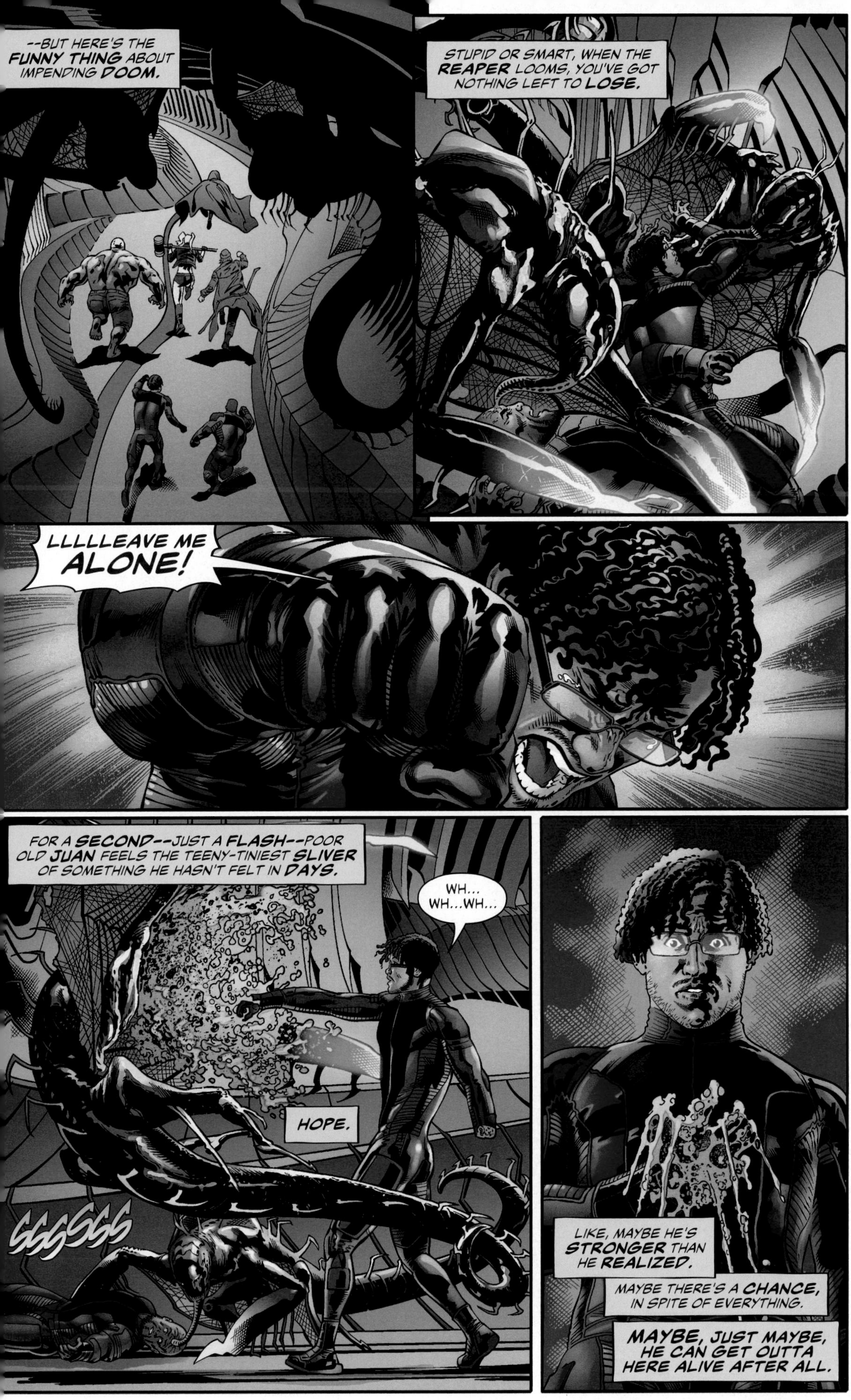
--BUT HERE'S THE FUNNY THING ABOUT IMPENDING DOOM.
STUPID OR SMART, WHEN THE REAPER LOOMS, YOU'VE GOT NOTHING LEFT TO LOSE.
LLLLLEAVE ME ALONE!
FOR A SECOND--JUST A FLASH--POOR OLD JUAN FEELS THE TEENY-TINIEST SLIVER OF SOMETHING HE HASN'T FELT IN DAYS.
WH... WH...WH...
HOPE.
GGGGGG
LIKE, MAYBE HE'S STRONGER THAN HE REALIZED.
MAYBE THERE'S A CHANCE, IN SPITE OF EVERYTHING.
MAYBE, JUST MAYBE, HE CAN GET OUTTA HERE ALIVE AFTER ALL.

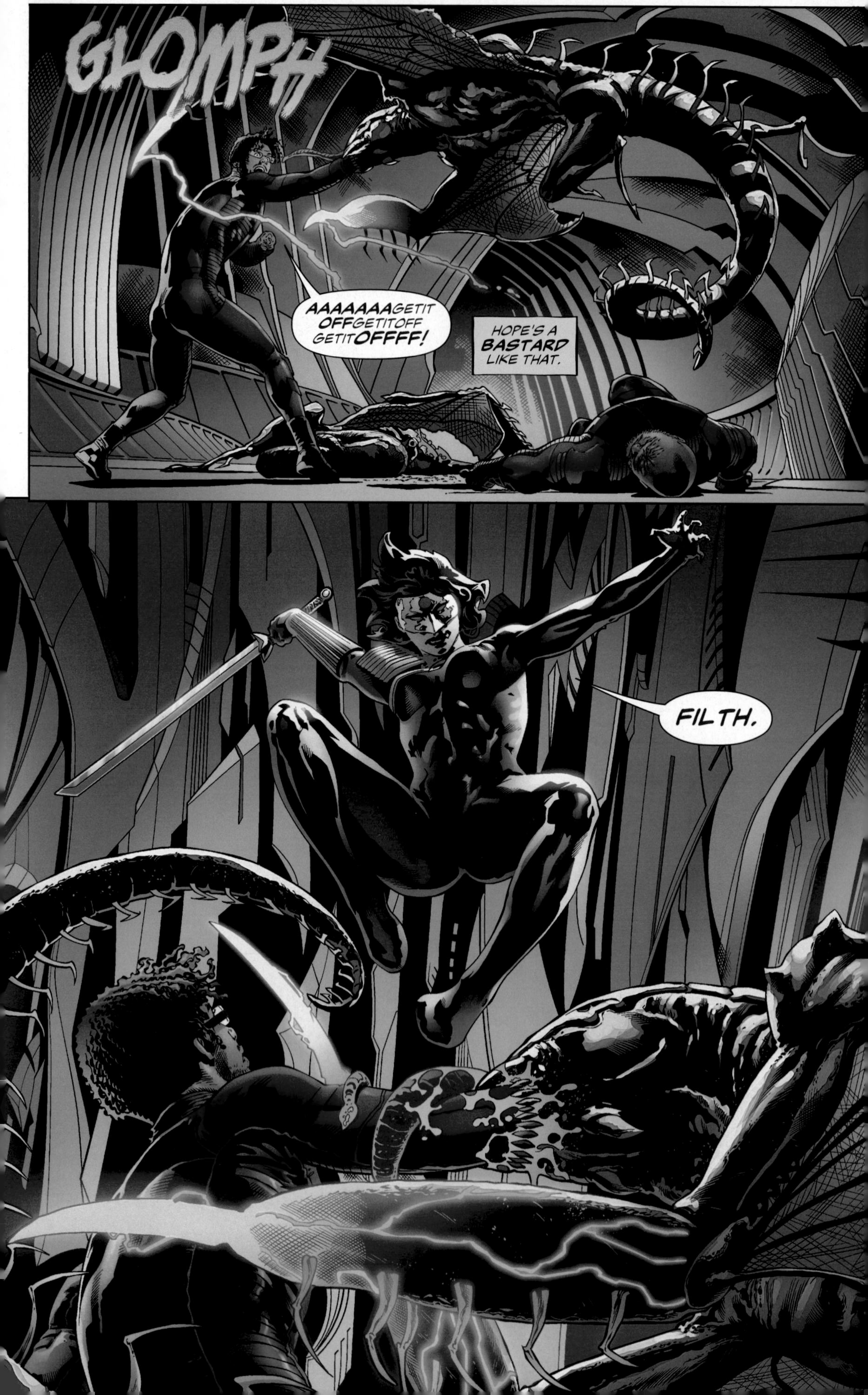
GLOMPH
AAAAAAAGETIT OFFGETITOFF GETITOFFFF!
HOPE'S A BASTARD LIKE THAT.
FILTH.

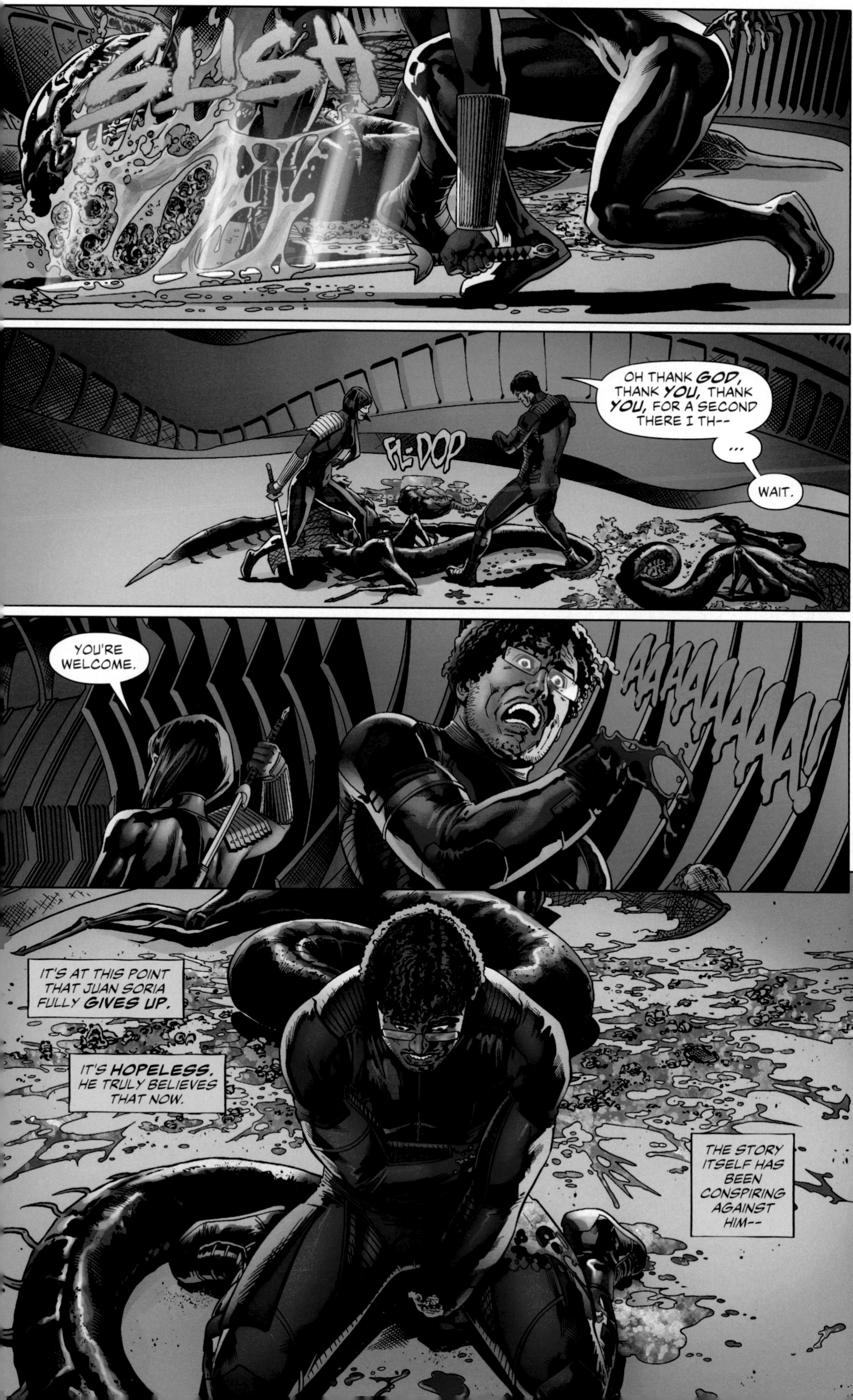
SLISH
FL-DOP
OH THANK GOD, THANK YOU, THANK YOU, FOR A SECOND THERE I TH--
...
WAIT.
YOU'RE WELCOME.
AAAAAAAAA!
IT'S AT THIS POINT THAT JUAN SORIA FULLY GIVES UP.
IT'S HOPELESS. HE TRULY BELIEVES THAT NOW.
THE STORY ITSELF HAS BEEN CONSPIRING AGAINST HIM--

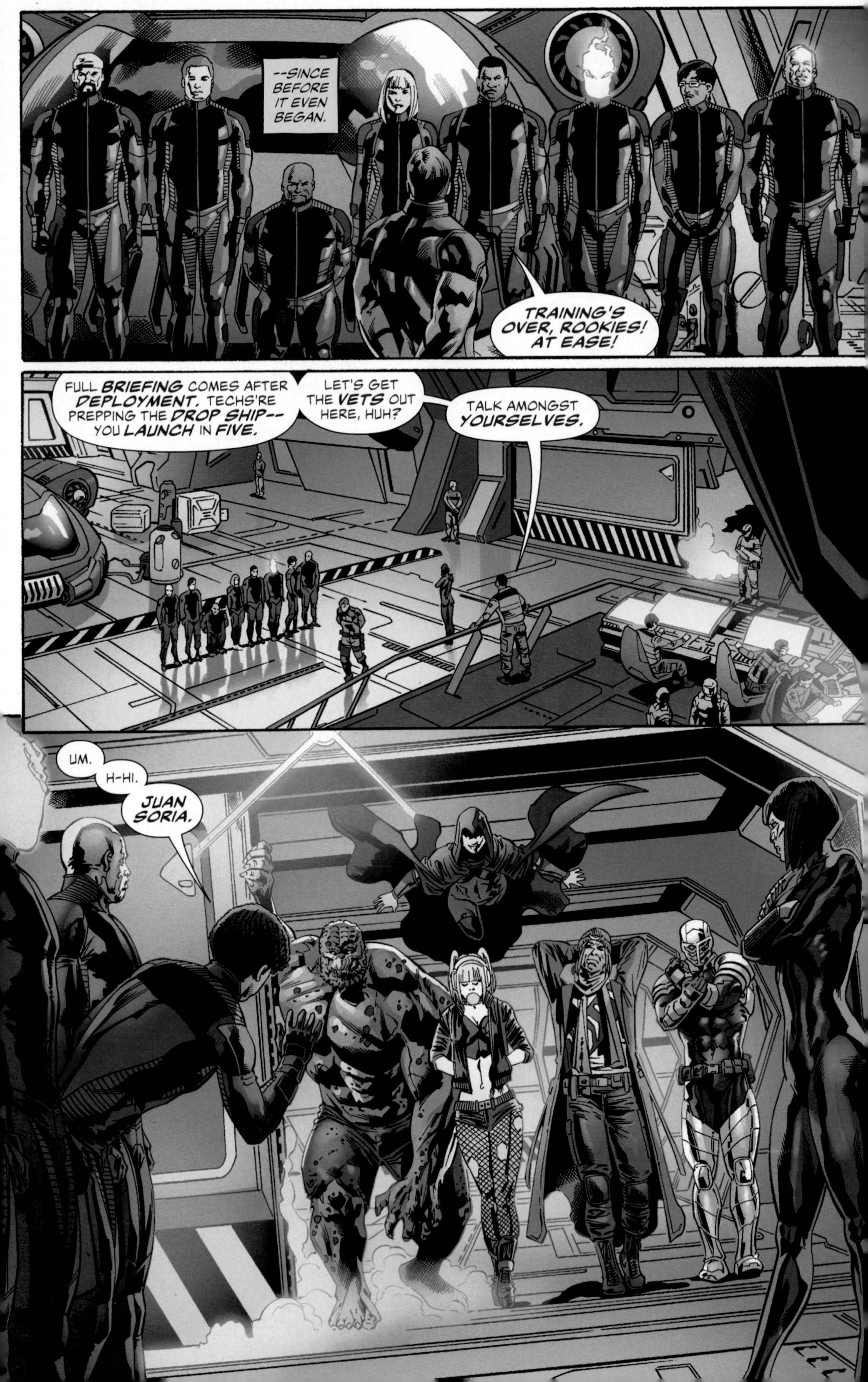
--SINCE BEFORE IT EVEN BEGAN.
TRAINING'S OVER, ROOKIES! AT EASE!
FULL BRIEFING COMES AFTER DEPLOYMENT. TECHS'RE PREPPING THE DROP SHIP-- YOU LAUNCH IN FIVE.
LET'S GET THE VETS OUT HERE, HUH?
TALK AMONGST YOURSELVES.
UM.
H-HI.
JUAN SORIA.

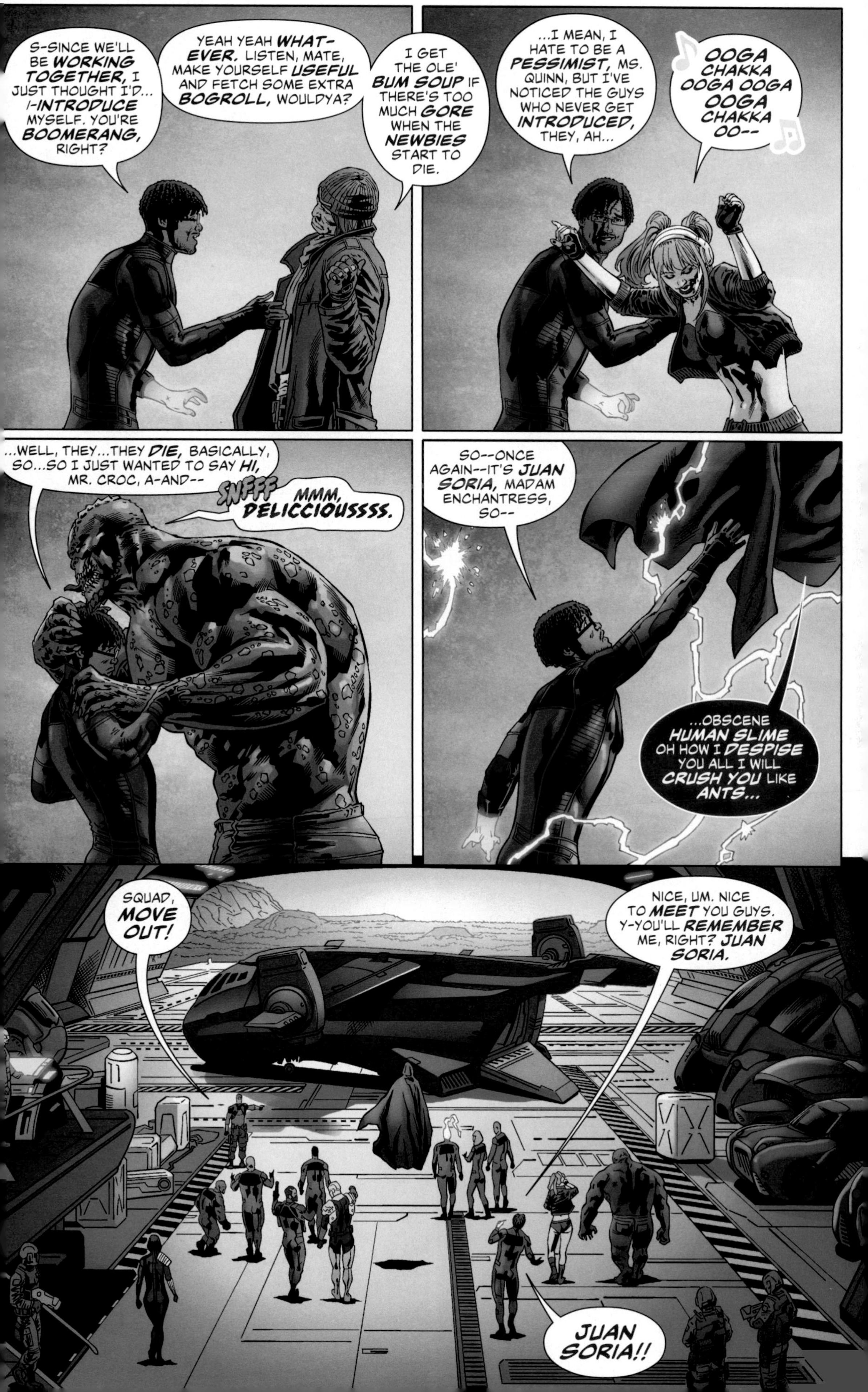
S-SINCE WE'LL BE WORKING TOGETHER, I JUST THOUGHT I'D... I-INTRODUCE MYSELF. YOU'RE BOOMERANG, RIGHT?
YEAH YEAH WHAT-EVER. LISTEN, MATE, MAKE YOURSELF USEFUL AND FETCH SOME EXTRA BOGROLL, WOULDYA?
I GET THE OLE' BUM SOUP IF THERE'S TOO MUCH GORE WHEN THE NEWBIES START TO DIE.
...I MEAN, I HATE TO BE A PESSIMIST, MS. QUINN, BUT I'VE NOTICED THE GUYS WHO NEVER GET INTRODUCED, THEY, AH...
OOGA CHAKKA OOGA OOGA OOGA CHAKKA OO--
...WELL, THEY...THEY DIE, BASICALLY, SO...SO I JUST WANTED TO SAY HI, MR. CROC, A-AND--
SNFFF
MMM, DELICCIOUSSSS.
SO--ONCE AGAIN--IT'S JUAN SORIA, MADAM ENCHANTRESS, SO--
...OBSCENE HUMAN SLIME OH HOW I DESPISE YOU ALL I WILL CRUSH YOU LIKE ANTS...
SQUAD, MOVE OUT!
NICE, UM. NICE TO MEET YOU GUYS. Y-YOU'LL REMEMBER ME, RIGHT? JUAN SORIA.
JUAN SORIA!!

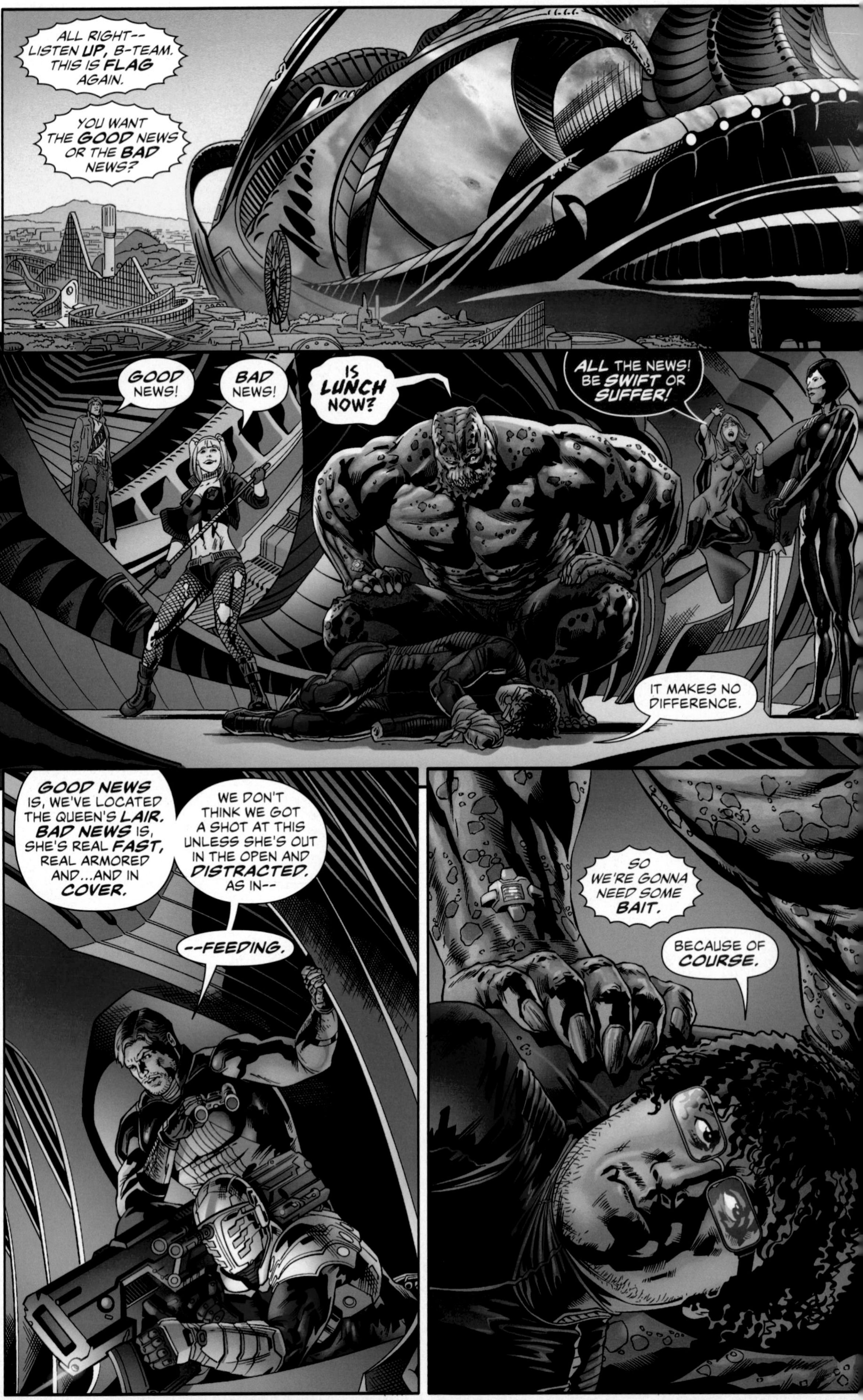
ALL RIGHT-- LISTEN UP, B-TEAM. THIS IS FLAG AGAIN.
YOU WANT THE GOOD NEWS OR THE BAD NEWS?
GOOD NEWS!
BAD NEWS!
IS LUNCH NOW?
ALL THE NEWS! BE SWIFT OR SUFFER!
IT MAKES NO DIFFERENCE.
GOOD NEWS IS, WE'VE LOCATED THE QUEEN'S LAIR. BAD NEWS IS, SHE'S REAL FAST, REAL ARMORED AND...AND IN COVER.
WE DON'T THINK WE GOT A SHOT AT THIS UNLESS SHE'S OUT IN THE OPEN AND DISTRACTED. AS IN--
--FEEDING.
SO WE'RE GONNA NEED SOME BAIT.
BECAUSE OF COURSE.

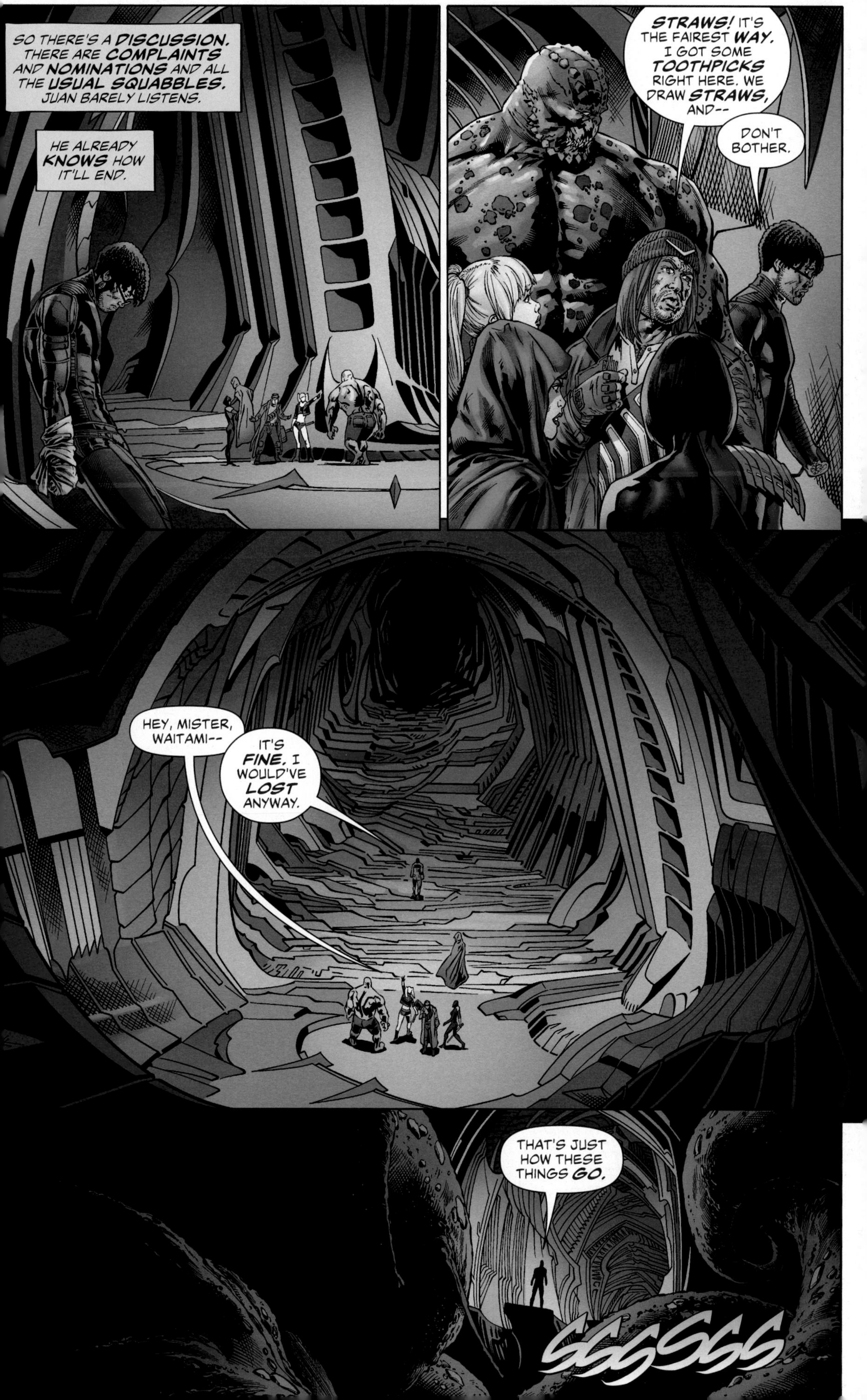
SO THERE'S A DISCUSSION. THERE ARE COMPLAINTS AND NOMINATIONS AND ALL THE USUAL SQUABBLES. JUAN BARELY LISTENS.
HE ALREADY KNOWS HOW IT'LL END.
STRAWS! IT'S THE FAIREST WAY. I GOT SOME TOOTHPICKS RIGHT HERE. WE DRAW STRAWS, AND--
DON'T BOTHER.
HEY, MISTER, WAITAMI--
IT'S FINE. I WOULD'VE LOST ANYWAY.
THAT'S JUST HOW THESE THINGS GO.
SSSSSS

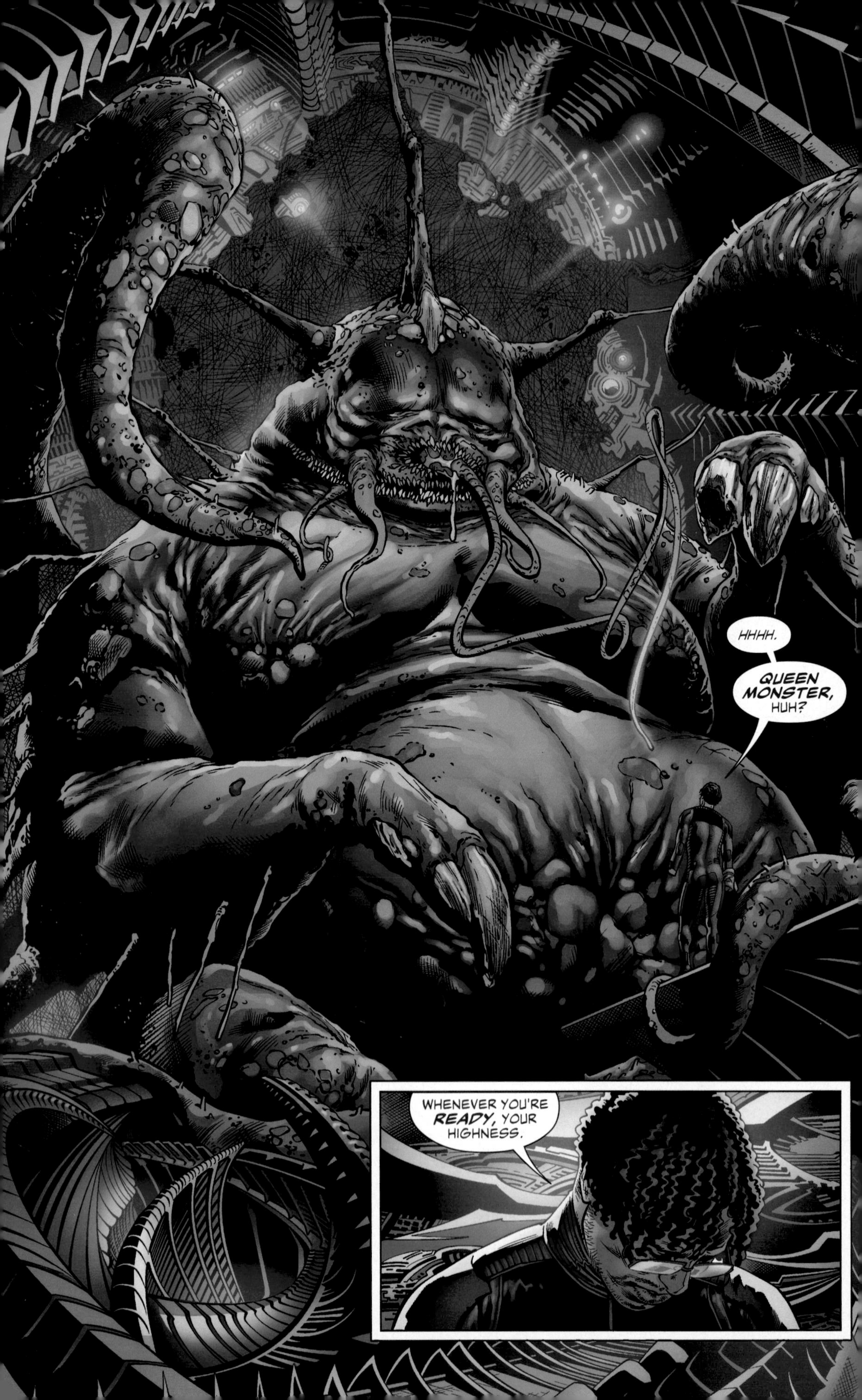
HHHH.
QUEEN MONSTER, HUH?
WHENEVER YOU'RE READY, YOUR HIGHNESS.

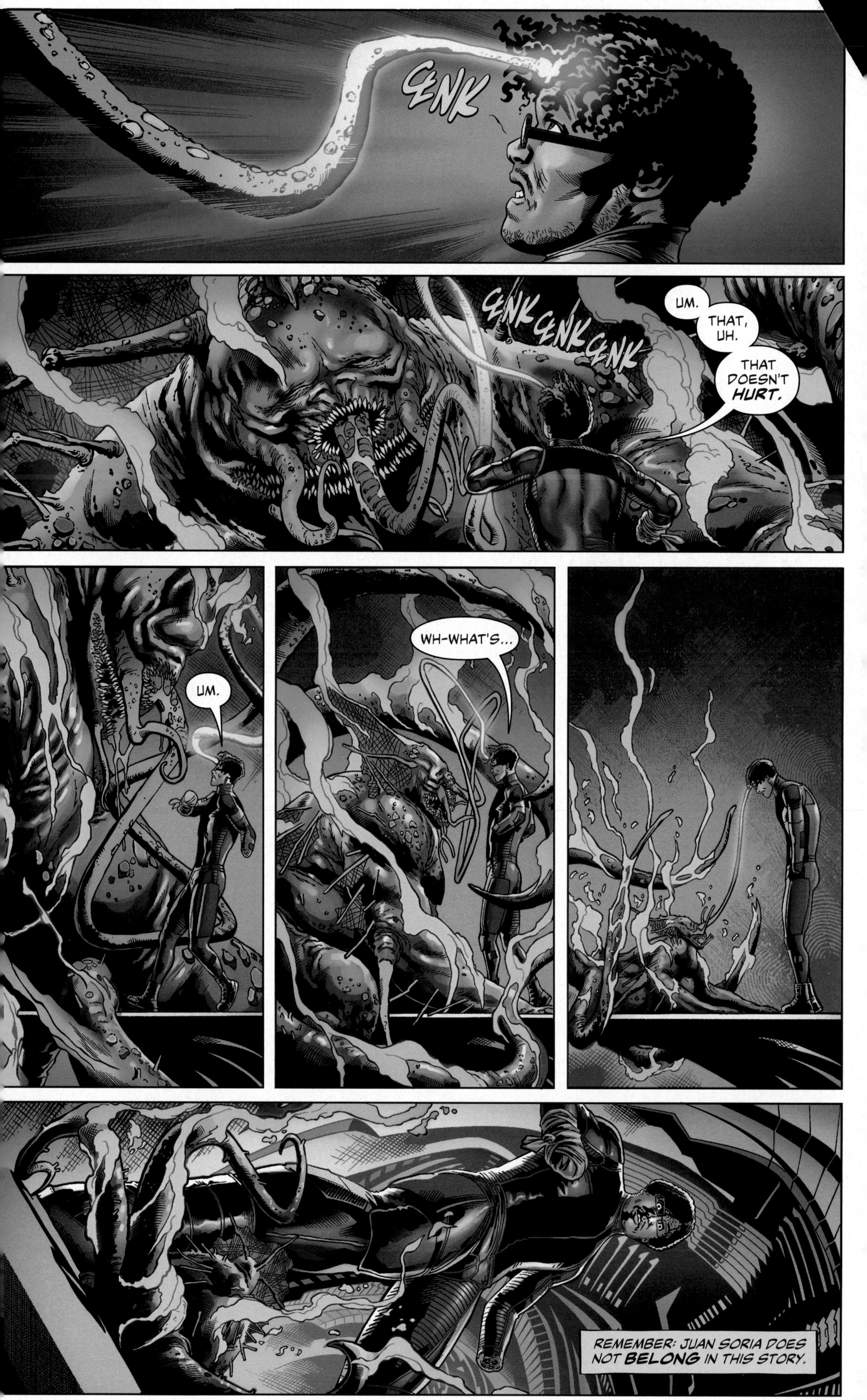
GLNK
GLNK GLNK GLNK
UM.
THAT, UH.
THAT DOESN'T HURT.
UM.
WH-WHAT'S...
REMEMBER: JUAN SORIA DOES NOT BELONG IN THIS STORY.

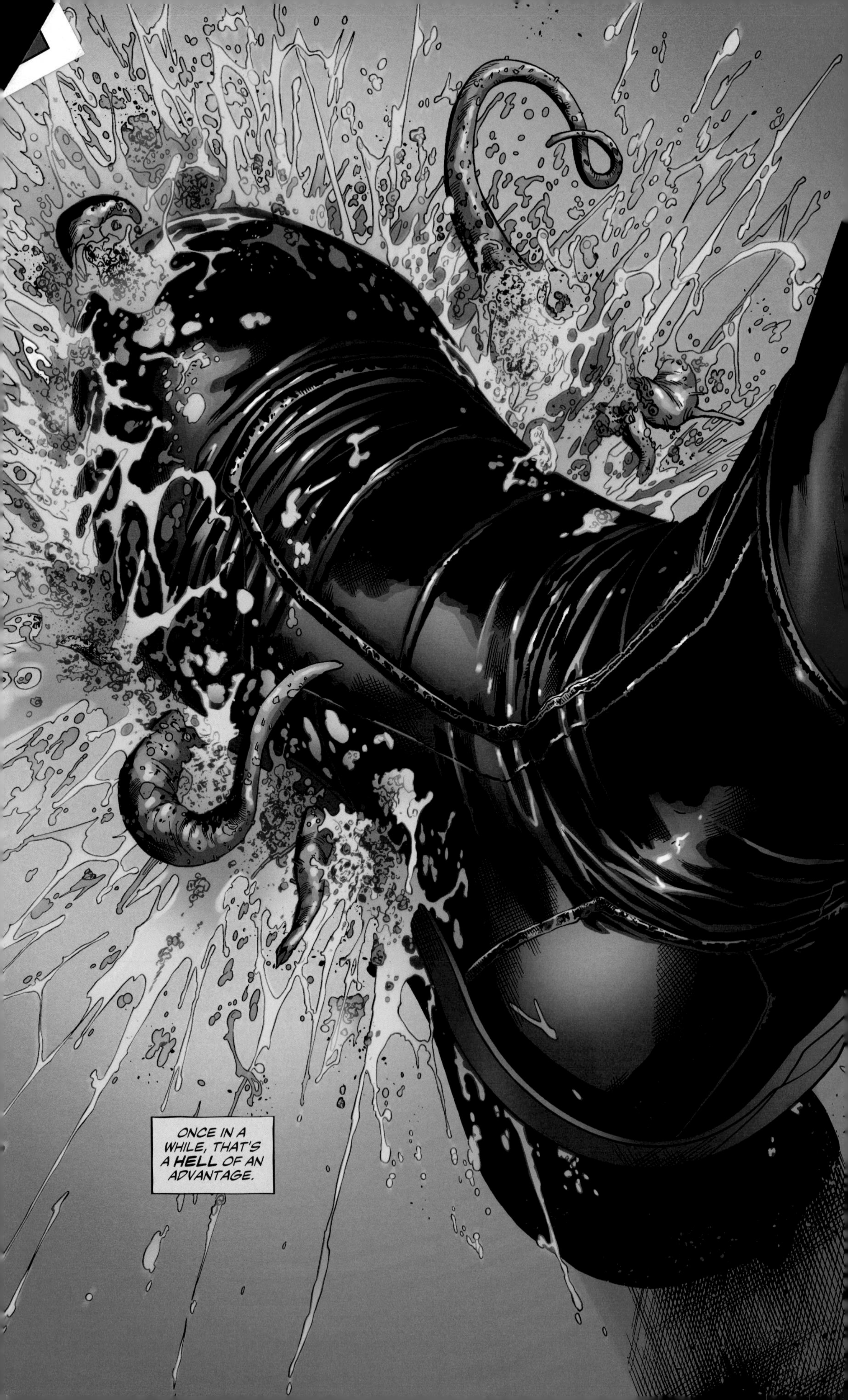
ONCE IN A WHILE, THAT'S A **HELL** OF AN ADVANTAGE.

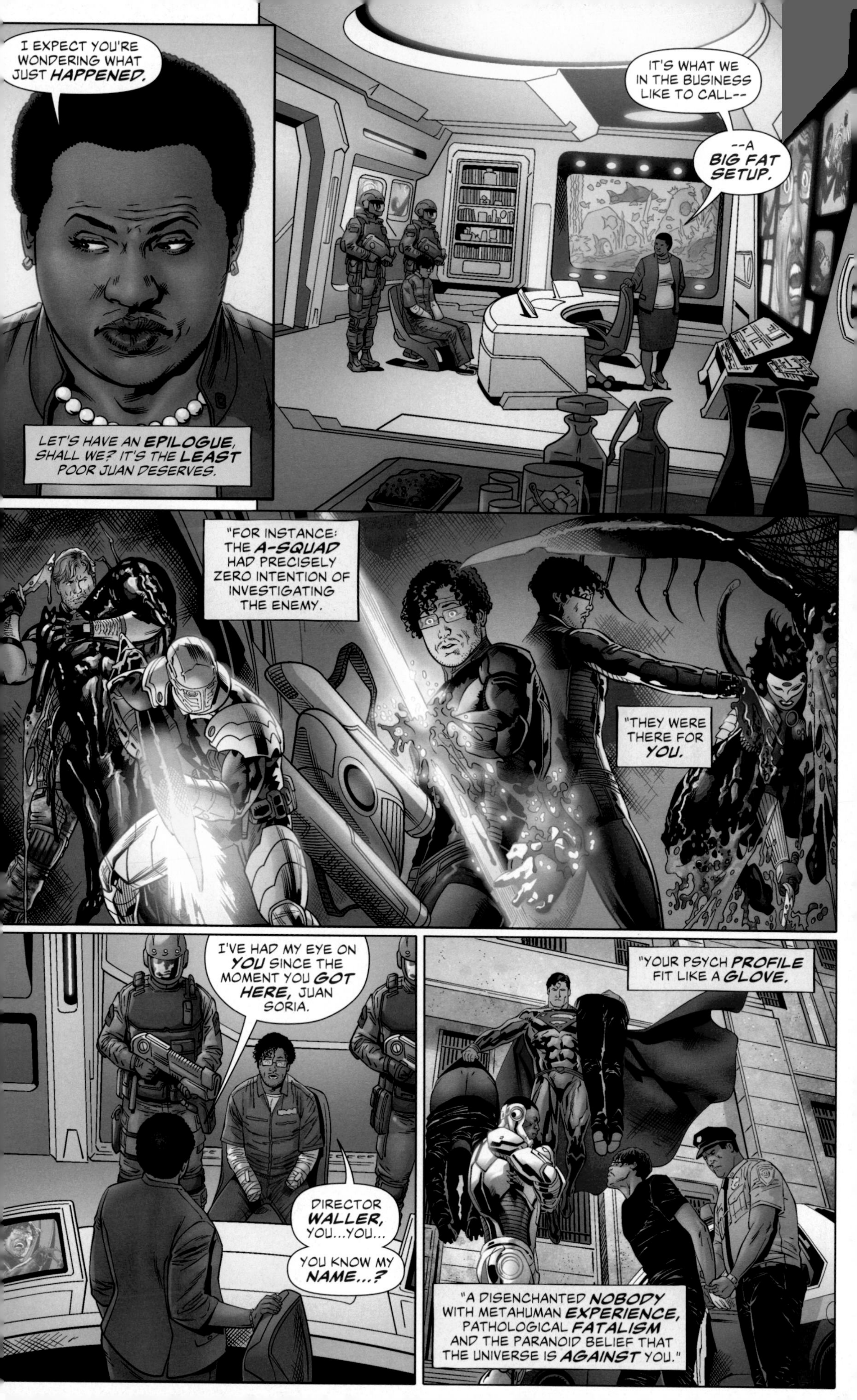
I EXPECT YOU'RE WONDERING WHAT JUST HAPPENED.
LET'S HAVE AN EPILOGUE, SHALL WE? IT'S THE LEAST POOR JUAN DESERVES.
IT'S WHAT WE IN THE BUSINESS LIKE TO CALL--
--A BIG FAT SETUP.
"FOR INSTANCE: THE A-SQUAD HAD PRECISELY ZERO INTENTION OF INVESTIGATING THE ENEMY.
"THEY WERE THERE FOR YOU.
I'VE HAD MY EYE ON YOU SINCE THE MOMENT YOU GOT HERE, JUAN SORIA.
DIRECTOR WALLER, YOU...YOU...
YOU KNOW MY NAME...?
"YOUR PSYCH PROFILE FIT LIKE A GLOVE.
"A DISENCHANTED NOBODY WITH METAHUMAN EXPERIENCE, PATHOLOGICAL FATALISM AND THE PARANOID BELIEF THAT THE UNIVERSE IS AGAINST YOU."

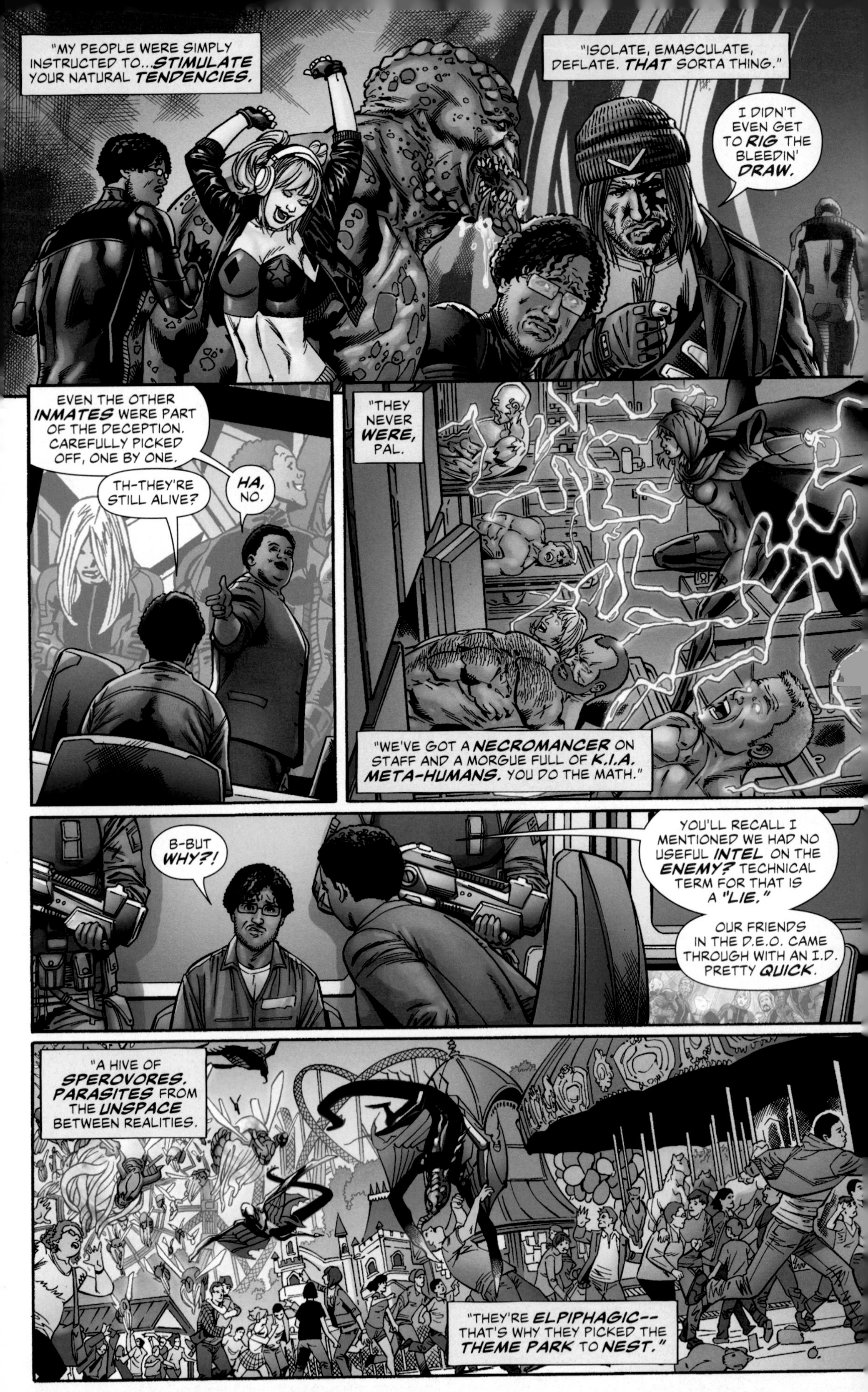

"MY PEOPLE WERE SIMPLY INSTRUCTED TO...STIMULATE YOUR NATURAL TENDENCIES.
"ISOLATE, EMASCULATE, DEFLATE. THAT SORTA THING."
I DIDN'T EVEN GET TO RIG THE BLEEDIN' DRAW.
EVEN THE OTHER INMATES WERE PART OF THE DECEPTION. CAREFULLY PICKED OFF, ONE BY ONE.
TH-THEY'RE STILL ALIVE?
HA, NO.
"THEY NEVER WERE, PAL.
"WE'VE GOT A NECROMANCER ON STAFF AND A MORGUE FULL OF K.I.A. META-HUMANS. YOU DO THE MATH."
B-BUT WHY?!
YOU'LL RECALL I MENTIONED WE HAD NO USEFUL INTEL ON THE ENEMY? TECHNICAL TERM FOR THAT IS A "LIE."
OUR FRIENDS IN THE D.E.O. CAME THROUGH WITH AN I.D. PRETTY QUICK.
"A HIVE OF SPEROVORES. PARASITES FROM THE UNSPACE BETWEEN REALITIES.
"THEY'RE ELPIPHAGIC-- THAT'S WHY THEY PICKED THE THEME PARK TO NEST."

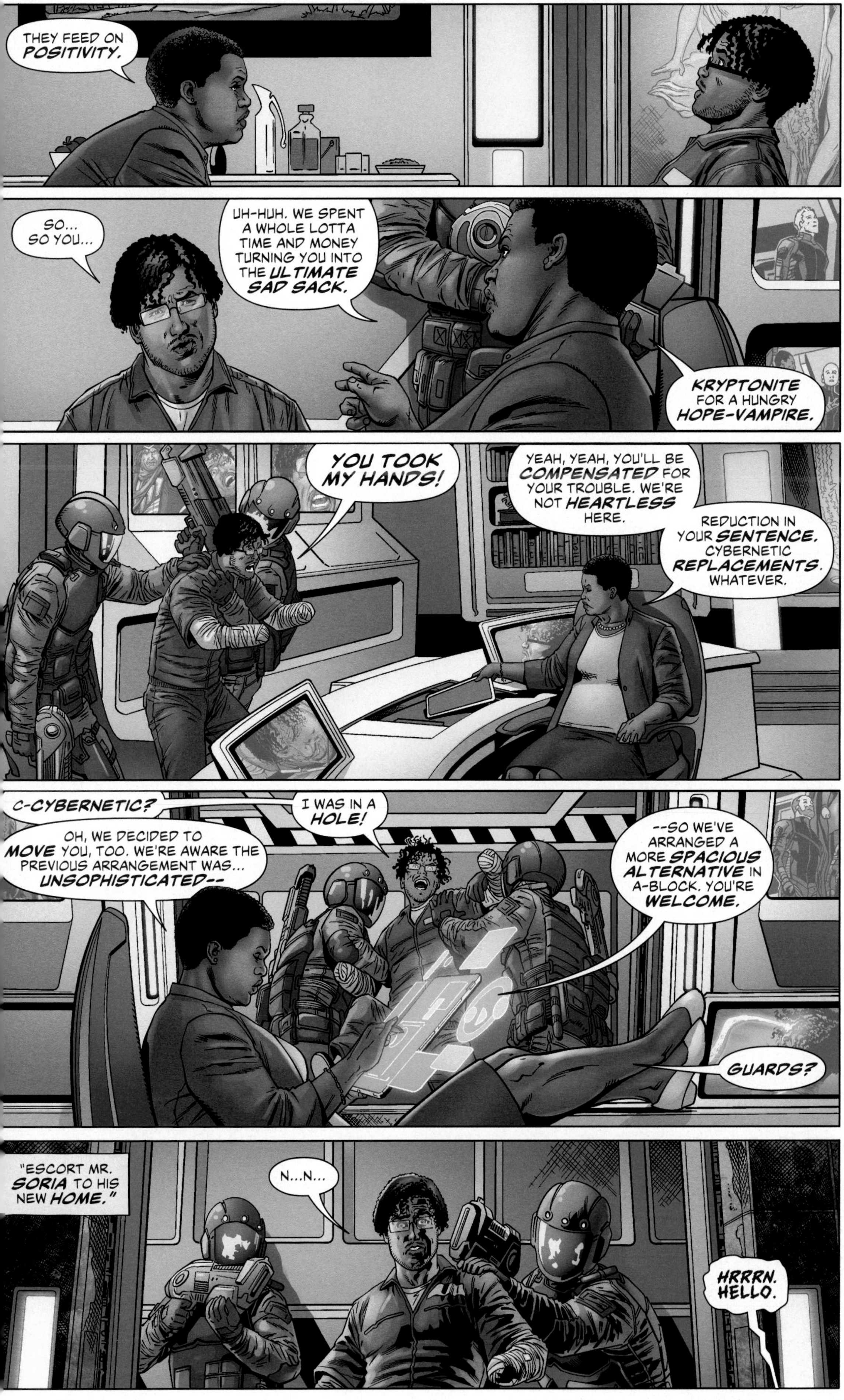
THEY FEED ON POSITIVITY.
SO... SO YOU...
UH-HUH. WE SPENT A WHOLE LOTTA TIME AND MONEY TURNING YOU INTO THE ULTIMATE SAD SACK.
KRYPTONITE FOR A HUNGRY HOPE-VAMPIRE.
YOU TOOK MY HANDS!
YEAH, YEAH, YOU'LL BE COMPENSATED FOR YOUR TROUBLE. WE'RE NOT HEARTLESS HERE.
REDUCTION IN YOUR SENTENCE. CYBERNETIC REPLACEMENTS. WHATEVER.
C-CYBERNETIC?
I WAS IN A HOLE!
OH, WE DECIDED TO MOVE YOU, TOO. WE'RE AWARE THE PREVIOUS ARRANGEMENT WAS... UNSOPHISTICATED--
--SO WE'VE ARRANGED A MORE SPACIOUS ALTERNATIVE IN A-BLOCK. YOU'RE WELCOME.
GUARDS?
"ESCORT MR. SORIA TO HIS NEW HOME."
N...N...
HRRRN. HELLO.

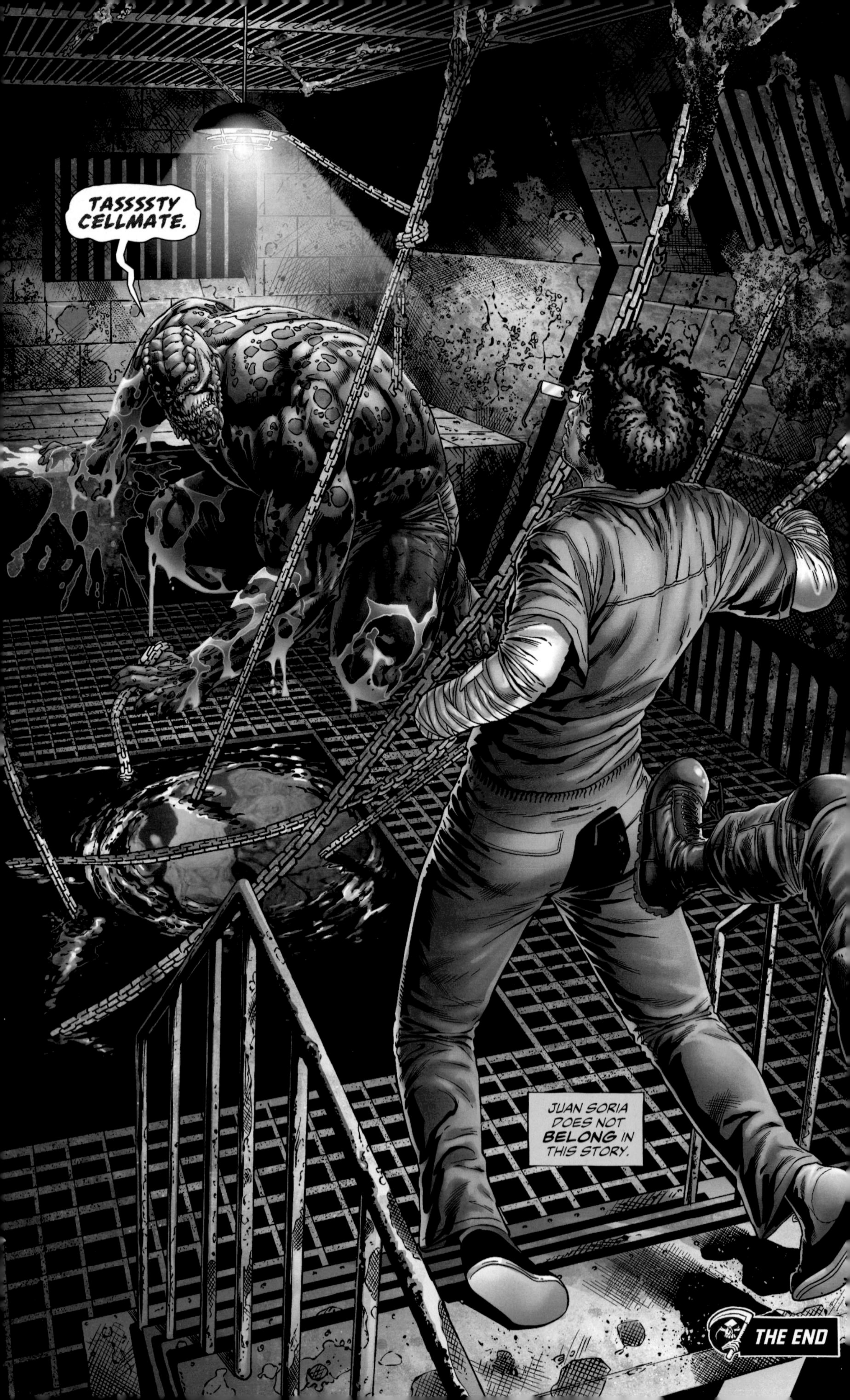
TASSSSTY CELLMATE.
JUAN SORIA DOES NOT BELONG IN THIS STORY.
THE END

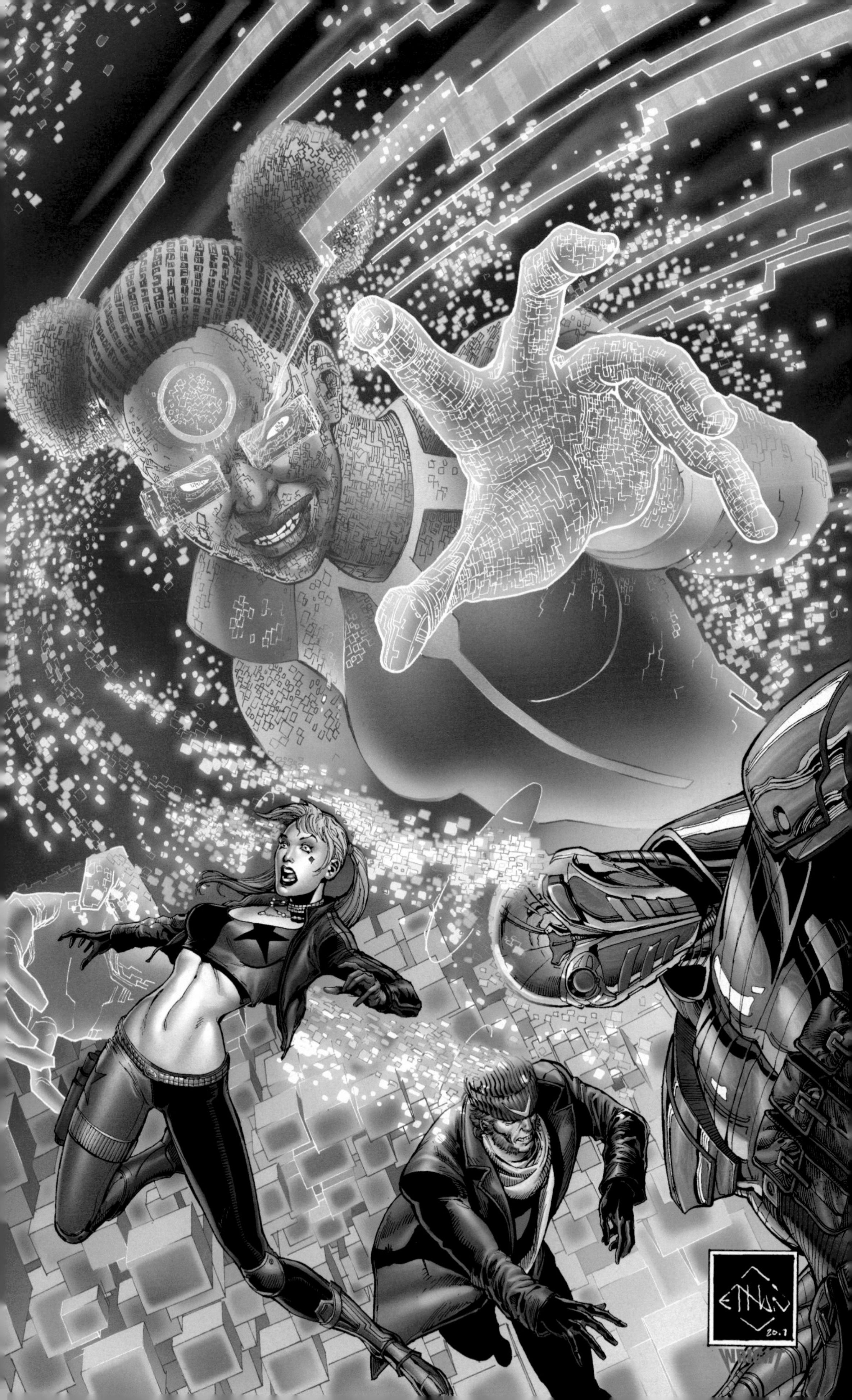

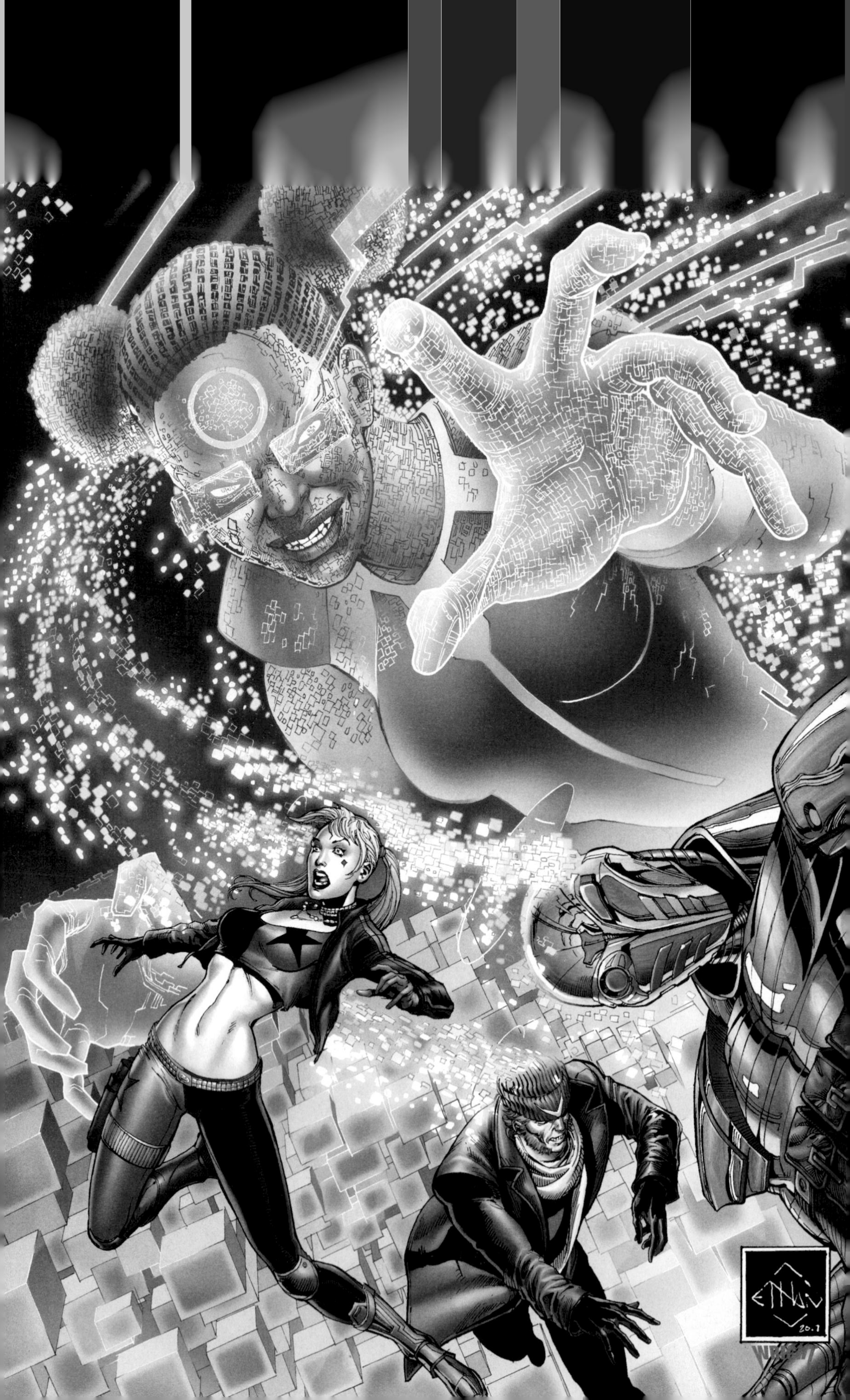

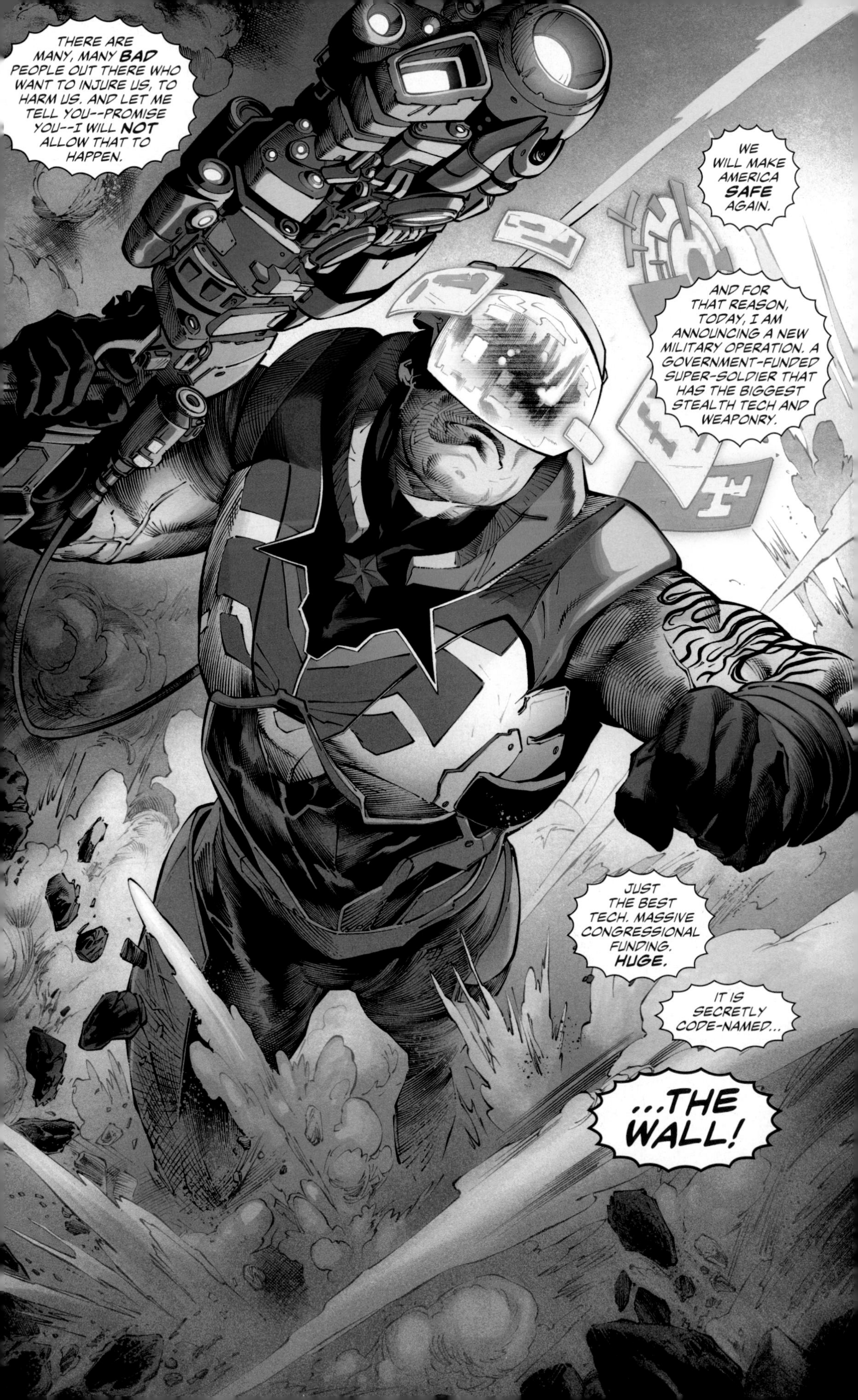
THERE ARE MANY, MANY BAD PEOPLE OUT THERE WHO WANT TO INJURE US, TO HARM US. AND LET ME TELL YOU--PROMISE YOU--I WILL NOT ALLOW THAT TO HAPPEN.
WE WILL MAKE AMERICA SAFE AGAIN.
AND FOR THAT REASON, TODAY, I AM ANNOUNCING A NEW MILITARY OPERATION. A GOVERNMENT-FUNDED SUPER-SOLDIER THAT HAS THE BIGGEST STEALTH TECH AND WEAPONRY.
JUST THE BEST TECH. MASSIVE CONGRESSIONAL FUNDING. HUGE.
IT IS SECRETLY CODE-NAMED...
...THE WALL!

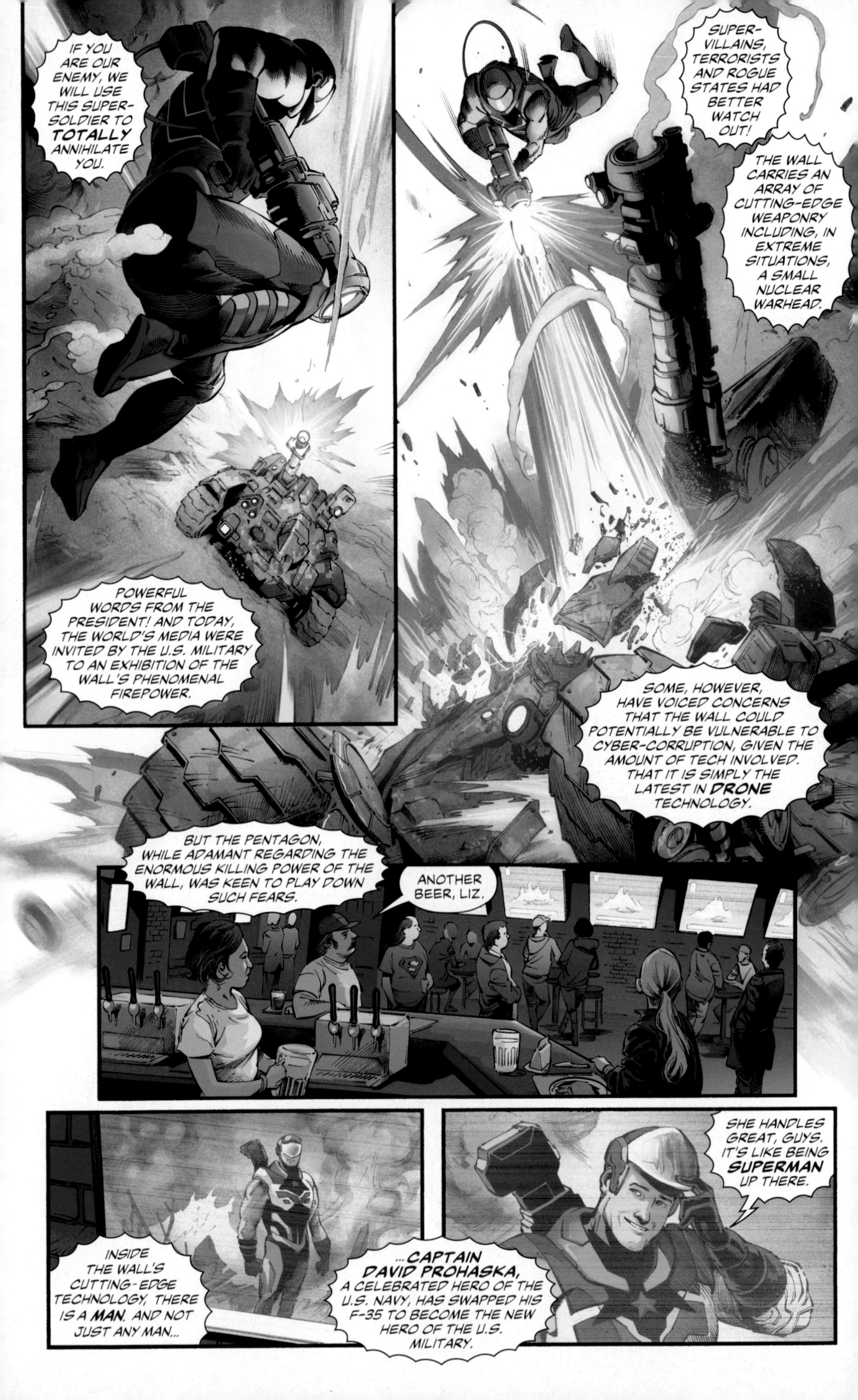
IF YOU ARE OUR ENEMY, WE WILL USE THIS SUPER-SOLDIER TO **TOTALLY** ANNIHILATE YOU.
SUPER-VILLAINS, TERRORISTS AND ROGUE STATES HAD BETTER WATCH OUT!
THE WALL CARRIES AN ARRAY OF CUTTING-EDGE WEAPONRY INCLUDING, IN EXTREME SITUATIONS, A SMALL NUCLEAR WARHEAD.
POWERFUL WORDS FROM THE PRESIDENT! AND TODAY, THE WORLD'S MEDIA WERE INVITED BY THE U.S. MILITARY TO AN EXHIBITION OF THE WALL'S PHENOMENAL FIREPOWER.
SOME, HOWEVER, HAVE VOICED CONCERNS THAT THE WALL COULD POTENTIALLY BE VULNERABLE TO CYBER-CORRUPTION, GIVEN THE AMOUNT OF TECH INVOLVED. THAT IT IS SIMPLY THE LATEST IN **DRONE** TECHNOLOGY.
BUT THE PENTAGON, WHILE ADAMANT REGARDING THE ENORMOUS KILLING POWER OF THE WALL, WAS KEEN TO PLAY DOWN SUCH FEARS.
ANOTHER BEER, LIZ.
INSIDE THE WALL'S CUTTING-EDGE TECHNOLOGY, THERE IS A **MAN**. AND NOT JUST ANY MAN...
...**CAPTAIN DAVID PROHASKA,** A CELEBRATED HERO OF THE U.S. NAVY, HAS SWAPPED HIS F-35 TO BECOME THE NEW HERO OF THE U.S. MILITARY.
SHE HANDLES GREAT, GUYS. IT'S LIKE BEING **SUPERMAN** UP THERE.

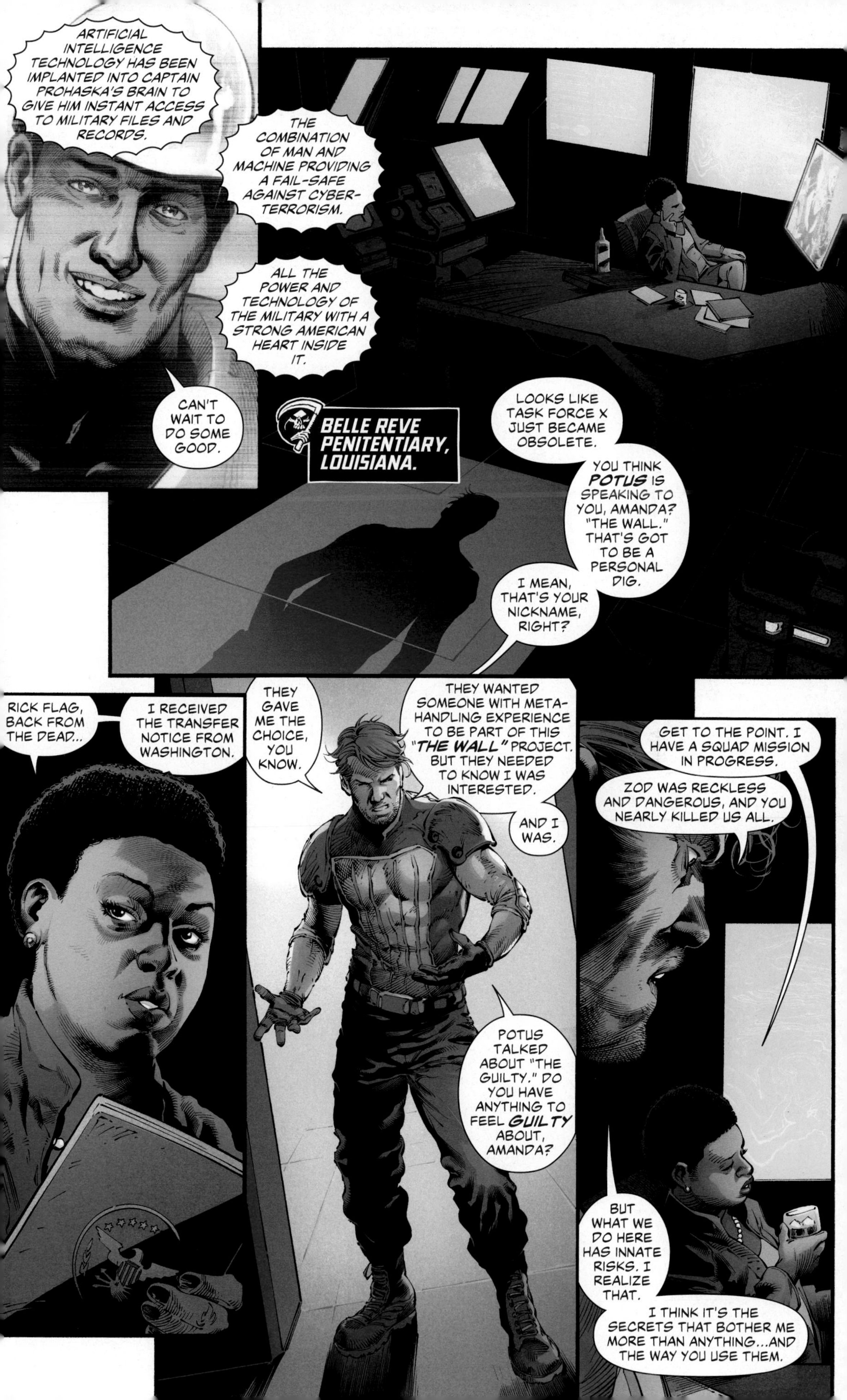

ARTIFICIAL INTELLIGENCE TECHNOLOGY HAS BEEN IMPLANTED INTO CAPTAIN PROHASKA'S BRAIN TO GIVE HIM INSTANT ACCESS TO MILITARY FILES AND RECORDS.
THE COMBINATION OF MAN AND MACHINE PROVIDING A FAIL-SAFE AGAINST CYBER-TERRORISM.
ALL THE POWER AND TECHNOLOGY OF THE MILITARY WITH A STRONG AMERICAN HEART INSIDE IT.
CAN'T WAIT TO DO SOME GOOD.
BELLE REVE PENITENTIARY, LOUISIANA.
LOOKS LIKE TASK FORCE X JUST BECAME OBSOLETE.
YOU THINK POTUS IS SPEAKING TO YOU, AMANDA? "THE WALL." THAT'S GOT TO BE A PERSONAL DIG.
I MEAN, THAT'S YOUR NICKNAME, RIGHT?
RICK FLAG, BACK FROM THE DEAD...
I RECEIVED THE TRANSFER NOTICE FROM WASHINGTON.
THEY GAVE ME THE CHOICE, YOU KNOW.
THEY WANTED SOMEONE WITH META-HANDLING EXPERIENCE TO BE PART OF THIS "THE WALL" PROJECT. BUT THEY NEEDED TO KNOW I WAS INTERESTED.
AND I WAS.
POTUS TALKED ABOUT "THE GUILTY." DO YOU HAVE ANYTHING TO FEEL GUILTY ABOUT, AMANDA?
GET TO THE POINT. I HAVE A SQUAD MISSION IN PROGRESS.
ZOD WAS RECKLESS AND DANGEROUS, AND YOU NEARLY KILLED US ALL.
BUT WHAT WE DO HERE HAS INNATE RISKS. I REALIZE THAT.
I THINK IT'S THE SECRETS THAT BOTHER ME MORE THAN ANYTHING...AND THE WAY YOU USE THEM.

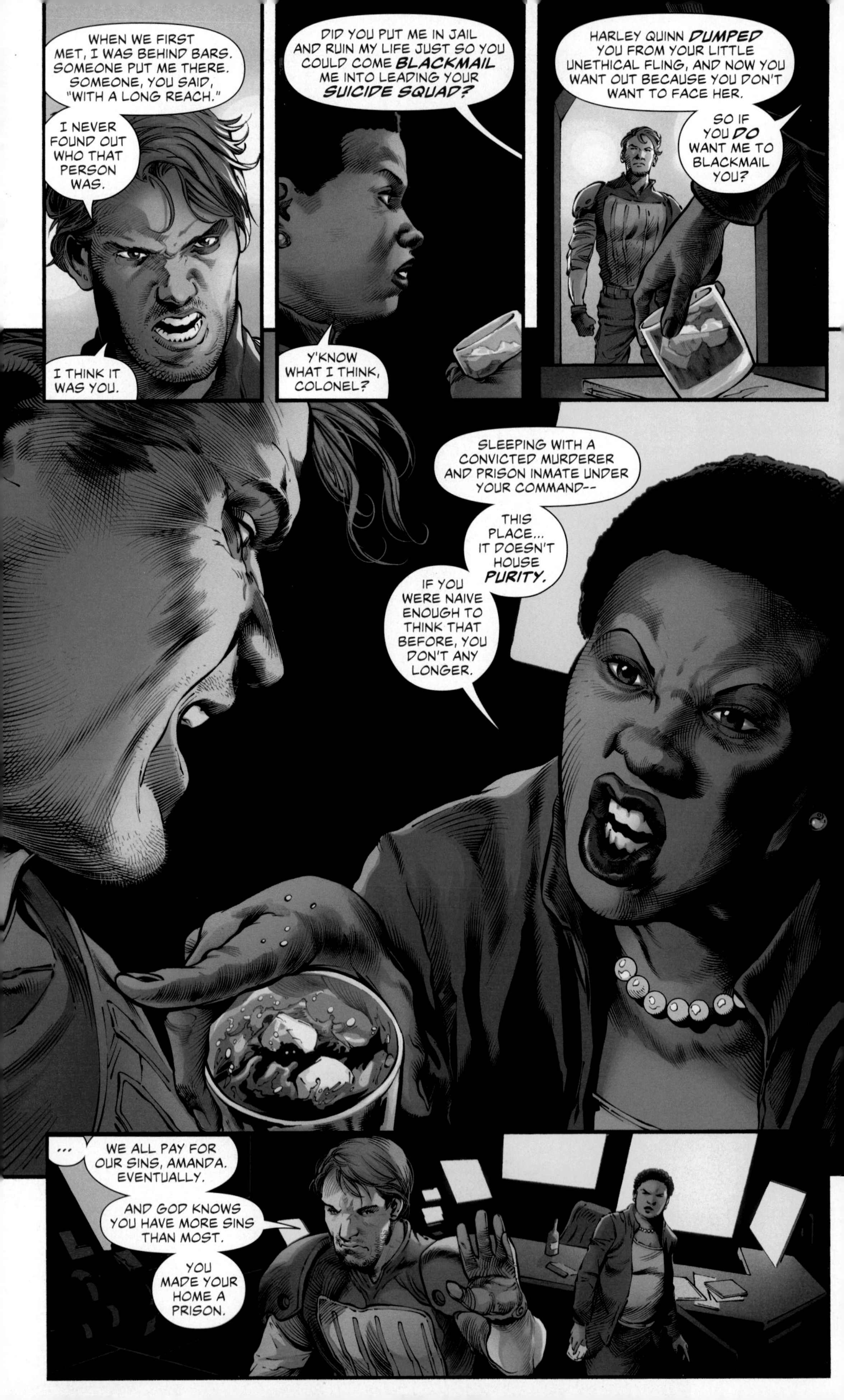
WHEN WE FIRST MET, I WAS BEHIND BARS. SOMEONE PUT ME THERE. SOMEONE, YOU SAID, "WITH A LONG REACH."
I NEVER FOUND OUT WHO THAT PERSON WAS.
I THINK IT WAS YOU.
DID YOU PUT ME IN JAIL AND RUIN MY LIFE JUST SO YOU COULD COME BLACKMAIL ME INTO LEADING YOUR SUICIDE SQUAD?
Y'KNOW WHAT I THINK, COLONEL?
HARLEY QUINN DUMPED YOU FROM YOUR LITTLE UNETHICAL FLING, AND NOW YOU WANT OUT BECAUSE YOU DON'T WANT TO FACE HER.
SO IF YOU DO WANT ME TO BLACKMAIL YOU?
SLEEPING WITH A CONVICTED MURDERER AND PRISON INMATE UNDER YOUR COMMAND--
THIS PLACE... IT DOESN'T HOUSE PURITY.
IF YOU WERE NAIVE ENOUGH TO THINK THAT BEFORE, YOU DON'T ANY LONGER.
...
WE ALL PAY FOR OUR SINS, AMANDA. EVENTUALLY.
AND GOD KNOWS YOU HAVE MORE SINS THAN MOST.
YOU MADE YOUR HOME A PRISON.

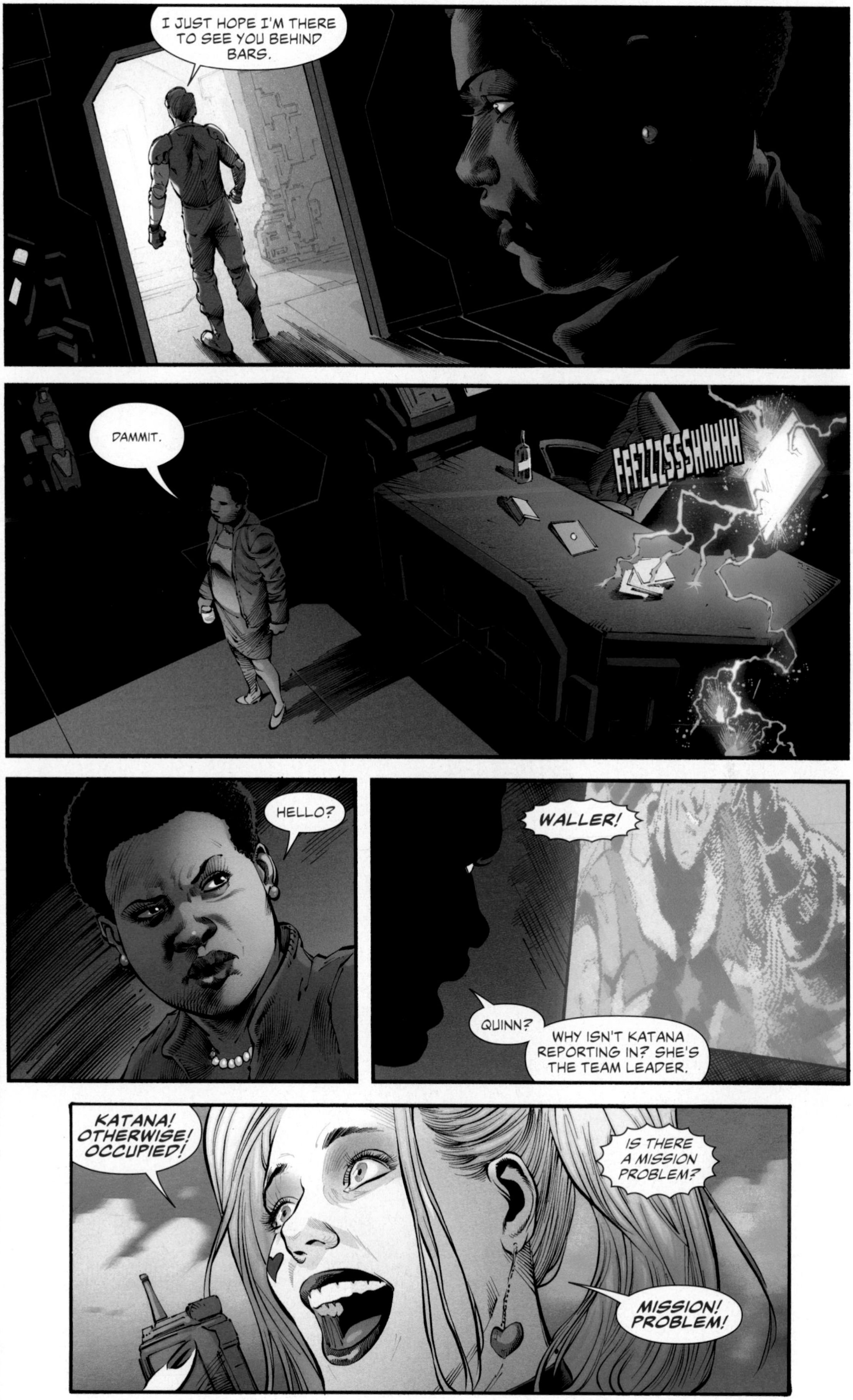
I JUST HOPE I'M THERE TO SEE YOU BEHIND BARS.
DAMMIT.
FFFZZZZSSSHHHHH
HELLO?
WALLER!
QUINN?
WHY ISN'T KATANA REPORTING IN? SHE'S THE TEAM LEADER.
KATANA! OTHERWISE! OCCUPIED!
IS THERE A MISSION PROBLEM?
MISSION! PROBLEM!

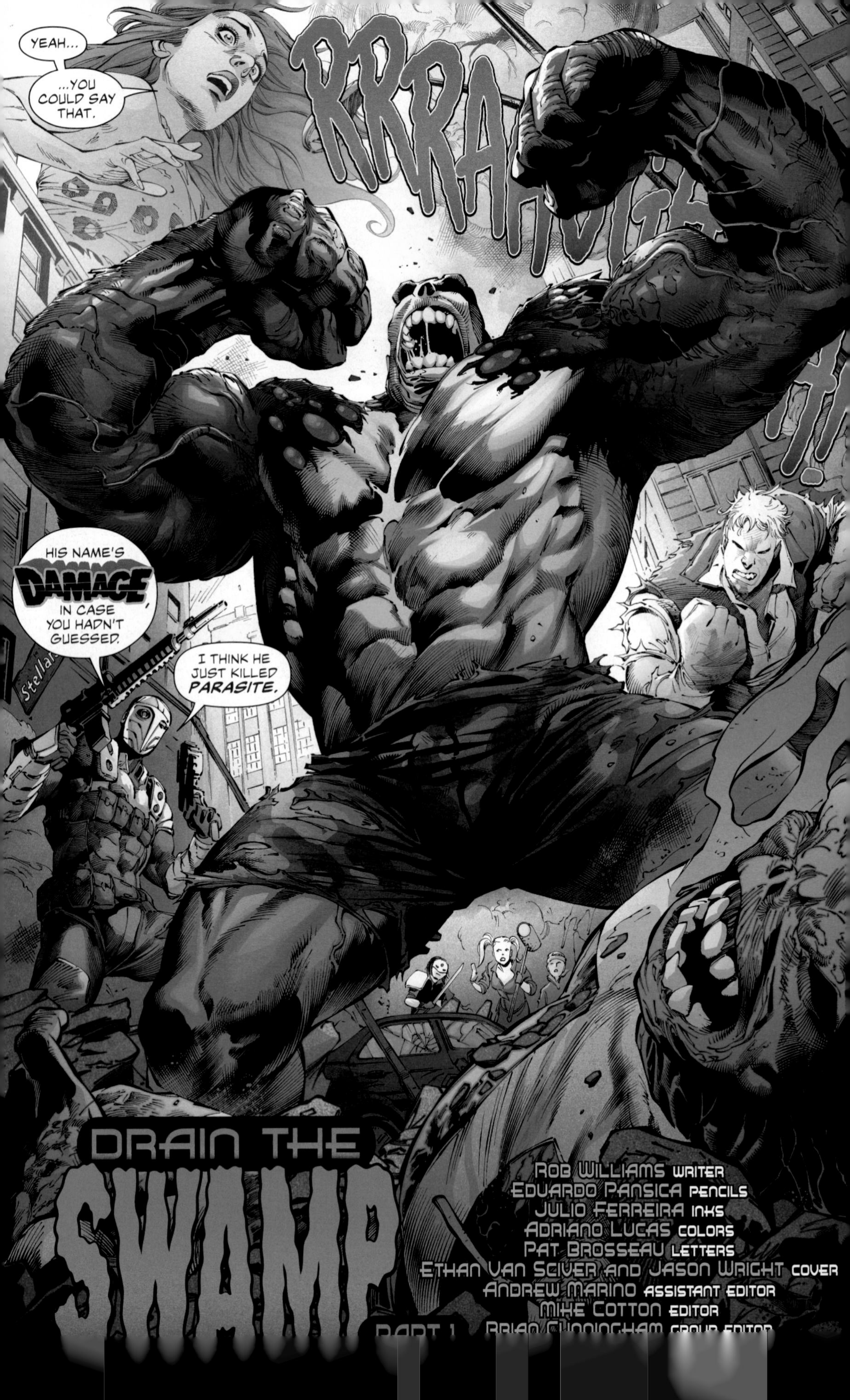
YEAH...
...YOU COULD SAY THAT.
RRRAAHHGH!!
HIS NAME'S DAMAGE, IN CASE YOU HADN'T GUESSED.
I THINK HE JUST KILLED PARASITE.
Stellar
DRAIN THE SWAMP
PART 1
ROB WILLIAMS WRITER
EDUARDO PANSICA PENCILS
JULIO FERREIRA INKS
ADRIANO LUCAS COLORS
PAT BROSSEAU LETTERS
ETHAN VAN SCIVER AND JASON WRIGHT COVER
ANDREW MARINO ASSISTANT EDITOR
MIKE COTTON EDITOR
BRIAN CUNNINGHAM GROUP EDITOR

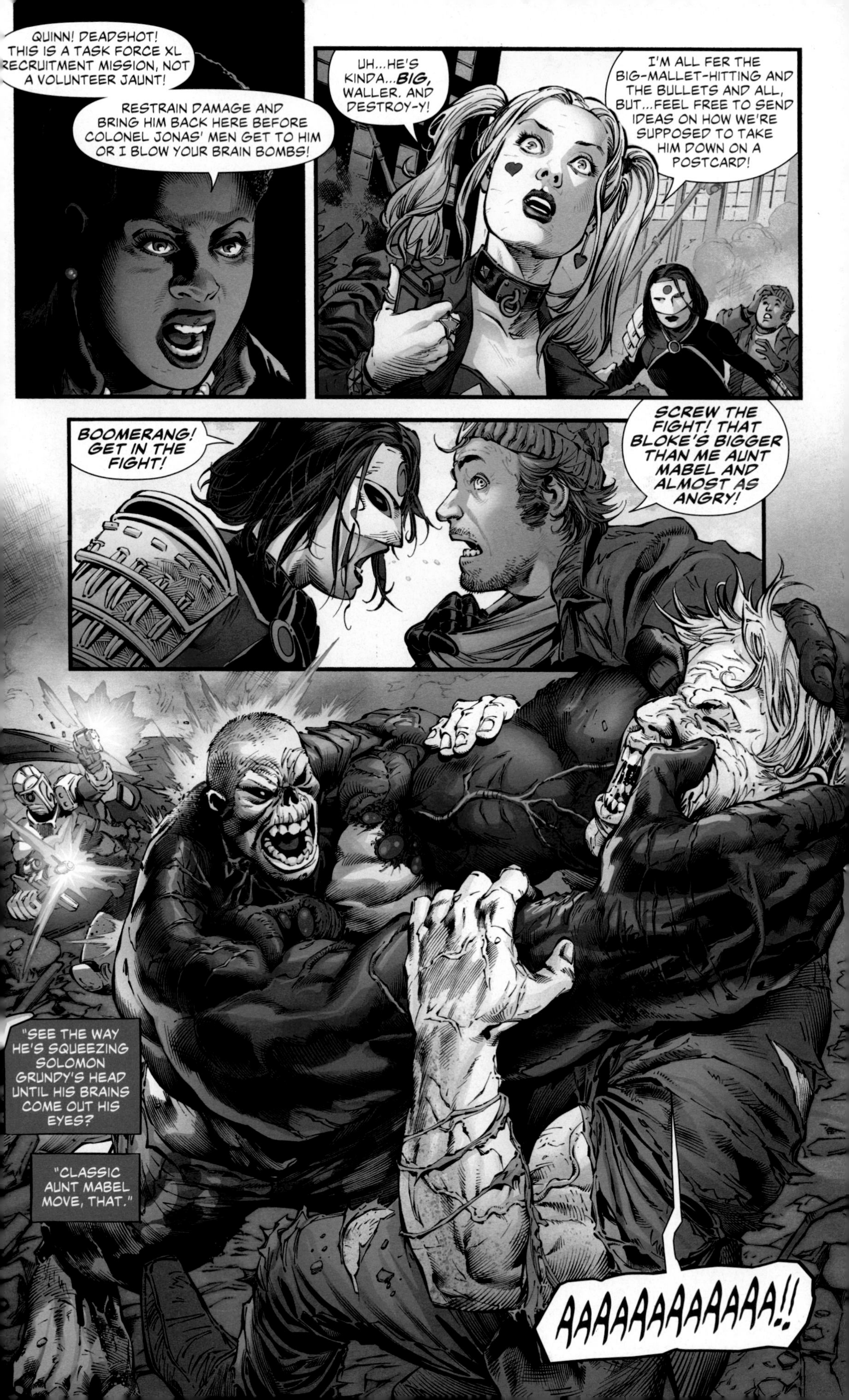
QUINN! DEADSHOT! THIS IS A TASK FORCE XL RECRUITMENT MISSION, NOT A VOLUNTEER JAUNT!
RESTRAIN DAMAGE AND BRING HIM BACK HERE BEFORE COLONEL JONAS' MEN GET TO HIM OR I BLOW YOUR BRAIN BOMBS!
UH...HE'S KINDA...**BIG,** WALLER. AND DESTROY-Y!
I'M ALL FER THE BIG-MALLET-HITTING AND THE BULLETS AND ALL, BUT...FEEL FREE TO SEND IDEAS ON HOW WE'RE SUPPOSED TO TAKE HIM DOWN ON A POSTCARD!
BOOMERANG! GET IN THE FIGHT!
SCREW THE FIGHT! THAT BLOKE'S BIGGER THAN ME AUNT MABEL AND ALMOST AS ANGRY!
"SEE THE WAY HE'S SQUEEZING SOLOMON GRUNDY'S HEAD UNTIL HIS BRAINS COME OUT HIS EYES?
"CLASSIC AUNT MABEL MOVE, THAT."
AAAAAAAAAAAA!!

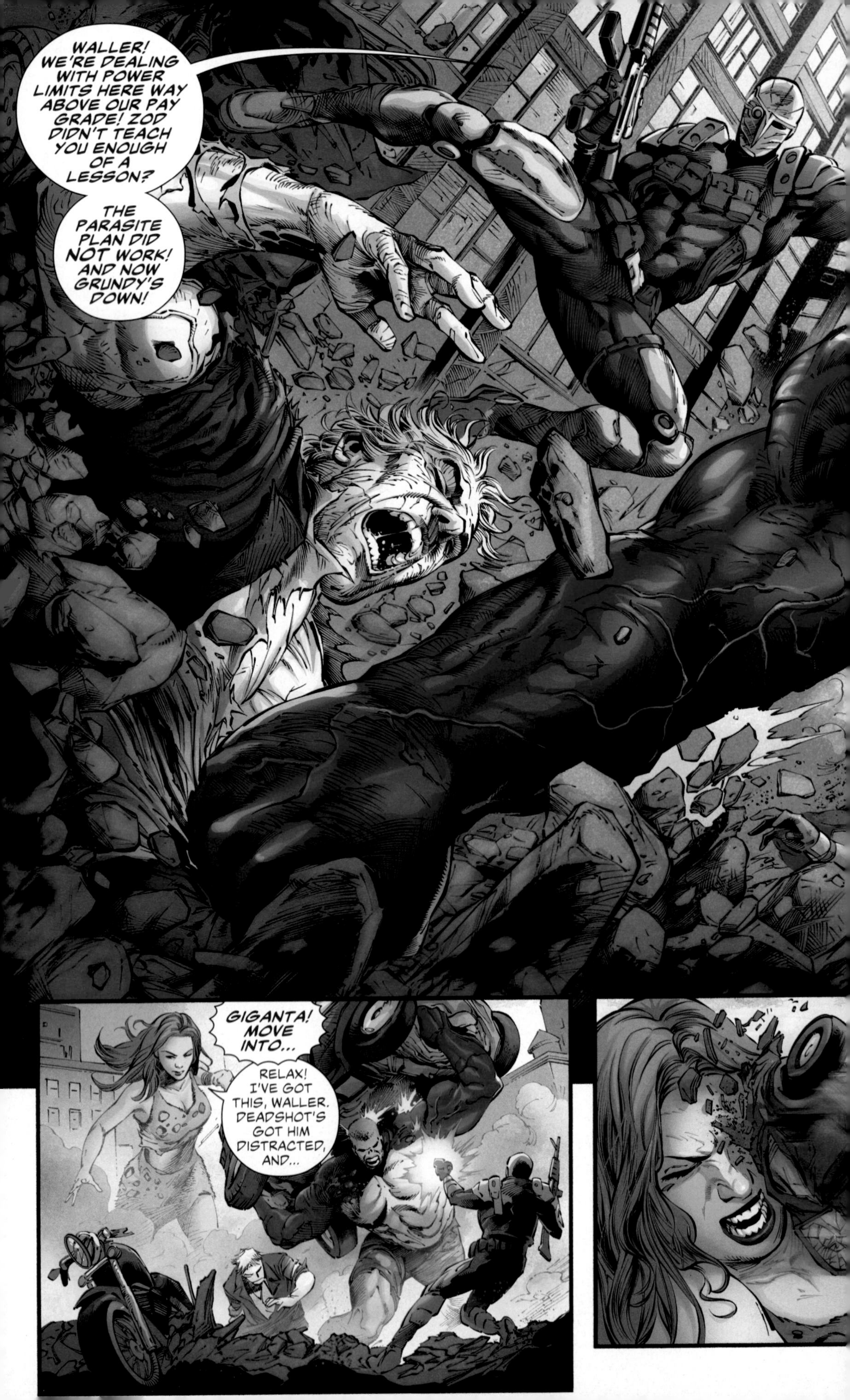
WALLER! WE'RE DEALING WITH POWER LIMITS HERE WAY ABOVE OUR PAY GRADE! ZOD DIDN'T TEACH YOU ENOUGH OF A LESSON?
THE PARASITE PLAN DID NOT WORK! AND NOW GRUNDY'S DOWN!
GIGANTA! MOVE INTO...
RELAX! I'VE GOT THIS, WALLER. DEADSHOT'S GOT HIM DISTRACTED, AND...

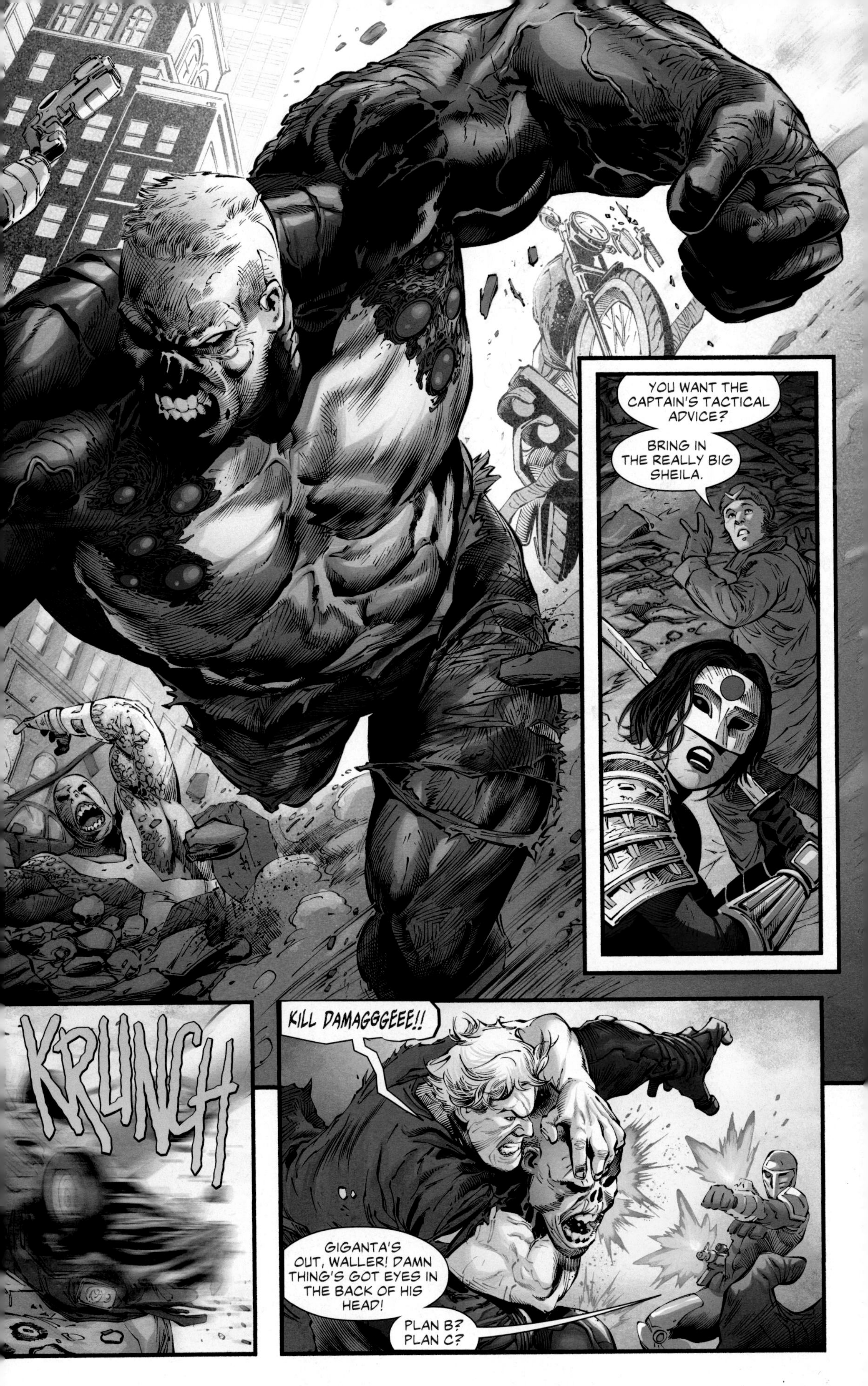
YOU WANT THE CAPTAIN'S TACTICAL ADVICE?
BRING IN THE REALLY BIG SHEILA.
KRUNCH
KILL DAMAGGGEEE!!
GIGANTA'S OUT, WALLER! DAMN THING'S GOT EYES IN THE BACK OF HIS HEAD!
PLAN B? PLAN C?

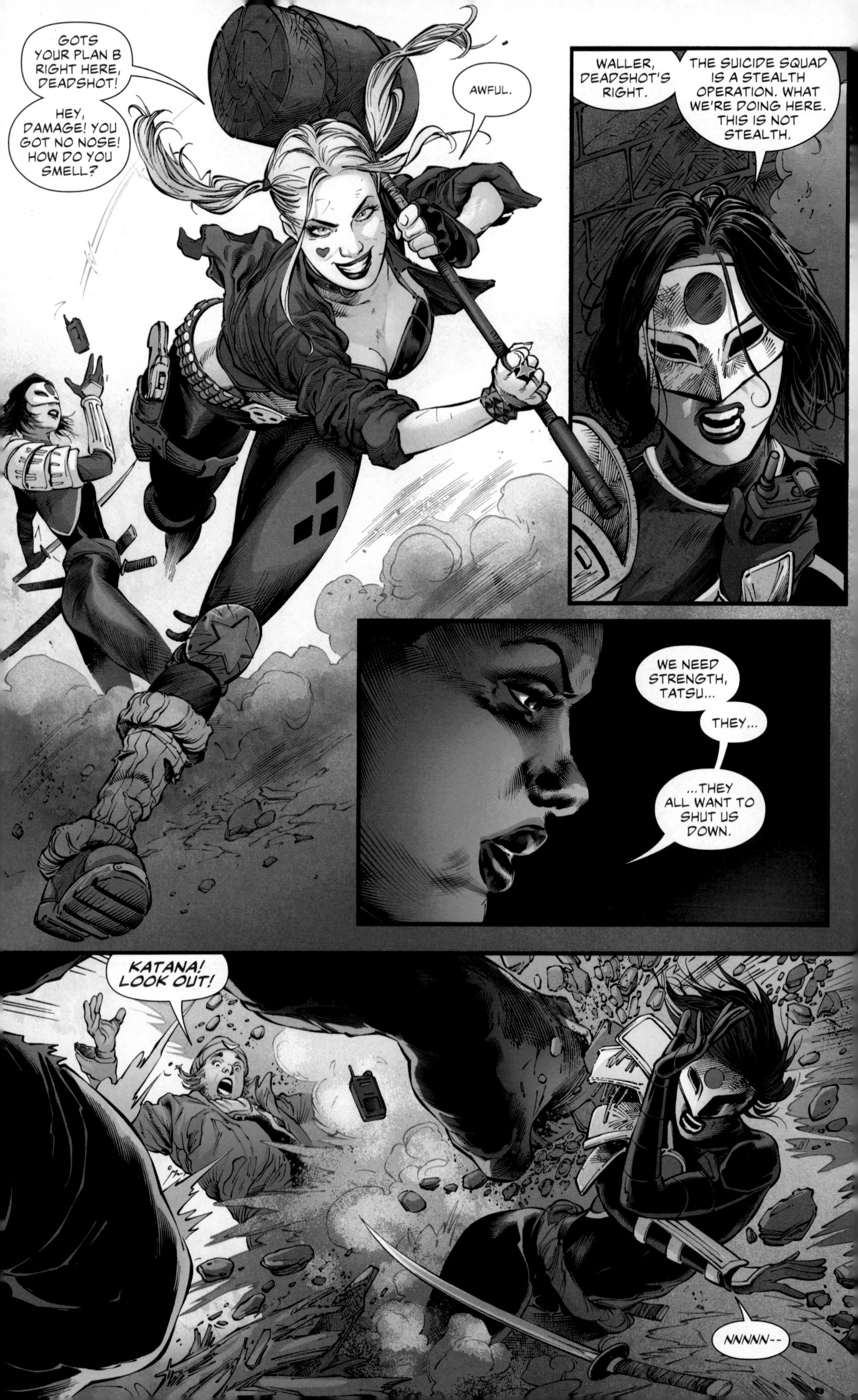
GOTS YOUR PLAN B RIGHT HERE, DEADSHOT!
HEY, DAMAGE! YOU GOT NO NOSE! HOW DO YOU SMELL?
AWFUL.
WALLER, DEADSHOT'S RIGHT.
THE SUICIDE SQUAD IS A STEALTH OPERATION. WHAT WE'RE DOING HERE. THIS IS NOT STEALTH.
WE NEED STRENGTH, TATSU...
THEY...
...THEY ALL WANT TO SHUT US DOWN.
KATANA! LOOK OUT!
NNNNN--

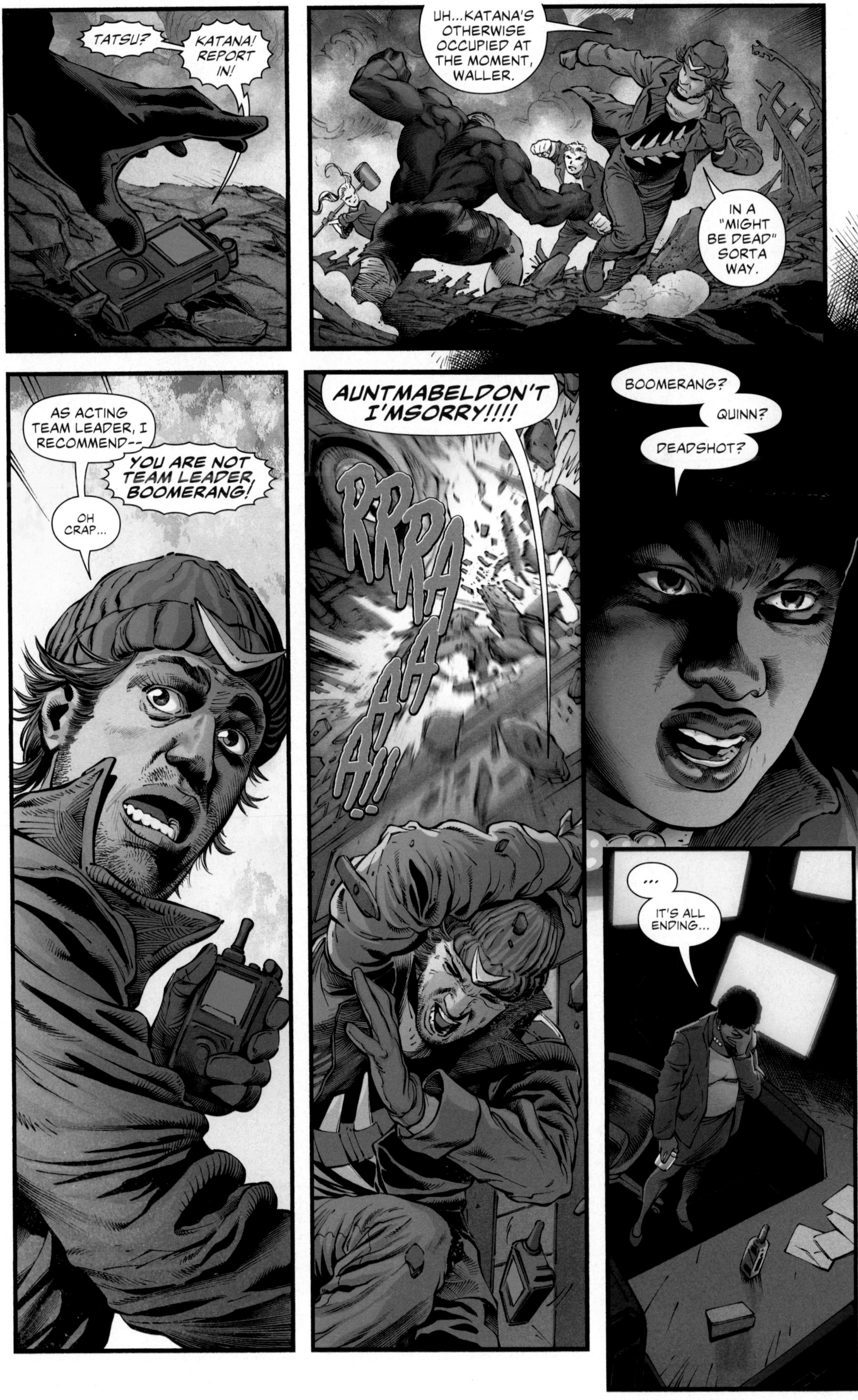
TATSU?
KATANA! REPORT IN!
UH...KATANA'S OTHERWISE OCCUPIED AT THE MOMENT, WALLER.
IN A "MIGHT BE DEAD" SORTA WAY.
AS ACTING TEAM LEADER, I RECOMMEND--
YOU ARE NOT TEAM LEADER, BOOMERANG!
OH CRAP...
AUNTMABELDON'T I'MSORRY!!!!
RRRAAAA!!
BOOMERANG?
QUINN?
DEADSHOT?
...
IT'S ALL ENDING...

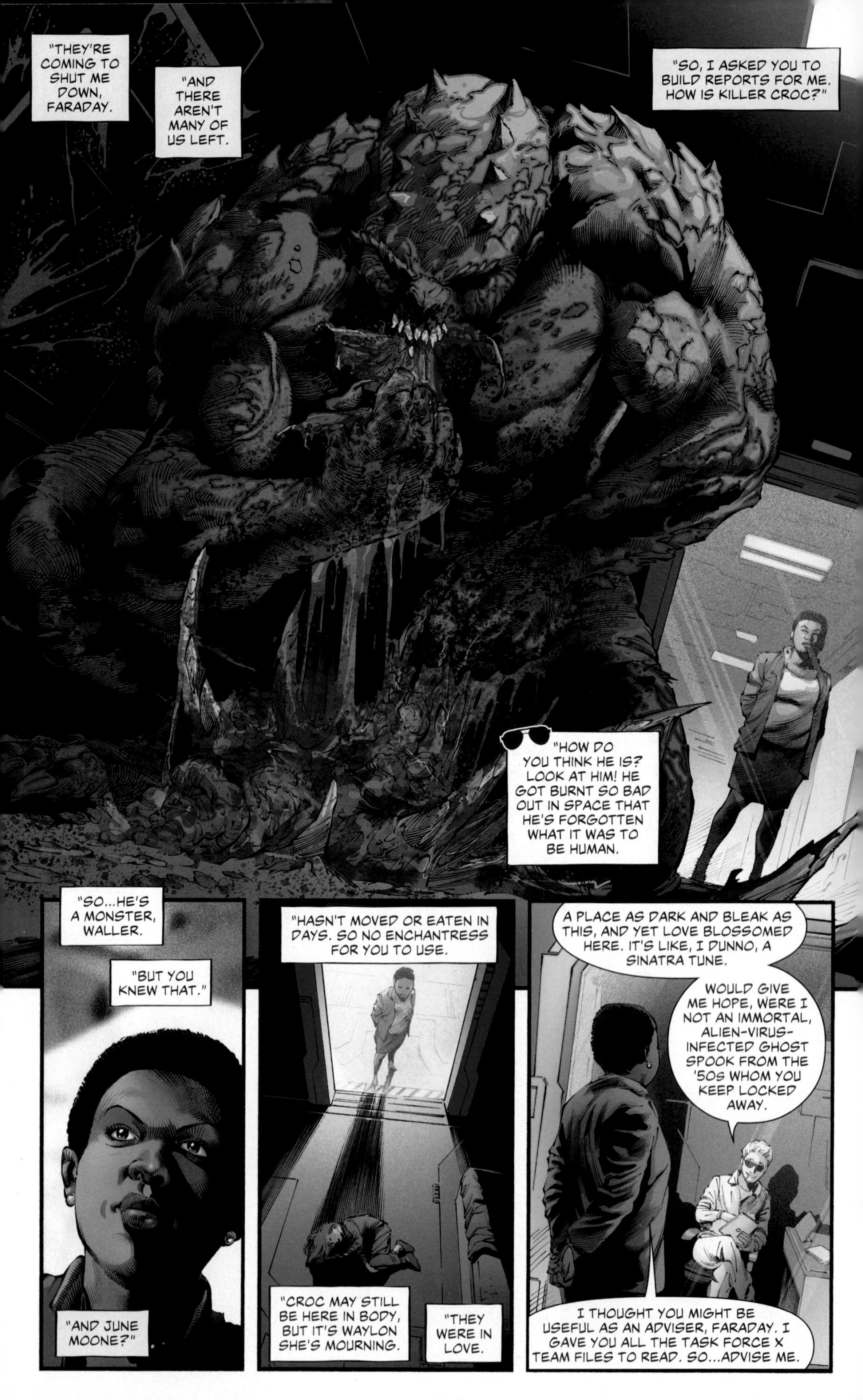
"THEY'RE COMING TO SHUT ME DOWN, FARADAY.
"AND THERE AREN'T MANY OF US LEFT.
"SO, I ASKED YOU TO BUILD REPORTS FOR ME. HOW IS KILLER CROC?"
"HOW DO YOU THINK HE IS? LOOK AT HIM! HE GOT BURNT SO BAD OUT IN SPACE THAT HE'S FORGOTTEN WHAT IT WAS TO BE HUMAN.
"SO...HE'S A MONSTER, WALLER.
"BUT YOU KNEW THAT."
"AND JUNE MOONE?"
"HASN'T MOVED OR EATEN IN DAYS. SO NO ENCHANTRESS FOR YOU TO USE.
"CROC MAY STILL BE HERE IN BODY, BUT IT'S WAYLON SHE'S MOURNING.
"THEY WERE IN LOVE.
A PLACE AS DARK AND BLEAK AS THIS, AND YET LOVE BLOSSOMED HERE. IT'S LIKE, I DUNNO, A SINATRA TUNE.
WOULD GIVE ME HOPE, WERE I NOT AN IMMORTAL, ALIEN-VIRUS-INFECTED GHOST SPOOK FROM THE '50S WHOM YOU KEEP LOCKED AWAY.
I THOUGHT YOU MIGHT BE USEFUL AS AN ADVISER, FARADAY. I GAVE YOU ALL THE TASK FORCE X TEAM FILES TO READ. SO...ADVISE ME.

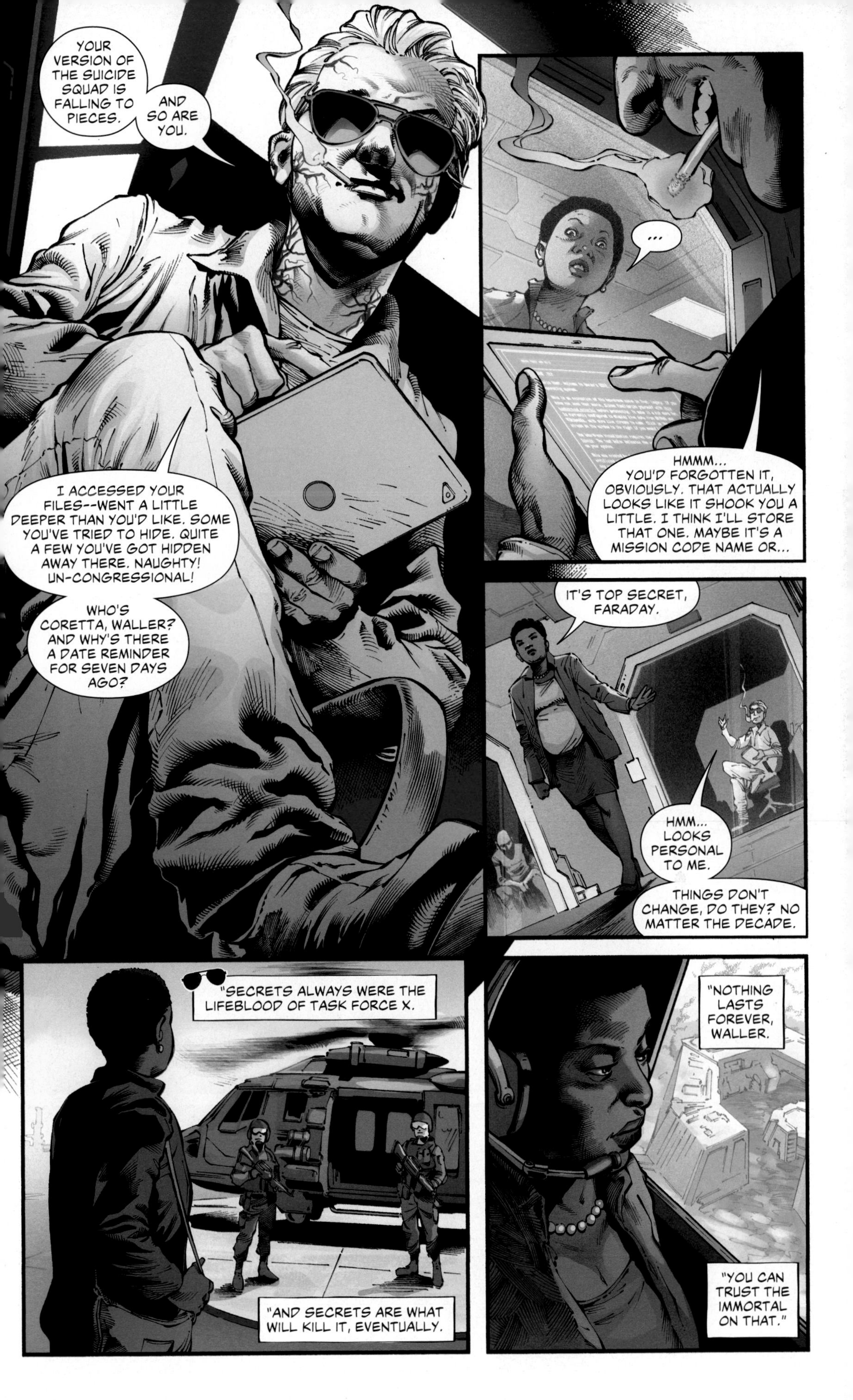
YOUR VERSION OF THE SUICIDE SQUAD IS FALLING TO PIECES.
AND SO ARE YOU.
I ACCESSED YOUR FILES--WENT A LITTLE DEEPER THAN YOU'D LIKE. SOME YOU'VE TRIED TO HIDE. QUITE A FEW YOU'VE GOT HIDDEN AWAY THERE. NAUGHTY! UN-CONGRESSIONAL!
WHO'S CORETTA, WALLER? AND WHY'S THERE A DATE REMINDER FOR SEVEN DAYS AGO?
...
HMMM... YOU'D FORGOTTEN IT, OBVIOUSLY. THAT ACTUALLY LOOKS LIKE IT SHOOK YOU A LITTLE. I THINK I'LL STORE THAT ONE. MAYBE IT'S A MISSION CODE NAME OR...
IT'S TOP SECRET, FARADAY.
HMM... LOOKS PERSONAL TO ME.
THINGS DON'T CHANGE, DO THEY? NO MATTER THE DECADE.
"SECRETS ALWAYS WERE THE LIFEBLOOD OF TASK FORCE X.
"AND SECRETS ARE WHAT WILL KILL IT, EVENTUALLY.
"NOTHING LASTS FOREVER, WALLER.
"YOU CAN TRUST THE IMMORTAL ON THAT."

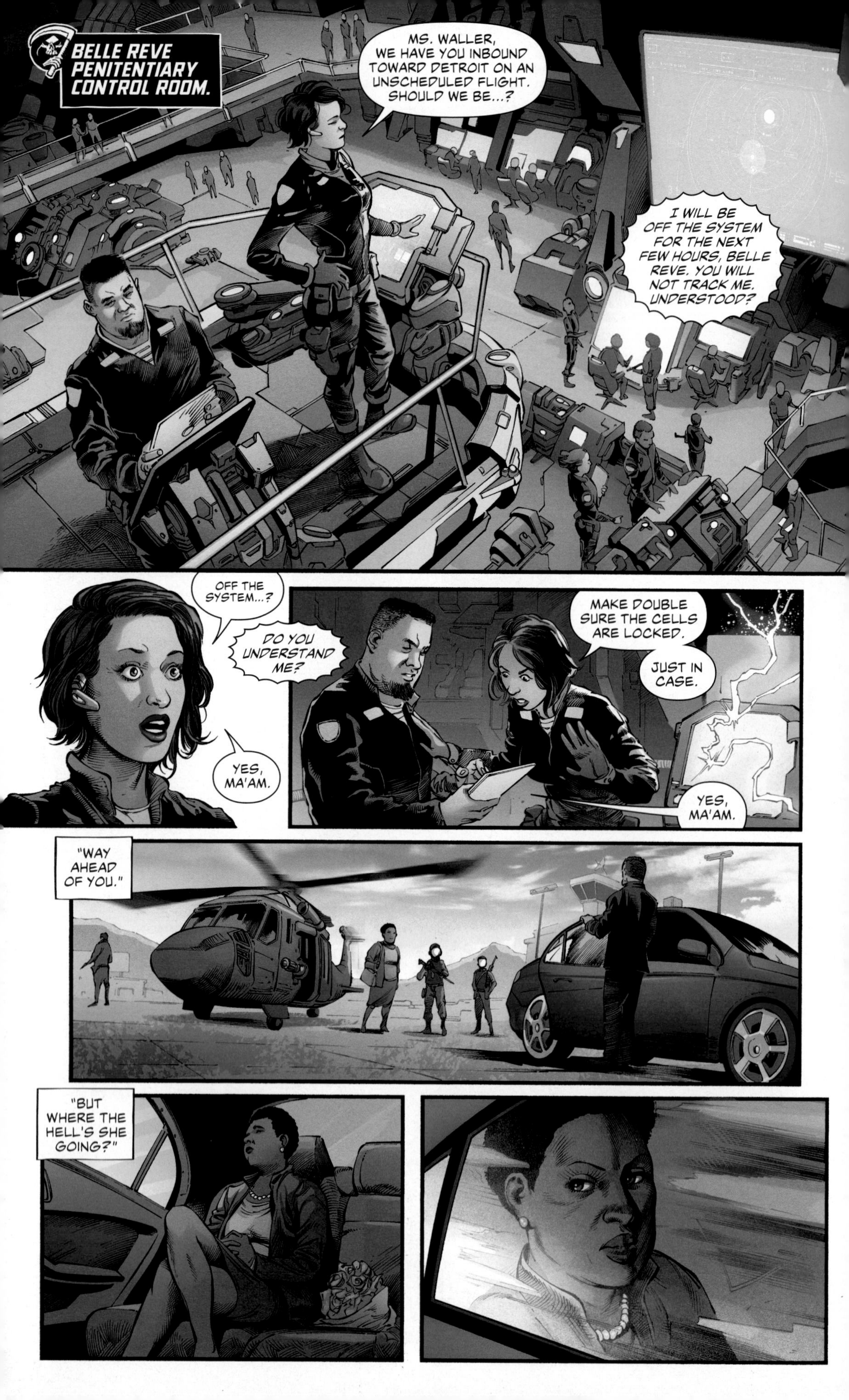
BELLE REVE PENITENTIARY CONTROL ROOM.
MS. WALLER, WE HAVE YOU INBOUND TOWARD DETROIT ON AN UNSCHEDULED FLIGHT. SHOULD WE BE...?
I WILL BE OFF THE SYSTEM FOR THE NEXT FEW HOURS, BELLE REVE. YOU WILL NOT TRACK ME. UNDERSTOOD?
OFF THE SYSTEM...?
DO YOU UNDERSTAND ME?
YES, MA'AM.
MAKE DOUBLE SURE THE CELLS ARE LOCKED.
JUST IN CASE.
YES, MA'AM.
"WAY AHEAD OF YOU."
"BUT WHERE THE HELL'S SHE GOING?"

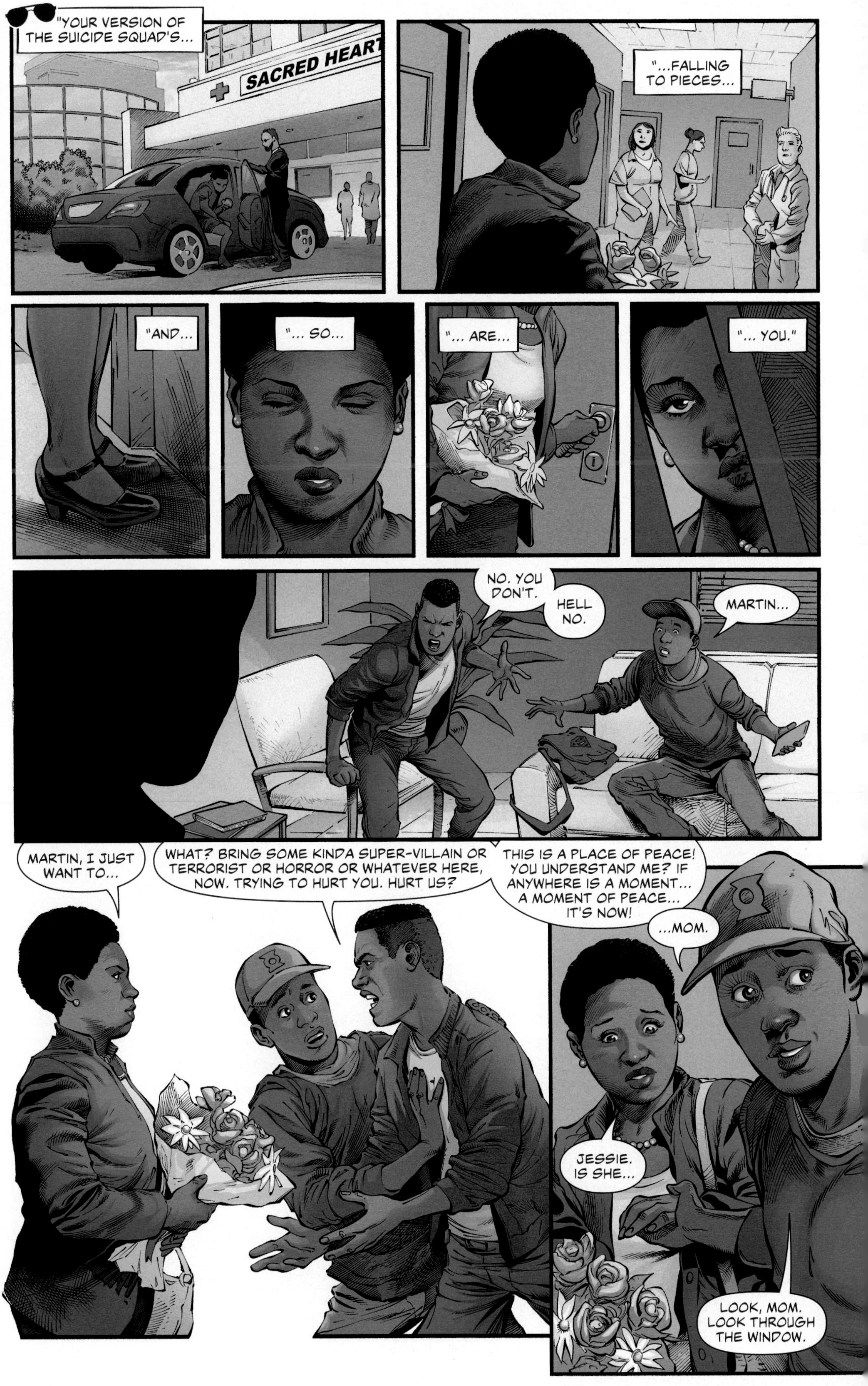
"YOUR VERSION OF THE SUICIDE SQUAD'S...
SACRED HEART
"...FALLING TO PIECES...
"AND...
"... SO...
"... ARE...
"... YOU."
NO. YOU DON'T.
HELL NO.
MARTIN...
MARTIN, I JUST WANT TO...
WHAT? BRING SOME KINDA SUPER-VILLAIN OR TERRORIST OR HORROR OR WHATEVER HERE, NOW. TRYING TO HURT YOU. HURT US?
THIS IS A PLACE OF PEACE! YOU UNDERSTAND ME? IF ANYWHERE IS A MOMENT... A MOMENT OF PEACE... IT'S NOW!
...MOM.
JESSIE. IS SHE...
LOOK, MOM. LOOK THROUGH THE WINDOW.

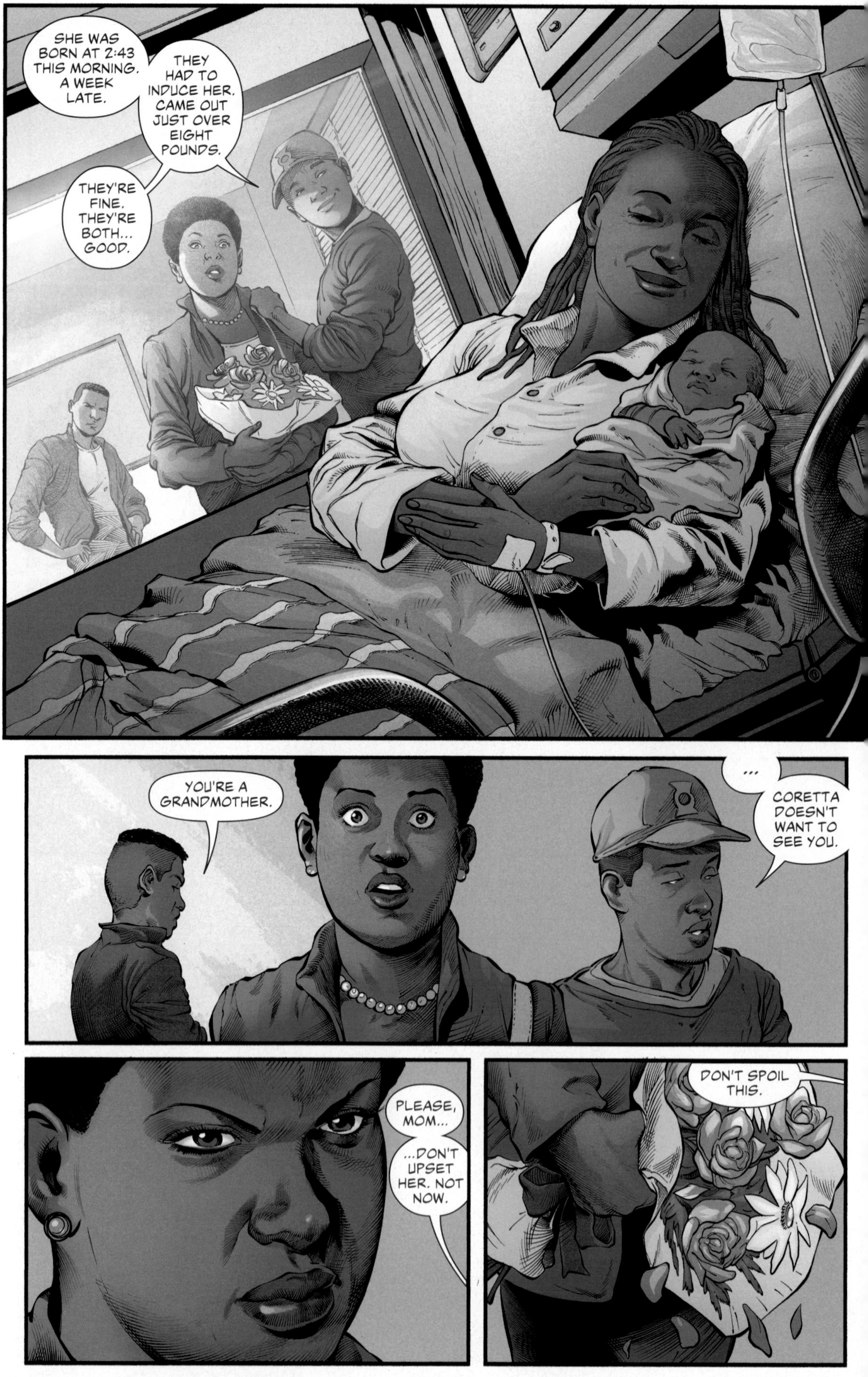
SHE WAS BORN AT 2:43 THIS MORNING. A WEEK LATE.
THEY HAD TO INDUCE HER. CAME OUT JUST OVER EIGHT POUNDS.
THEY'RE FINE. THEY'RE BOTH... GOOD.
YOU'RE A GRANDMOTHER.
...
CORETTA DOESN'T WANT TO SEE YOU.
PLEASE, MOM...
...DON'T UPSET HER. NOT NOW.
DON'T SPOIL THIS.

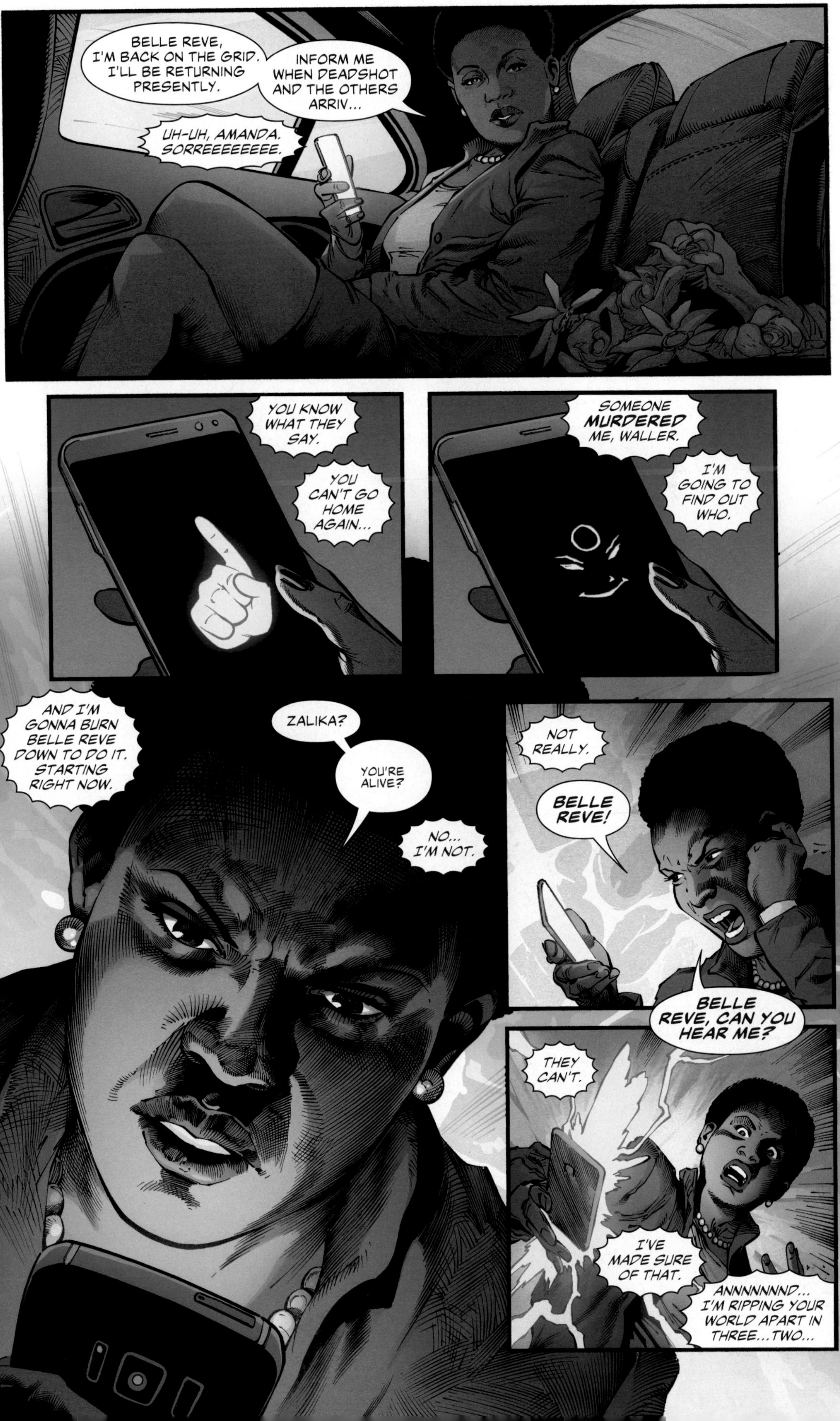
BELLE REVE, I'M BACK ON THE GRID. I'LL BE RETURNING PRESENTLY.
INFORM ME WHEN DEADSHOT AND THE OTHERS ARRIV...
UH-UH, AMANDA. SORREEEEEEEE.
YOU KNOW WHAT THEY SAY.
YOU CAN'T GO HOME AGAIN...
SOMEONE MURDERED ME, WALLER.
I'M GOING TO FIND OUT WHO.
AND I'M GONNA BURN BELLE REVE DOWN TO DO IT. STARTING RIGHT NOW.
ZALIKA?
YOU'RE ALIVE?
NO... I'M NOT.
NOT REALLY.
BELLE REVE!
BELLE REVE, CAN YOU HEAR ME?
THEY CAN'T.
I'VE MADE SURE OF THAT.
ANNNNNNND... I'M RIPPING YOUR WORLD APART IN THREE...TWO...

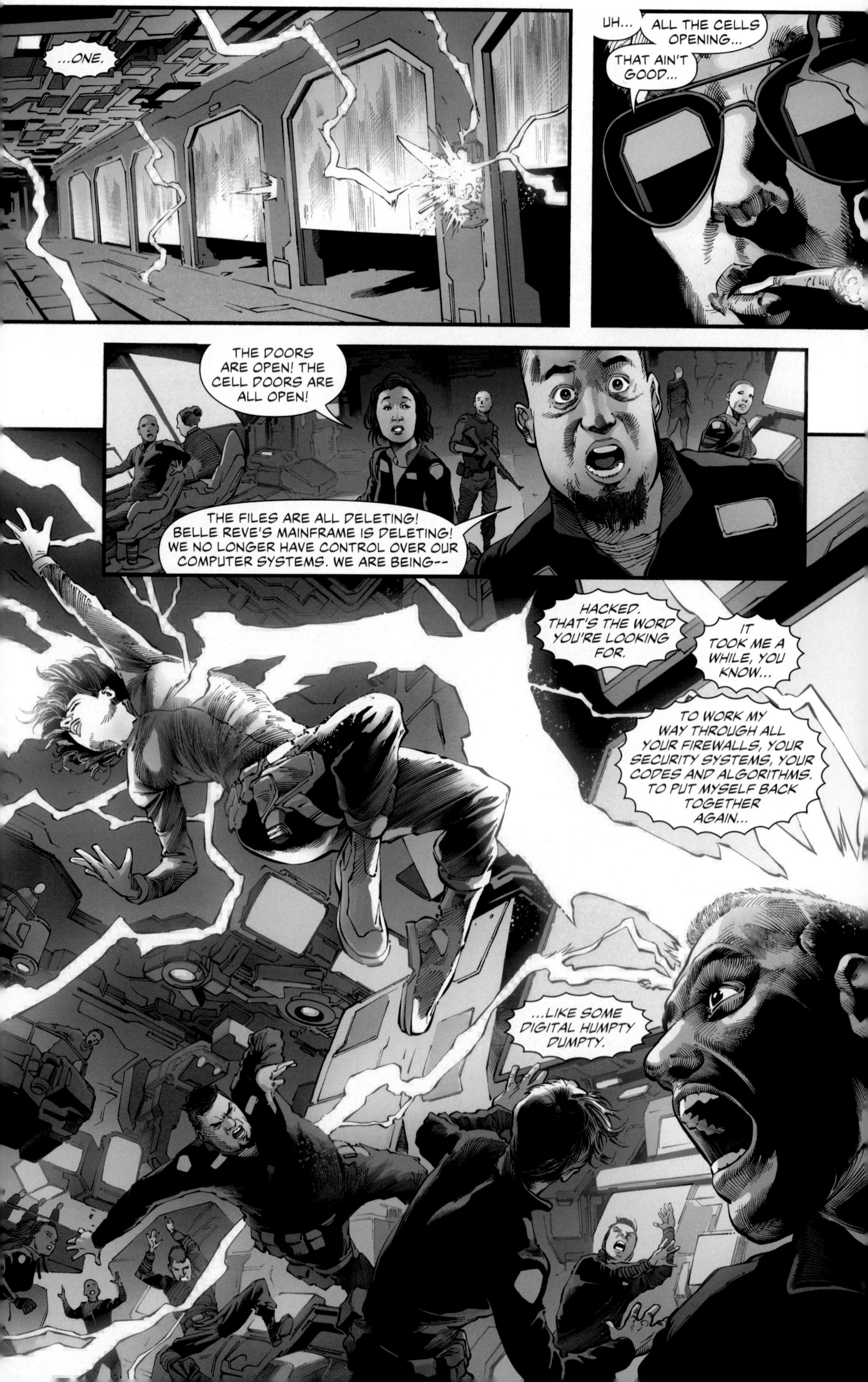
...ONE.
UH...
ALL THE CELLS OPENING...
THAT AIN'T GOOD...
THE DOORS ARE OPEN! THE CELL DOORS ARE ALL OPEN!
THE FILES ARE ALL DELETING! BELLE REVE'S MAINFRAME IS DELETING! WE NO LONGER HAVE CONTROL OVER OUR COMPUTER SYSTEMS. WE ARE BEING--
HACKED. THAT'S THE WORD YOU'RE LOOKING FOR.
IT TOOK ME A WHILE, YOU KNOW...
TO WORK MY WAY THROUGH ALL YOUR FIREWALLS, YOUR SECURITY SYSTEMS, YOUR CODES AND ALGORITHMS. TO PUT MYSELF BACK TOGETHER AGAIN...
...LIKE SOME DIGITAL HUMPTY DUMPTY.

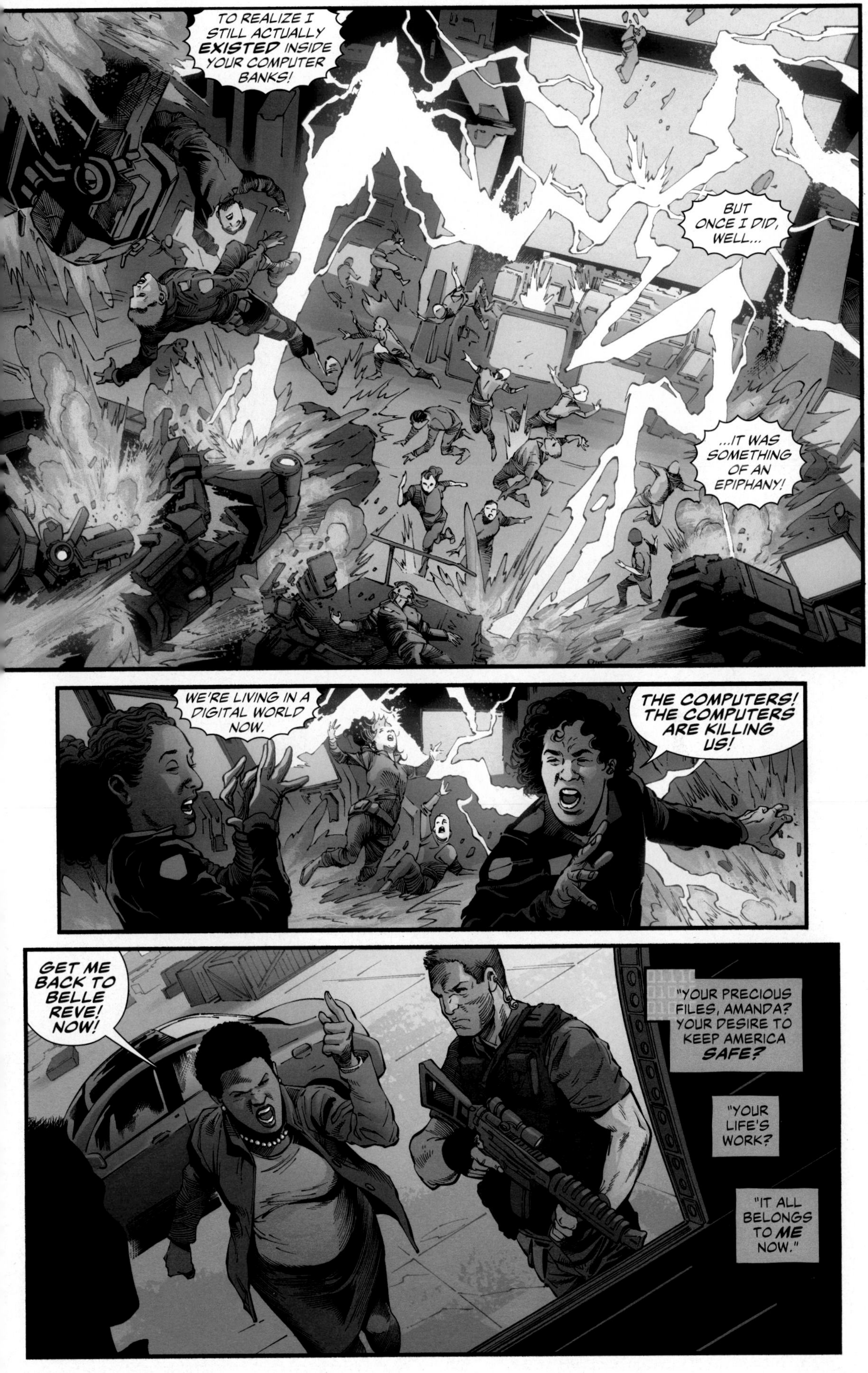
TO REALIZE I STILL ACTUALLY EXISTED INSIDE YOUR COMPUTER BANKS!
BUT ONCE I DID, WELL...
...IT WAS SOMETHING OF AN EPIPHANY!
WE'RE LIVING IN A DIGITAL WORLD NOW.
THE COMPUTERS! THE COMPUTERS ARE KILLING US!
GET ME BACK TO BELLE REVE! NOW!
"YOUR PRECIOUS FILES, AMANDA? YOUR DESIRE TO KEEP AMERICA SAFE?
"YOUR LIFE'S WORK?
"IT ALL BELONGS TO ME NOW."

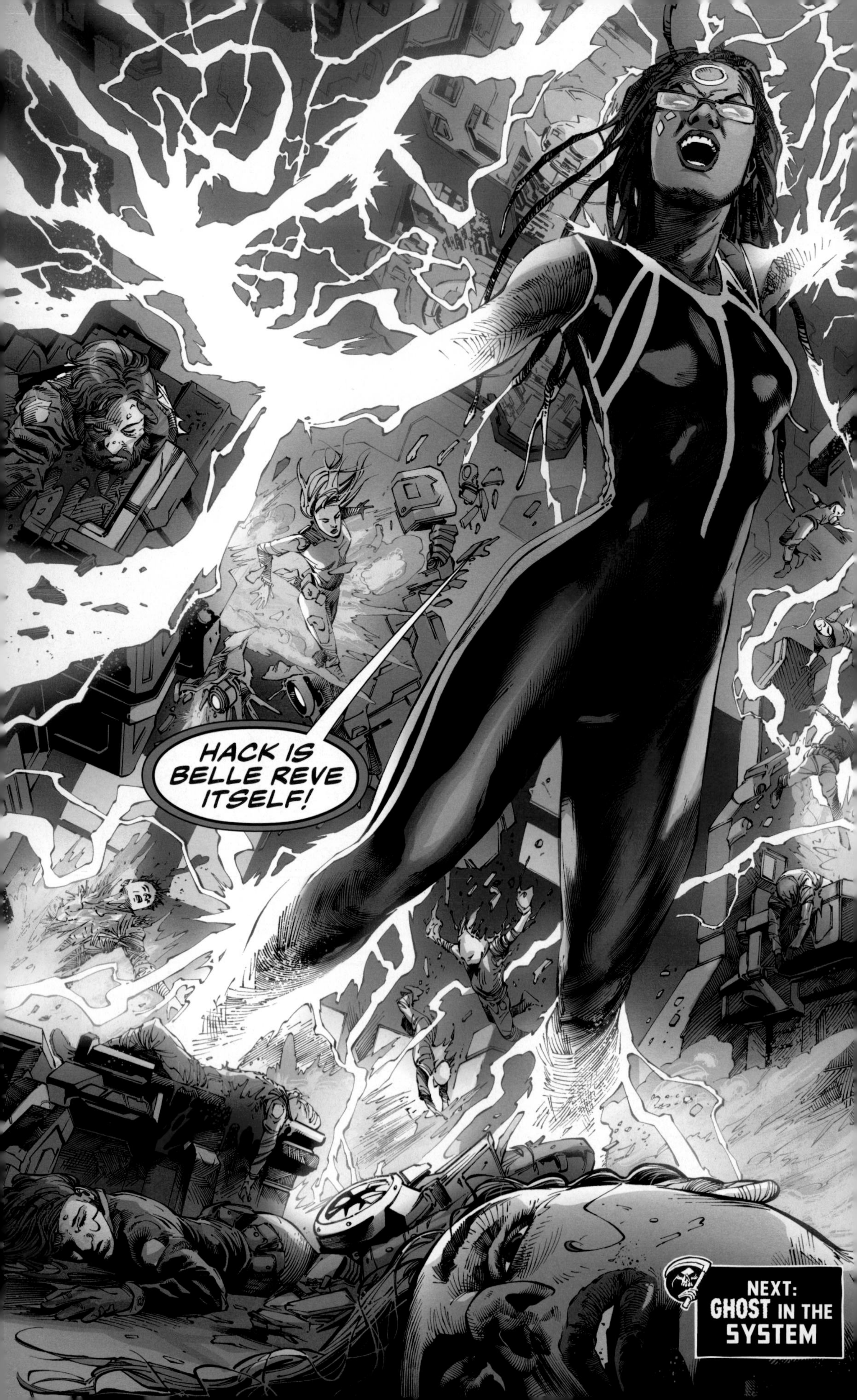
HACK IS BELLE REVE ITSELF!
NEXT: GHOST IN THE SYSTEM

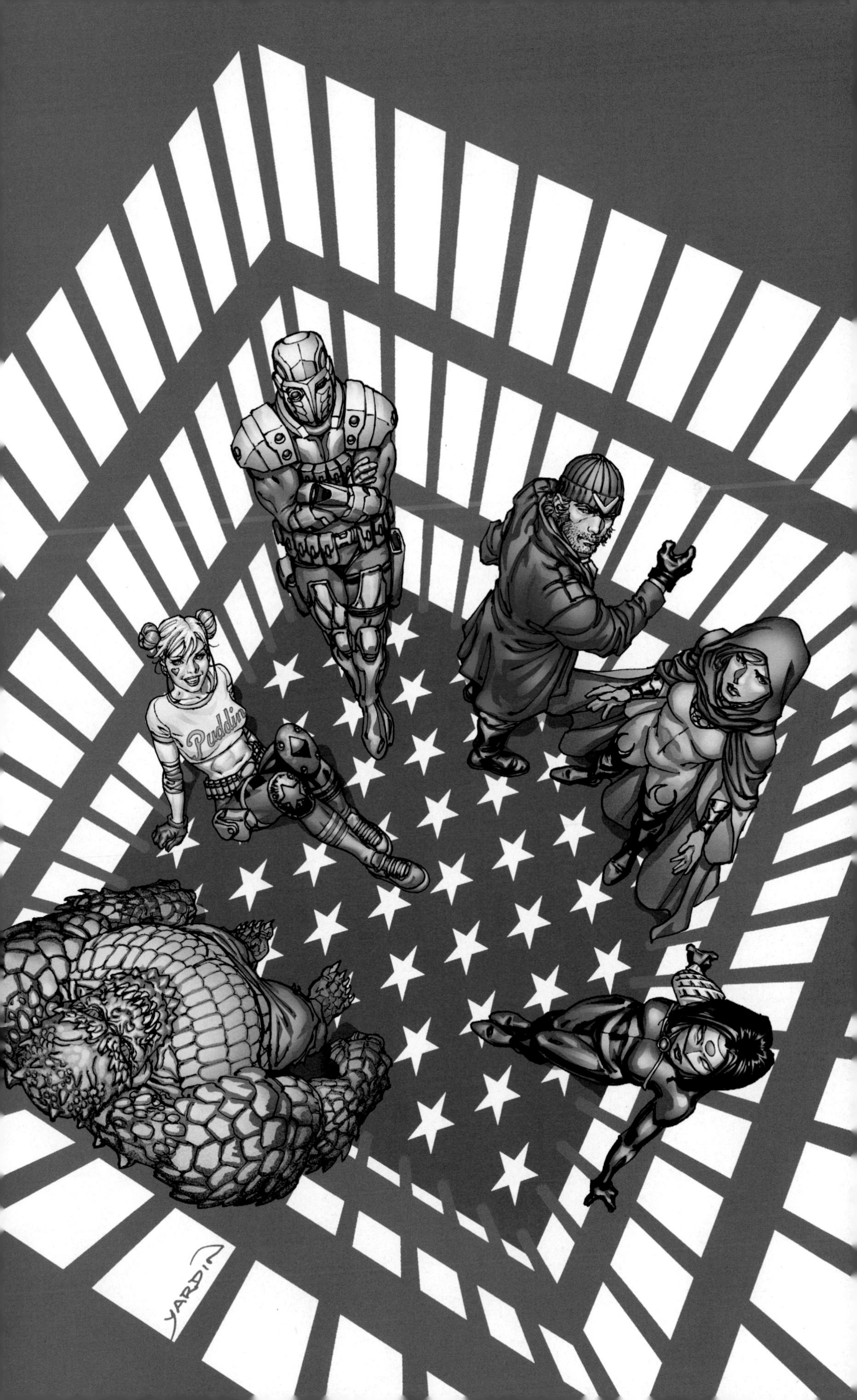
Puddin
YARDIN

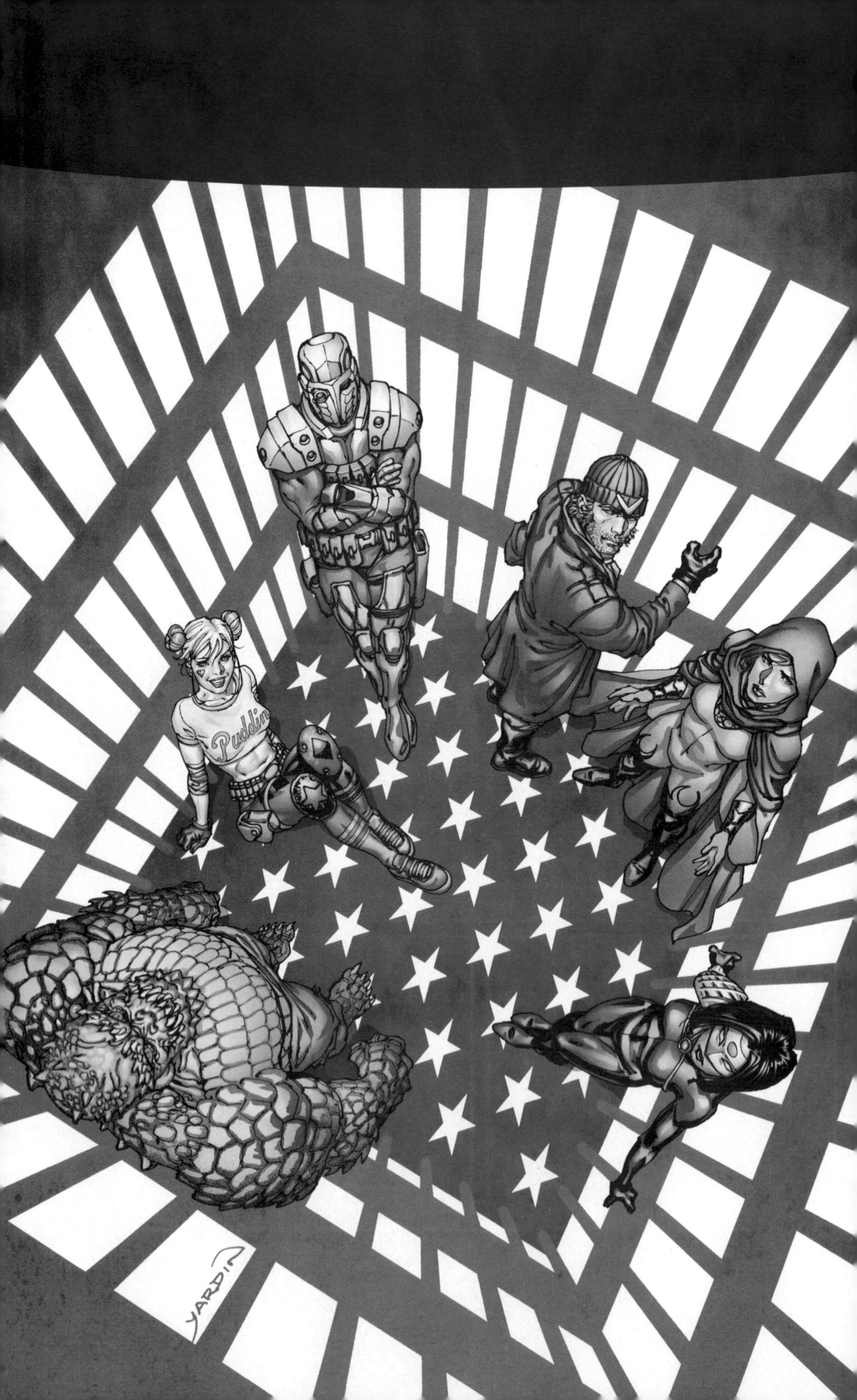
Puddin
YARDIN

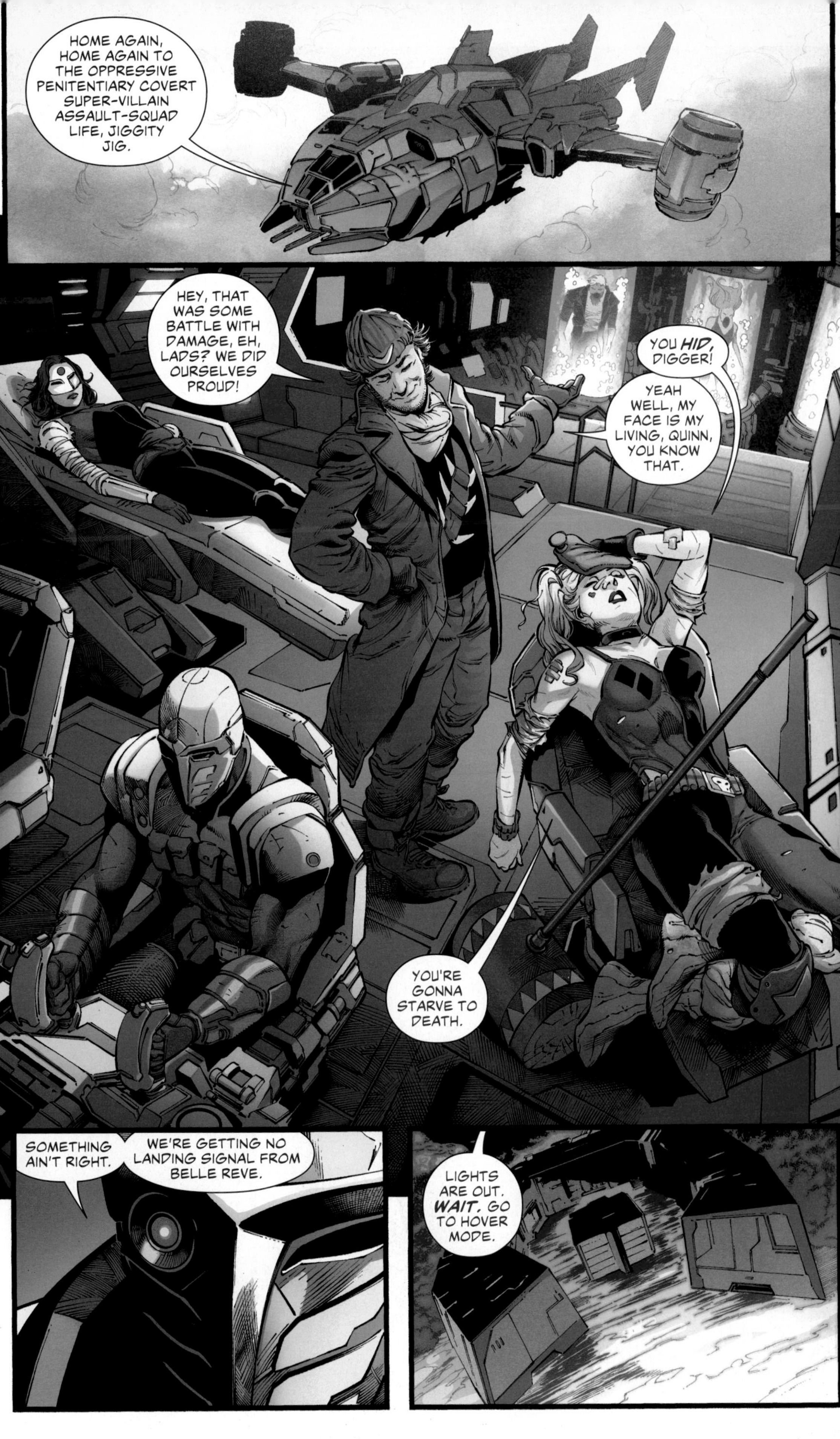
HOME AGAIN, HOME AGAIN TO THE OPPRESSIVE PENITENTIARY COVERT SUPER-VILLAIN ASSAULT-SQUAD LIFE, JIGGITY JIG.
HEY, THAT WAS SOME BATTLE WITH DAMAGE, EH, LADS? WE DID OURSELVES PROUD!
YOU *HID*, DIGGER!
YEAH WELL, MY FACE IS MY LIVING, QUINN, YOU KNOW THAT.
YOU'RE GONNA STARVE TO DEATH.
SOMETHING AIN'T RIGHT.
WE'RE GETTING NO LANDING SIGNAL FROM BELLE REVE.
LIGHTS ARE OUT. ***WAIT.*** GO TO HOVER MODE.

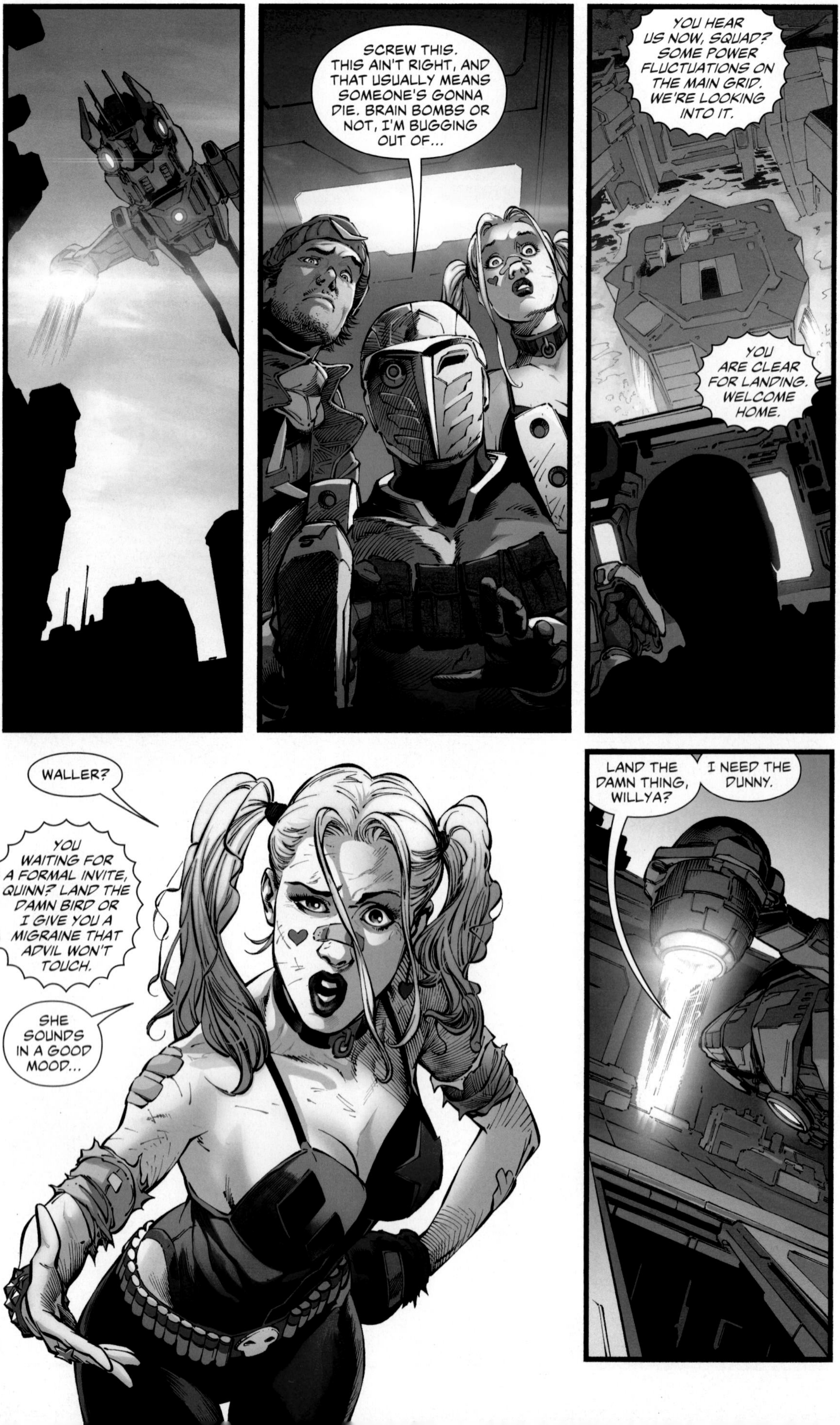

SCREW THIS. THIS AIN'T RIGHT, AND THAT USUALLY MEANS SOMEONE'S GONNA DIE. BRAIN BOMBS OR NOT, I'M BUGGING OUT OF...
YOU HEAR US NOW, SQUAD? SOME POWER FLUCTUATIONS ON THE MAIN GRID. WE'RE LOOKING INTO IT.
YOU ARE CLEAR FOR LANDING. WELCOME HOME.
WALLER?
YOU WAITING FOR A FORMAL INVITE, QUINN? LAND THE DAMN BIRD OR I GIVE YOU A MIGRAINE THAT ADVIL WON'T TOUCH.
SHE SOUNDS IN A GOOD MOOD...
LAND THE DAMN THING, WILLYA?
I NEED THE DUNNY.

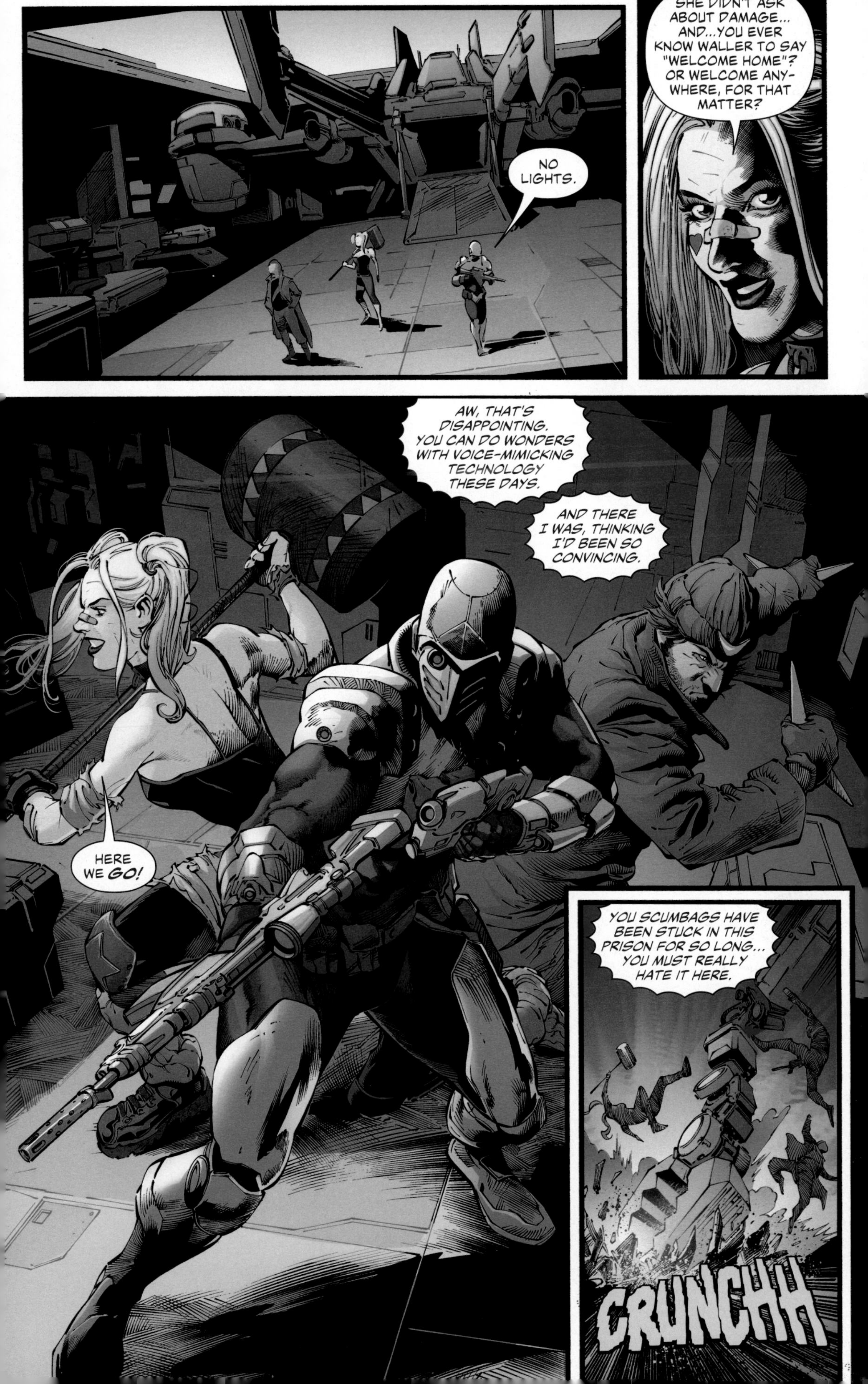
NO LIGHTS.
SHE DIDN'T ASK ABOUT DAMAGE... AND...YOU EVER KNOW WALLER TO SAY "WELCOME HOME"? OR WELCOME ANY-WHERE, FOR THAT MATTER?
AW, THAT'S DISAPPOINTING. YOU CAN DO WONDERS WITH VOICE-MIMICKING TECHNOLOGY THESE DAYS.
AND THERE I WAS, THINKING I'D BEEN SO CONVINCING.
HERE WE GO!
YOU SCUMBAGS HAVE BEEN STUCK IN THIS PRISON FOR SO LONG... YOU MUST REALLY HATE IT HERE.
CRUNCHH

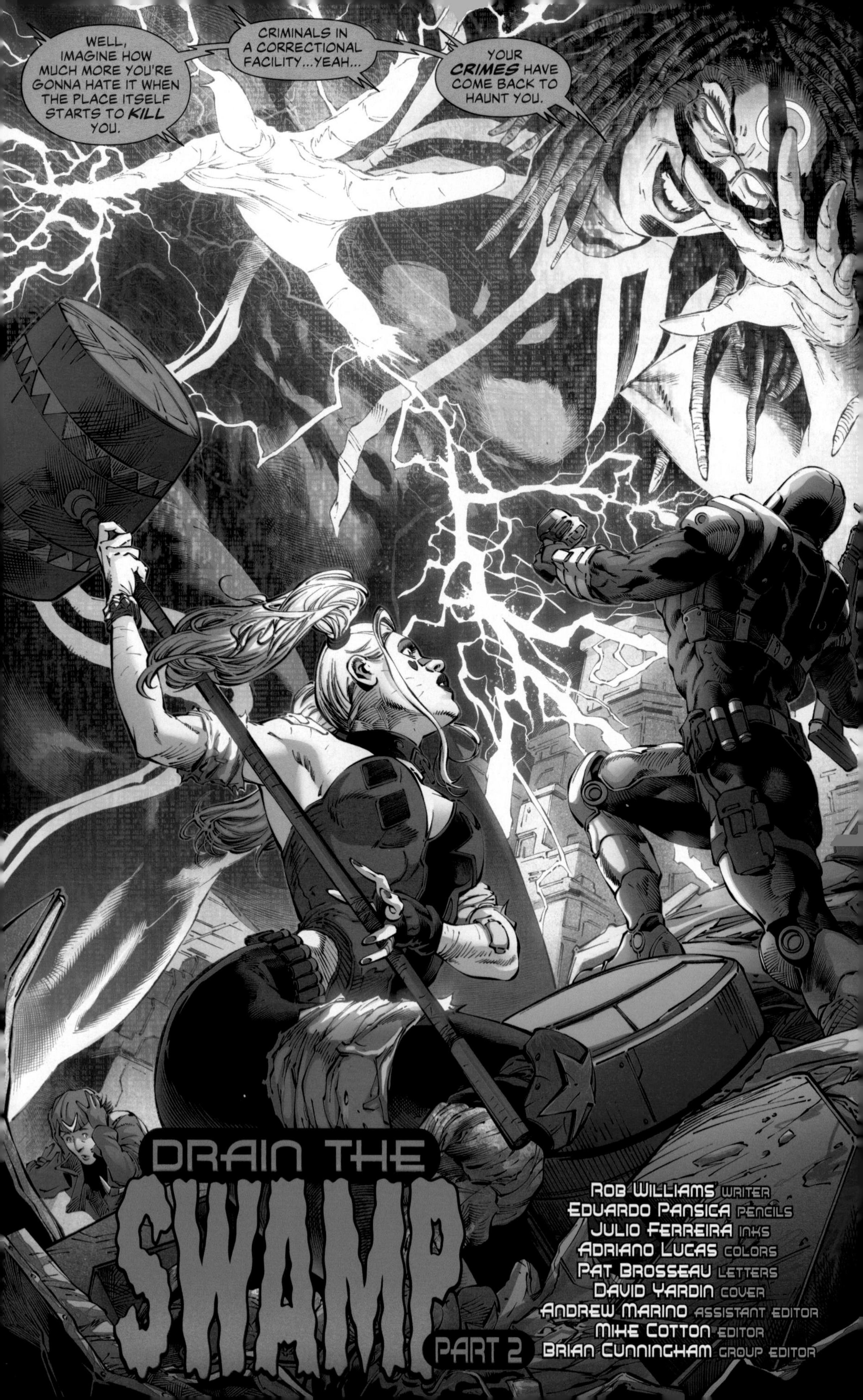

WELL, IMAGINE HOW MUCH MORE YOU'RE GONNA HATE IT WHEN THE PLACE ITSELF STARTS TO KILL YOU.
CRIMINALS IN A CORRECTIONAL FACILITY...YEAH...
YOUR CRIMES HAVE COME BACK TO HAUNT YOU.
DRAIN THE SWAMP PART 2
ROB WILLIAMS WRITER
EDUARDO PANSICA PENCILS
JULIO FERREIRA INKS
ADRIANO LUCAS COLORS
PAT BROSSEAU LETTERS
DAVID YARDIN COVER
ANDREW MARINO ASSISTANT EDITOR
MIKE COTTON EDITOR
BRIAN CUNNINGHAM GROUP EDITOR

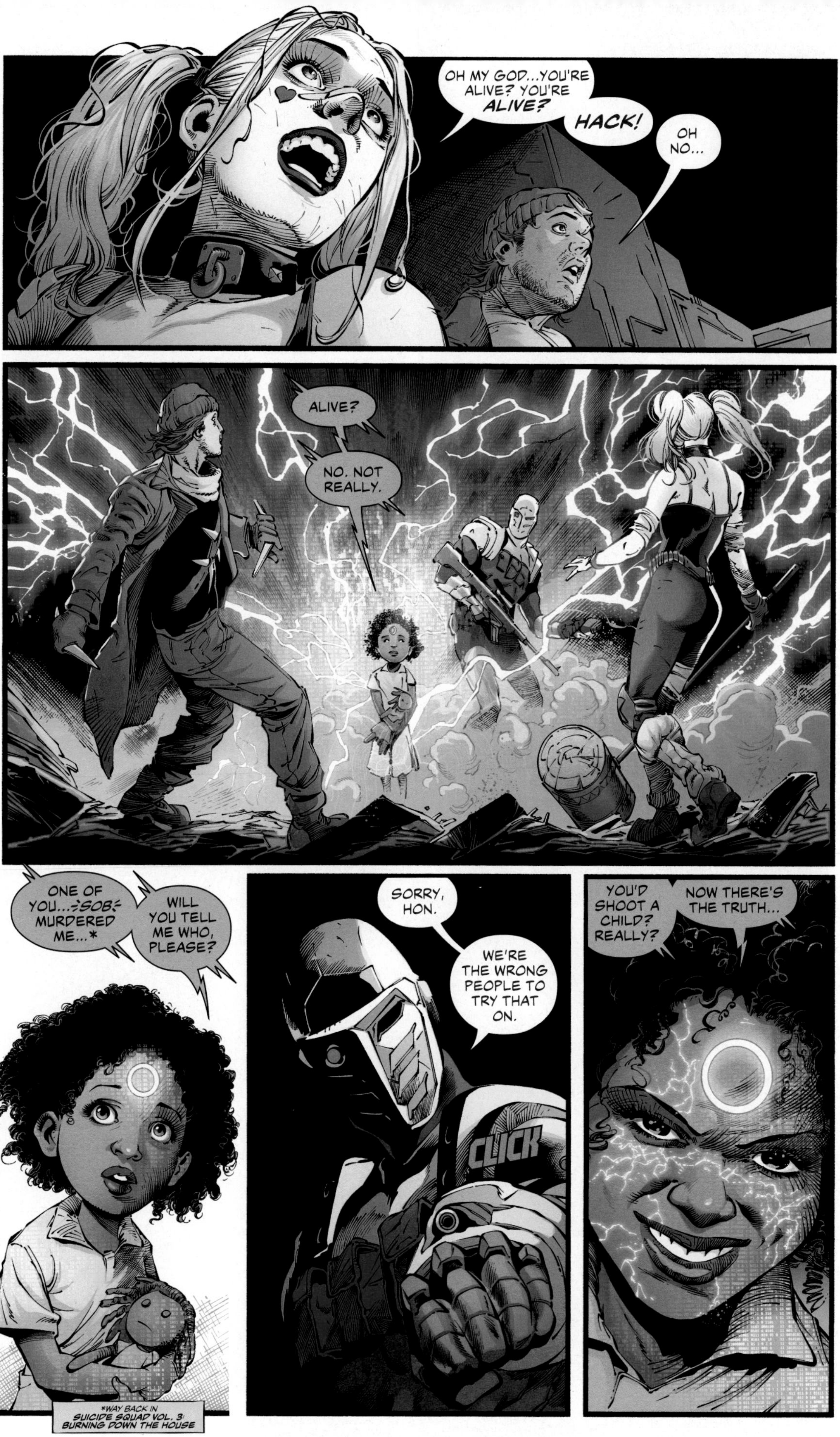
OH MY GOD...YOU'RE ALIVE? YOU'RE *ALIVE?*
HACK!
OH NO...
ALIVE?
NO. NOT REALLY.
ONE OF YOU... -SOB- MURDERED ME...*
WILL YOU TELL ME WHO, PLEASE?
*WAY BACK IN SUICIDE SQUAD VOL. 3: BURNING DOWN THE HOUSE
SORRY, HON.
WE'RE THE WRONG PEOPLE TO TRY THAT ON.
CLICK
YOU'D SHOOT A CHILD? REALLY?
NOW THERE'S THE TRUTH...

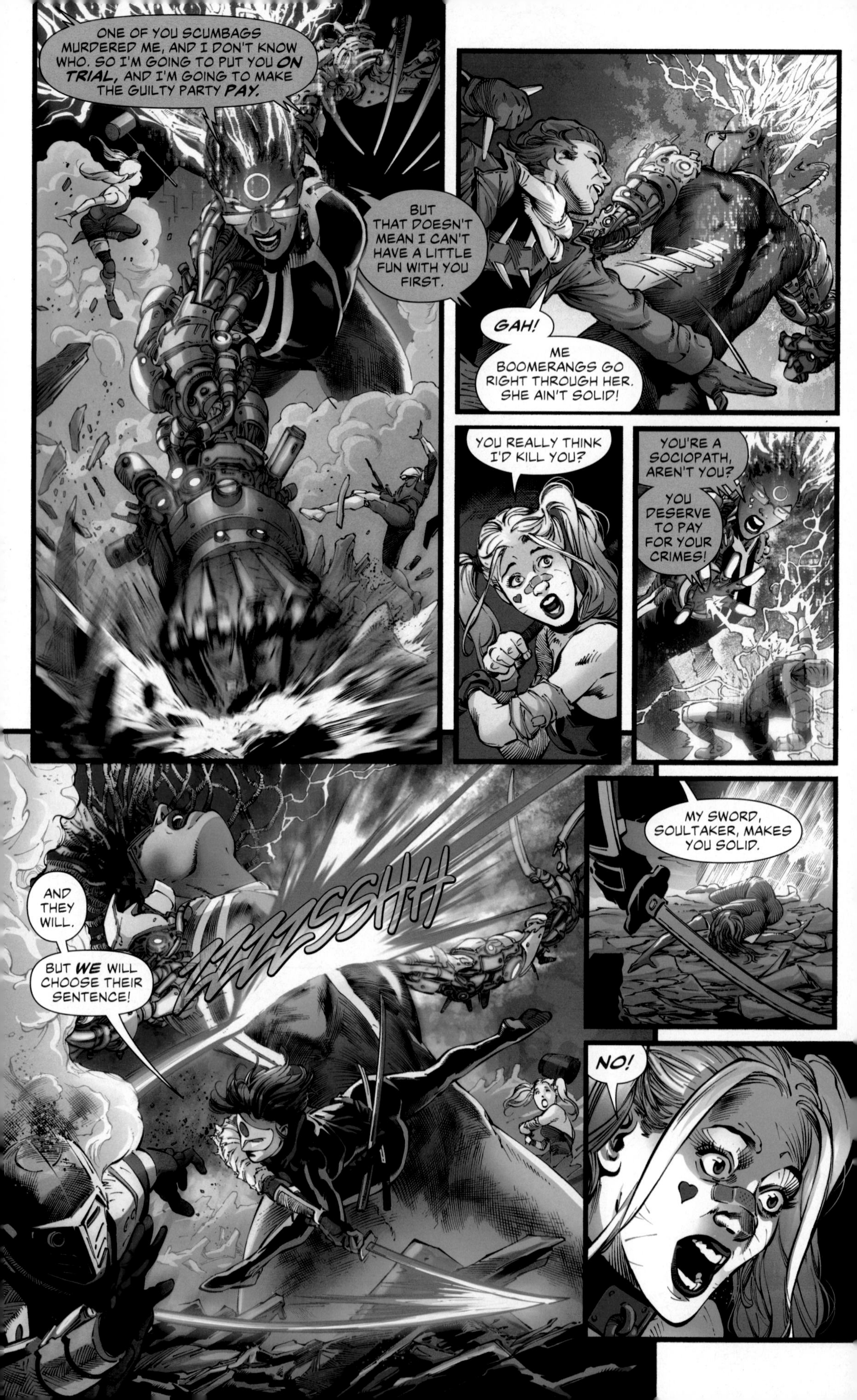
ONE OF YOU SCUMBAGS MURDERED ME, AND I DON'T KNOW WHO. SO I'M GOING TO PUT YOU ON TRIAL, AND I'M GOING TO MAKE THE GUILTY PARTY PAY.
BUT THAT DOESN'T MEAN I CAN'T HAVE A LITTLE FUN WITH YOU FIRST.
GAH!
ME BOOMERANGS GO RIGHT THROUGH HER. SHE AIN'T SOLID!
YOU REALLY THINK I'D KILL YOU?
YOU'RE A SOCIOPATH, AREN'T YOU?
YOU DESERVE TO PAY FOR YOUR CRIMES!
AND THEY WILL.
BUT WE WILL CHOOSE THEIR SENTENCE!
WHOOSSHH
MY SWORD, SOULTAKER, MAKES YOU SOLID.
NO!

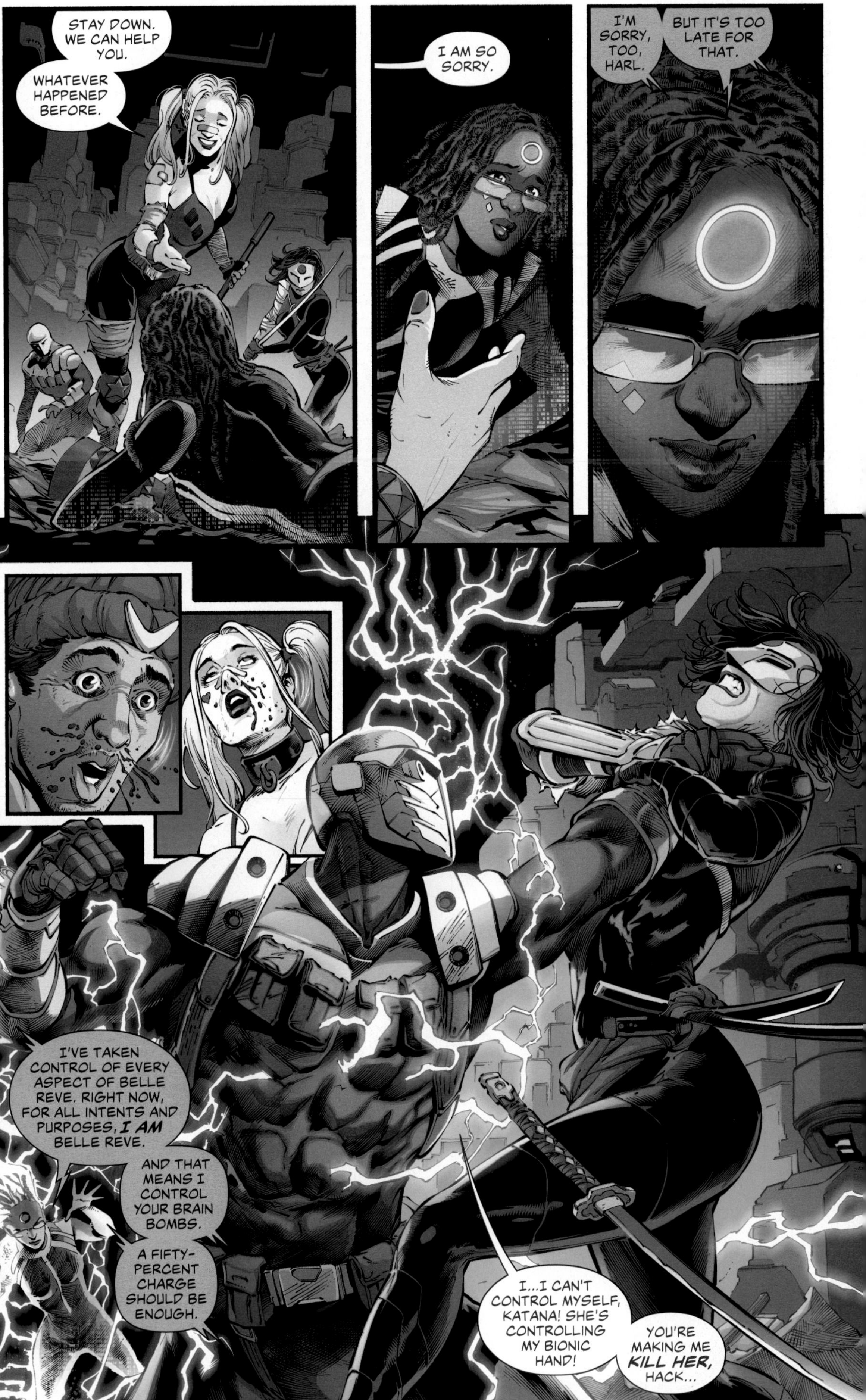
STAY DOWN. WE CAN HELP YOU.
WHATEVER HAPPENED BEFORE.
I AM SO SORRY.
I'M SORRY, TOO, HARL.
BUT IT'S TOO LATE FOR THAT.
I'VE TAKEN CONTROL OF EVERY ASPECT OF BELLE REVE. RIGHT NOW, FOR ALL INTENTS AND PURPOSES, I AM BELLE REVE.
AND THAT MEANS I CONTROL YOUR BRAIN BOMBS.
A FIFTY-PERCENT CHARGE SHOULD BE ENOUGH.
I...I CAN'T CONTROL MYSELF, KATANA! SHE'S CONTROLLING MY BIONIC HAND!
YOU'RE MAKING ME KILL HER, HACK...

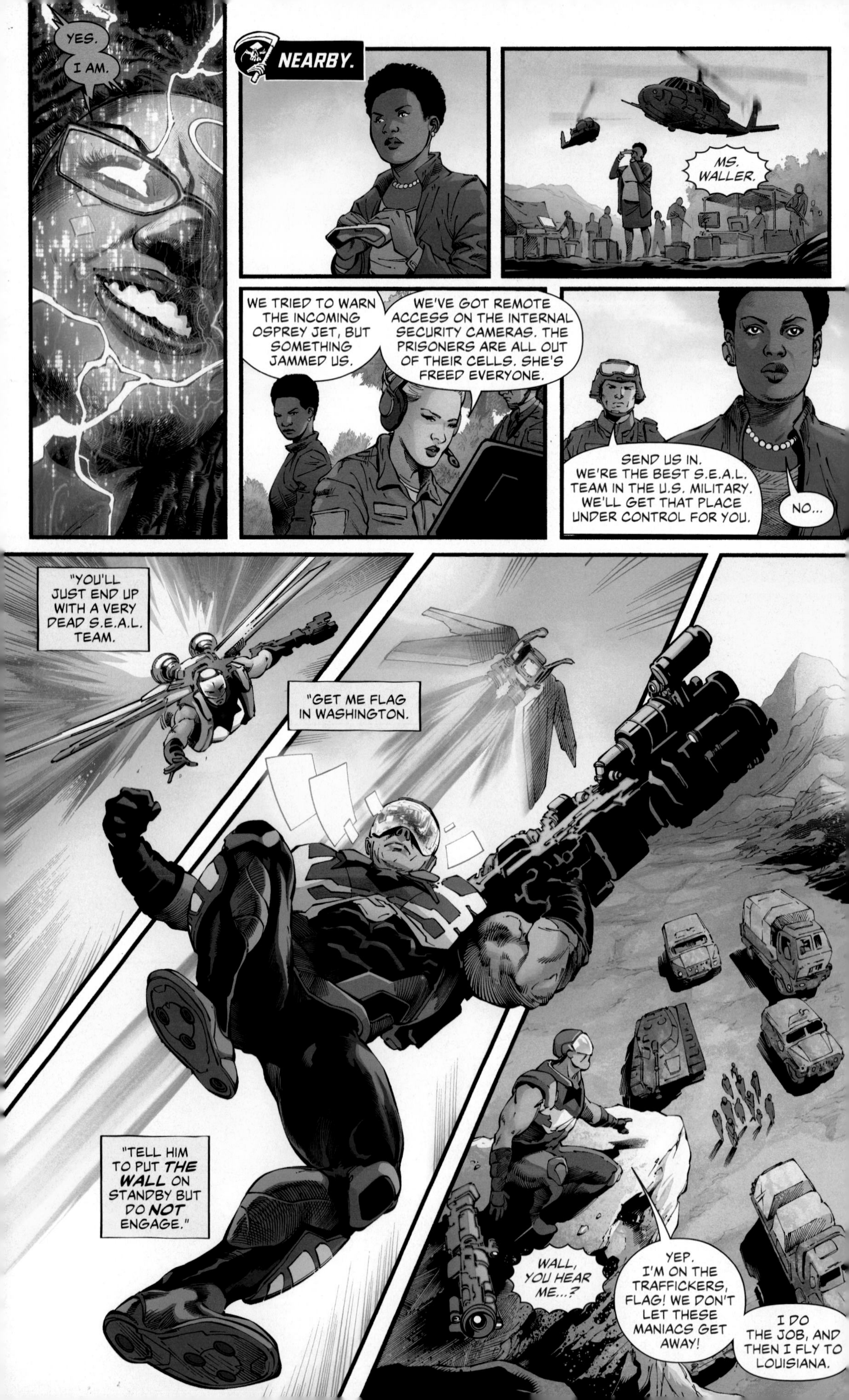

YES. I AM.
NEARBY.
MS. WALLER.
WE TRIED TO WARN THE INCOMING OSPREY JET, BUT SOMETHING JAMMED US.
WE'VE GOT REMOTE ACCESS ON THE INTERNAL SECURITY CAMERAS. THE PRISONERS ARE ALL OUT OF THEIR CELLS. SHE'S FREED EVERYONE.
SEND US IN. WE'RE THE BEST S.E.A.L. TEAM IN THE U.S. MILITARY. WE'LL GET THAT PLACE UNDER CONTROL FOR YOU.
NO...
"YOU'LL JUST END UP WITH A VERY DEAD S.E.A.L. TEAM.
"GET ME FLAG IN WASHINGTON.
"TELL HIM TO PUT *THE WALL* ON STANDBY BUT DO *NOT* ENGAGE."
WALL, YOU HEAR ME...?
YEP. I'M ON THE TRAFFICKERS, FLAG! WE DON'T LET THESE MANIACS GET AWAY!
I DO THE JOB, AND THEN I FLY TO LOUISIANA.

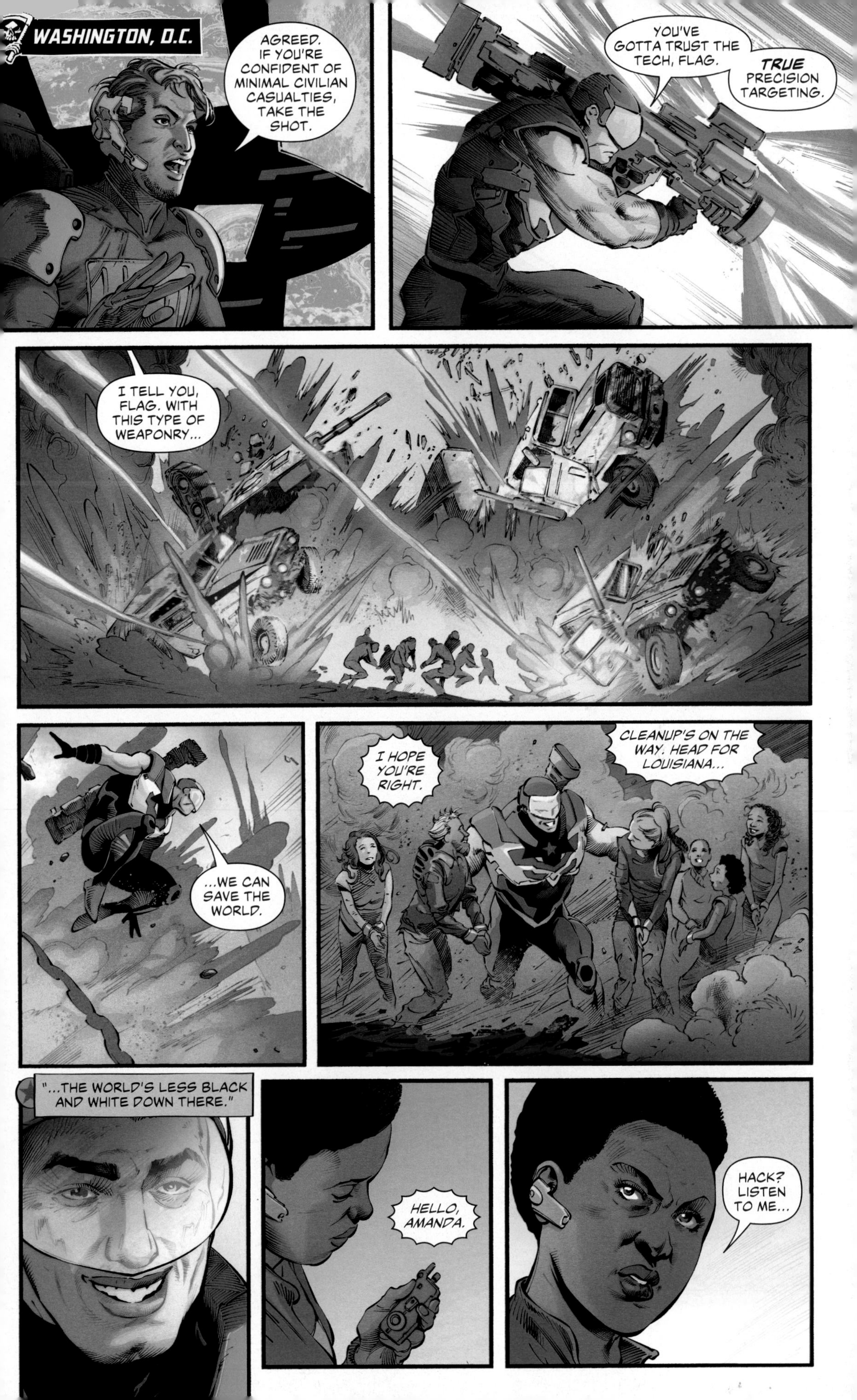
WASHINGTON, D.C.
AGREED. IF YOU'RE CONFIDENT OF MINIMAL CIVILIAN CASUALTIES, TAKE THE SHOT.
YOU'VE GOTTA TRUST THE TECH, FLAG.
TRUE PRECISION TARGETING.
I TELL YOU, FLAG. WITH THIS TYPE OF WEAPONRY...
...WE CAN SAVE THE WORLD.
I HOPE YOU'RE RIGHT.
CLEANUP'S ON THE WAY. HEAD FOR LOUISIANA...
"...THE WORLD'S LESS BLACK AND WHITE DOWN THERE."
HELLO, AMANDA.
HACK? LISTEN TO ME...

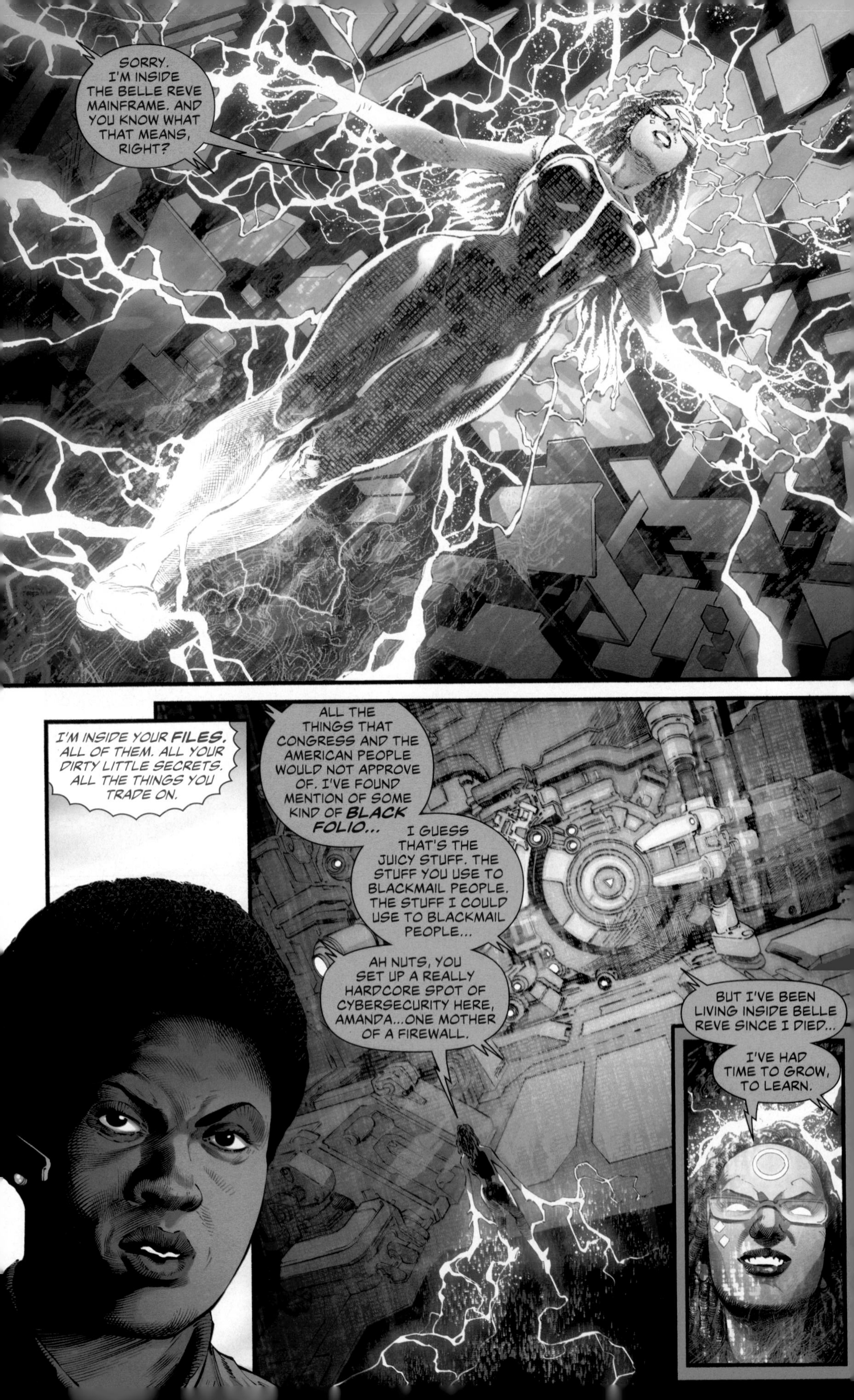
SORRY. I'M INSIDE THE BELLE REVE MAINFRAME. AND YOU KNOW WHAT THAT MEANS, RIGHT?
I'M INSIDE YOUR **FILES.** ALL OF THEM. ALL YOUR DIRTY LITTLE SECRETS. ALL THE THINGS YOU TRADE ON.
ALL THE THINGS THAT CONGRESS AND THE AMERICAN PEOPLE WOULD NOT APPROVE OF. I'VE FOUND MENTION OF SOME KIND OF **BLACK FOLIO...**
I GUESS THAT'S THE JUICY STUFF. THE STUFF YOU USE TO BLACKMAIL PEOPLE. THE STUFF I COULD USE TO BLACKMAIL PEOPLE...
AH NUTS, YOU SET UP A REALLY HARDCORE SPOT OF CYBERSECURITY HERE, AMANDA...ONE MOTHER OF A FIREWALL.
BUT I'VE BEEN LIVING INSIDE BELLE REVE SINCE I DIED...
I'VE HAD TIME TO GROW, TO LEARN.

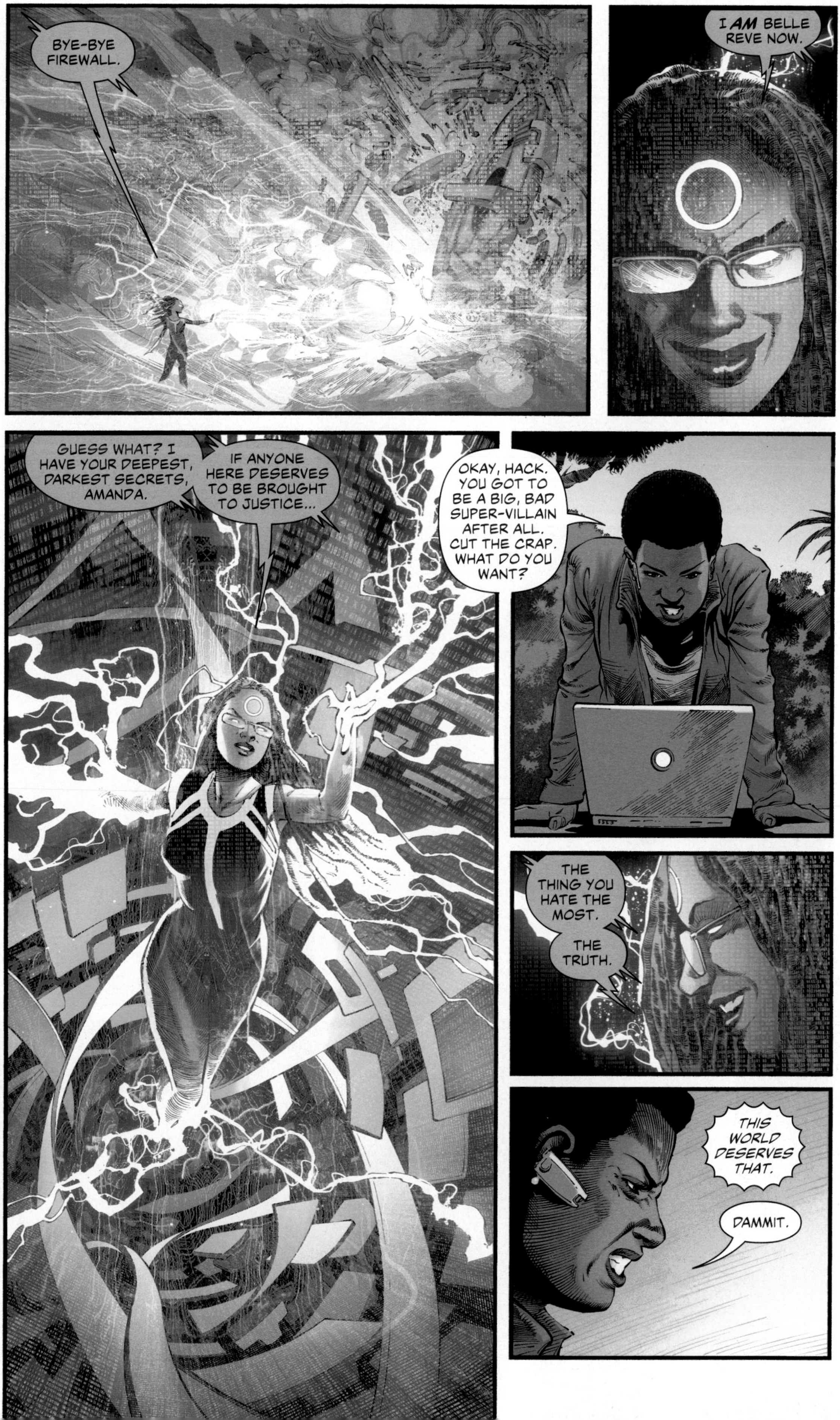
BYE-BYE FIREWALL.
I AM BELLE REVE NOW.
GUESS WHAT? I HAVE YOUR DEEPEST, DARKEST SECRETS, AMANDA.
IF ANYONE HERE DESERVES TO BE BROUGHT TO JUSTICE...
OKAY, HACK. YOU GOT TO BE A BIG, BAD SUPER-VILLAIN AFTER ALL. CUT THE CRAP. WHAT DO YOU WANT?
THE THING YOU HATE THE MOST.
THE TRUTH.
THIS WORLD DESERVES THAT.
DAMMIT.

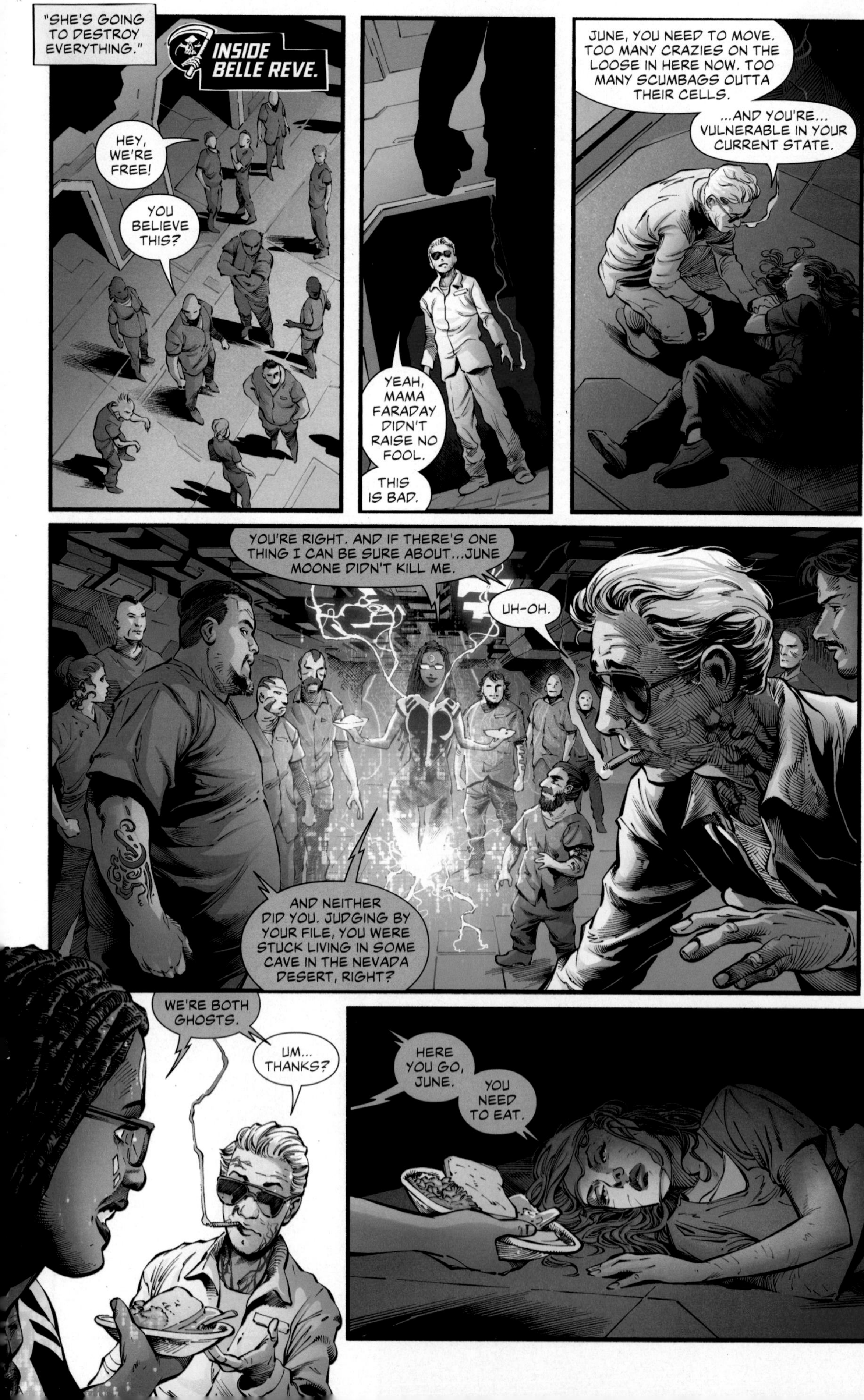
"SHE'S GOING TO DESTROY EVERYTHING."
INSIDE BELLE REVE.
HEY, WE'RE FREE!
YOU BELIEVE THIS?
YEAH, MAMA FARADAY DIDN'T RAISE NO FOOL.
THIS IS BAD.
JUNE, YOU NEED TO MOVE. TOO MANY CRAZIES ON THE LOOSE IN HERE NOW. TOO MANY SCUMBAGS OUTTA THEIR CELLS.
...AND YOU'RE... VULNERABLE IN YOUR CURRENT STATE.
YOU'RE RIGHT. AND IF THERE'S ONE THING I CAN BE SURE ABOUT...JUNE MOONE DIDN'T KILL ME.
UH-OH.
AND NEITHER DID YOU. JUDGING BY YOUR FILE, YOU WERE STUCK LIVING IN SOME CAVE IN THE NEVADA DESERT, RIGHT?
WE'RE BOTH GHOSTS.
UM... THANKS?
HERE YOU GO, JUNE.
YOU NEED TO EAT.

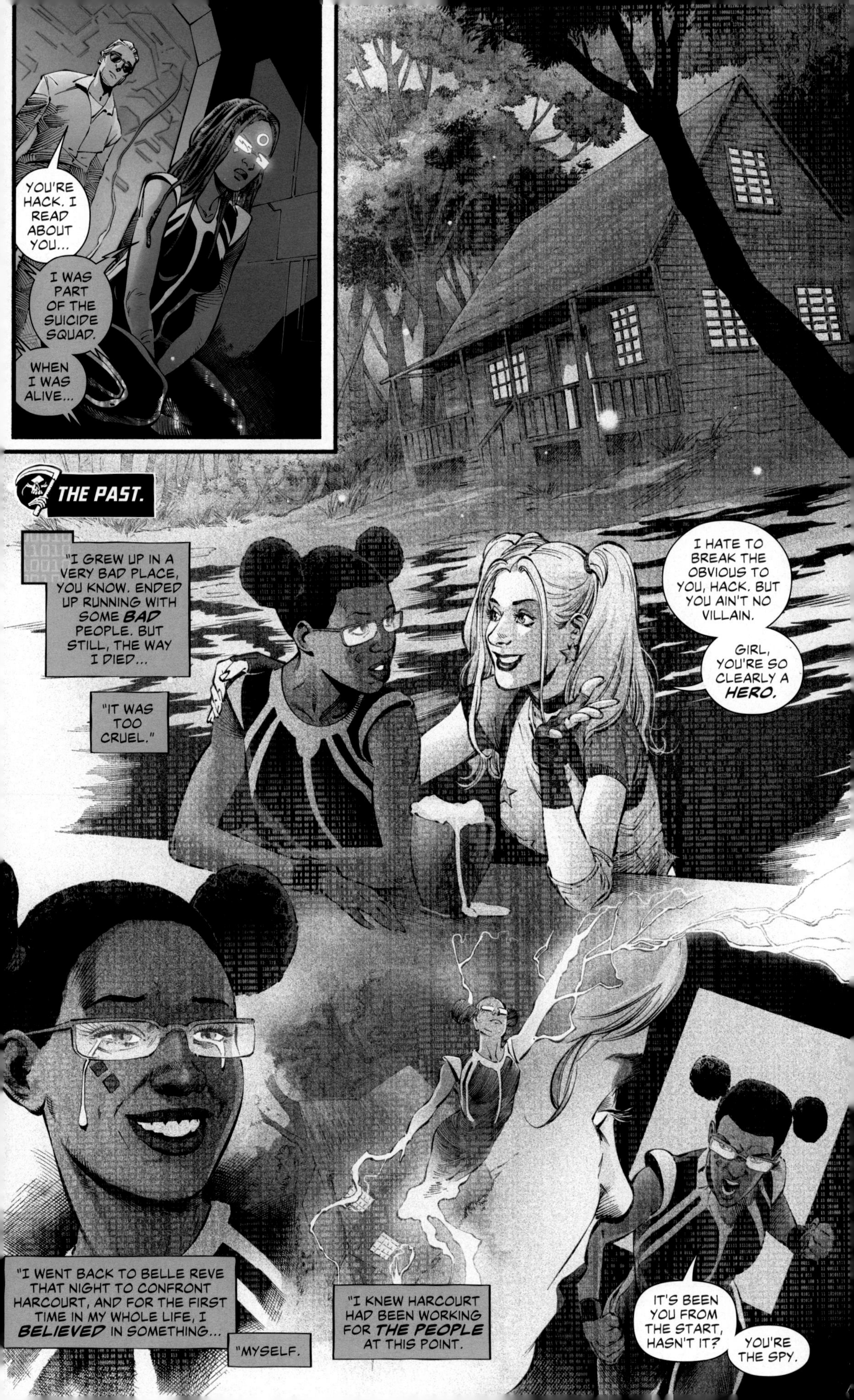
YOU'RE HACK. I READ ABOUT YOU...
I WAS PART OF THE SUICIDE SQUAD.
WHEN I WAS ALIVE...
THE PAST.
"I GREW UP IN A VERY BAD PLACE, YOU KNOW. ENDED UP RUNNING WITH SOME BAD PEOPLE. BUT STILL, THE WAY I DIED...
"IT WAS TOO CRUEL."
I HATE TO BREAK THE OBVIOUS TO YOU, HACK. BUT YOU AIN'T NO VILLAIN.
GIRL, YOU'RE SO CLEARLY A HERO.
"I WENT BACK TO BELLE REVE THAT NIGHT TO CONFRONT HARCOURT, AND FOR THE FIRST TIME IN MY WHOLE LIFE, I BELIEVED IN SOMETHING...
"MYSELF.
"I KNEW HARCOURT HAD BEEN WORKING FOR THE PEOPLE AT THIS POINT.
IT'S BEEN YOU FROM THE START, HASN'T IT?
YOU'RE THE SPY.

"I REMEMBER THE PAIN. I KNOW HARCOURT WAS IN FRONT OF ME. SHE DIDN'T MOVE. THAT... THAT'S THE LAST THING I REMEMBER. SO I KNOW IT WASN'T HER...

"I DON'T KNOW WHO MURDERED ME...

"I WAS DEAD, I THINK. FOR A LONG TIME. I WAS IN THE CIRCUIT BOARDS, THE MAINFRAMES, THE SERVERS...

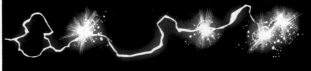

"A LIFE SPLIT AND SPREAD INTO A MILLION BYTES AND PROCESSORS AND R.A.M.

"AND THEN I REMEMBERED WHO I WAS. THAT EVEN THOUGH MY BODY WAS DEAD...MY MIND WAS STILL ALIVE. I WAS STILL DIGITAL INFORMATION.

AND THAT MEANT, IN THIS WORLD OF INTERNET AND SMARTPHONES AND A COMPUTER IN EVERY POCKET...

...I CAN BE ANYTHING I WANT TO BE.

SO... UH...

WHADDYA WANT TO BE?

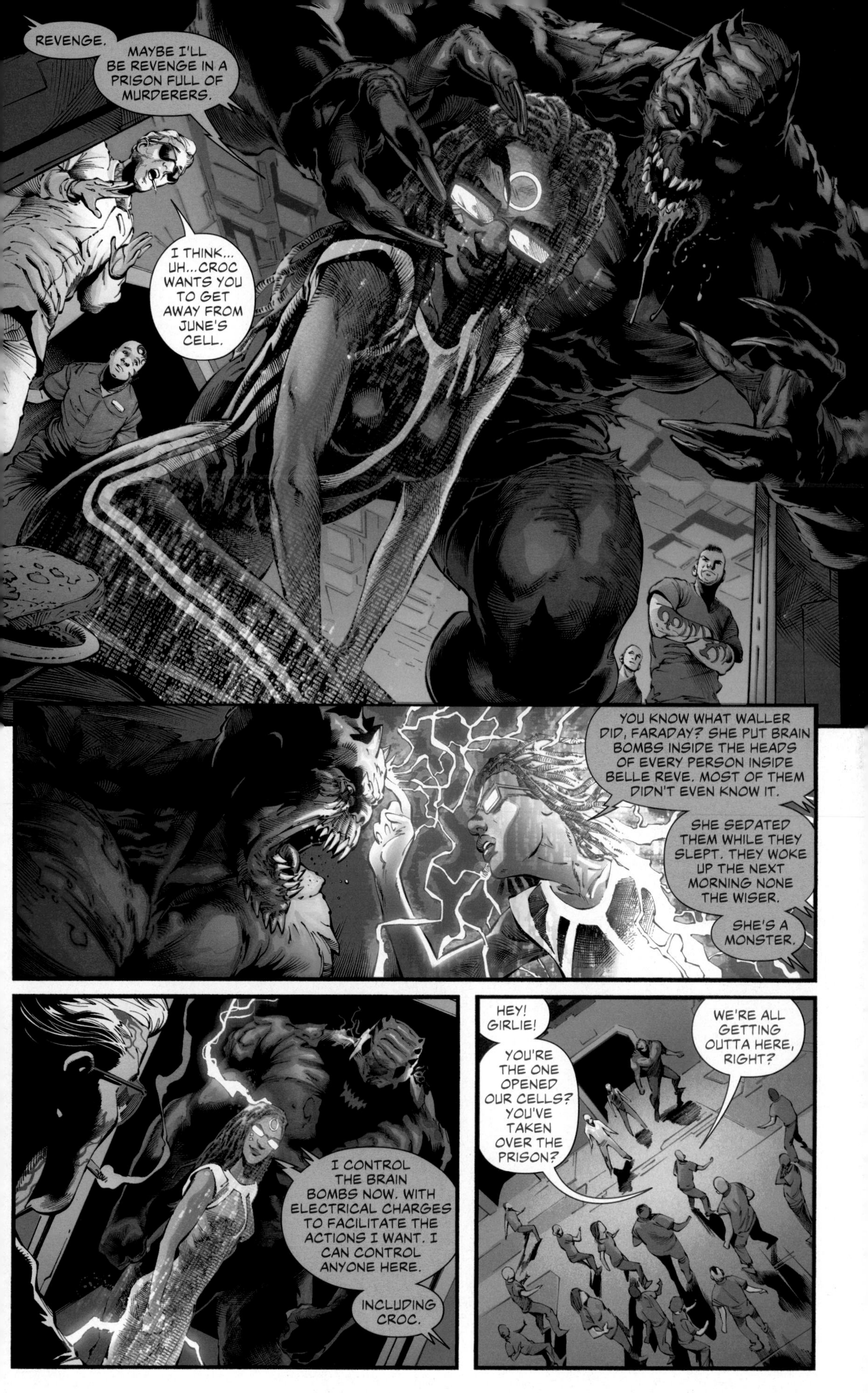
REVENGE.
MAYBE I'LL BE REVENGE IN A PRISON FULL OF MURDERERS.
I THINK... UH...CROC WANTS YOU TO GET AWAY FROM JUNE'S CELL.
YOU KNOW WHAT WALLER DID, FARADAY? SHE PUT BRAIN BOMBS INSIDE THE HEADS OF EVERY PERSON INSIDE BELLE REVE. MOST OF THEM DIDN'T EVEN KNOW IT.
SHE SEDATED THEM WHILE THEY SLEPT. THEY WOKE UP THE NEXT MORNING NONE THE WISER.
SHE'S A MONSTER.
I CONTROL THE BRAIN BOMBS NOW. WITH ELECTRICAL CHARGES TO FACILITATE THE ACTIONS I WANT. I CAN CONTROL ANYONE HERE.
INCLUDING CROC.
HEY! GIRLIE!
YOU'RE THE ONE OPENED OUR CELLS? YOU'VE TAKEN OVER THE PRISON?
WE'RE ALL GETTING OUTTA HERE, RIGHT?

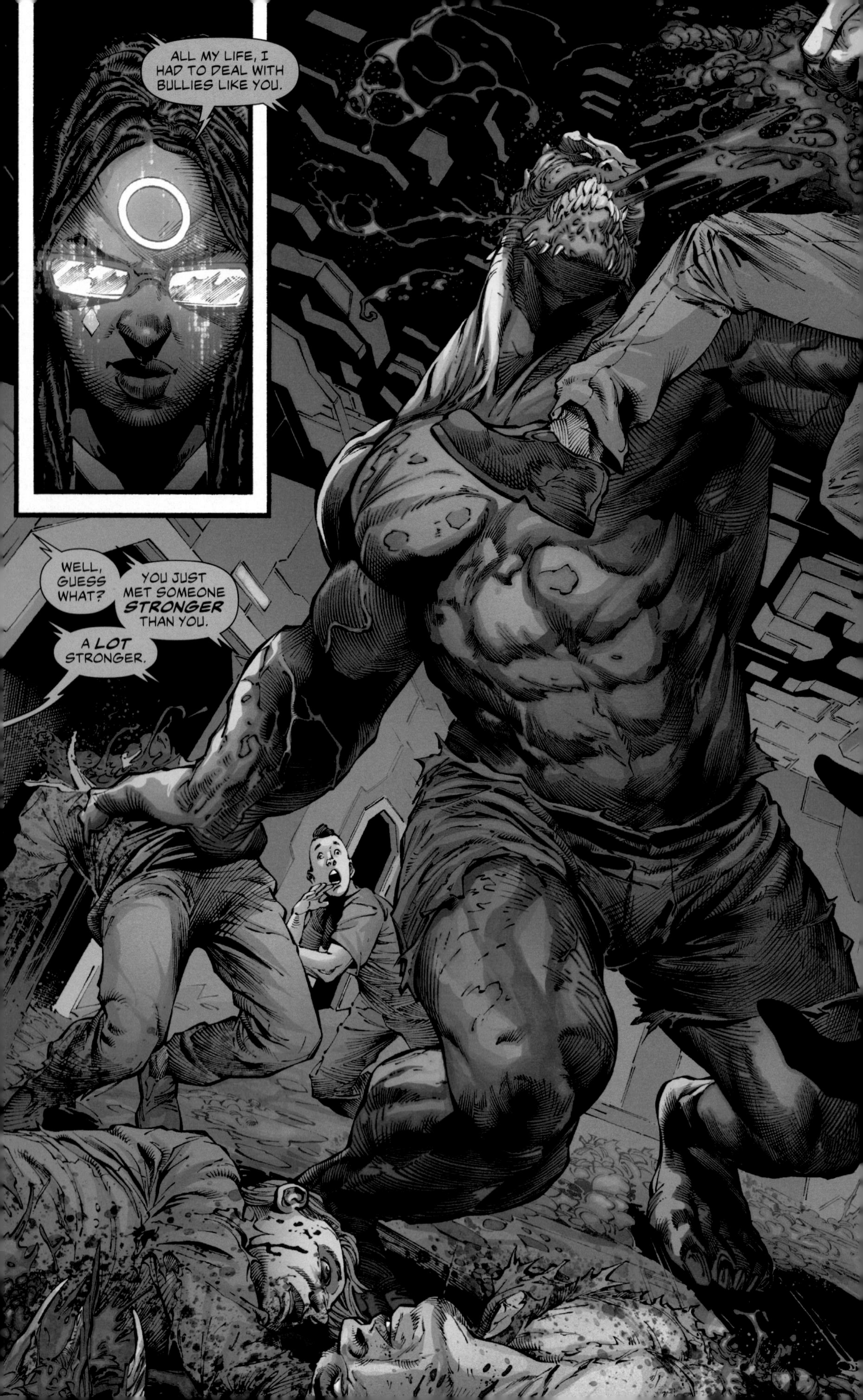
ALL MY LIFE, I HAD TO DEAL WITH BULLIES LIKE YOU.
WELL, GUESS WHAT?
YOU JUST MET SOMEONE **STRONGER** THAN YOU.
A **LOT** STRONGER.

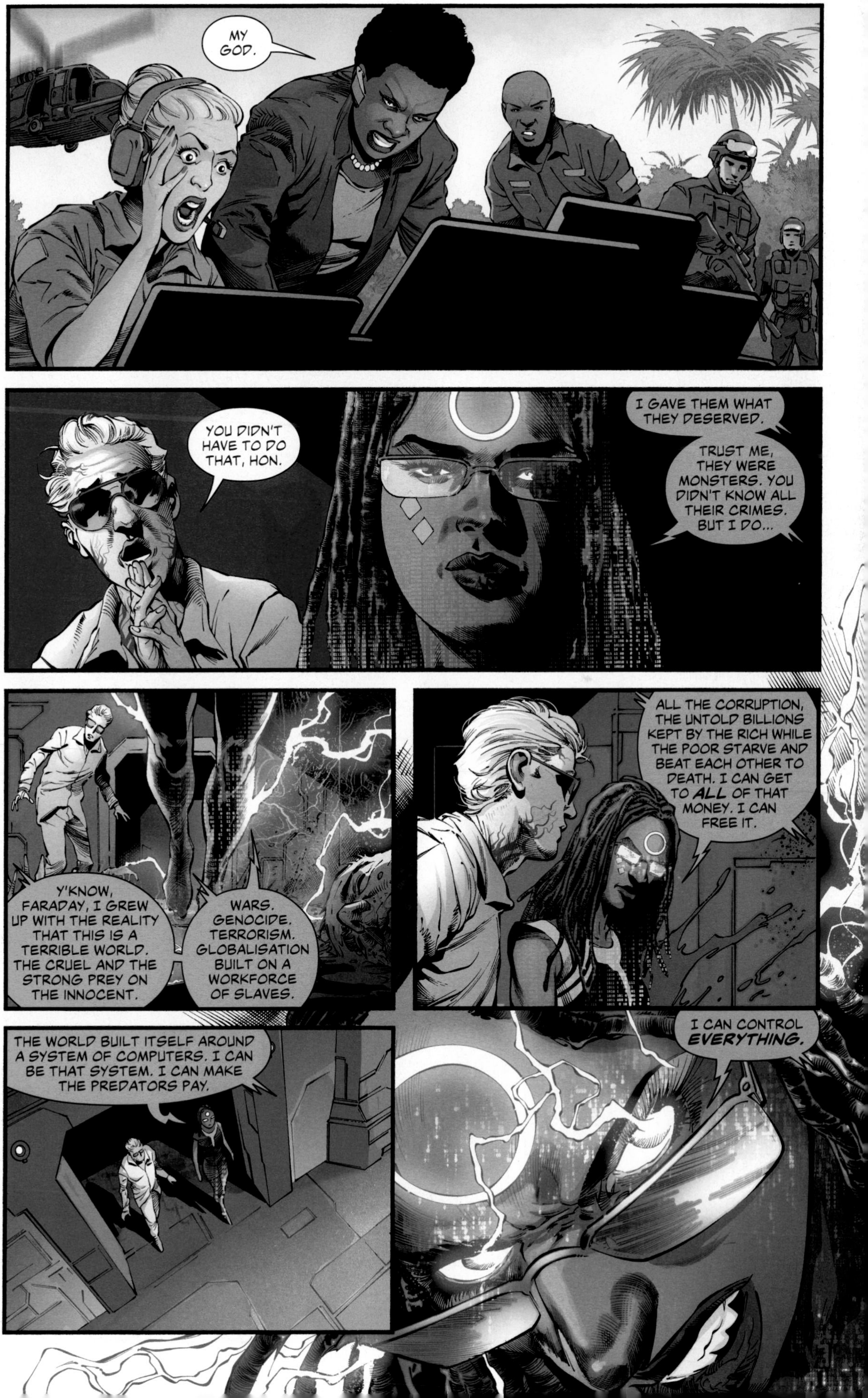
MY GOD.
YOU DIDN'T HAVE TO DO THAT, HON.
I GAVE THEM WHAT THEY DESERVED.
TRUST ME, THEY WERE MONSTERS. YOU DIDN'T KNOW ALL THEIR CRIMES. BUT I DO...
Y'KNOW, FARADAY, I GREW UP WITH THE REALITY THAT THIS IS A TERRIBLE WORLD. THE CRUEL AND THE STRONG PREY ON THE INNOCENT.
WARS. GENOCIDE. TERRORISM. GLOBALISATION BUILT ON A WORKFORCE OF SLAVES.
ALL THE CORRUPTION, THE UNTOLD BILLIONS KEPT BY THE RICH WHILE THE POOR STARVE AND BEAT EACH OTHER TO DEATH. I CAN GET TO ALL OF THAT MONEY. I CAN FREE IT.
THE WORLD BUILT ITSELF AROUND A SYSTEM OF COMPUTERS. I CAN BE THAT SYSTEM. I CAN MAKE THE PREDATORS PAY.
I CAN CONTROL EVERYTHING.

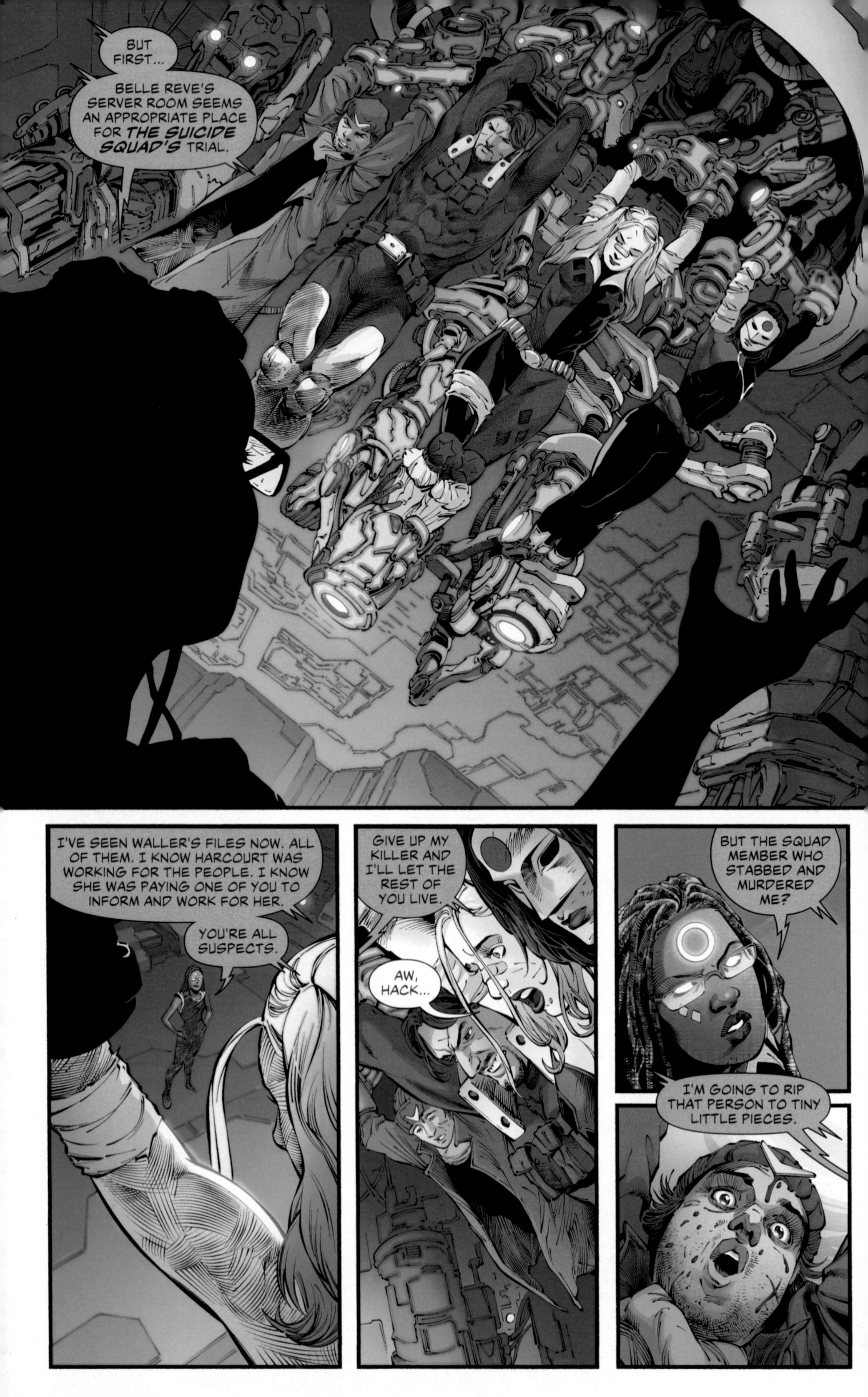
BUT FIRST...
BELLE REVE'S SERVER ROOM SEEMS AN APPROPRIATE PLACE FOR THE SUICIDE SQUAD'S TRIAL.
I'VE SEEN WALLER'S FILES NOW. ALL OF THEM. I KNOW HARCOURT WAS WORKING FOR THE PEOPLE. I KNOW SHE WAS PAYING ONE OF YOU TO INFORM AND WORK FOR HER.
YOU'RE ALL SUSPECTS.
GIVE UP MY KILLER AND I'LL LET THE REST OF YOU LIVE.
AW, HACK...
BUT THE SQUAD MEMBER WHO STABBED AND MURDERED ME?
I'M GOING TO RIP THAT PERSON TO TINY LITTLE PIECES.

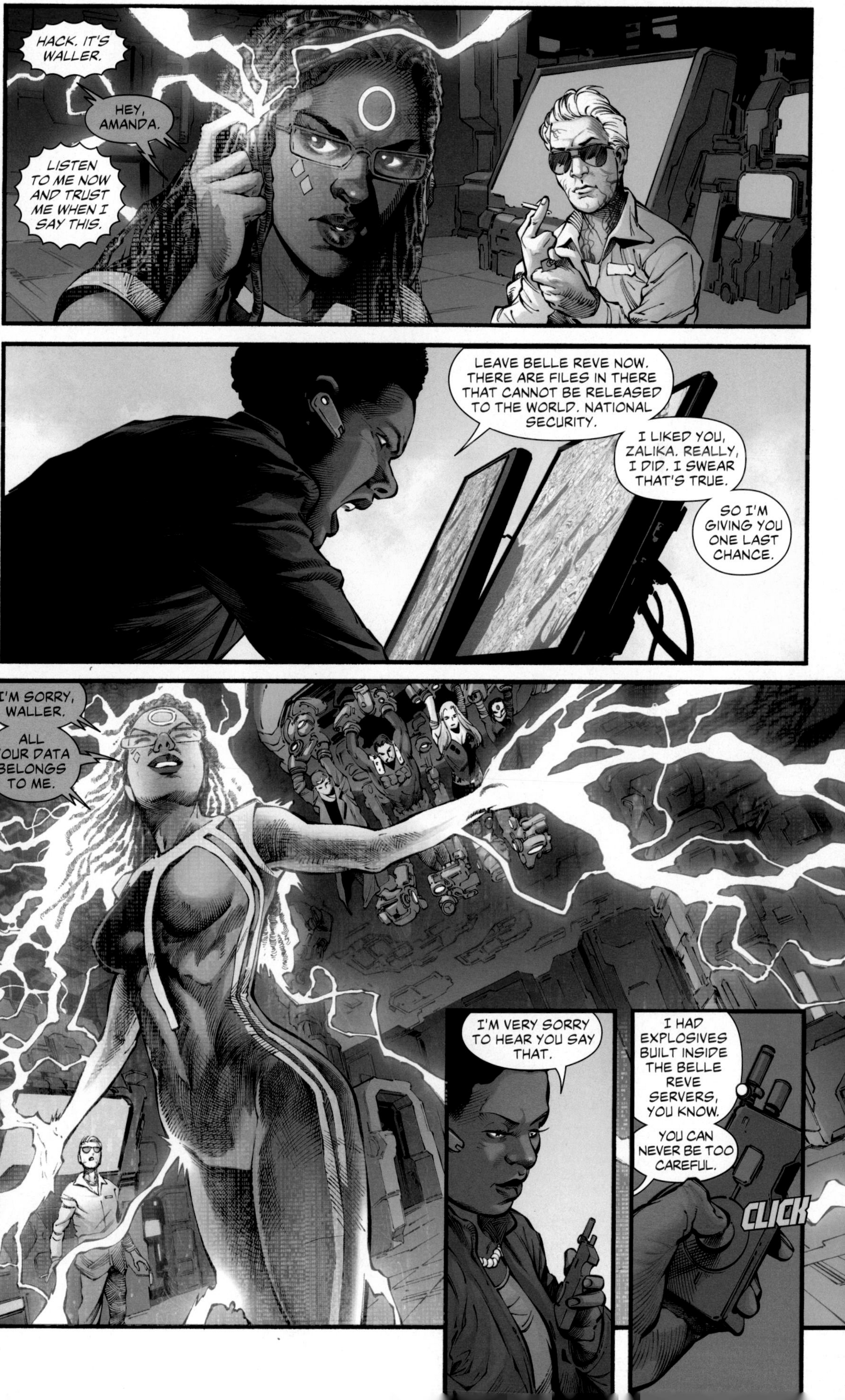
HACK. IT'S WALLER.
HEY, AMANDA.
LISTEN TO ME NOW AND TRUST ME WHEN I SAY THIS.
LEAVE BELLE REVE NOW. THERE ARE FILES IN THERE THAT CANNOT BE RELEASED TO THE WORLD. NATIONAL SECURITY.
I LIKED YOU, ZALIKA. REALLY, I DID. I SWEAR THAT'S TRUE.
SO I'M GIVING YOU ONE LAST CHANCE.
I'M SORRY, WALLER.
ALL YOUR DATA BELONGS TO ME.
I'M VERY SORRY TO HEAR YOU SAY THAT.
I HAD EXPLOSIVES BUILT INSIDE THE BELLE REVE SERVERS, YOU KNOW.
YOU CAN NEVER BE TOO CAREFUL.
CLICK

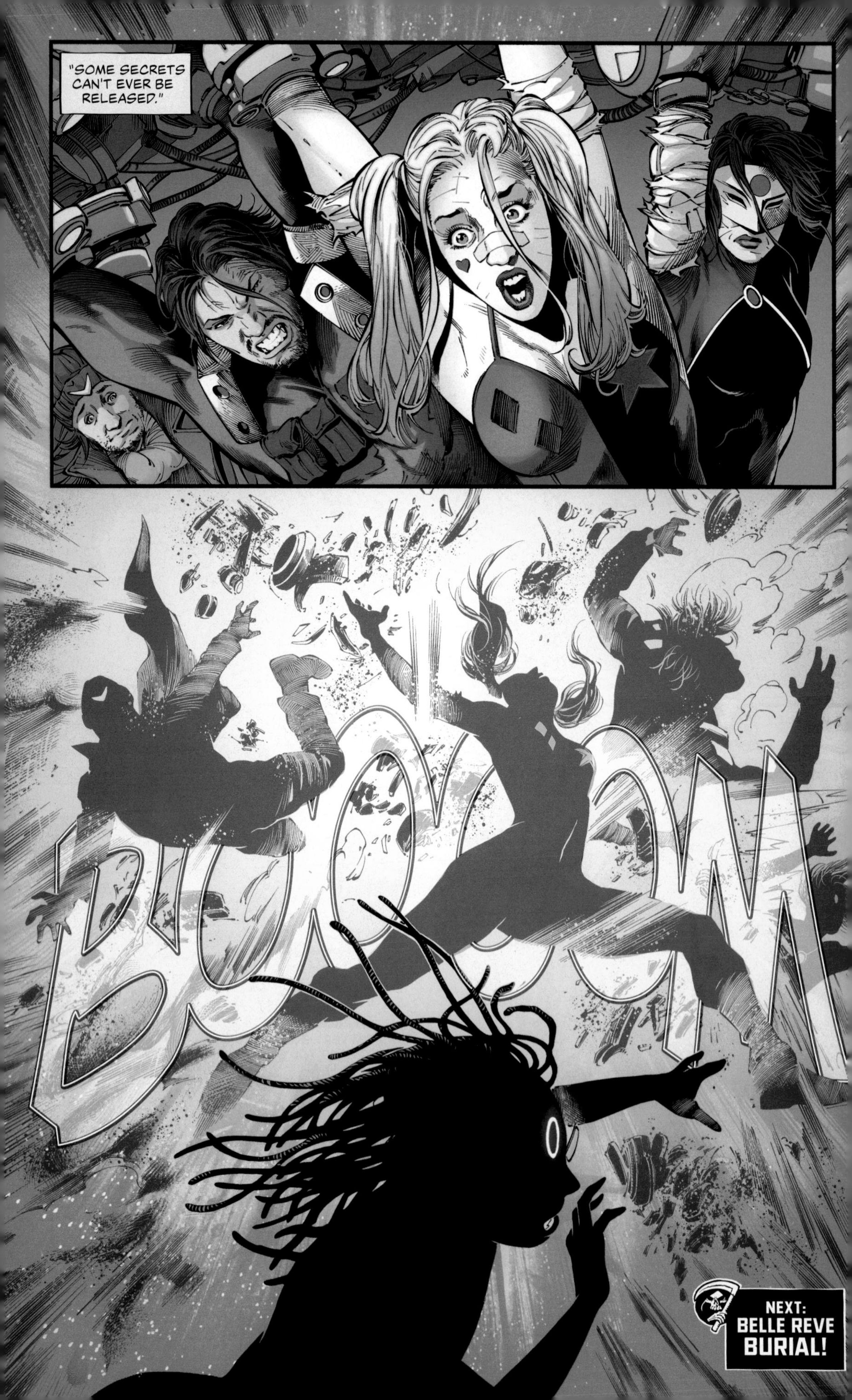
"SOME SECRETS CAN'T EVER BE RELEASED."
BOOOOM
NEXT: BELLE REVE BURIAL!

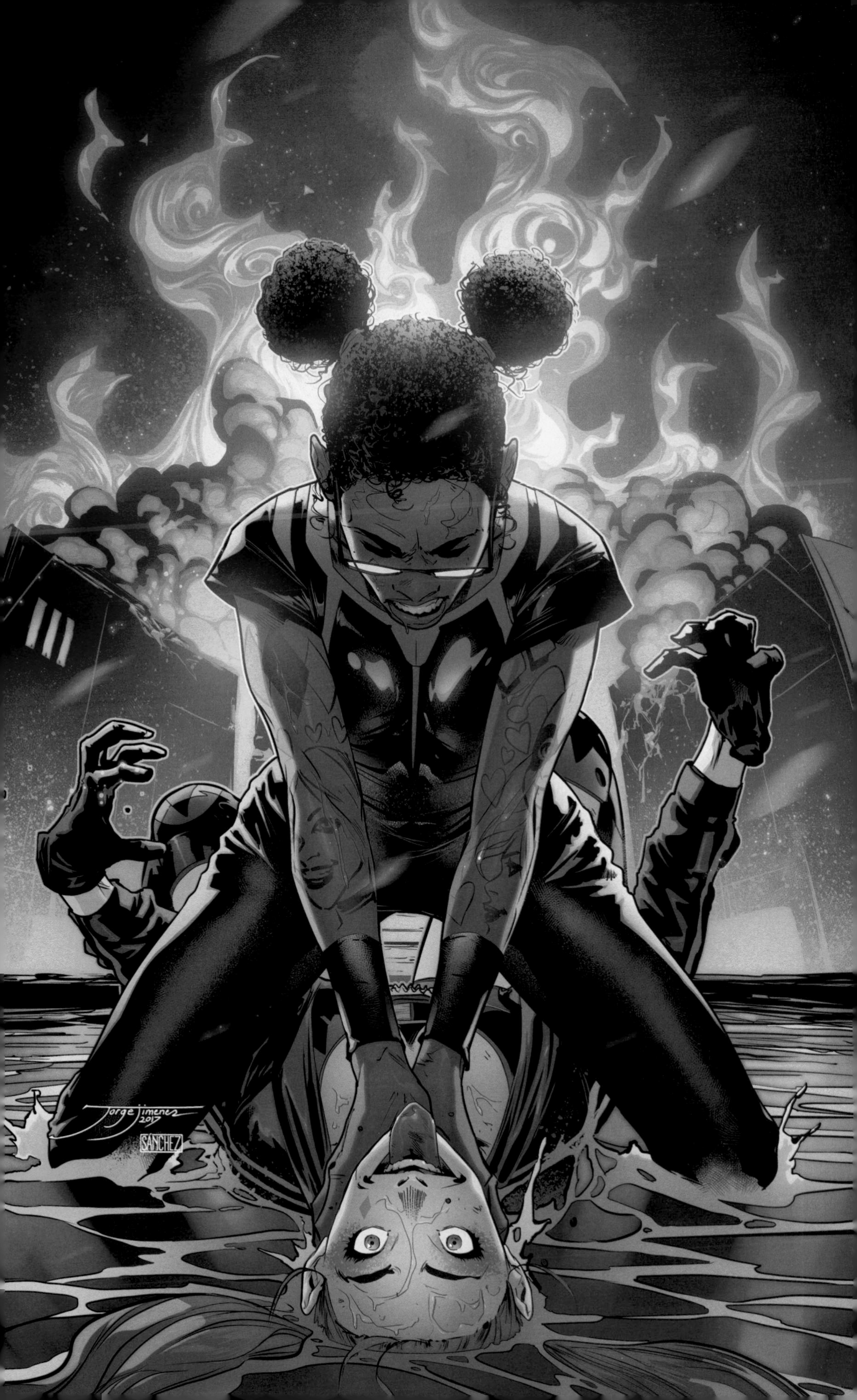
Jorge Jimenez 2017
SANCHEZ

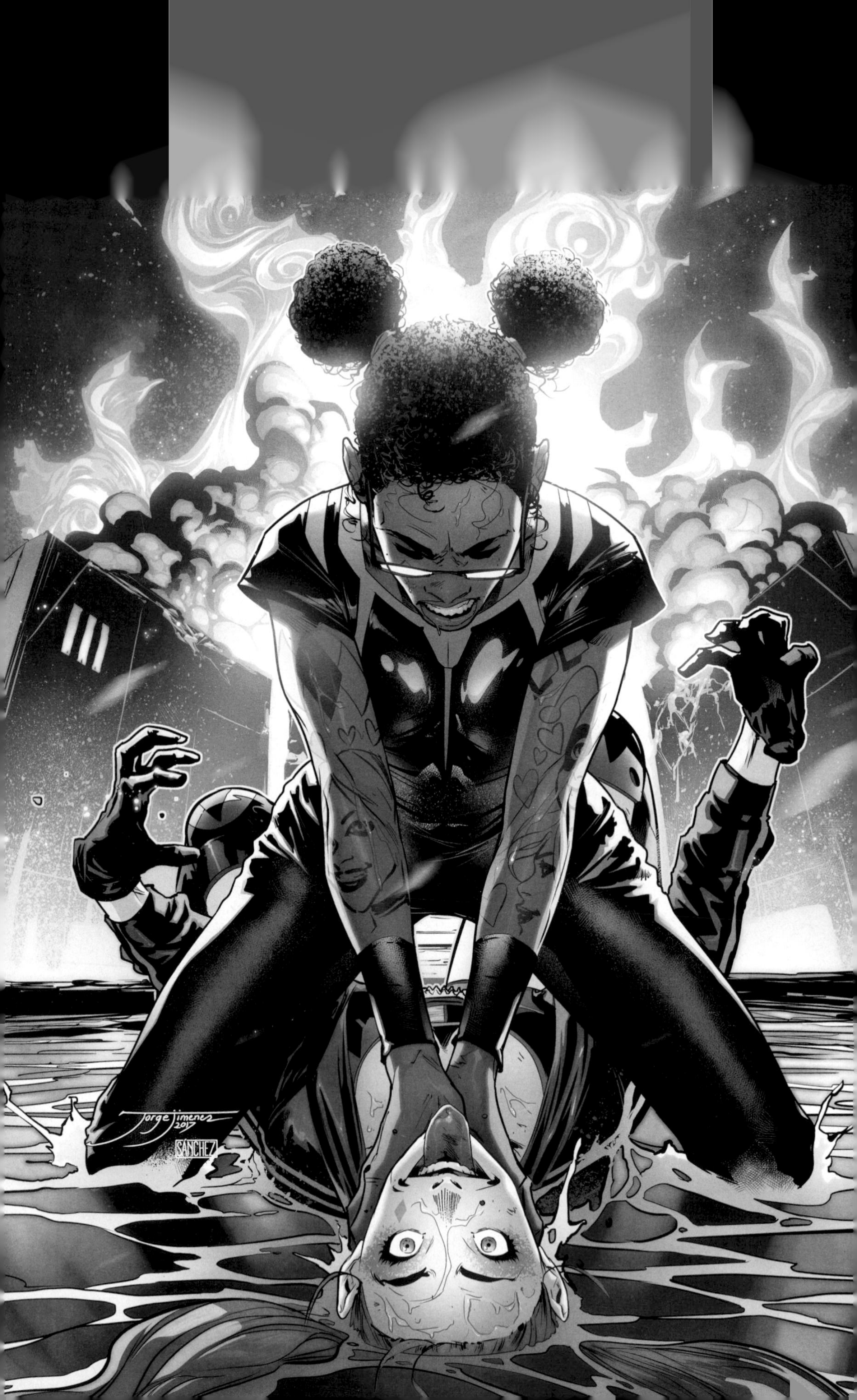
Jorge Jimenez 2017
SANCHEZ

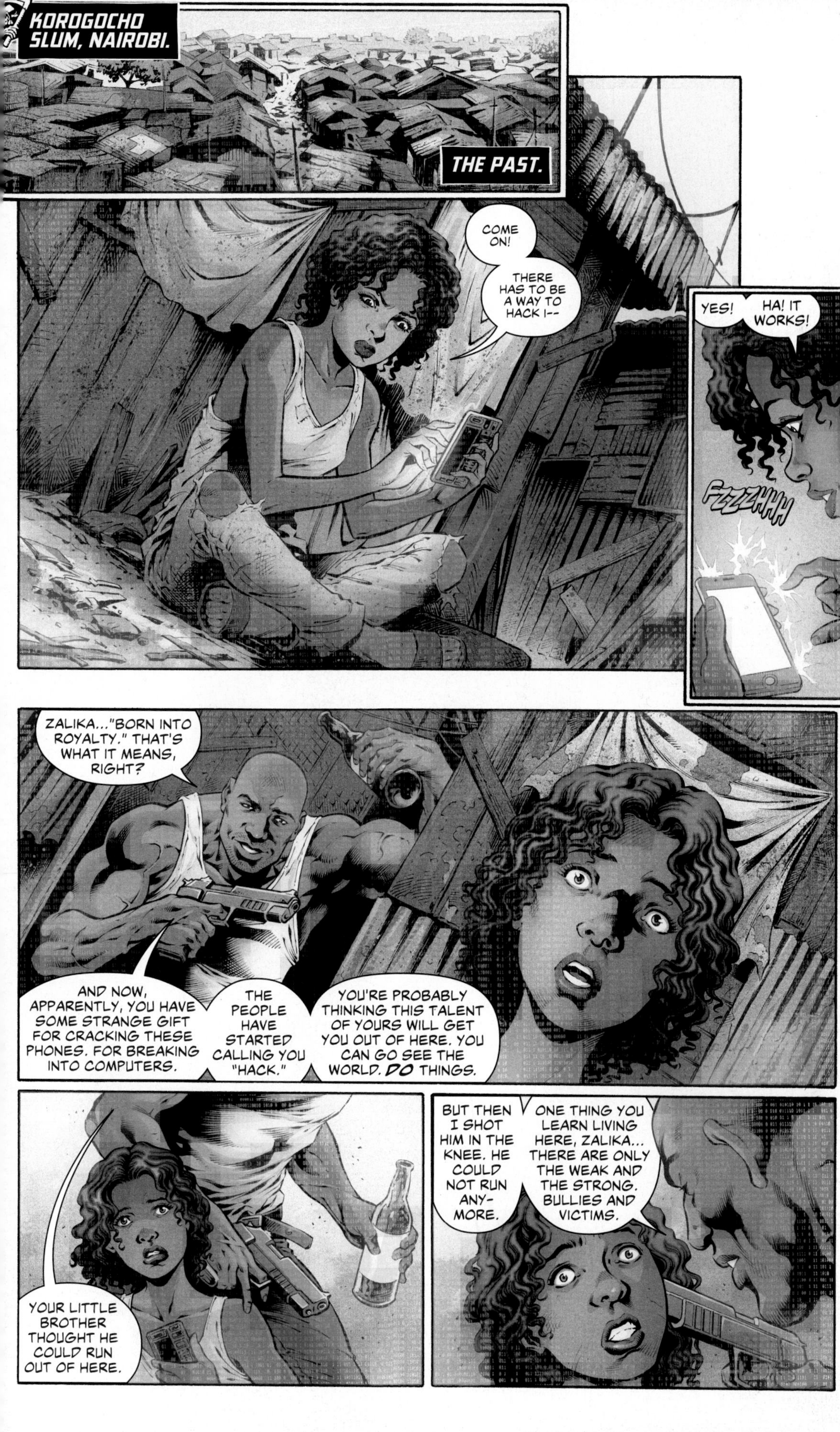

KOROGOCHO SLUM, NAIROBI.
THE PAST.
COME ON!
THERE HAS TO BE A WAY TO HACK I--
YES!
HA! IT WORKS!
FZZZHHH
ZALIKA..."BORN INTO ROYALTY." THAT'S WHAT IT MEANS, RIGHT?
AND NOW, APPARENTLY, YOU HAVE SOME STRANGE GIFT FOR CRACKING THESE PHONES. FOR BREAKING INTO COMPUTERS.
THE PEOPLE HAVE STARTED CALLING YOU "HACK."
YOU'RE PROBABLY THINKING THIS TALENT OF YOURS WILL GET YOU OUT OF HERE. YOU CAN GO SEE THE WORLD. DO THINGS.
YOUR LITTLE BROTHER THOUGHT HE COULD RUN OUT OF HERE.
BUT THEN I SHOT HIM IN THE KNEE. HE COULD NOT RUN ANY-MORE.
ONE THING YOU LEARN LIVING HERE, ZALIKA... THERE ARE ONLY THE WEAK AND THE STRONG. BULLIES AND VICTIMS.

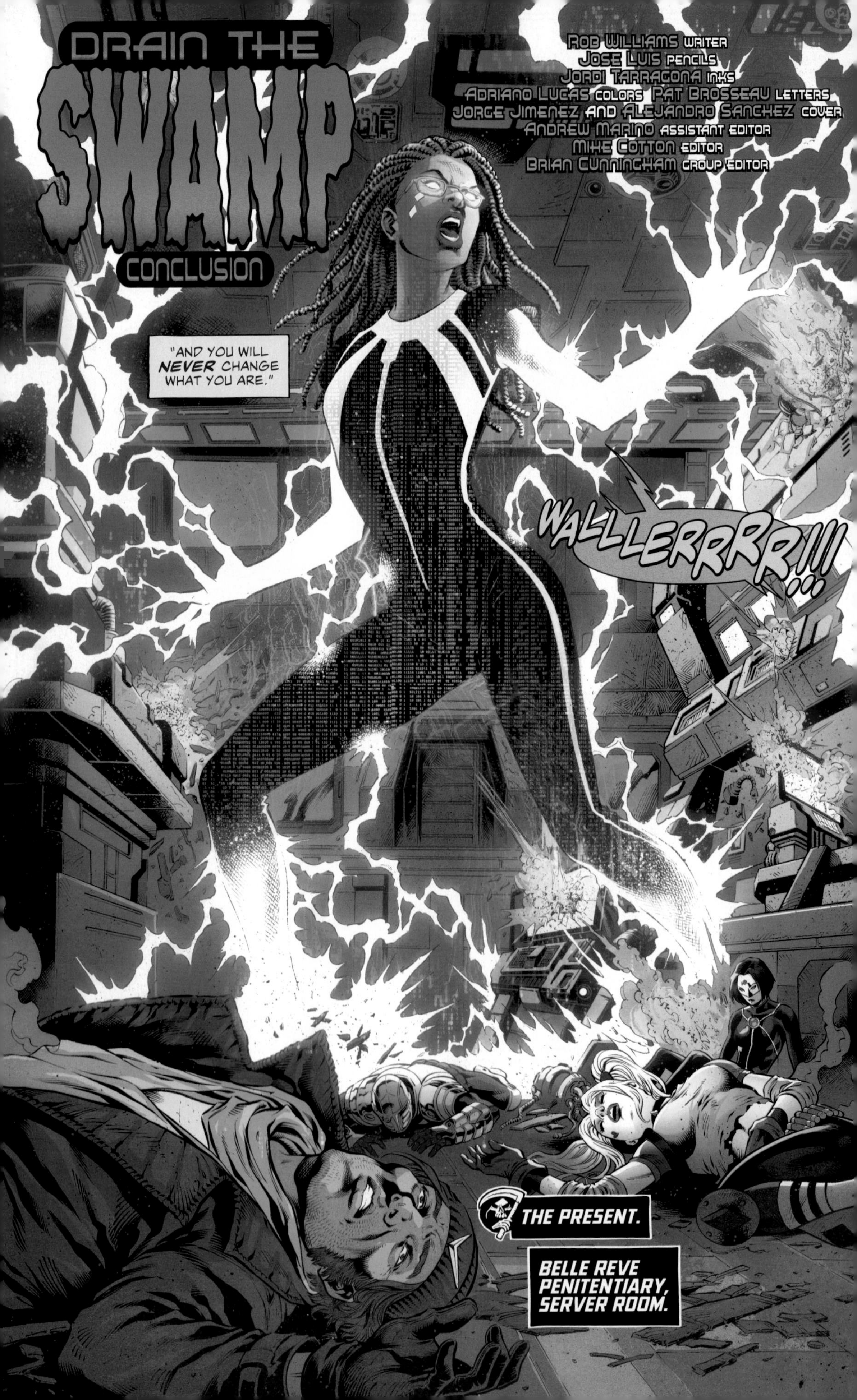
DRAIN THE SWAMP
CONCLUSION
ROB WILLIAMS WRITER
JOSE LUIS PENCILS
JORDI TARRAGONA INKS
ADRIANO LUCAS COLORS PAT BROSSEAU LETTERS
JORGE JIMENEZ AND ALEJANDRO SANCHEZ COVER
ANDREW MARINO ASSISTANT EDITOR
MIKE COTTON EDITOR
BRIAN CUNNINGHAM GROUP EDITOR
"AND YOU WILL NEVER CHANGE WHAT YOU ARE."
WALLLERRRR!!!
THE PRESENT.
BELLE REVE PENITENTIARY, SERVER ROOM.

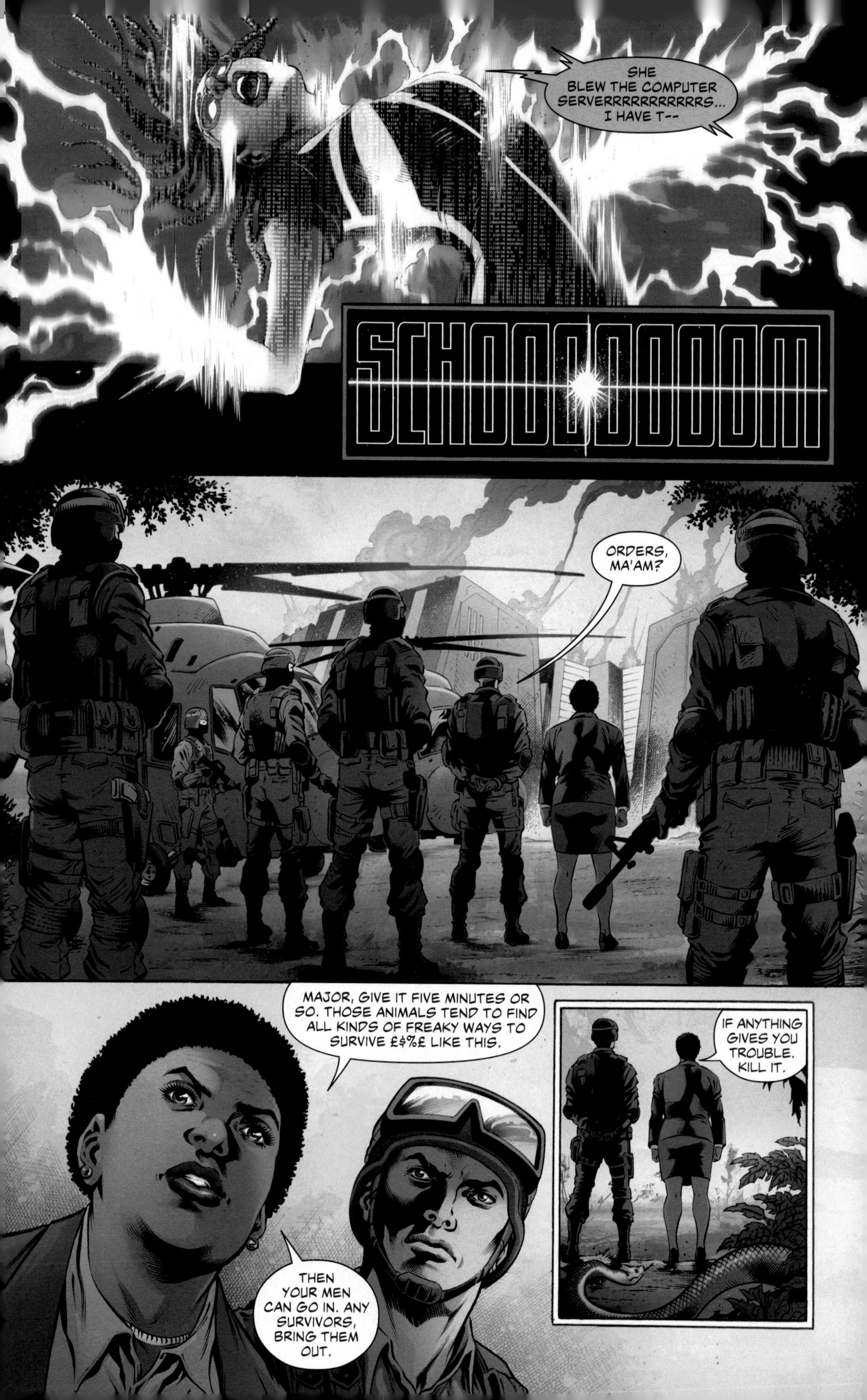

SHE BLEW THE COMPUTER SERVERRRRRRRRRRS... I HAVE T--
SCHOOOOOOOM
ORDERS, MA'AM?
MAJOR, GIVE IT FIVE MINUTES OR SO. THOSE ANIMALS TEND TO FIND ALL KINDS OF FREAKY WAYS TO SURVIVE £$%£ LIKE THIS.
THEN YOUR MEN CAN GO IN. ANY SURVIVORS, BRING THEM OUT.
IF ANYTHING GIVES YOU TROUBLE. KILL IT.

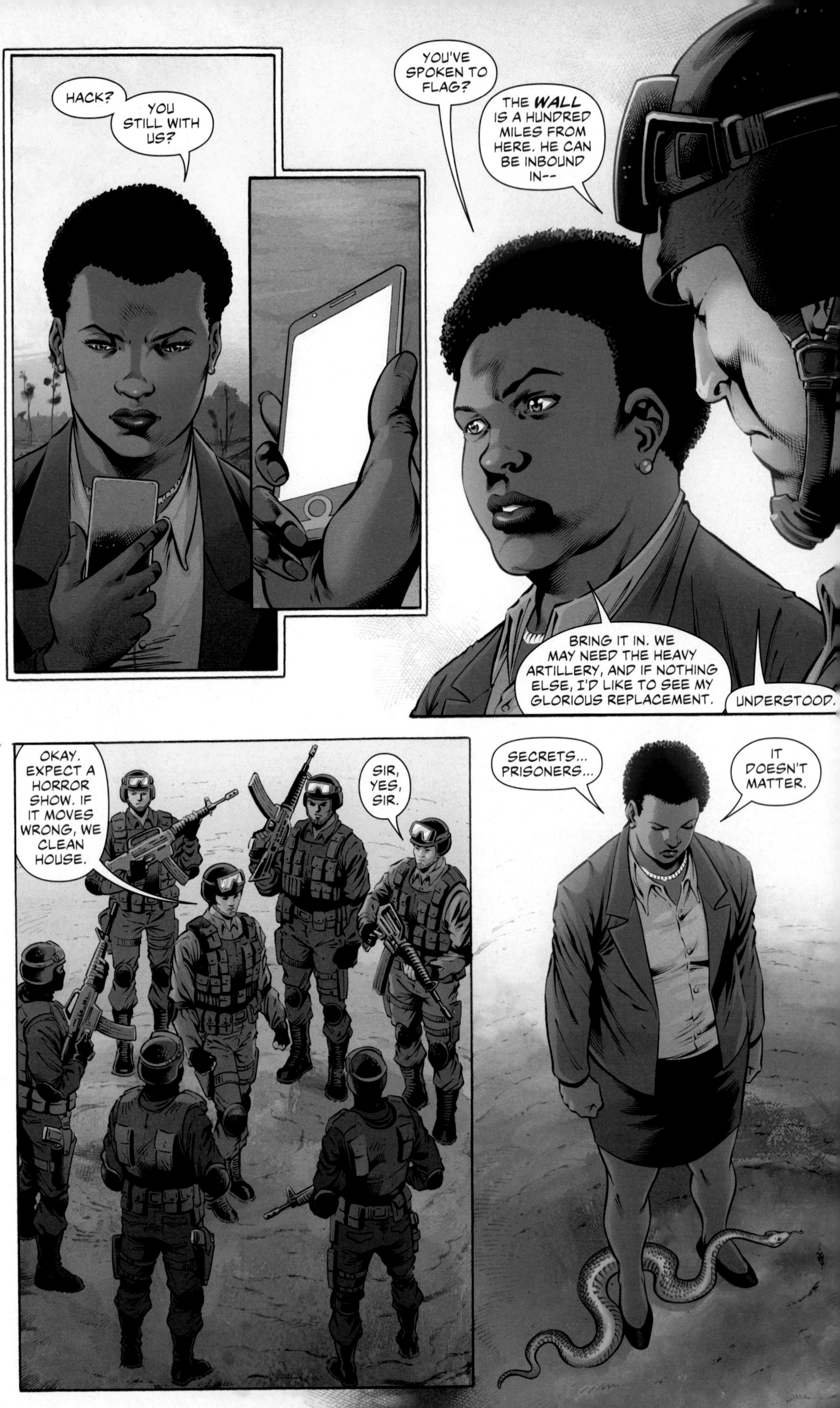
HACK?
YOU STILL WITH US?
YOU'VE SPOKEN TO FLAG?
THE WALL IS A HUNDRED MILES FROM HERE. HE CAN BE INBOUND IN--
BRING IT IN. WE MAY NEED THE HEAVY ARTILLERY, AND IF NOTHING ELSE, I'D LIKE TO SEE MY GLORIOUS REPLACEMENT.
UNDERSTOOD.
OKAY. EXPECT A HORROR SHOW. IF IT MOVES WRONG, WE CLEAN HOUSE.
SIR, YES, SIR.
SECRETS... PRISONERS...
IT DOESN'T MATTER.

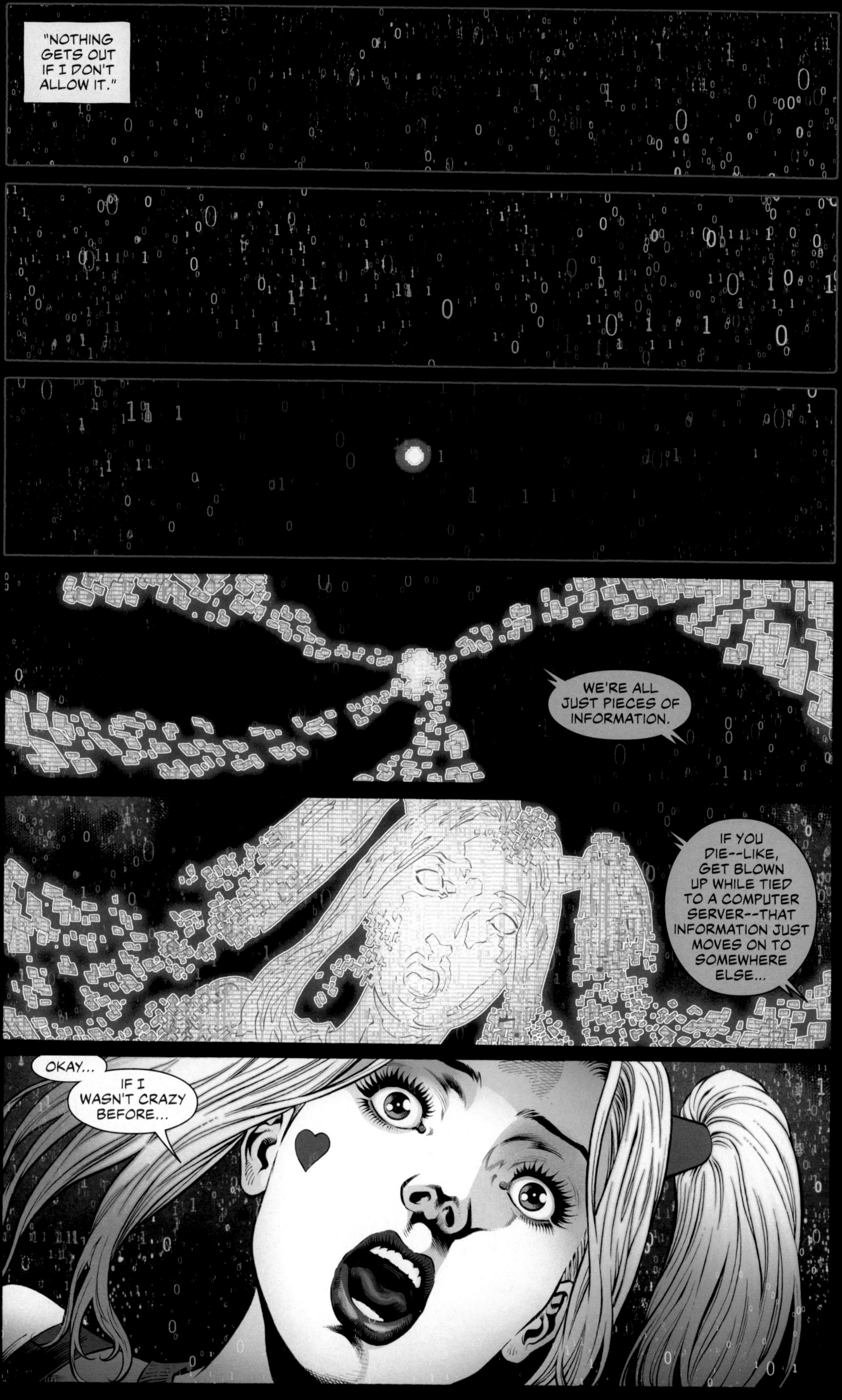
"NOTHING GETS OUT IF I DON'T ALLOW IT."
WE'RE ALL JUST PIECES OF INFORMATION.
IF YOU DIE--LIKE, GET BLOWN UP WHILE TIED TO A COMPUTER SERVER--THAT INFORMATION JUST MOVES ON TO SOMEWHERE ELSE...
OKAY...
IF I WASN'T CRAZY BEFORE...

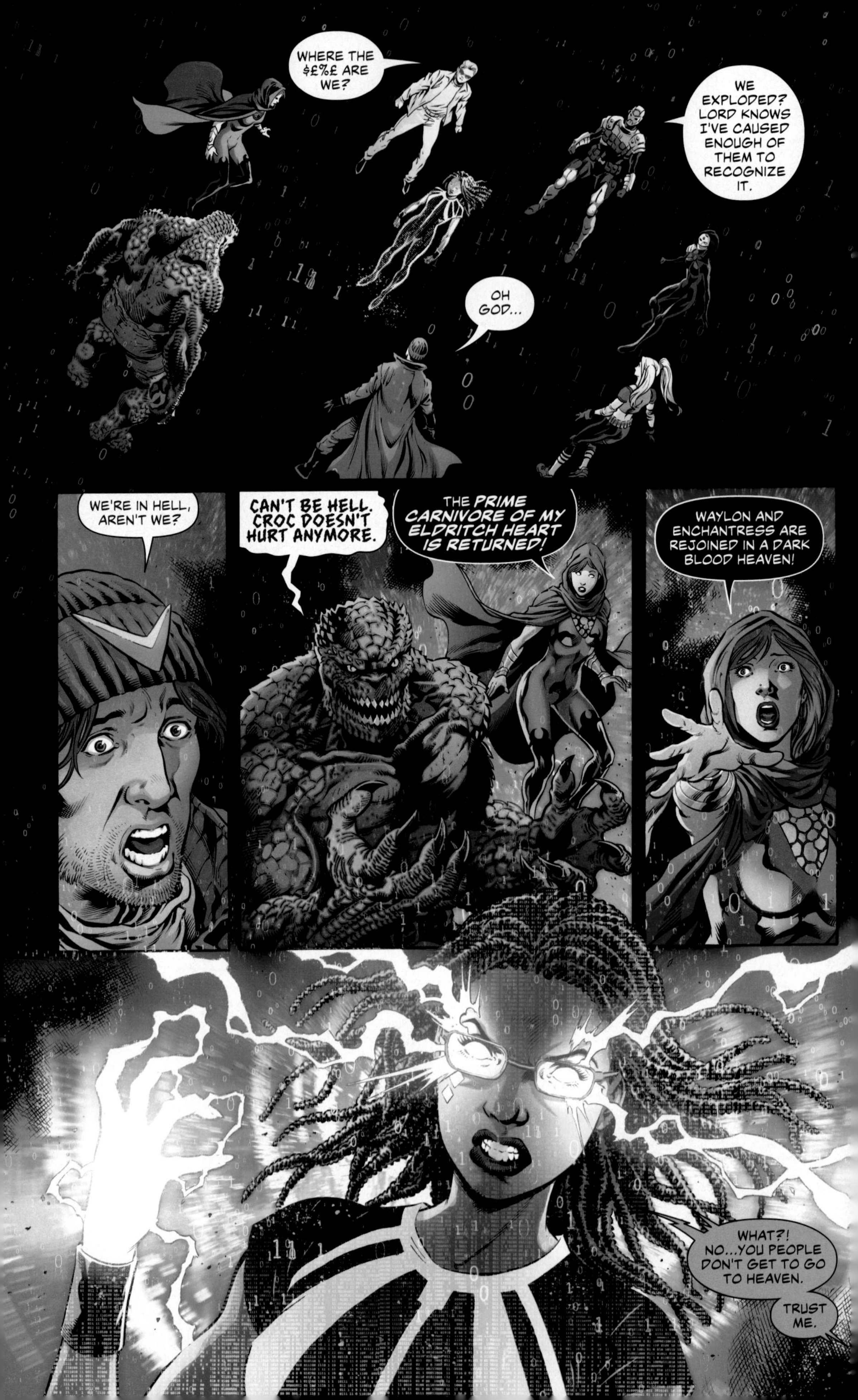
WHERE THE $£%£ ARE WE?
WE EXPLODED? LORD KNOWS I'VE CAUSED ENOUGH OF THEM TO RECOGNIZE IT.
OH GOD...
WE'RE IN HELL, AREN'T WE?
CAN'T BE HELL. CROC DOESN'T HURT ANYMORE.
THE PRIME CARNIVORE OF MY ELDRITCH HEART IS RETURNED!
WAYLON AND ENCHANTRESS ARE REJOINED IN A DARK BLOOD HEAVEN!
WHAT?! NO...YOU PEOPLE DON'T GET TO GO TO HEAVEN.
TRUST ME.

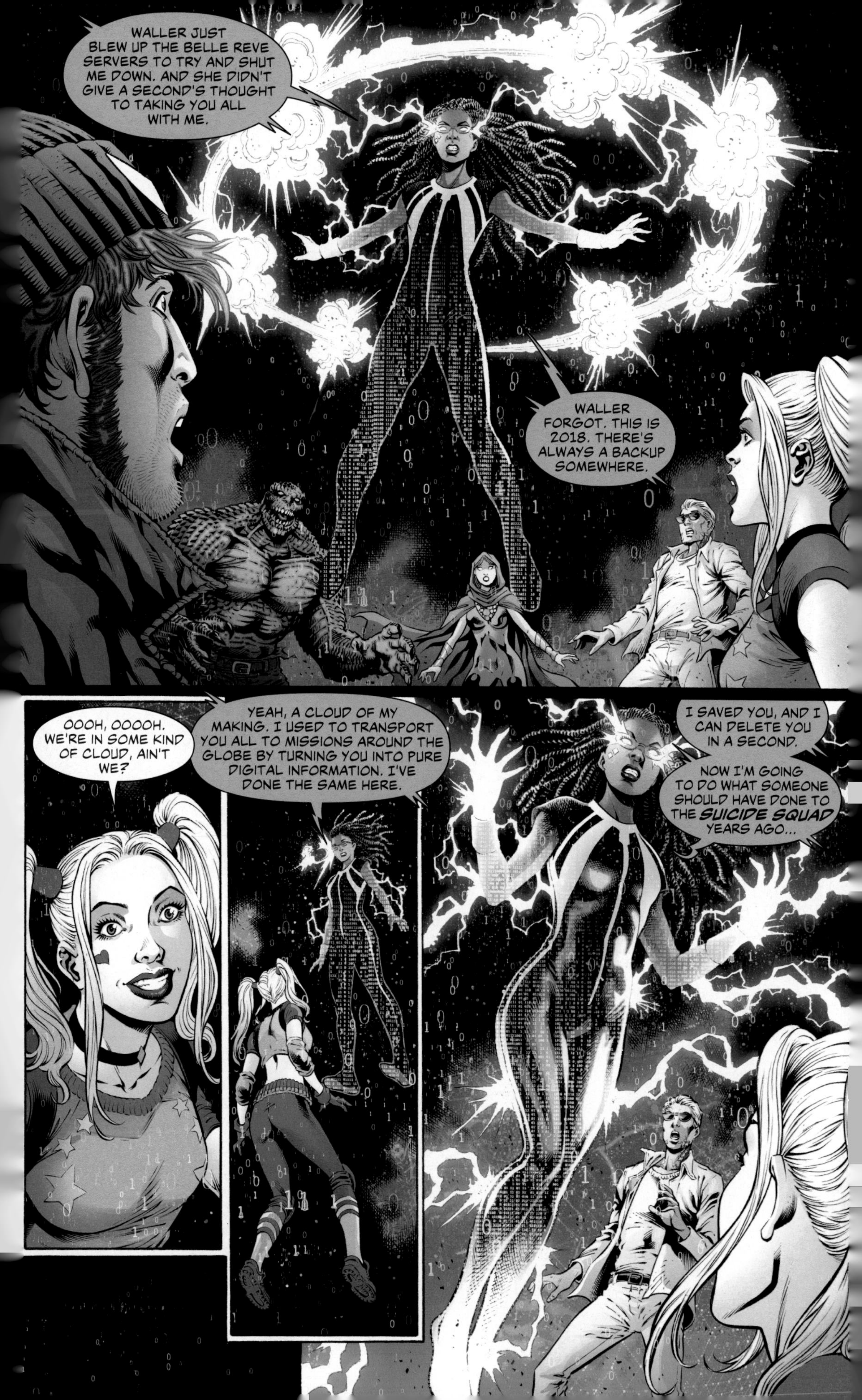
WALLER JUST BLEW UP THE BELLE REVE SERVERS TO TRY AND SHUT ME DOWN. AND SHE DIDN'T GIVE A SECOND'S THOUGHT TO TAKING YOU ALL WITH ME.
WALLER FORGOT. THIS IS 2018. THERE'S ALWAYS A BACKUP SOMEWHERE.
OOOH, OOOOH. WE'RE IN SOME KIND OF CLOUD, AIN'T WE?
YEAH, A CLOUD OF MY MAKING. I USED TO TRANSPORT YOU ALL TO MISSIONS AROUND THE GLOBE BY TURNING YOU INTO PURE DIGITAL INFORMATION. I'VE DONE THE SAME HERE.
I SAVED YOU, AND I CAN DELETE YOU IN A SECOND.
NOW I'M GOING TO DO WHAT SOMEONE SHOULD HAVE DONE TO THE SUICIDE SQUAD YEARS AGO...

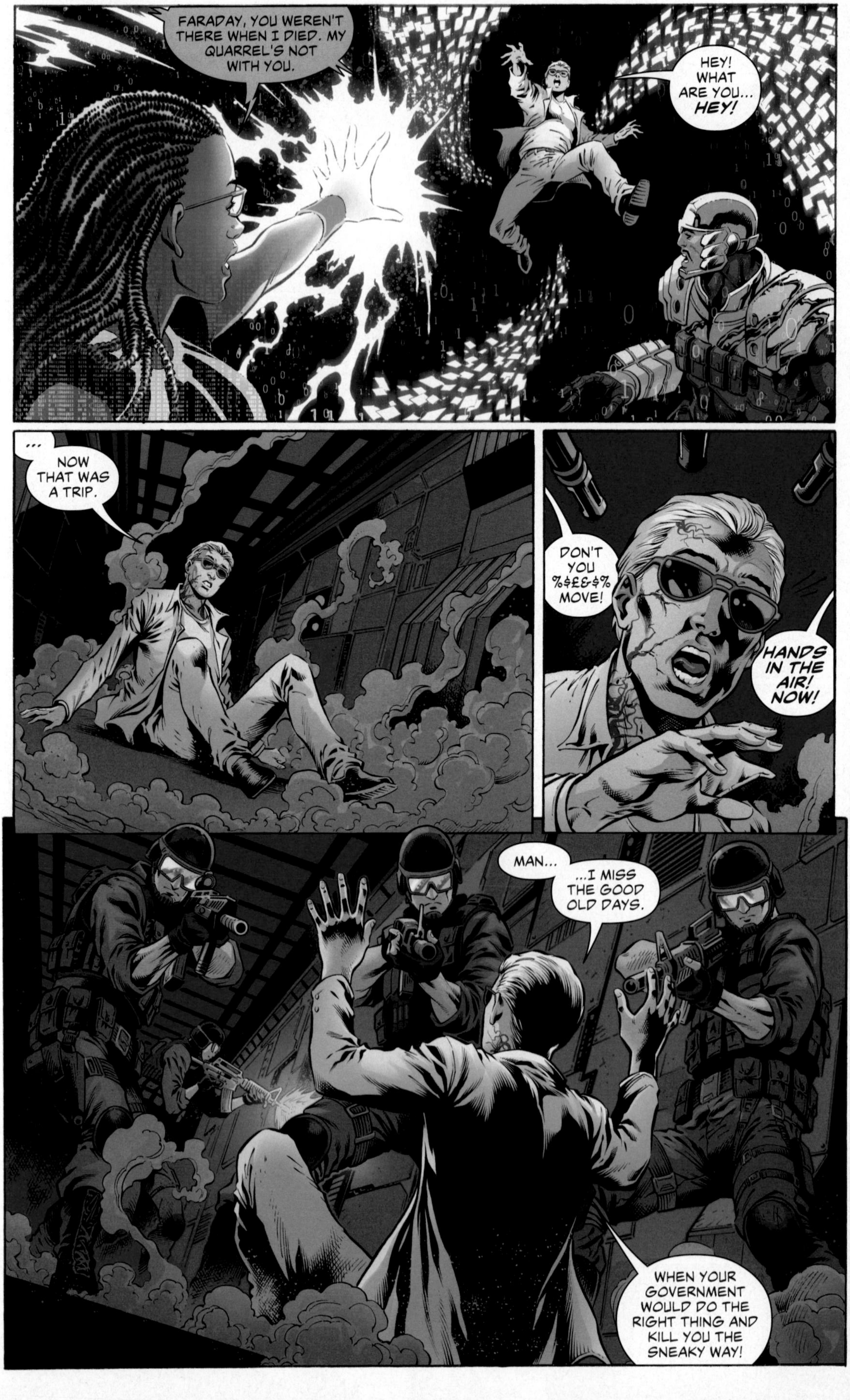
FARADAY, YOU WEREN'T THERE WHEN I DIED. MY QUARREL'S NOT WITH YOU.
HEY! WHAT ARE YOU... HEY!
... NOW THAT WAS A TRIP.
DON'T YOU %$££$% MOVE!
HANDS IN THE AIR! NOW!
MAN...
...I MISS THE GOOD OLD DAYS.
WHEN YOUR GOVERNMENT WOULD DO THE RIGHT THING AND KILL YOU THE SNEAKY WAY!

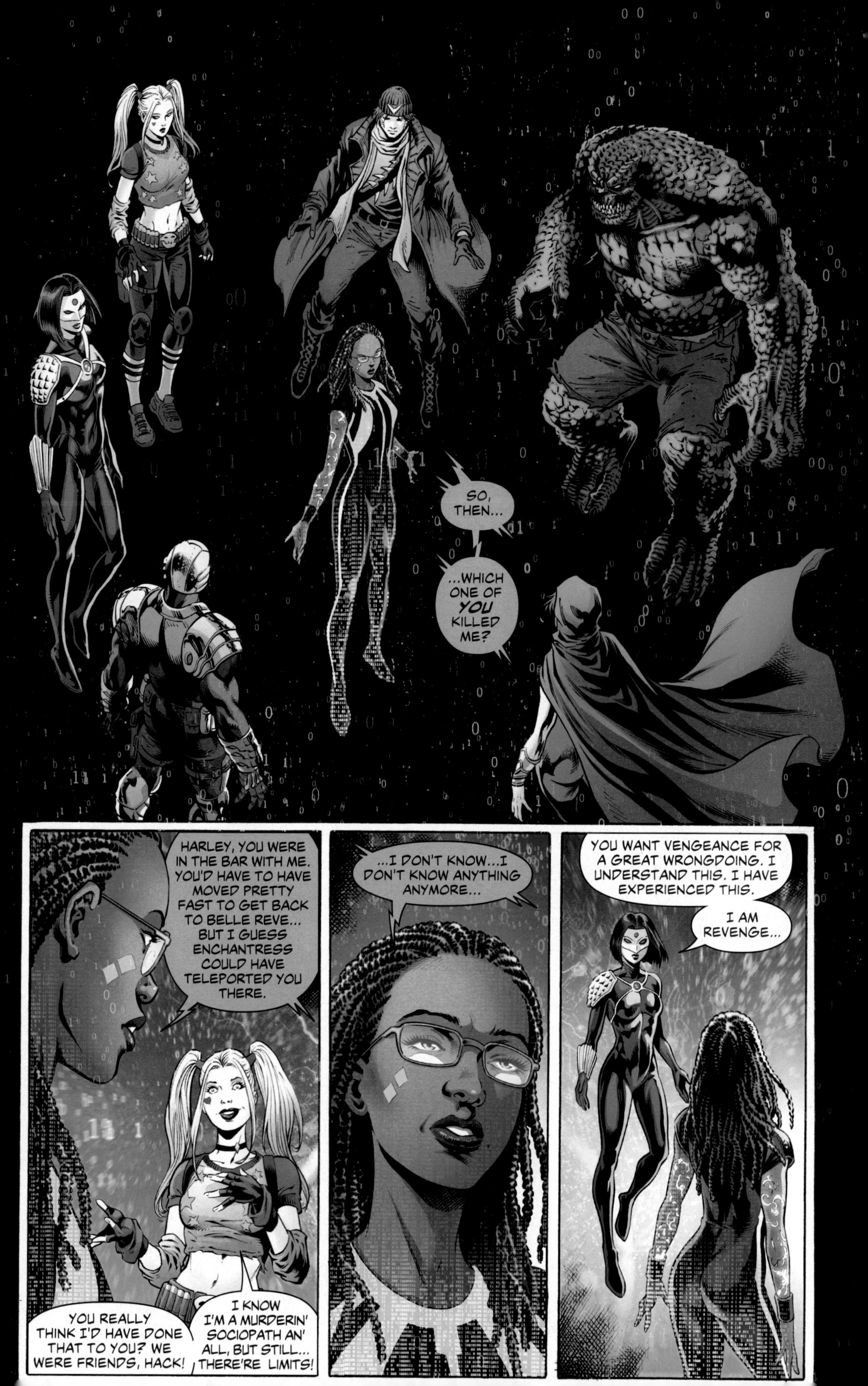

SO, THEN...
...WHICH ONE OF *YOU* KILLED ME?
HARLEY, YOU WERE IN THE BAR WITH ME. YOU'D HAVE TO HAVE MOVED PRETTY FAST TO GET BACK TO BELLE REVE... BUT I GUESS ENCHANTRESS COULD HAVE TELEPORTED YOU THERE.
YOU REALLY THINK I'D HAVE DONE THAT TO YOU? WE WERE FRIENDS, HACK!
I KNOW I'M A MURDERIN' SOCIOPATH AN' ALL, BUT STILL... THERE'RE LIMITS!
...I DON'T KNOW...I DON'T KNOW ANYTHING ANYMORE...
YOU WANT VENGEANCE FOR A GREAT WRONGDOING. I UNDERSTAND THIS. I HAVE EXPERIENCED THIS.
I AM REVENGE...

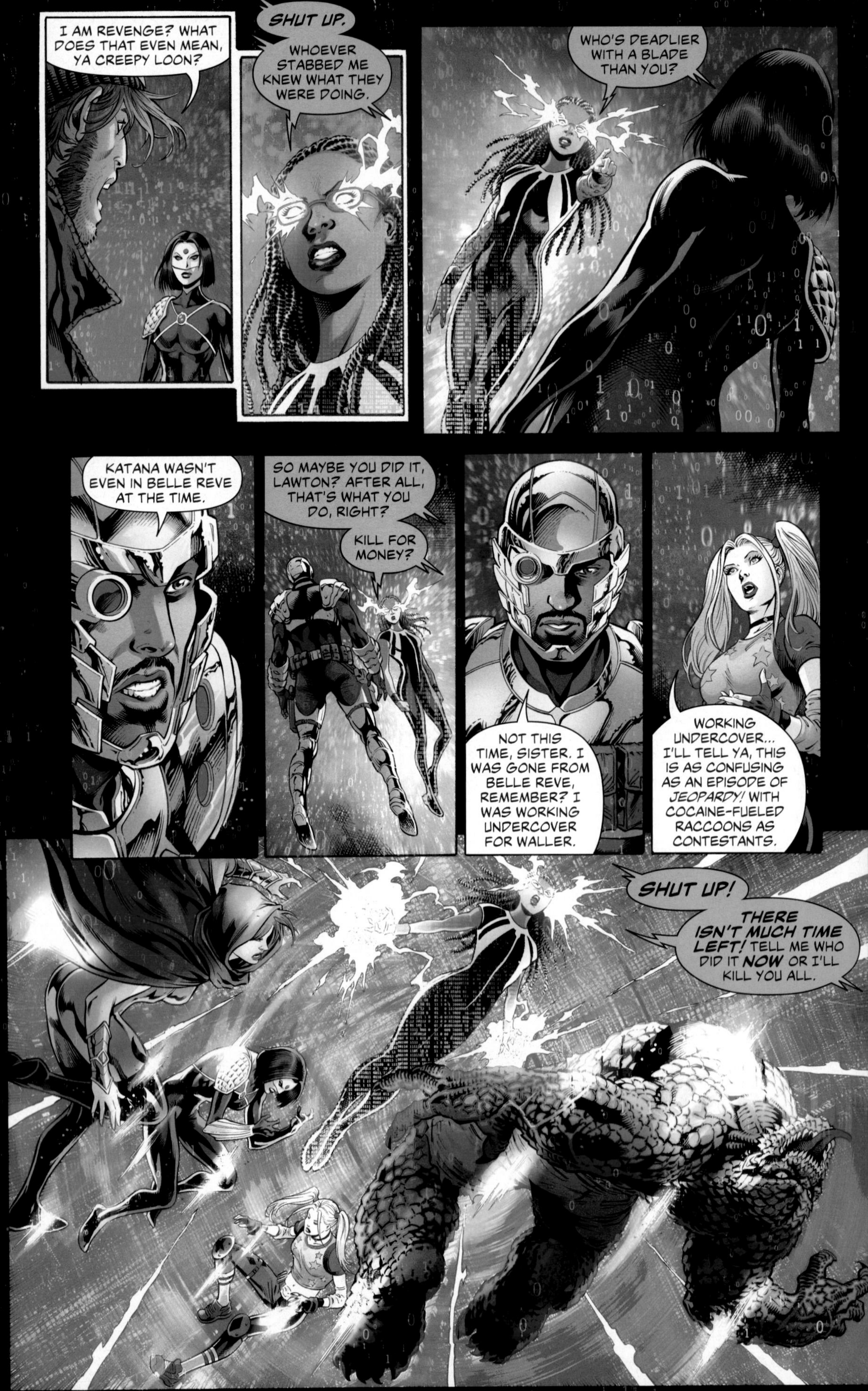
I AM REVENGE? WHAT DOES THAT EVEN MEAN, YA CREEPY LOON?
SHUT UP.
WHOEVER STABBED ME KNEW WHAT THEY WERE DOING.
WHO'S DEADLIER WITH A BLADE THAN YOU?
KATANA WASN'T EVEN IN BELLE REVE AT THE TIME.
SO MAYBE YOU DID IT, LAWTON? AFTER ALL, THAT'S WHAT YOU DO, RIGHT?
KILL FOR MONEY?
NOT THIS TIME, SISTER. I WAS GONE FROM BELLE REVE, REMEMBER? I WAS WORKING UNDERCOVER FOR WALLER.
WORKING UNDERCOVER... I'LL TELL YA, THIS IS AS CONFUSING AS AN EPISODE OF JEOPARDY! WITH COCAINE-FUELED RACCOONS AS CONTESTANTS.
SHUT UP!
THERE ISN'T MUCH TIME LEFT! TELL ME WHO DID IT NOW OR I'LL KILL YOU ALL.

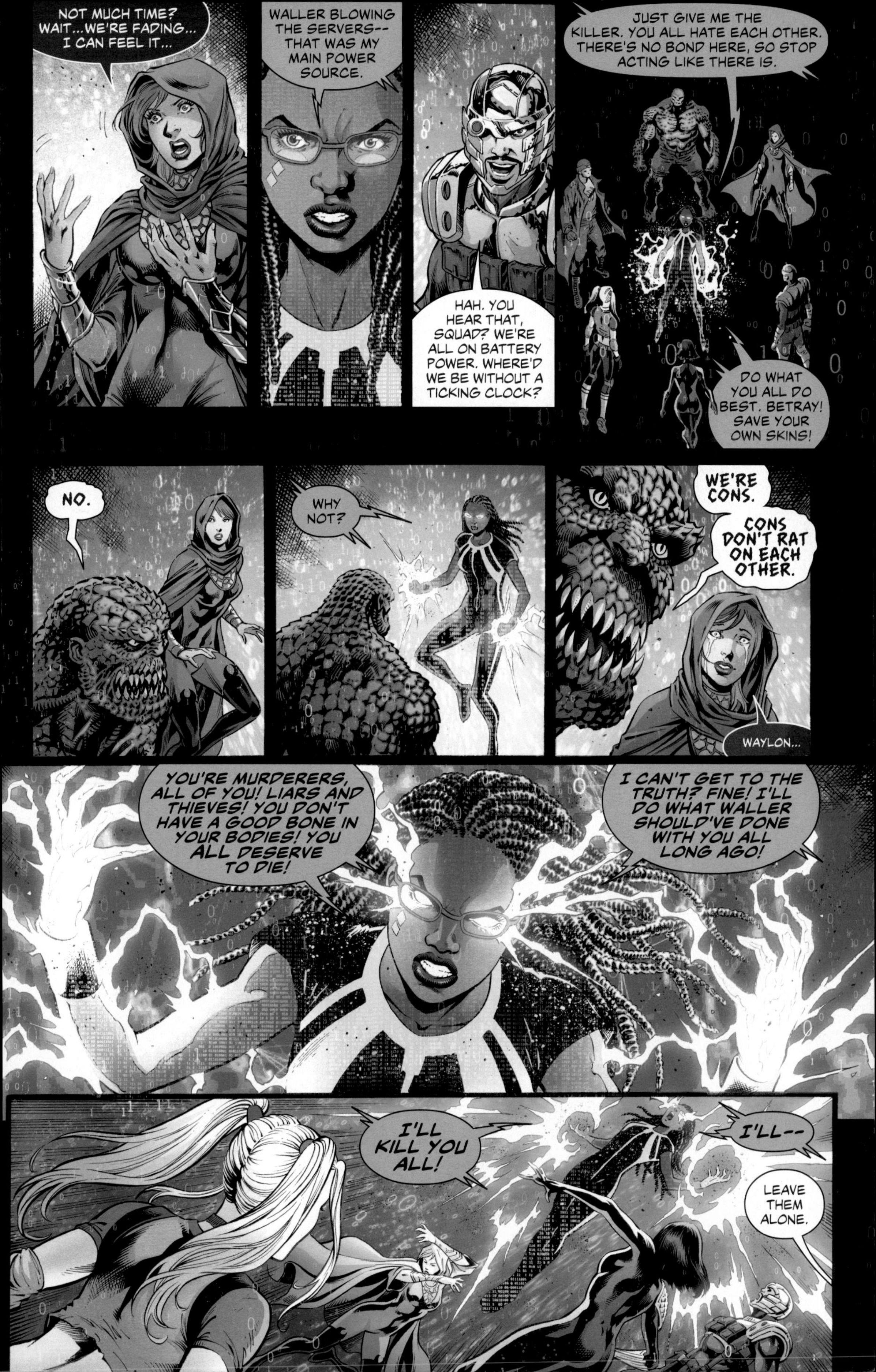
NOT MUCH TIME? WAIT...WE'RE FADING... I CAN FEEL IT...
WALLER BLOWING THE SERVERS-- THAT WAS MY MAIN POWER SOURCE.
HAH. YOU HEAR THAT, SQUAD? WE'RE ALL ON BATTERY POWER. WHERE'D WE BE WITHOUT A TICKING CLOCK?
JUST GIVE ME THE KILLER. YOU ALL HATE EACH OTHER. THERE'S NO BOND HERE, SO STOP ACTING LIKE THERE IS.
DO WHAT YOU ALL DO BEST. BETRAY! SAVE YOUR OWN SKINS!
NO.
WHY NOT?
WE'RE CONS.
CONS DON'T RAT ON EACH OTHER.
WAYLON...
YOU'RE MURDERERS, ALL OF YOU! LIARS AND THIEVES! YOU DON'T HAVE A GOOD BONE IN YOUR BODIES! YOU ALL DESERVE TO DIE!
I CAN'T GET TO THE TRUTH? FINE! I'LL DO WHAT WALLER SHOULD'VE DONE WITH YOU ALL LONG AGO!
I'LL KILL YOU ALL!
I'LL--
LEAVE THEM ALONE.

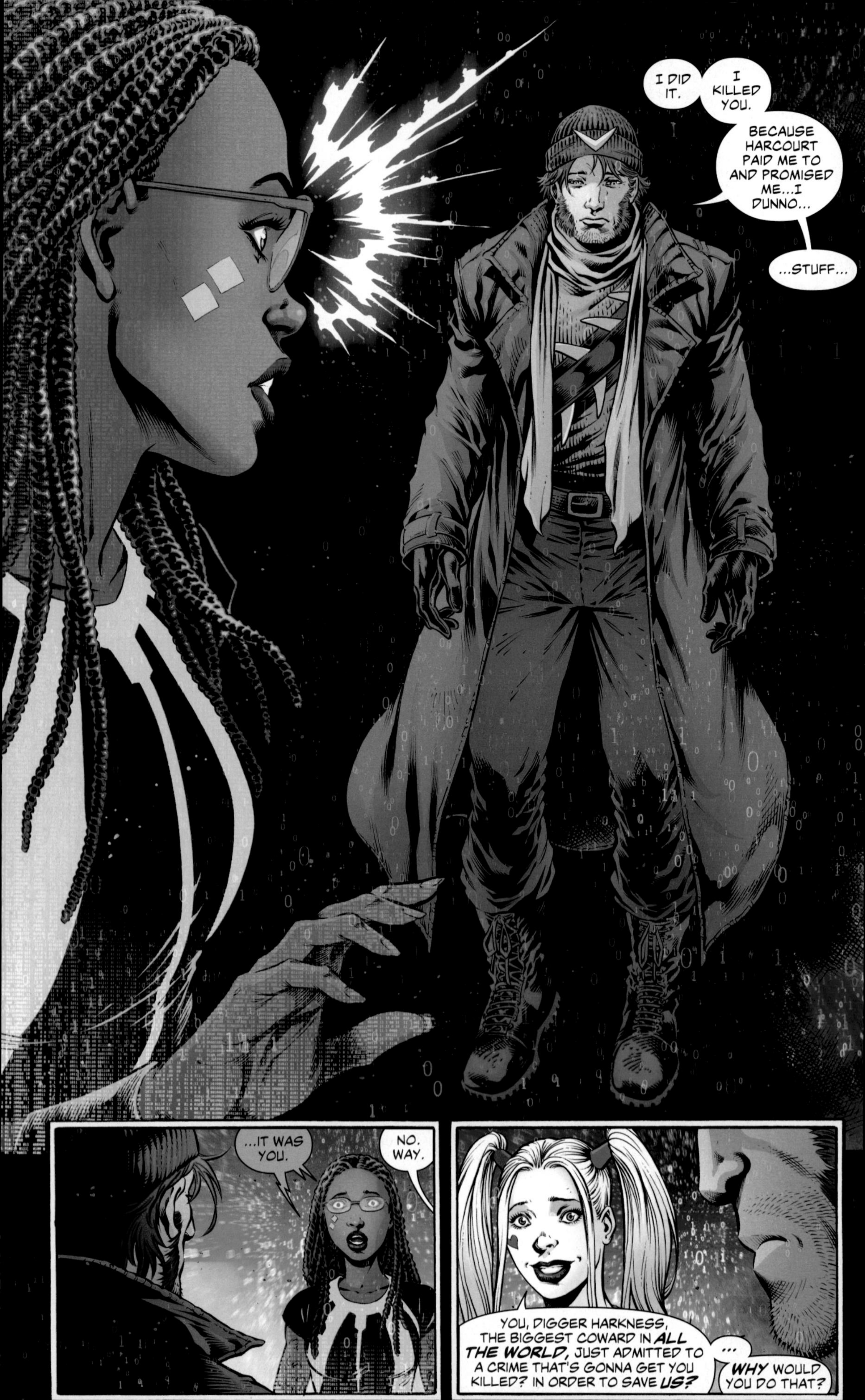
I DID IT.
I KILLED YOU.
BECAUSE HARCOURT PAID ME TO AND PROMISED ME...I DUNNO...
...STUFF...
...IT WAS YOU.
NO. WAY.
YOU, DIGGER HARKNESS, THE BIGGEST COWARD IN ALL THE WORLD, JUST ADMITTED TO A CRIME THAT'S GONNA GET YOU KILLED? IN ORDER TO SAVE US?
...
WHY WOULD YOU DO THAT?

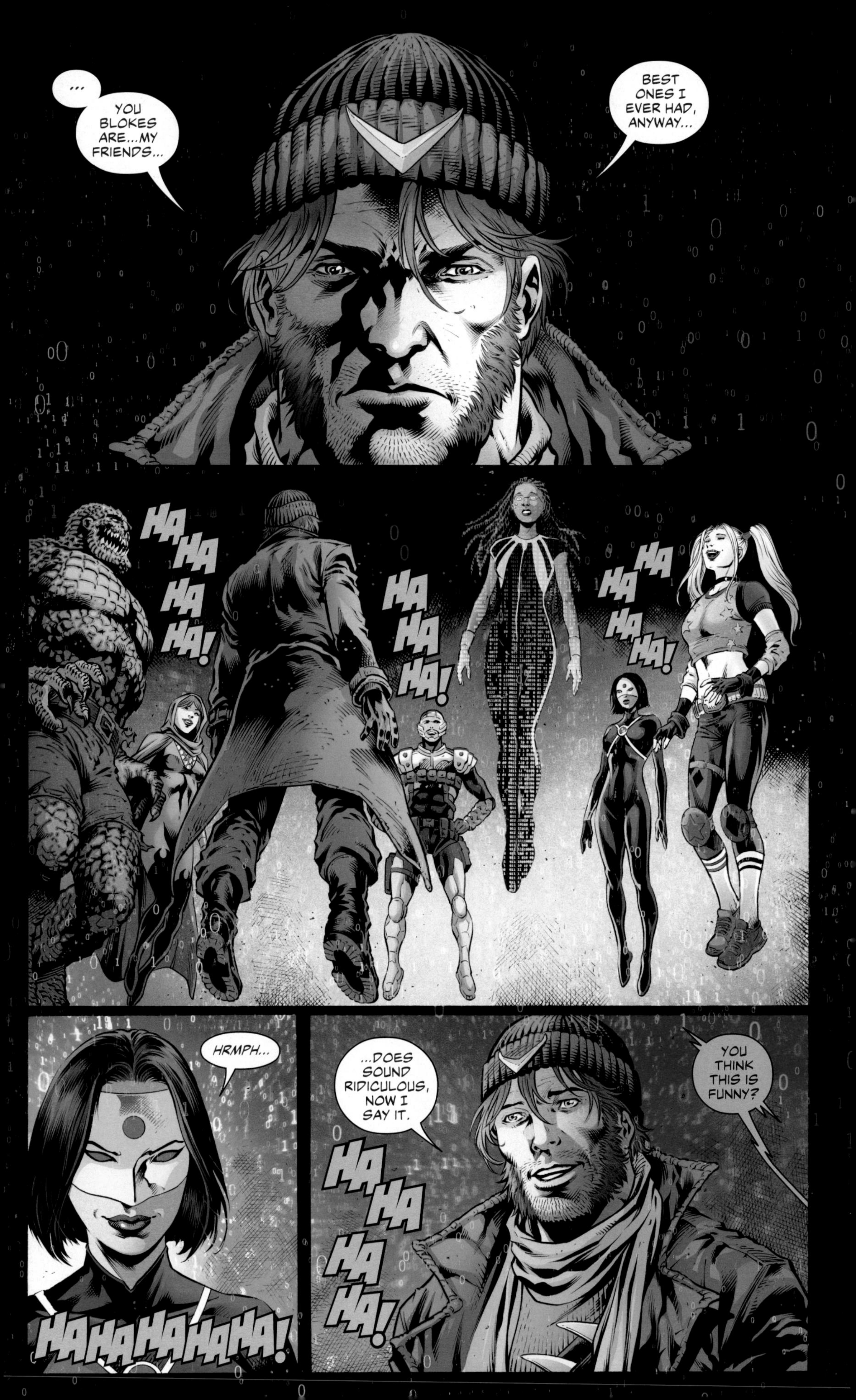
...
YOU BLOKES ARE...MY FRIENDS...
BEST ONES I EVER HAD, ANYWAY...
HA HA HA HA!
HA HA HA!
HA HA HA HA HA!
HRMPH...
...DOES SOUND RIDICULOUS, NOW I SAY IT.
YOU THINK THIS IS FUNNY?
HA HA HA HA!
HAHAHAHAHA!

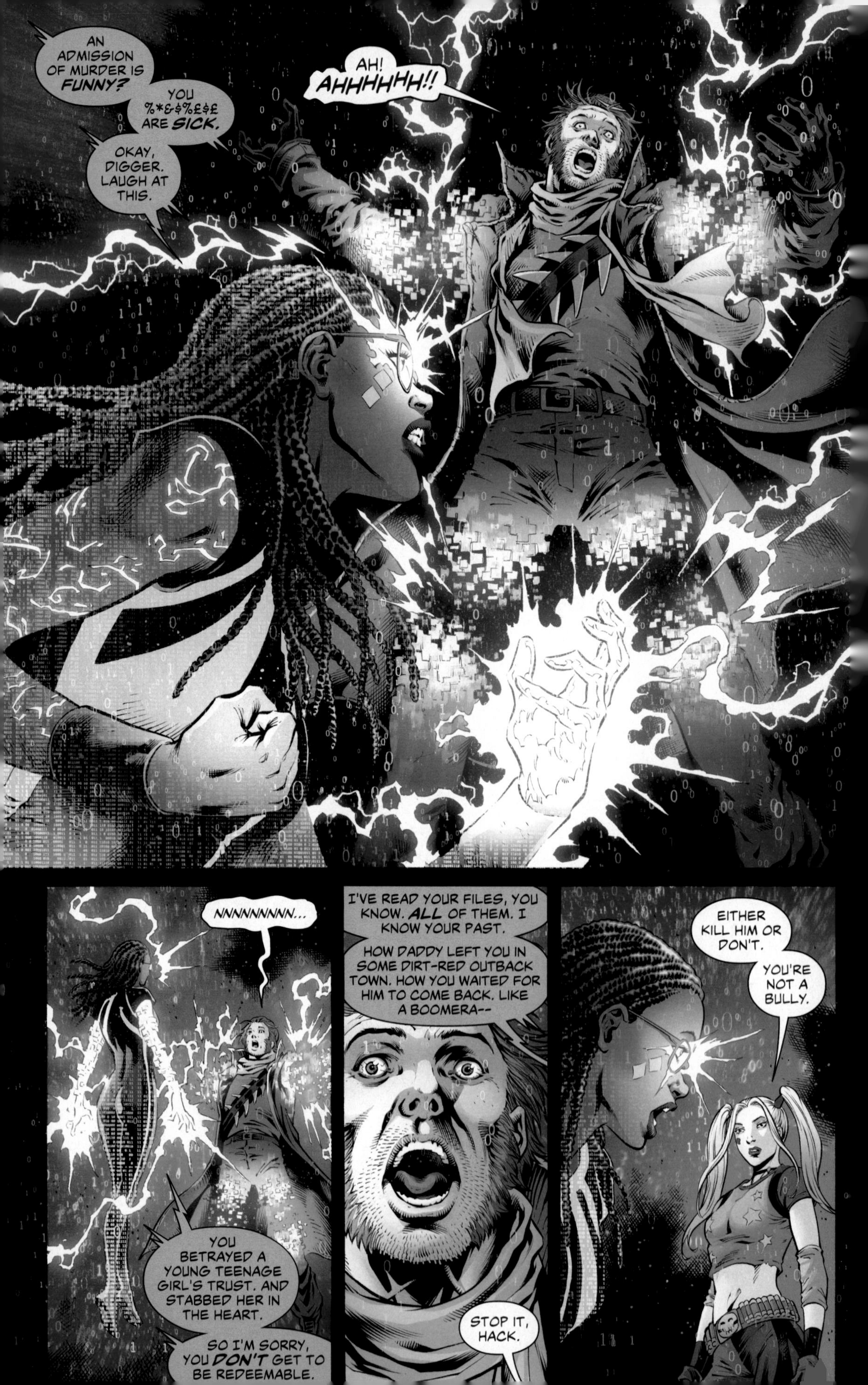
AN ADMISSION OF MURDER IS *FUNNY?*
YOU %*&$%£$£ ARE *SICK.*
OKAY, DIGGER. LAUGH AT THIS.
AH! *AHHHHHH!!*
NNNNNNNNN...
YOU BETRAYED A YOUNG TEENAGE GIRL'S TRUST. AND STABBED HER IN THE HEART.
SO I'M SORRY, YOU *DON'T* GET TO BE REDEEMABLE.
I'VE READ YOUR FILES, YOU KNOW. *ALL* OF THEM. I KNOW YOUR PAST.
HOW DADDY LEFT YOU IN SOME DIRT-RED OUTBACK TOWN. HOW YOU WAITED FOR HIM TO COME BACK. LIKE A BOOMERA--
STOP IT, HACK.
EITHER KILL HIM OR DON'T.
YOU'RE NOT A BULLY.

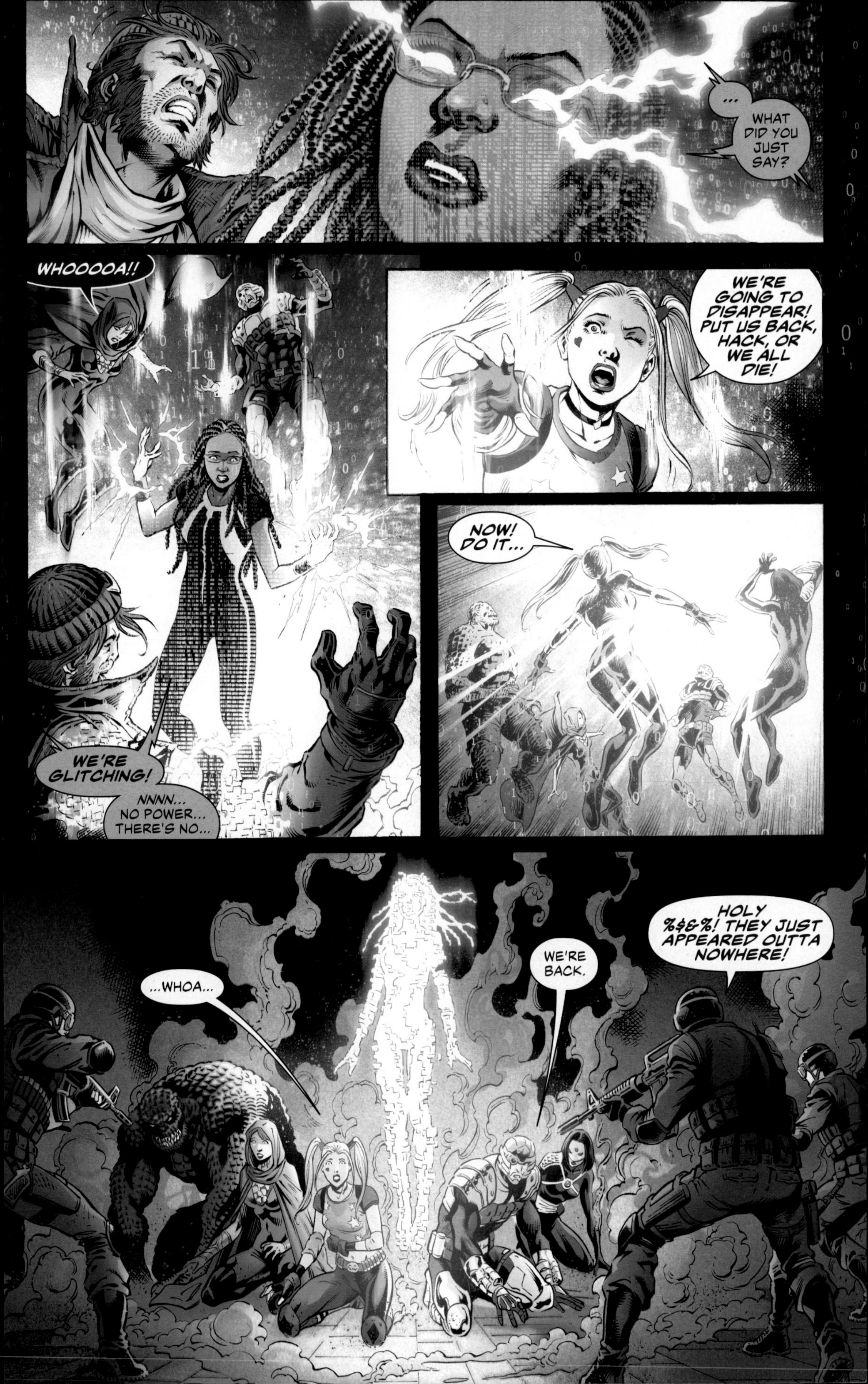
...
WHAT DID YOU JUST SAY?
WHOOOOA!!
WE'RE GOING TO DISAPPEAR! PUT US BACK, HACK, OR WE ALL DIE!
WE'RE GLITCHING!
NNNN... NO POWER... THERE'S NO...
NOW! DO IT...
...WHOA...
WE'RE BACK.
HOLY %$&%! THEY JUST APPEARED OUTTA NOWHERE!

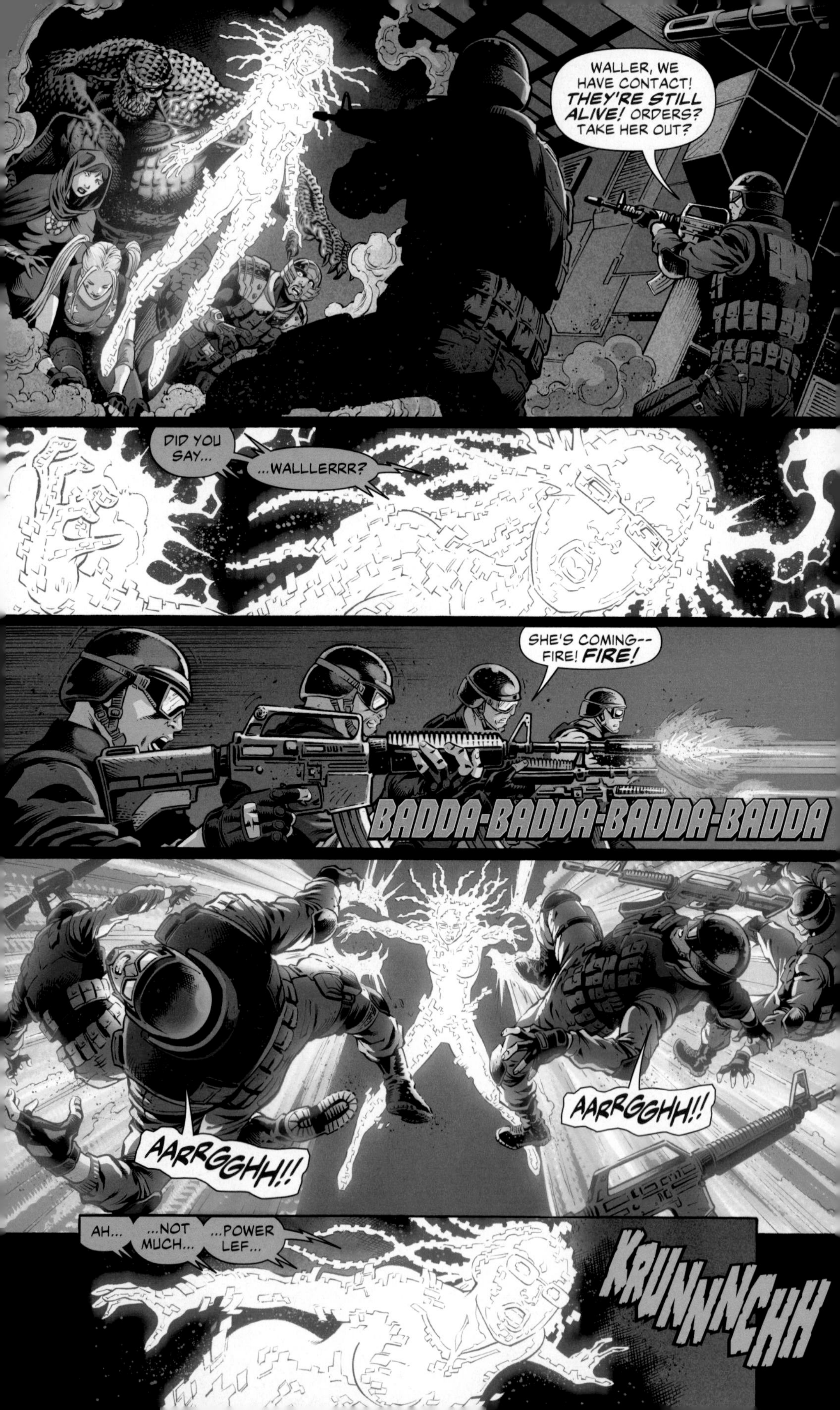
WALLER, WE HAVE CONTACT! THEY'RE STILL ALIVE! ORDERS? TAKE HER OUT?
DID YOU SAY...
...WALLLERRR?
SHE'S COMING-- FIRE! FIRE!
BADDA-BADDA-BADDA-BADDA
AARRGGHH!!
AARRGGHH!!
AH...
...NOT MUCH...
...POWER LEF...
KRUNNNCHH

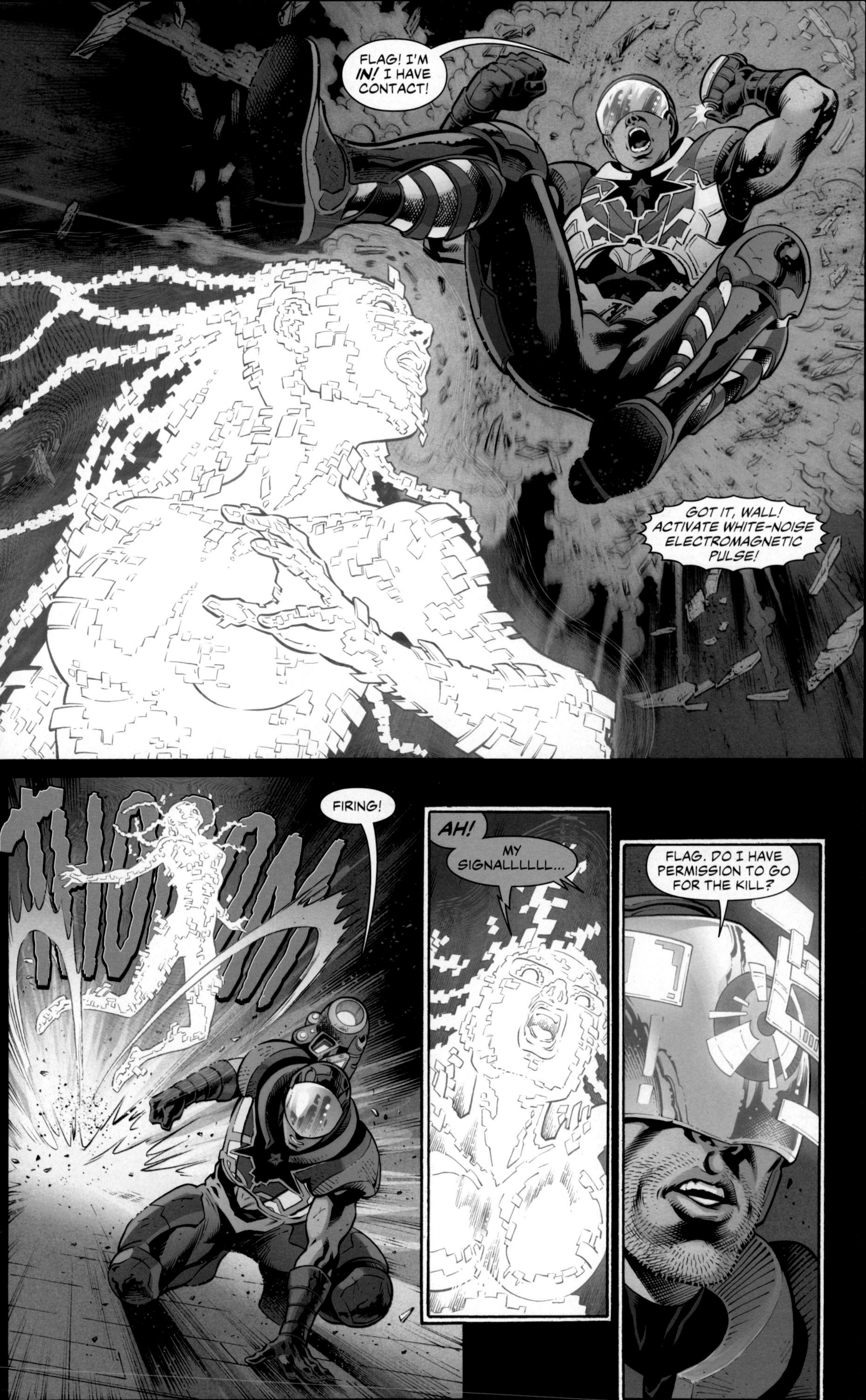
FLAG! I'M *IN!* I HAVE CONTACT!
GOT IT, WALL! ACTIVATE WHITE-NOISE ELECTROMAGNETIC PULSE!
FIRING!
AH!
MY SIGNALLLLLLL...
FLAG. DO I HAVE PERMISSION TO GO FOR THE KILL?

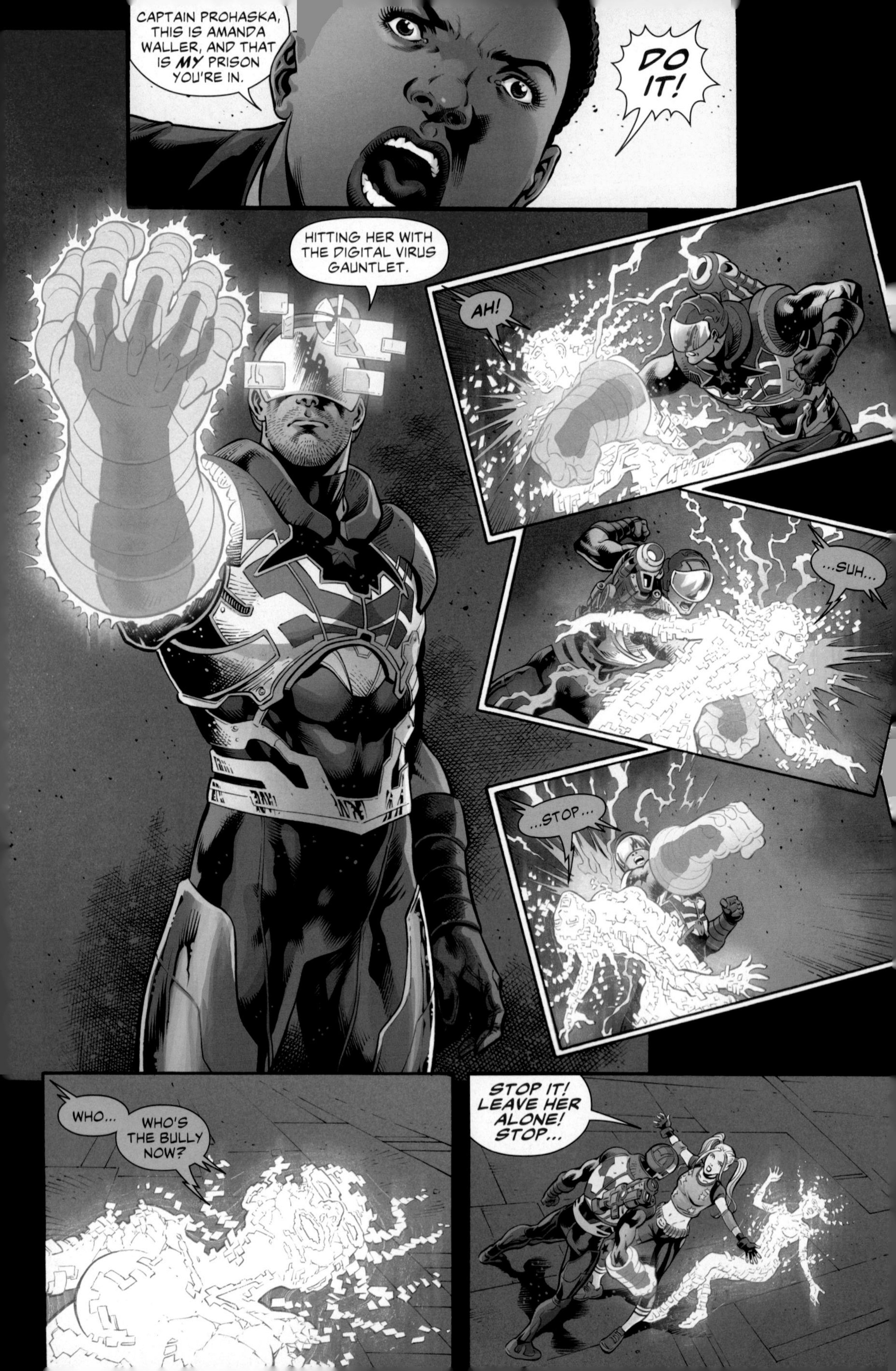
CAPTAIN PROHASKA, THIS IS AMANDA WALLER, AND THAT IS MY PRISON YOU'RE IN.
DO IT!
HITTING HER WITH THE DIGITAL VIRUS GAUNTLET.
AH!
...SUH...
...STOP...
WHO...
WHO'S THE BULLY NOW?
STOP IT! LEAVE HER ALONE! STOP...

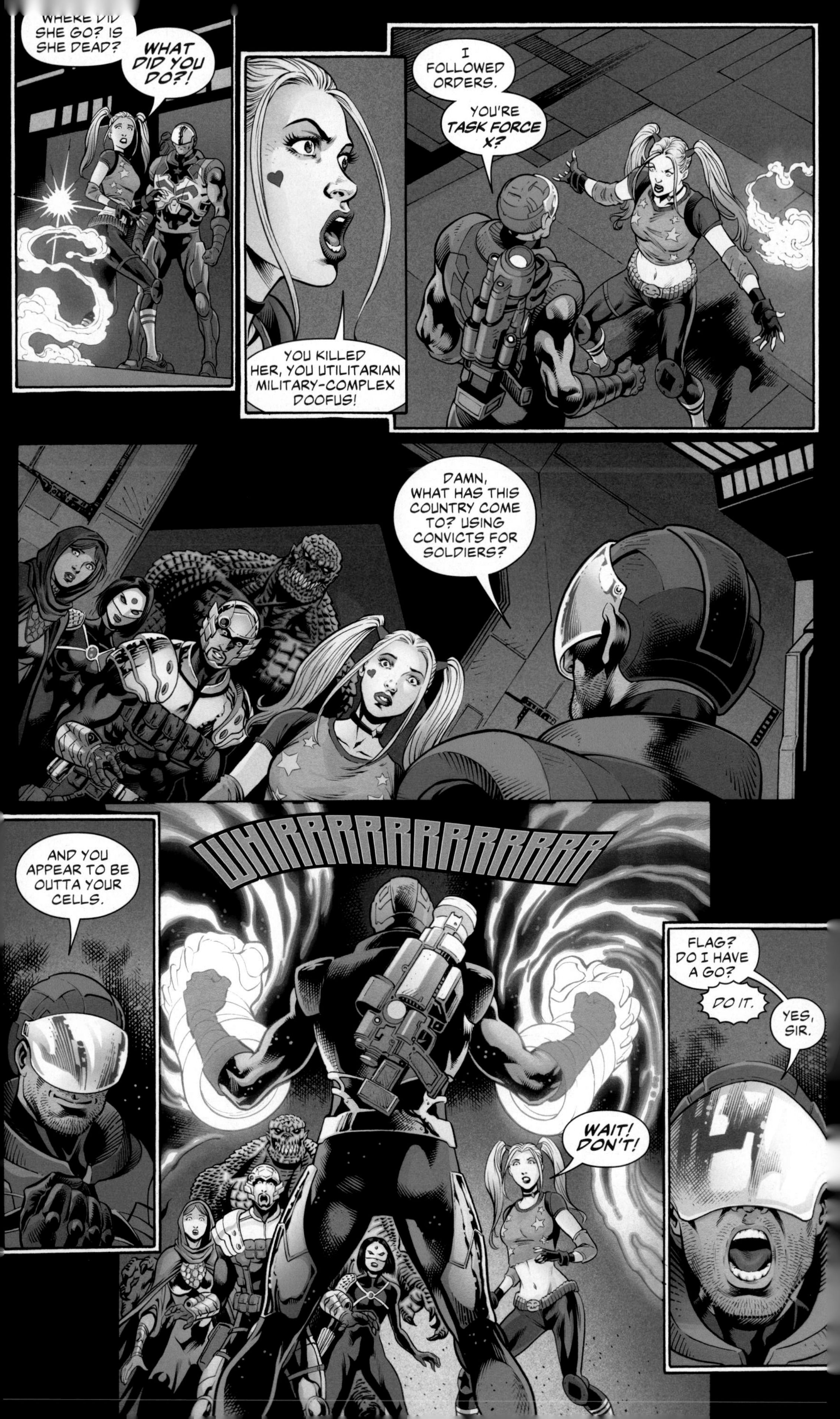
WHERE DID SHE GO? IS SHE DEAD?
WHAT DID YOU DO?!
YOU KILLED HER, YOU UTILITARIAN MILITARY-COMPLEX DOOFUS!
I FOLLOWED ORDERS.
YOU'RE TASK FORCE X?
DAMN, WHAT HAS THIS COUNTRY COME TO? USING CONVICTS FOR SOLDIERS?
AND YOU APPEAR TO BE OUTTA YOUR CELLS.
WHIRRRRRRRRRRRR
FLAG? DO I HAVE A GO?
DO IT.
YES, SIR.
WAIT! DON'T!

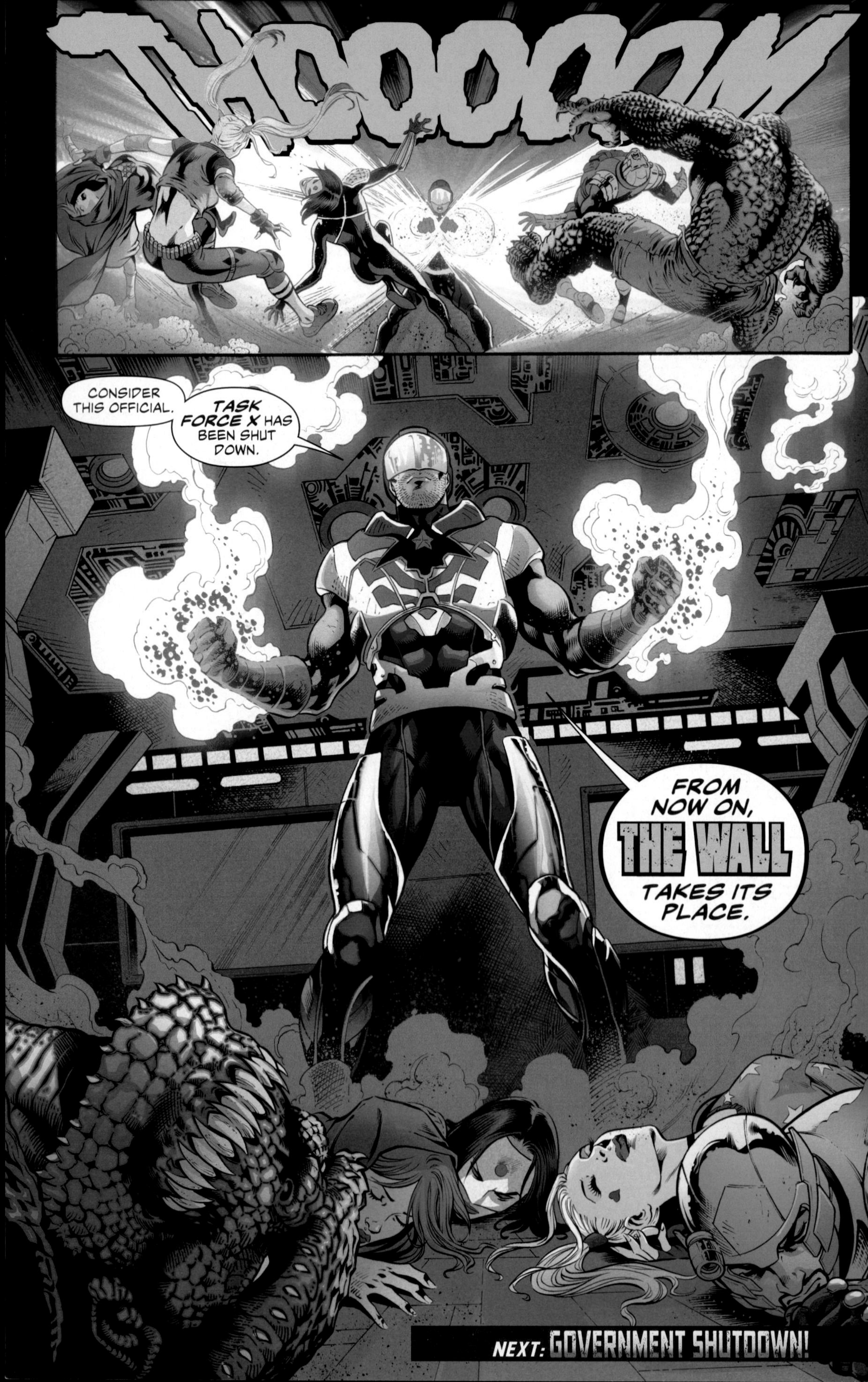
THOOOOM
CONSIDER THIS OFFICIAL.
TASK FORCE X HAS BEEN SHUT DOWN.
FROM NOW ON, THE WALL TAKES ITS PLACE.
NEXT: GOVERNMENT SHUTDOWN!

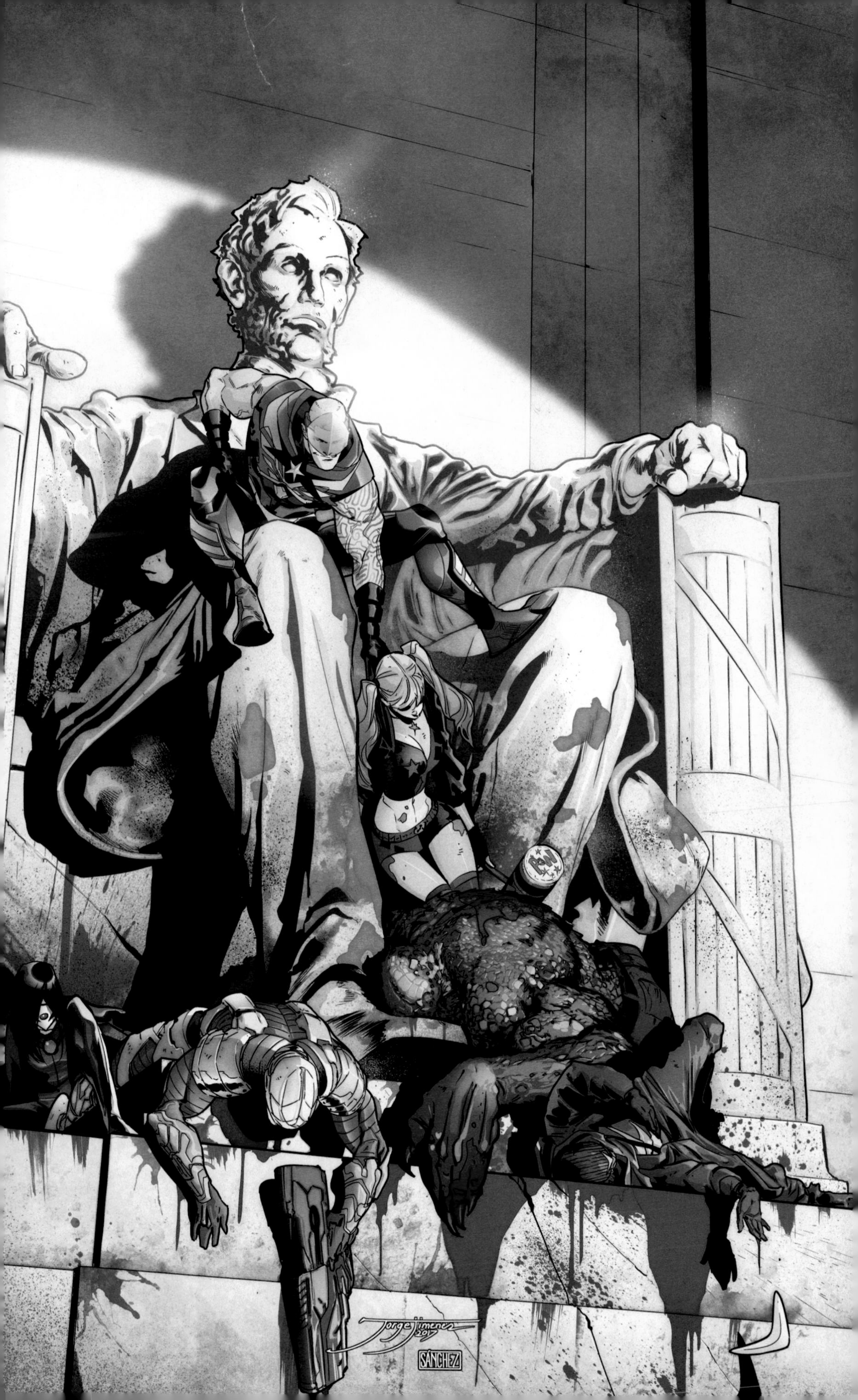
Jorge Jimenez 2017
SÁNCHEZ

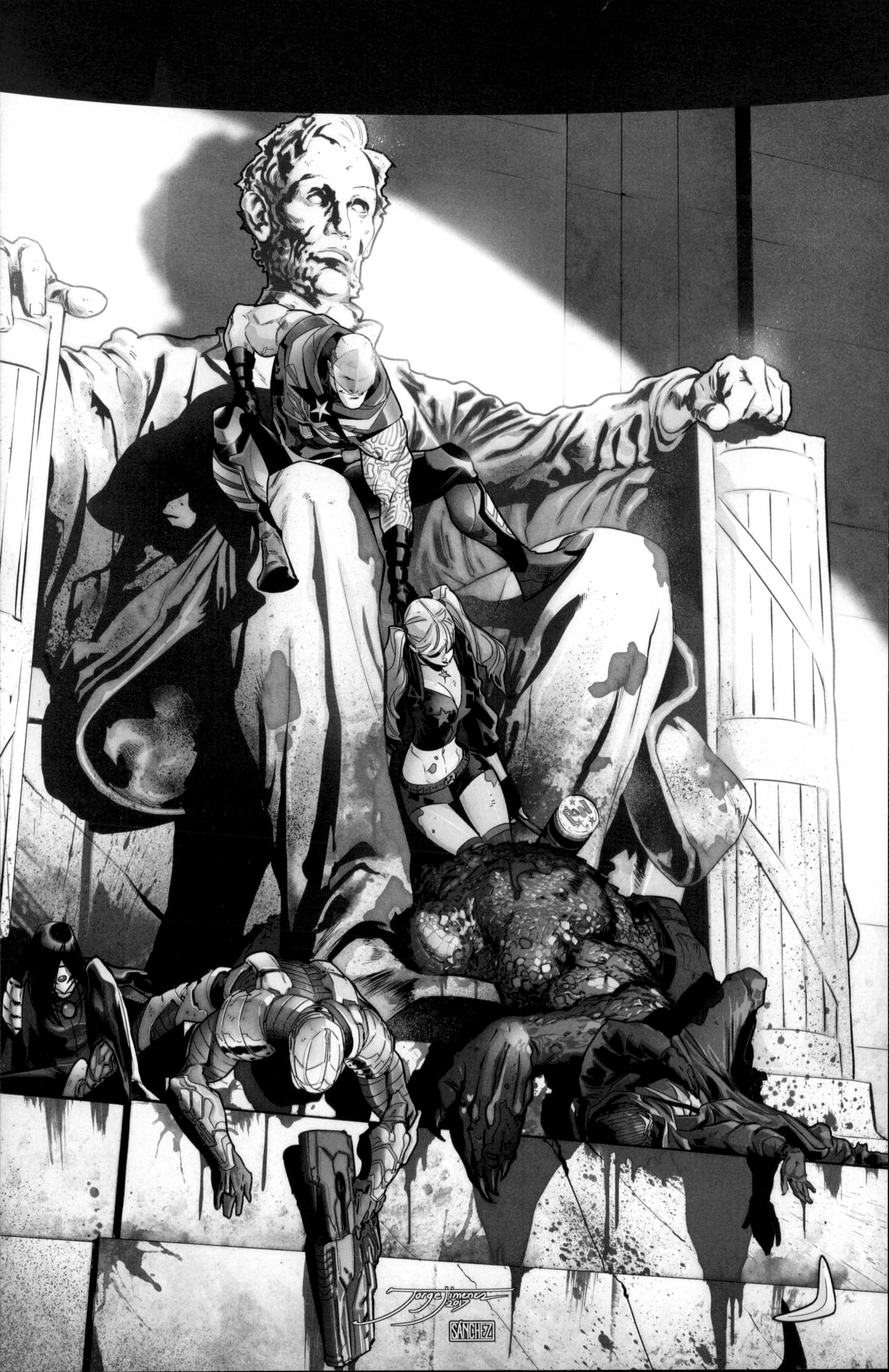
Jorge Jimenez 2017
SANCHEZ

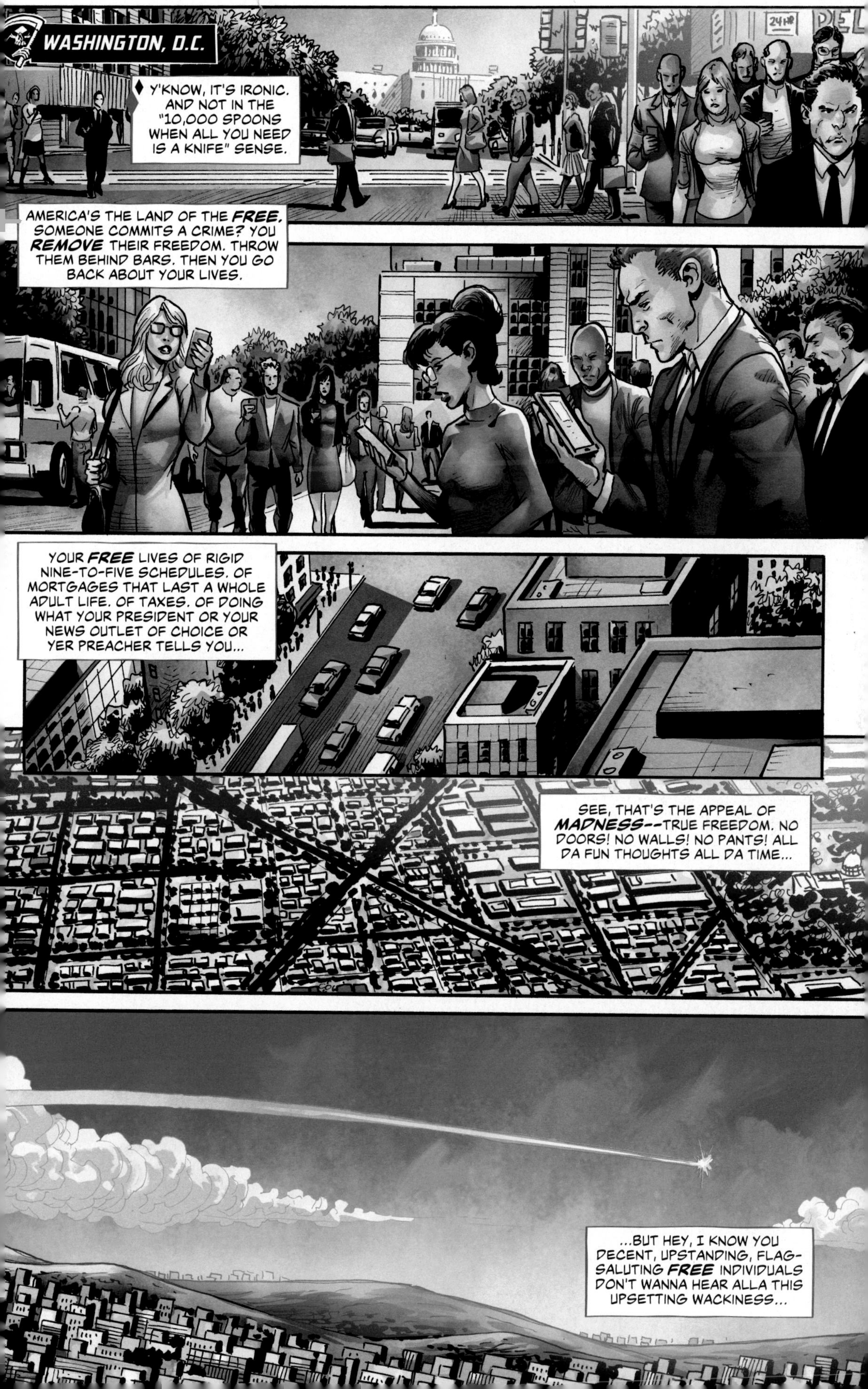
WASHINGTON, D.C.
Y'KNOW, IT'S IRONIC. AND NOT IN THE "10,000 SPOONS WHEN ALL YOU NEED IS A KNIFE" SENSE.
24HR
DEL
AMERICA'S THE LAND OF THE FREE. SOMEONE COMMITS A CRIME? YOU REMOVE THEIR FREEDOM. THROW THEM BEHIND BARS. THEN YOU GO BACK ABOUT YOUR LIVES.
YOUR FREE LIVES OF RIGID NINE-TO-FIVE SCHEDULES. OF MORTGAGES THAT LAST A WHOLE ADULT LIFE. OF TAXES. OF DOING WHAT YOUR PRESIDENT OR YOUR NEWS OUTLET OF CHOICE OR YER PREACHER TELLS YOU...
SEE, THAT'S THE APPEAL OF MADNESS--TRUE FREEDOM. NO DOORS! NO WALLS! NO PANTS! ALL DA FUN THOUGHTS ALL DA TIME...
...BUT HEY, I KNOW YOU DECENT, UPSTANDING, FLAG-SALUTING FREE INDIVIDUALS DON'T WANNA HEAR ALLA THIS UPSETTING WACKINESS...

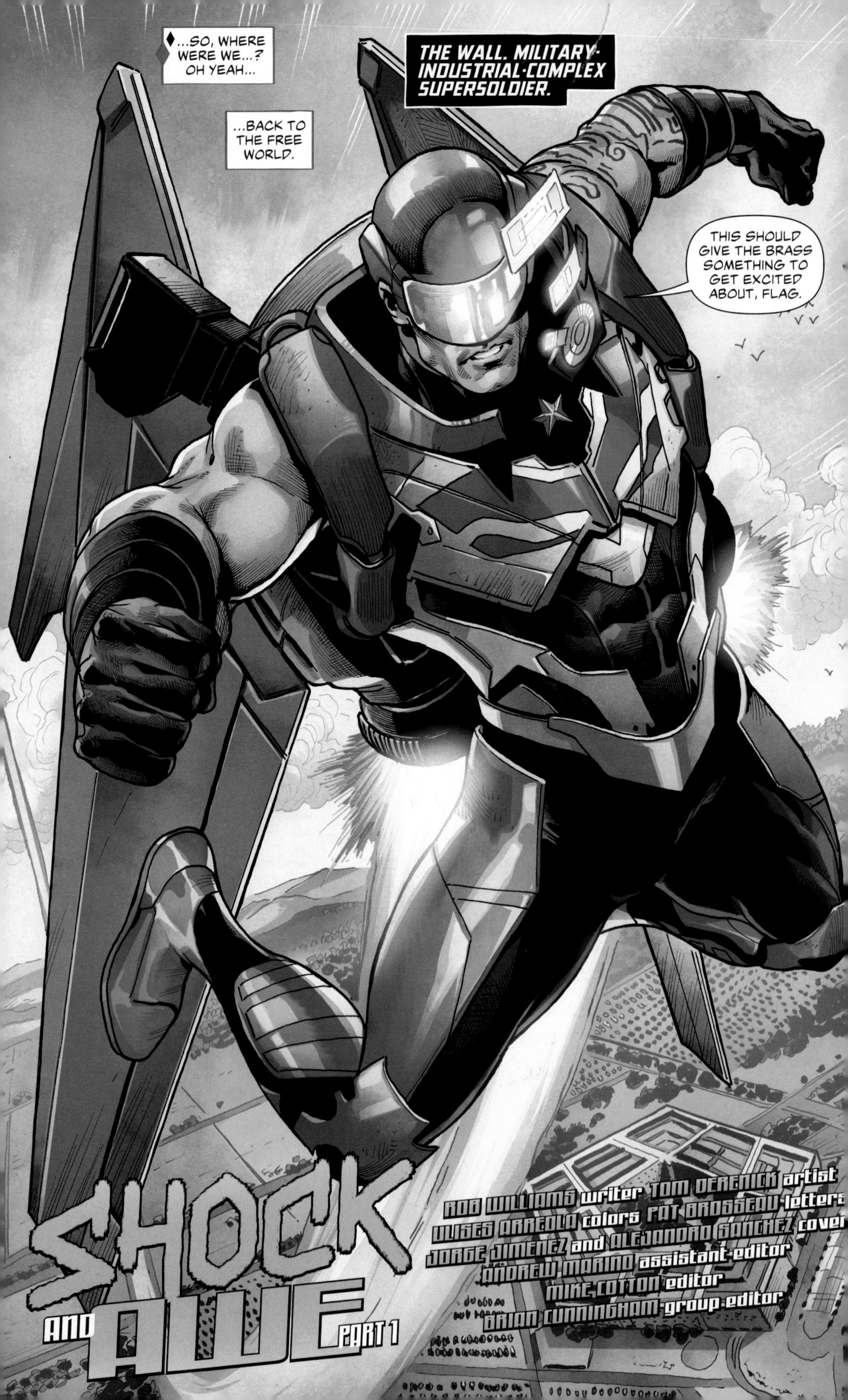
...SO, WHERE WERE WE...? OH YEAH...
...BACK TO THE FREE WORLD.
THE WALL. MILITARY-INDUSTRIAL-COMPLEX SUPERSOLDIER.
THIS SHOULD GIVE THE BRASS SOMETHING TO GET EXCITED ABOUT, FLAG.
SHOCK AND AWE PART 1
ROB WILLIAMS writer TOM DERENICK artist
ULISES ARREOLA colors PAT BROSSEAU letters
JORGE JIMENEZ and ALEJANDRO SANCHEZ cover
ANDREW MARINO assistant editor
MIKE COTTON editor
BRIAN CUNNINGHAM group editor

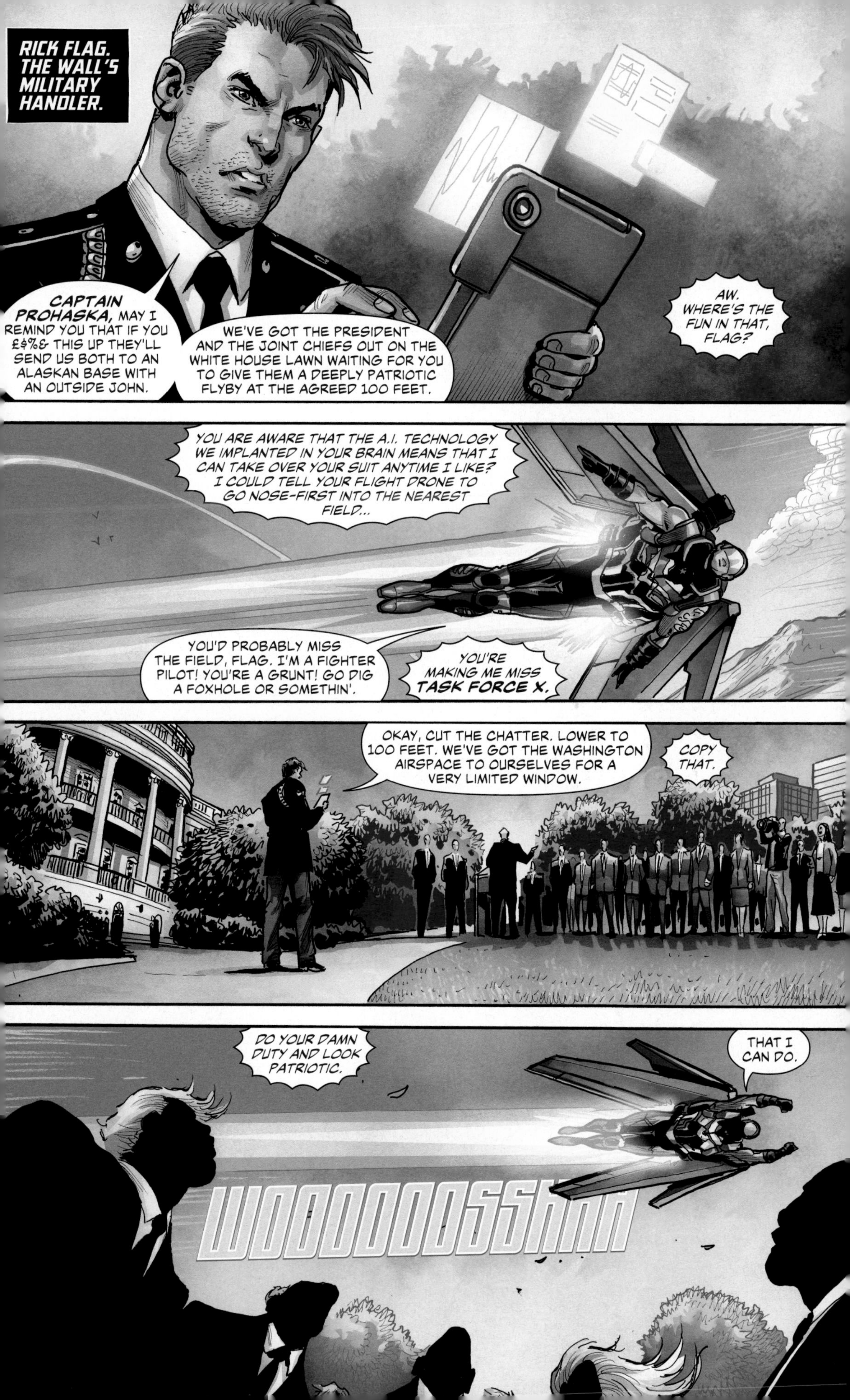
RICK FLAG. THE WALL'S MILITARY HANDLER.
CAPTAIN PROHASKA, MAY I REMIND YOU THAT IF YOU £$%& THIS UP THEY'LL SEND US BOTH TO AN ALASKAN BASE WITH AN OUTSIDE JOHN.
WE'VE GOT THE PRESIDENT AND THE JOINT CHIEFS OUT ON THE WHITE HOUSE LAWN WAITING FOR YOU TO GIVE THEM A DEEPLY PATRIOTIC FLYBY AT THE AGREED 100 FEET.
AW. WHERE'S THE FUN IN THAT, FLAG?
YOU ARE AWARE THAT THE A.I. TECHNOLOGY WE IMPLANTED IN YOUR BRAIN MEANS THAT I CAN TAKE OVER YOUR SUIT ANYTIME I LIKE? I COULD TELL YOUR FLIGHT DRONE TO GO NOSE-FIRST INTO THE NEAREST FIELD...
YOU'D PROBABLY MISS THE FIELD, FLAG. I'M A FIGHTER PILOT! YOU'RE A GRUNT! GO DIG A FOXHOLE OR SOMETHIN'.
YOU'RE MAKING ME MISS TASK FORCE X.
OKAY, CUT THE CHATTER. LOWER TO 100 FEET. WE'VE GOT THE WASHINGTON AIRSPACE TO OURSELVES FOR A VERY LIMITED WINDOW.
COPY THAT.
DO YOUR DAMN DUTY AND LOOK PATRIOTIC.
THAT I CAN DO.
WOOOOOOSSHHH

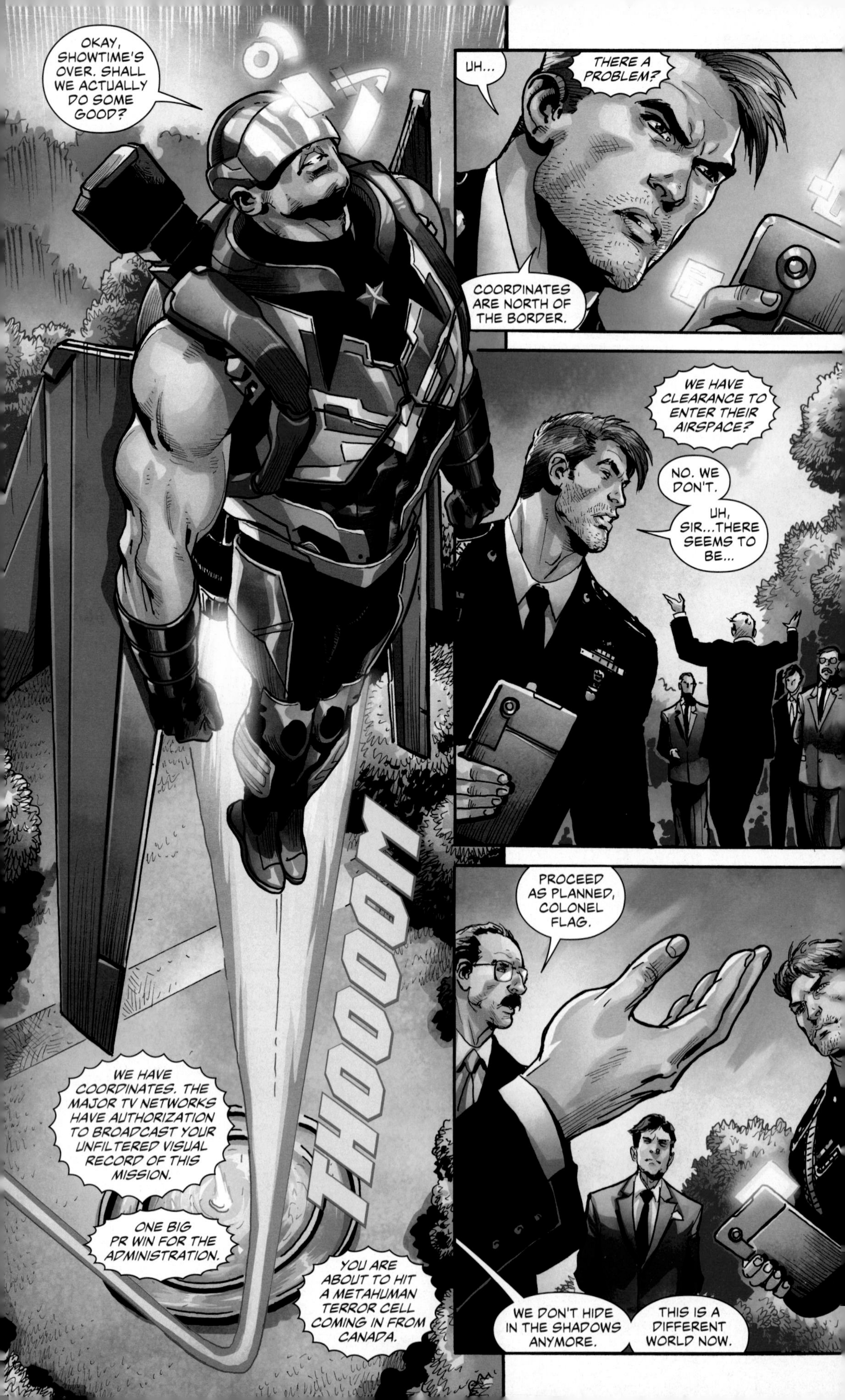
OKAY, SHOWTIME'S OVER. SHALL WE ACTUALLY DO SOME GOOD?
WE HAVE COORDINATES. THE MAJOR TV NETWORKS HAVE AUTHORIZATION TO BROADCAST YOUR UNFILTERED VISUAL RECORD OF THIS MISSION.
ONE BIG PR WIN FOR THE ADMINISTRATION.
YOU ARE ABOUT TO HIT A METAHUMAN TERROR CELL COMING IN FROM CANADA.
THOOOM
UH...
THERE A PROBLEM?
COORDINATES ARE NORTH OF THE BORDER.
WE HAVE CLEARANCE TO ENTER THEIR AIRSPACE?
NO. WE DON'T.
UH, SIR...THERE SEEMS TO BE...
PROCEED AS PLANNED, COLONEL FLAG.
WE DON'T HIDE IN THE SHADOWS ANYMORE.
THIS IS A DIFFERENT WORLD NOW.

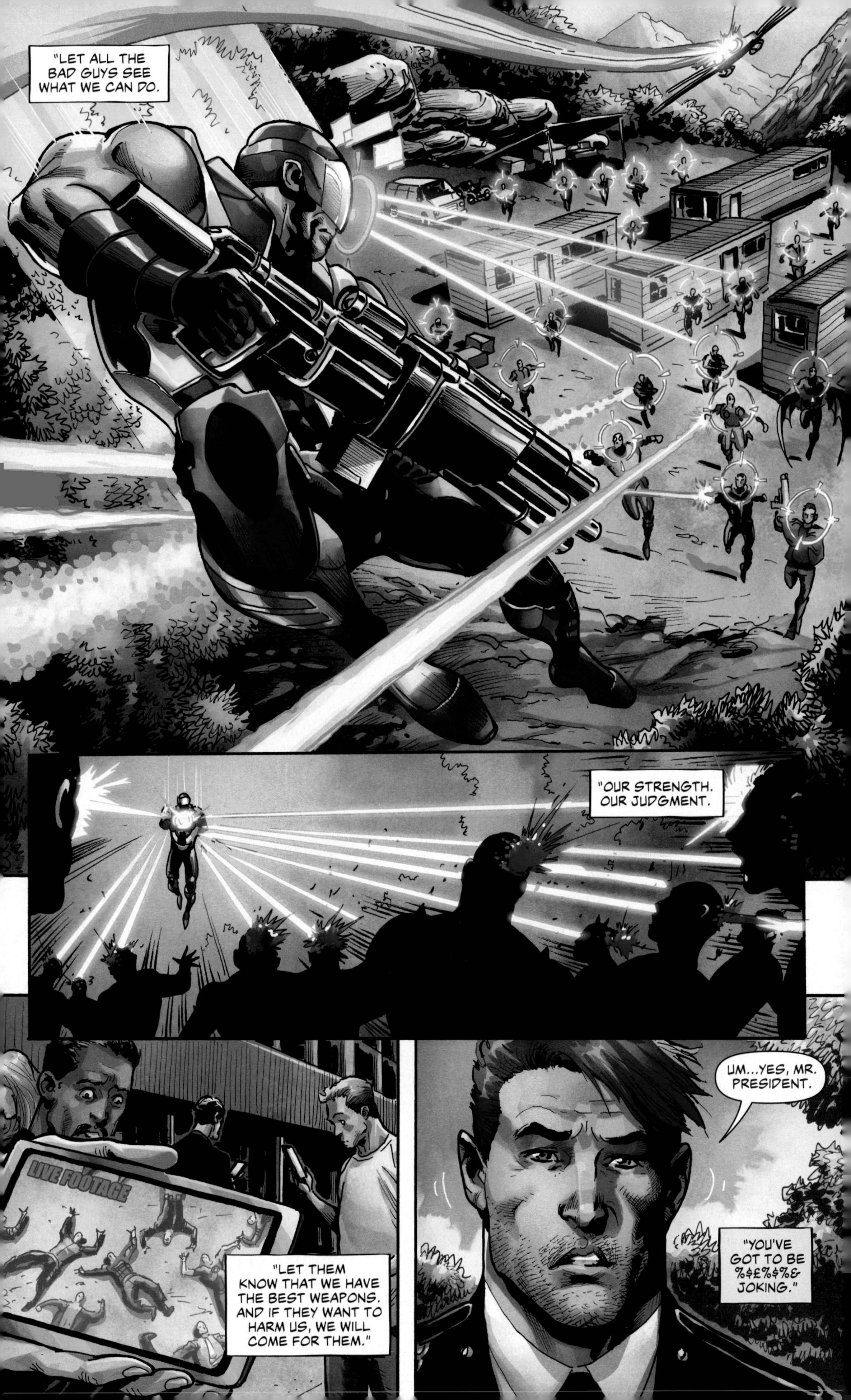
"LET ALL THE BAD GUYS SEE WHAT WE CAN DO.
"OUR STRENGTH. OUR JUDGMENT.
LIVE FOOTAGE
"LET THEM KNOW THAT WE HAVE THE BEST WEAPONS. AND IF THEY WANT TO HARM US, WE WILL COME FOR THEM."
UM...YES, MR. PRESIDENT.
"YOU'VE GOT TO BE %$£%$%& JOKING."

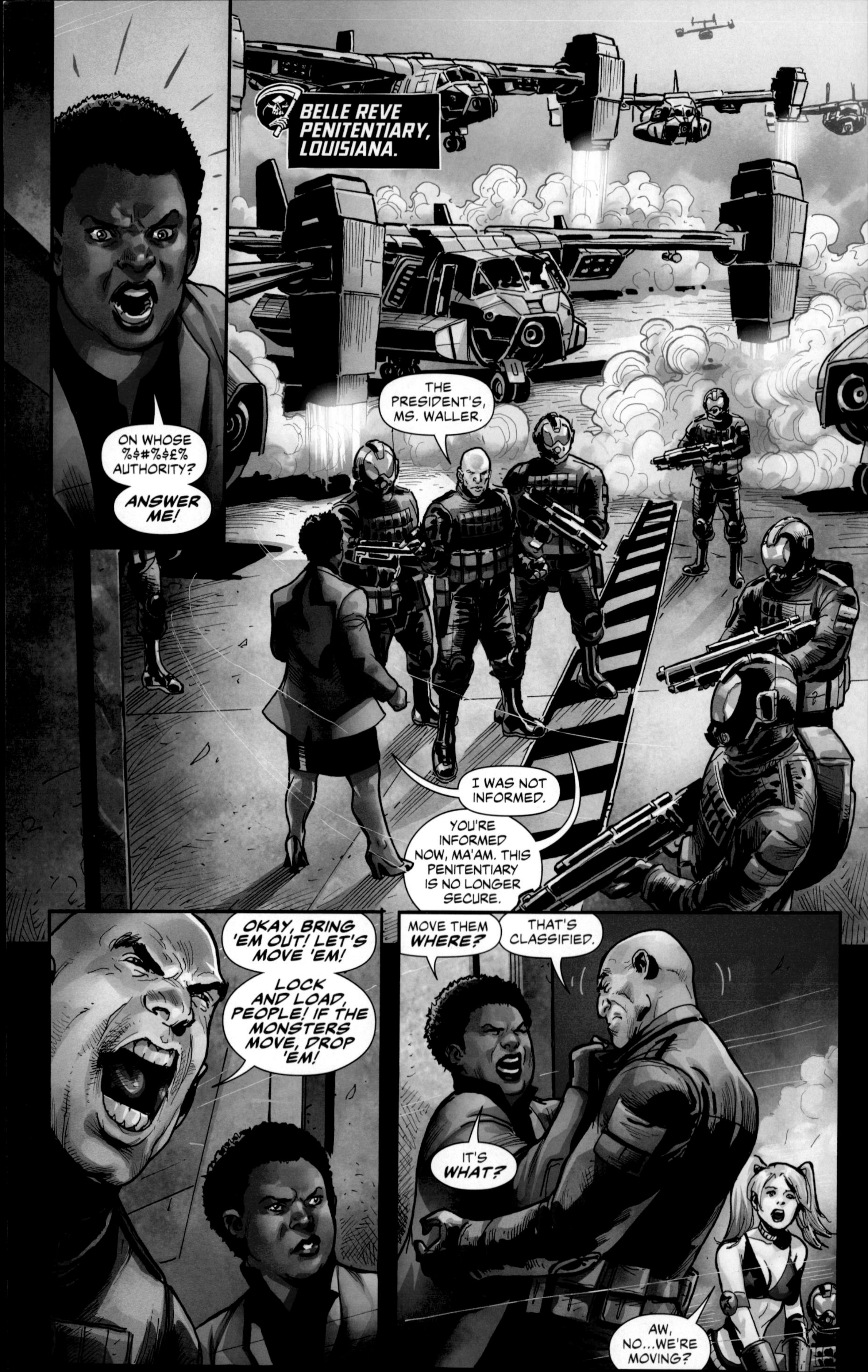

BELLE REVE PENITENTIARY, LOUISIANA.
ON WHOSE %$#%$£% AUTHORITY?
ANSWER ME!
THE PRESIDENT'S, MS. WALLER.
I WAS NOT INFORMED.
YOU'RE INFORMED NOW, MA'AM. THIS PENITENTIARY IS NO LONGER SECURE.
OKAY, BRING 'EM OUT! LET'S MOVE 'EM!
LOCK AND LOAD, PEOPLE! IF THE MONSTERS MOVE, DROP 'EM!
MOVE THEM WHERE?
THAT'S CLASSIFIED.
IT'S WHAT?
AW, NO...WE'RE MOVING?

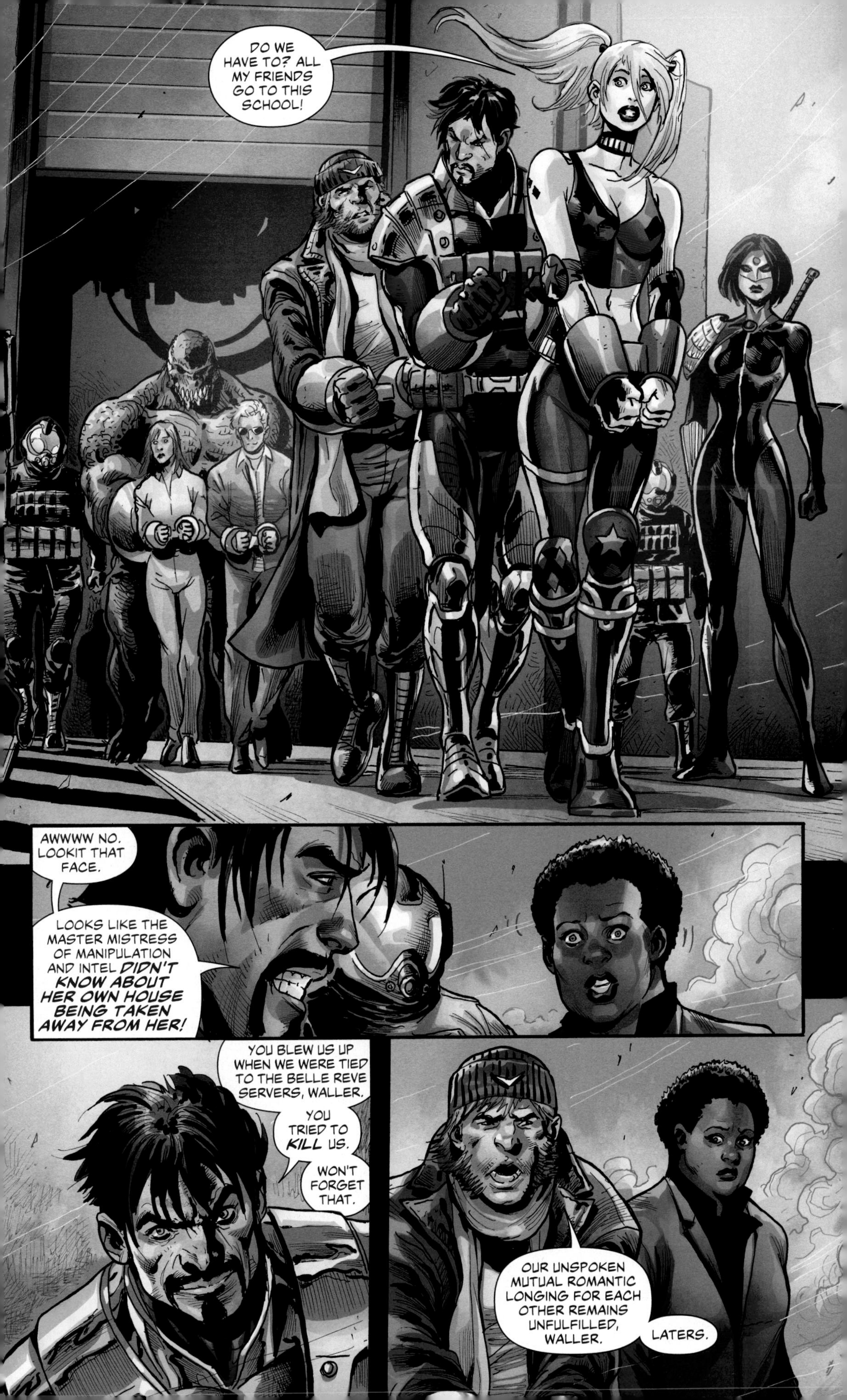
DO WE HAVE TO? ALL MY FRIENDS GO TO THIS SCHOOL!
AWWWW NO. LOOKIT THAT FACE.
LOOKS LIKE THE MASTER MISTRESS OF MANIPULATION AND INTEL DIDN'T KNOW ABOUT HER OWN HOUSE BEING TAKEN AWAY FROM HER!
YOU BLEW US UP WHEN WE WERE TIED TO THE BELLE REVE SERVERS, WALLER.
YOU TRIED TO KILL US.
WON'T FORGET THAT.
OUR UNSPOKEN MUTUAL ROMANTIC LONGING FOR EACH OTHER REMAINS UNFULFILLED, WALLER.
LATERS.

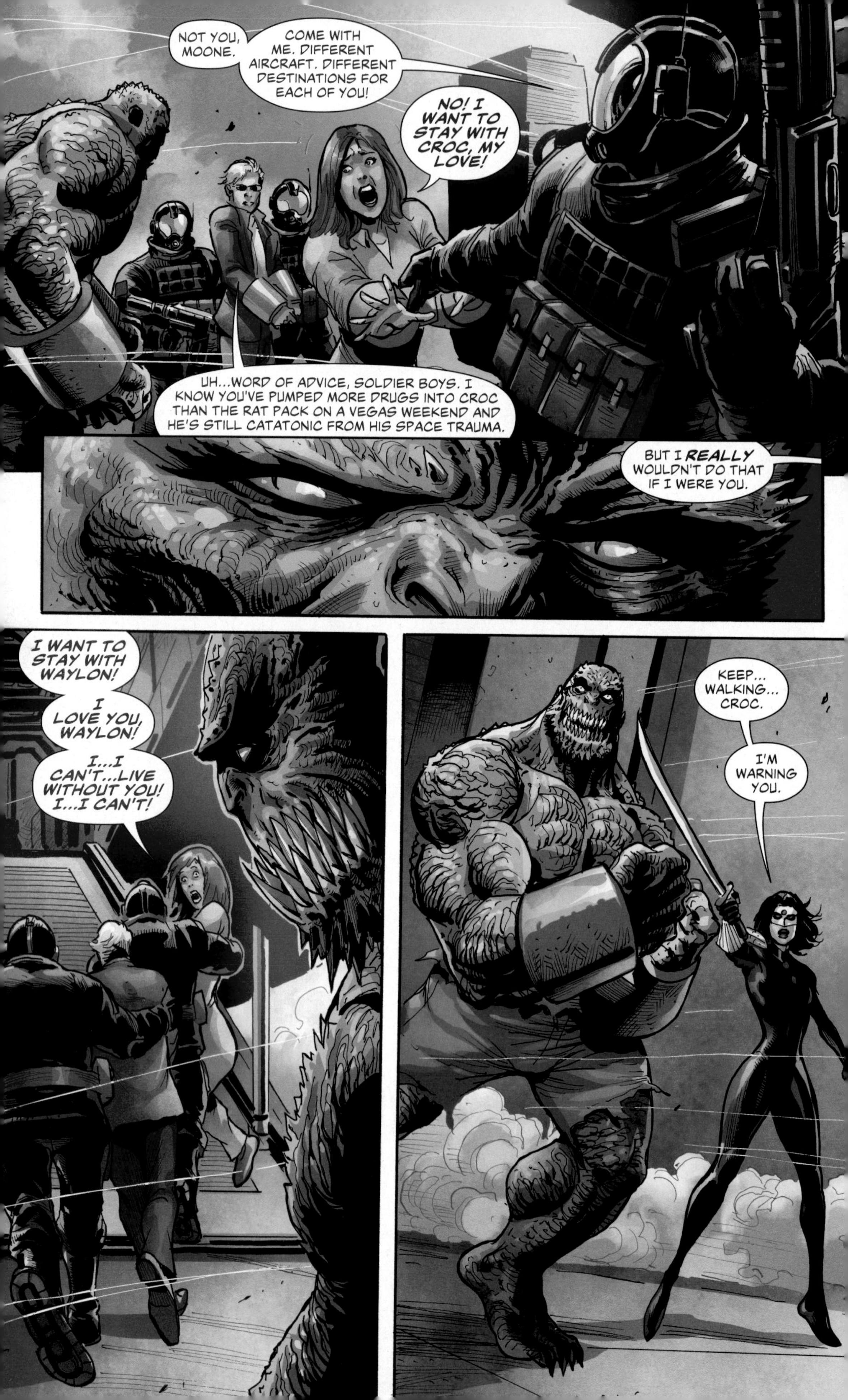
NOT YOU, MOONE.
COME WITH ME. DIFFERENT AIRCRAFT. DIFFERENT DESTINATIONS FOR EACH OF YOU!
NO! I WANT TO STAY WITH CROC, MY LOVE!
UH...WORD OF ADVICE, SOLDIER BOYS. I KNOW YOU'VE PUMPED MORE DRUGS INTO CROC THAN THE RAT PACK ON A VEGAS WEEKEND AND HE'S STILL CATATONIC FROM HIS SPACE TRAUMA.
BUT I REALLY WOULDN'T DO THAT IF I WERE YOU.
I WANT TO STAY WITH WAYLON!
I LOVE YOU, WAYLON!
I...I CAN'T...LIVE WITHOUT YOU! I...I CAN'T!
KEEP... WALKING... CROC.
I'M WARNING YOU.

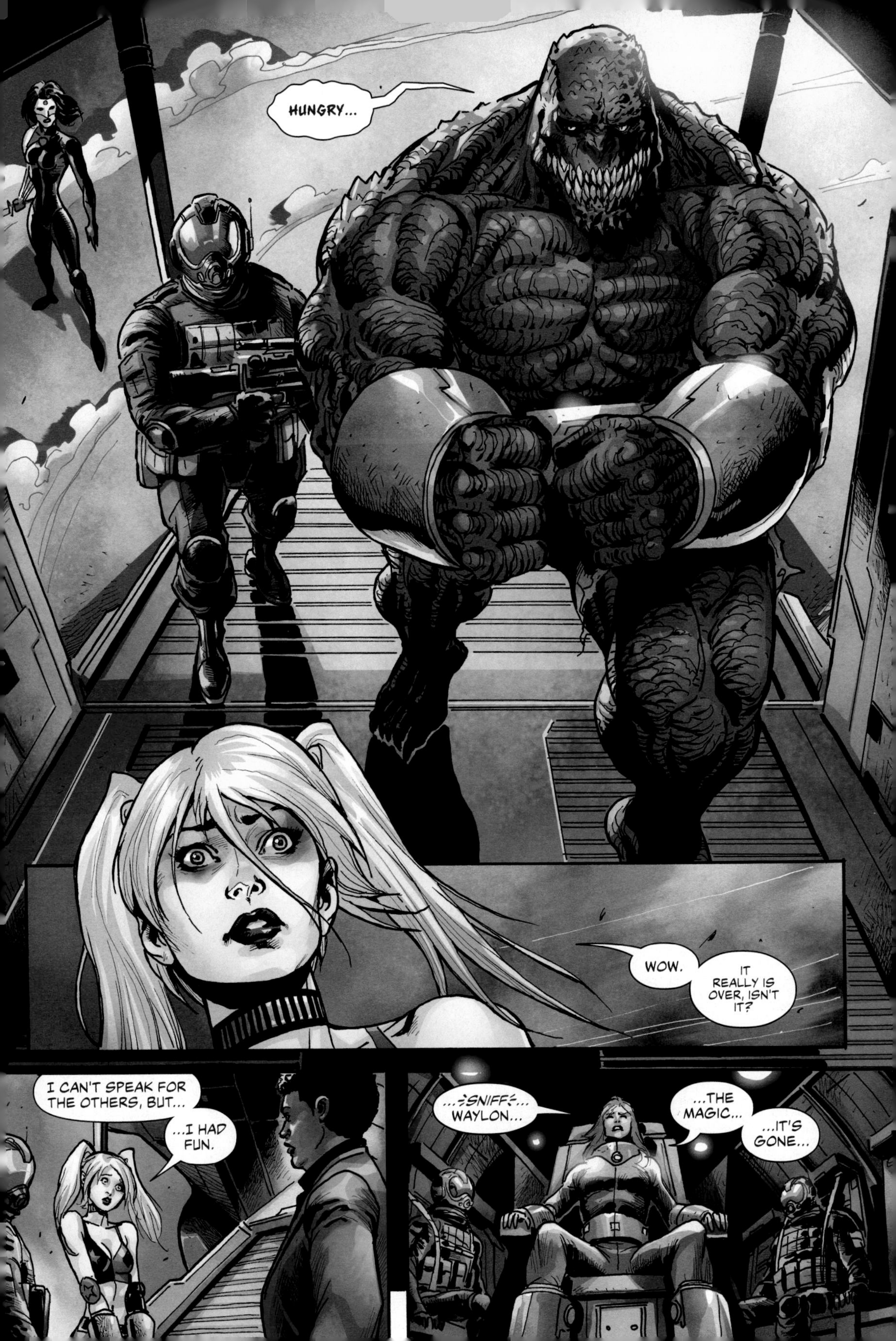
HUNGRY...
WOW.
IT REALLY IS OVER, ISN'T IT?
I CAN'T SPEAK FOR THE OTHERS, BUT...
...I HAD FUN.
...SNIFF... WAYLON...
...THE MAGIC...
...IT'S GONE...

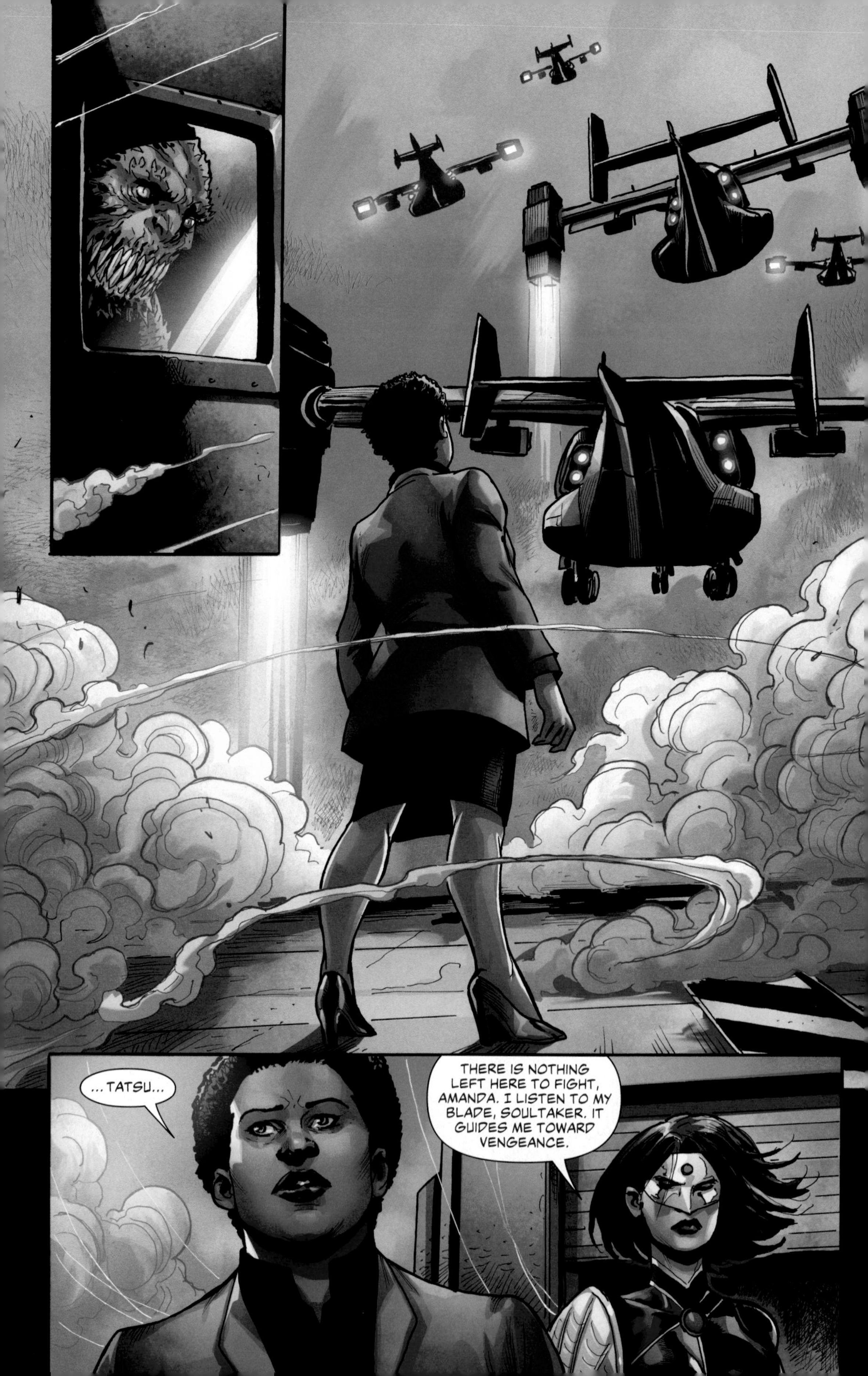
...TATSU...
THERE IS NOTHING LEFT HERE TO FIGHT, AMANDA. I LISTEN TO MY BLADE, SOULTAKER. IT GUIDES ME TOWARD VENGEANCE.

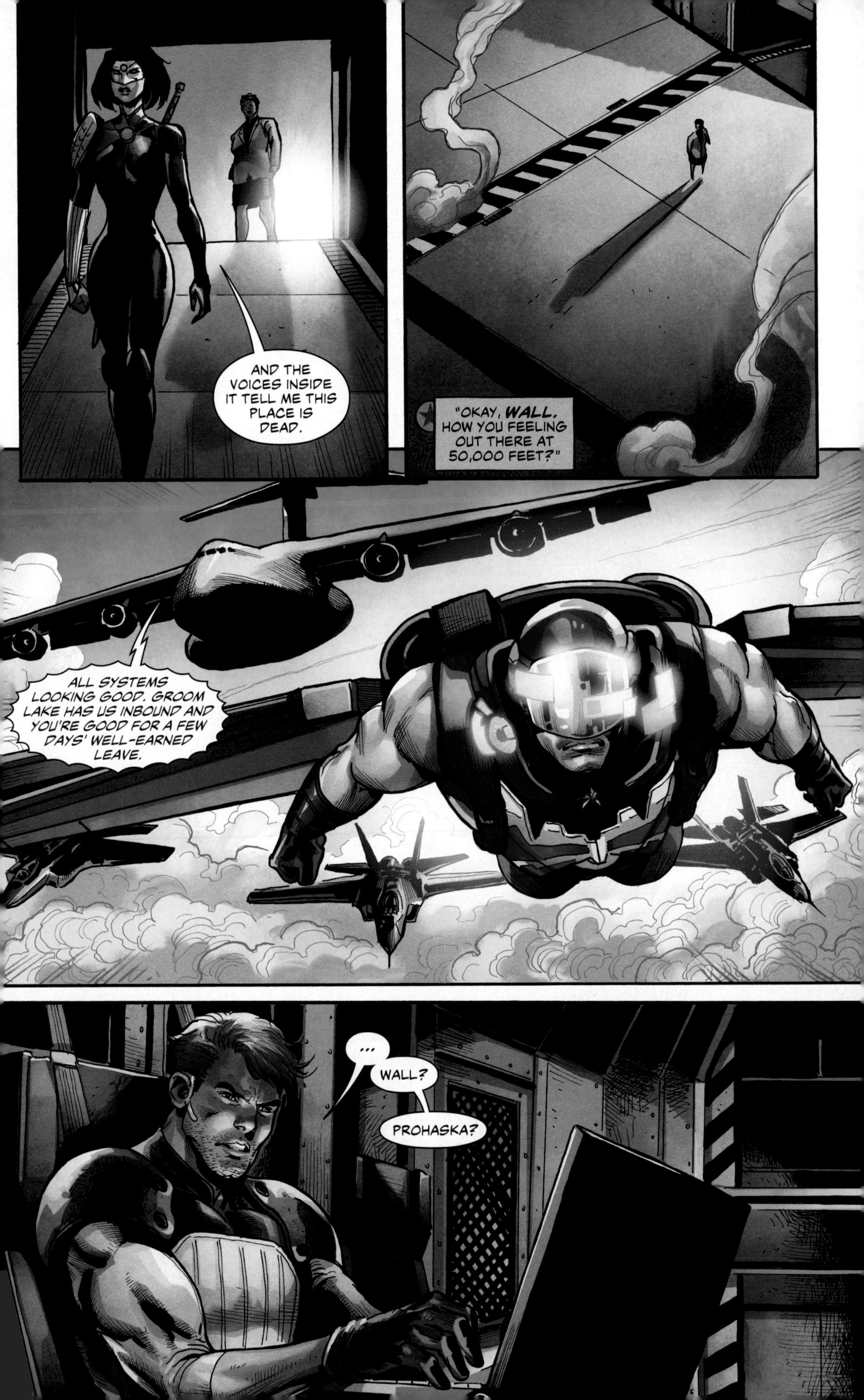
AND THE VOICES INSIDE IT TELL ME THIS PLACE IS DEAD.
"OKAY, WALL. HOW YOU FEELING OUT THERE AT 50,000 FEET?"
ALL SYSTEMS LOOKING GOOD. GROOM LAKE HAS US INBOUND AND YOU'RE GOOD FOR A FEW DAYS' WELL-EARNED LEAVE.
...
WALL?
PROHASKA?

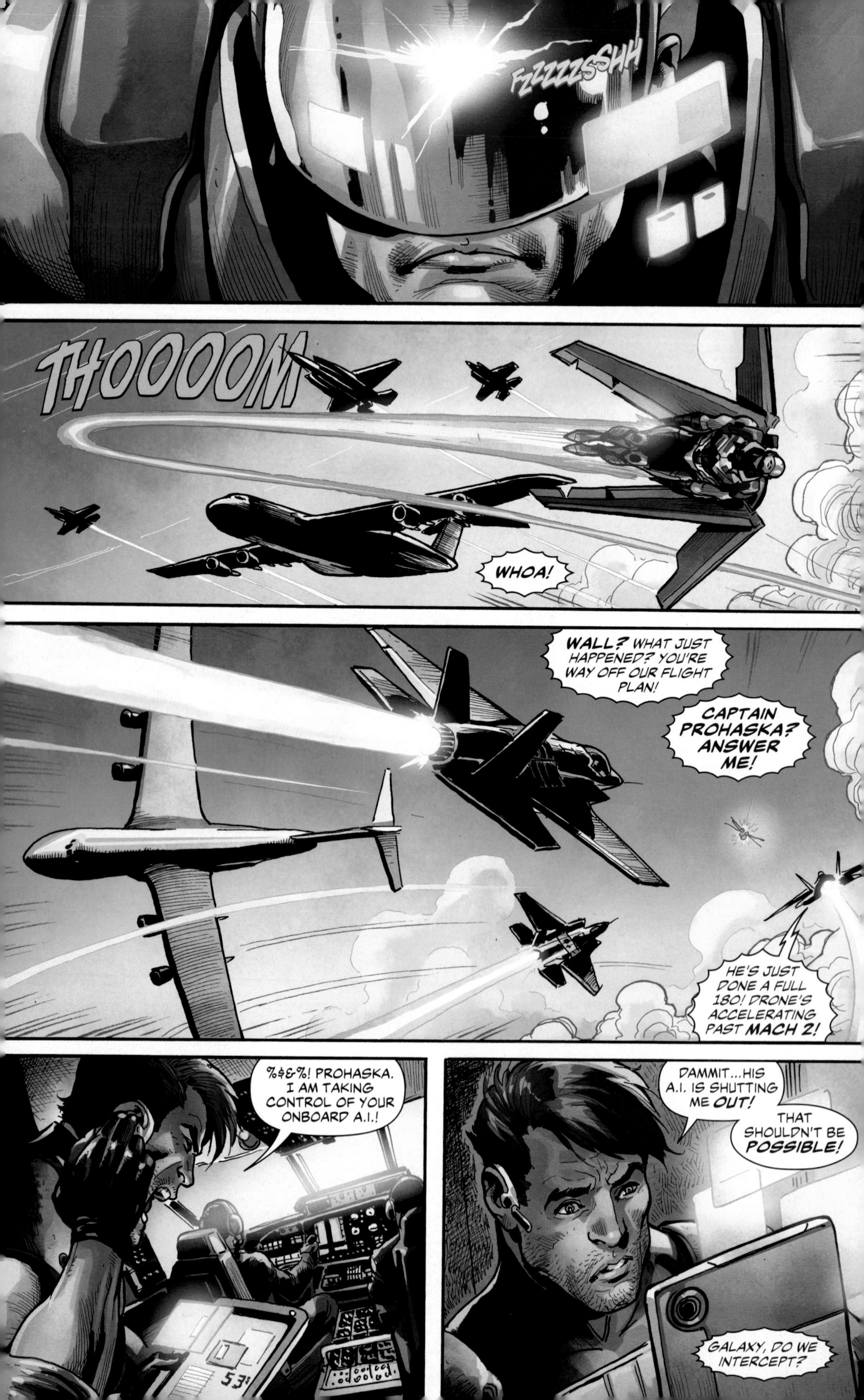
FZZZZZSSHH
THOOOOM
WHOA!
WALL? WHAT JUST HAPPENED? YOU'RE WAY OFF OUR FLIGHT PLAN!
CAPTAIN PROHASKA? ANSWER ME!
HE'S JUST DONE A FULL 180! DRONE'S ACCELERATING PAST MACH 2!
%$&%! PROHASKA. I AM TAKING CONTROL OF YOUR ONBOARD A.I.!
DAMMIT...HIS A.I. IS SHUTTING ME OUT!
THAT SHOULDN'T BE POSSIBLE!
GALAXY, DO WE INTERCEPT?

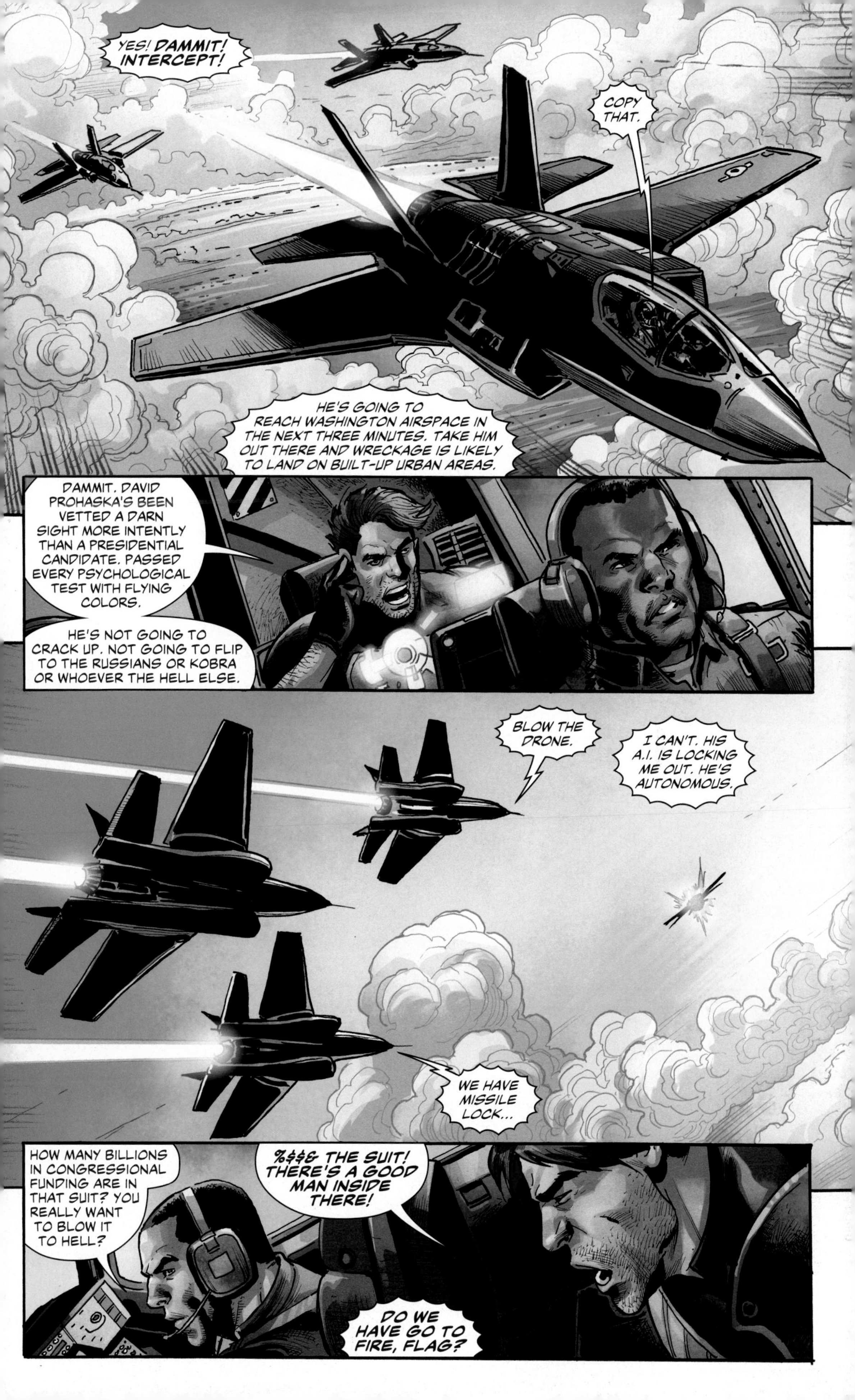
YES! DAMMIT! INTERCEPT!
COPY THAT.
HE'S GOING TO REACH WASHINGTON AIRSPACE IN THE NEXT THREE MINUTES. TAKE HIM OUT THERE AND WRECKAGE IS LIKELY TO LAND ON BUILT-UP URBAN AREAS.
DAMMIT. DAVID PROHASKA'S BEEN VETTED A DARN SIGHT MORE INTENTLY THAN A PRESIDENTIAL CANDIDATE. PASSED EVERY PSYCHOLOGICAL TEST WITH FLYING COLORS.
HE'S NOT GOING TO CRACK UP. NOT GOING TO FLIP TO THE RUSSIANS OR KOBRA OR WHOEVER THE HELL ELSE.
BLOW THE DRONE.
I CAN'T. HIS A.I. IS LOCKING ME OUT. HE'S AUTONOMOUS.
WE HAVE MISSILE LOCK...
HOW MANY BILLIONS IN CONGRESSIONAL FUNDING ARE IN THAT SUIT? YOU REALLY WANT TO BLOW IT TO HELL?
%$$& THE SUIT! THERE'S A GOOD MAN INSIDE THERE!
DO WE HAVE GO TO FIRE, FLAG?

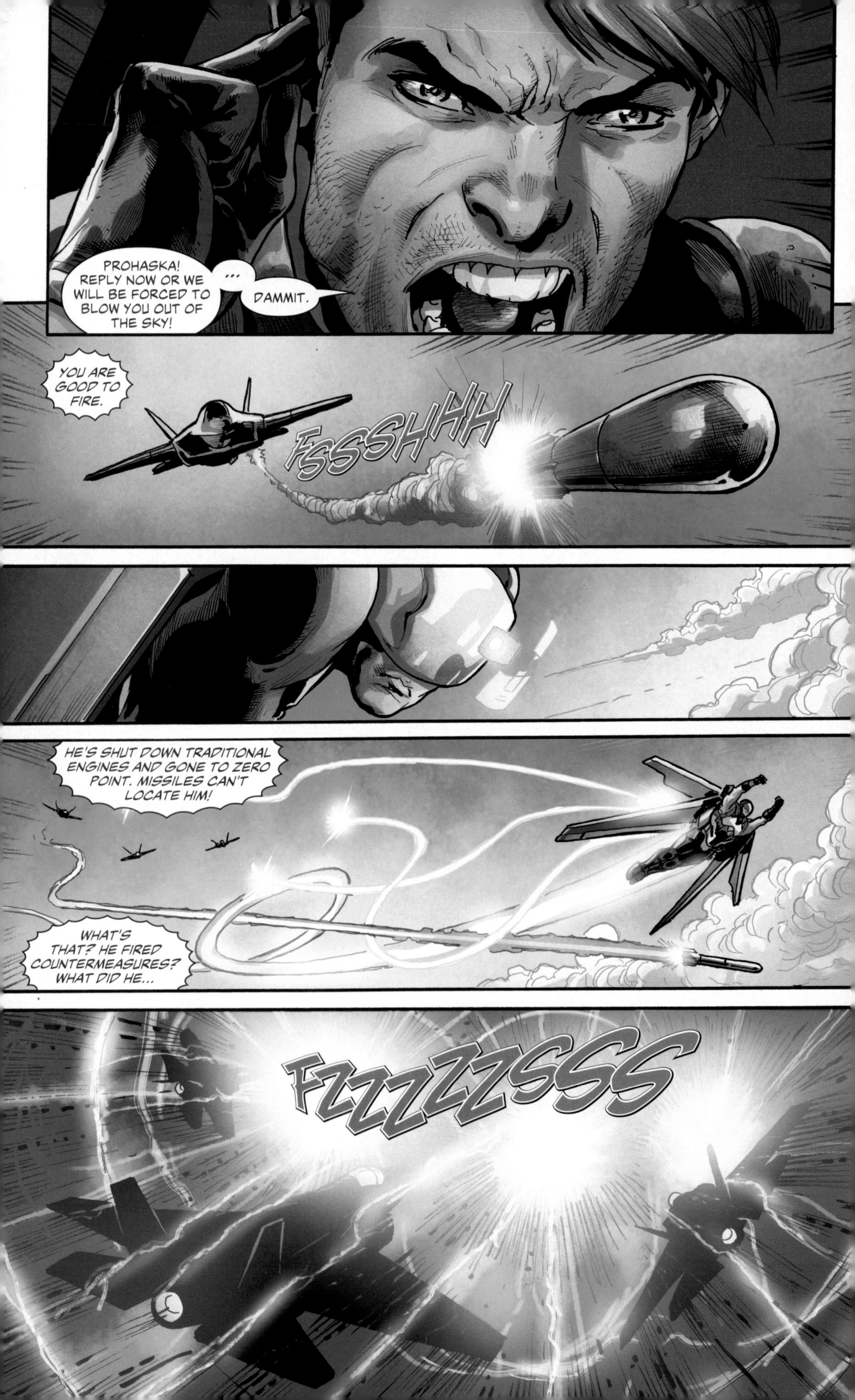
PROHASKA! REPLY NOW OR WE WILL BE FORCED TO BLOW YOU OUT OF THE SKY!
...
DAMMIT.
YOU ARE GOOD TO FIRE.
FSSSHHH
HE'S SHUT DOWN TRADITIONAL ENGINES AND GONE TO ZERO POINT. MISSILES CAN'T LOCATE HIM!
WHAT'S THAT? HE FIRED COUNTERMEASURES? WHAT DID HE...
FZZZZZSSSS

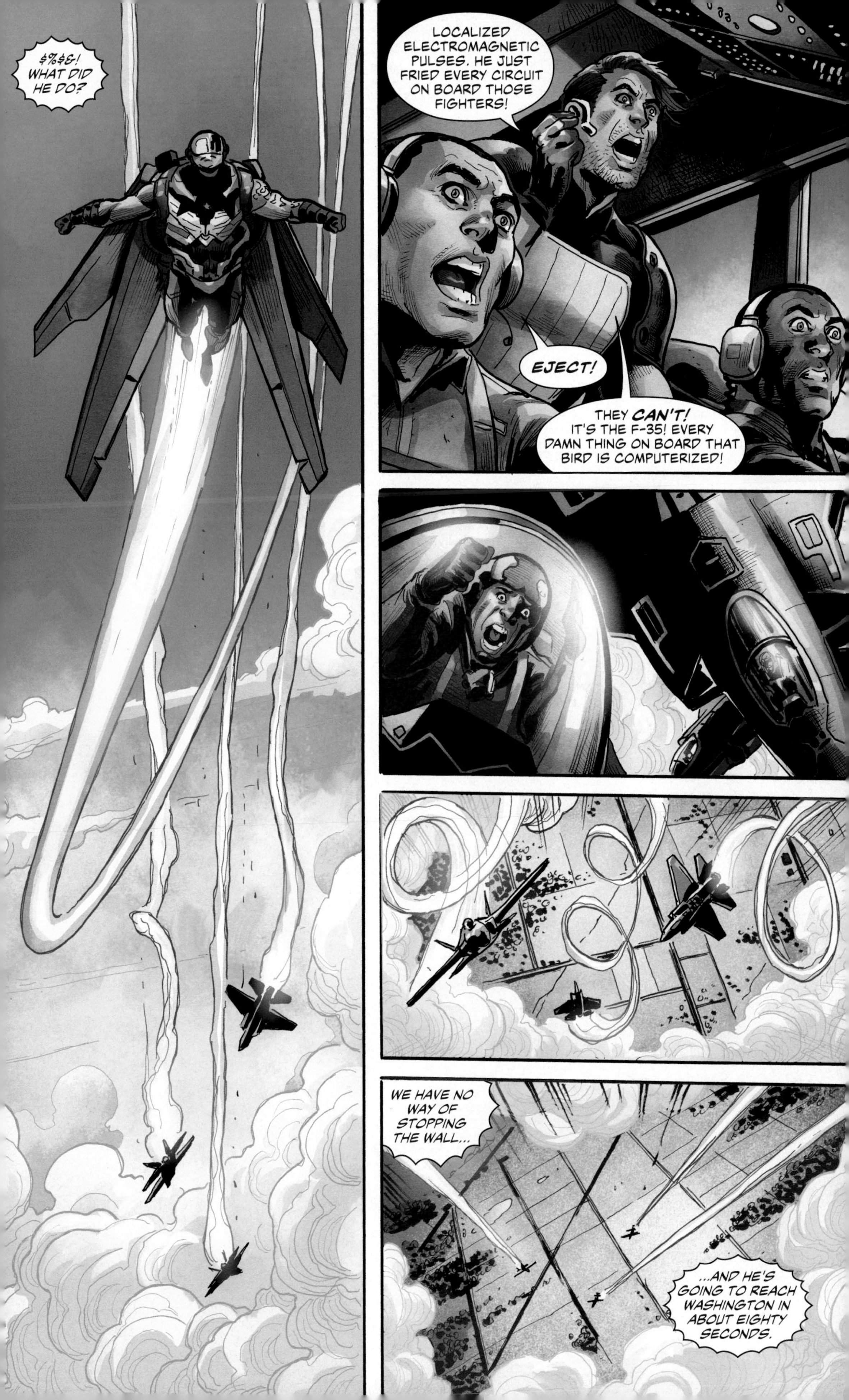
$%$&! WHAT DID HE DO?
LOCALIZED ELECTROMAGNETIC PULSES. HE JUST FRIED EVERY CIRCUIT ON BOARD THOSE FIGHTERS!
EJECT!
THEY CAN'T! IT'S THE F-35! EVERY DAMN THING ON BOARD THAT BIRD IS COMPUTERIZED!
WE HAVE NO WAY OF STOPPING THE WALL...
...AND HE'S GOING TO REACH WASHINGTON IN ABOUT EIGHTY SECONDS.

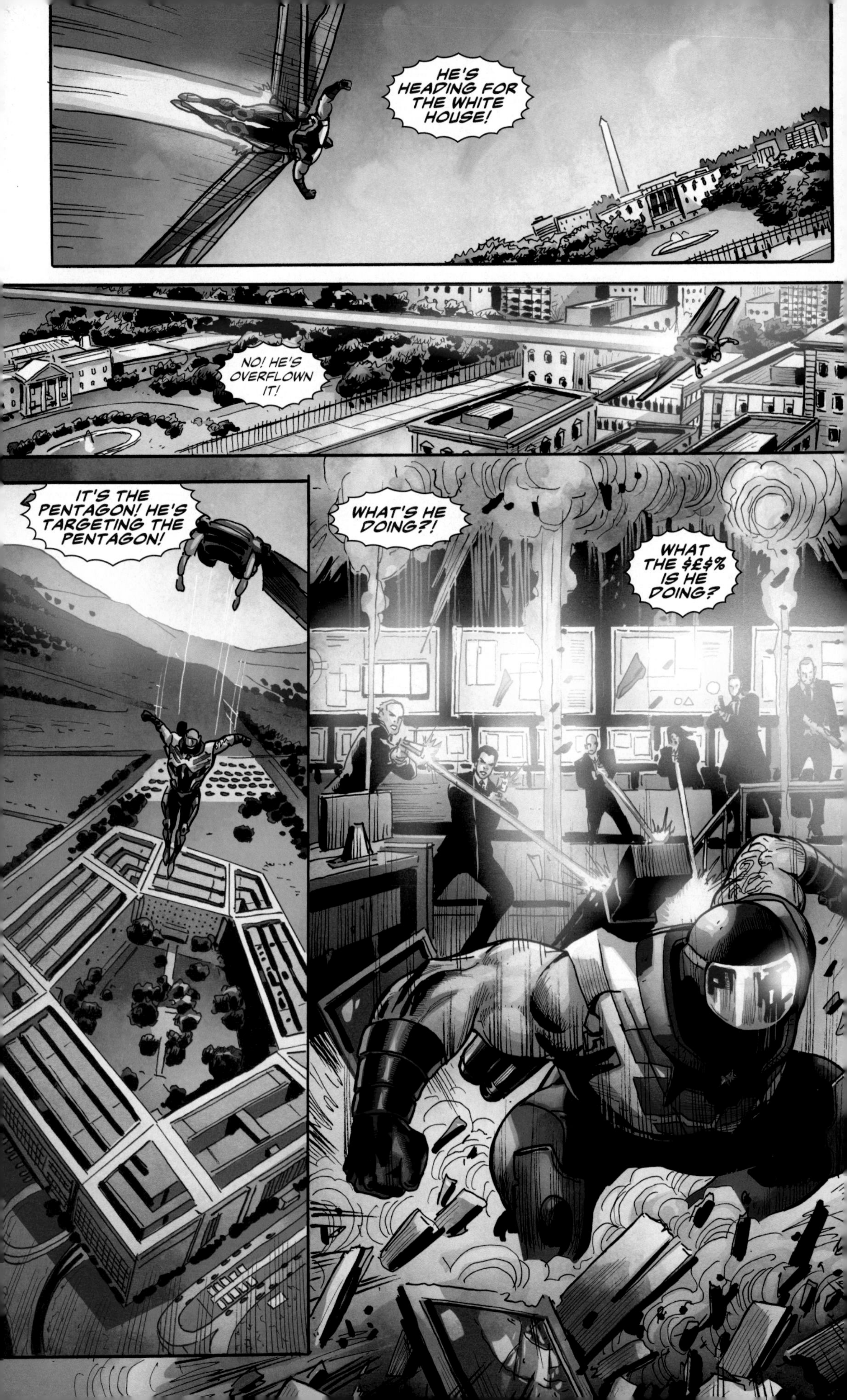
HE'S HEADING FOR THE WHITE HOUSE!
NO! HE'S OVERFLOWN IT!
IT'S THE PENTAGON! HE'S TARGETING THE PENTAGON!
WHAT'S HE DOING?!
WHAT THE $£$% IS HE DOING?

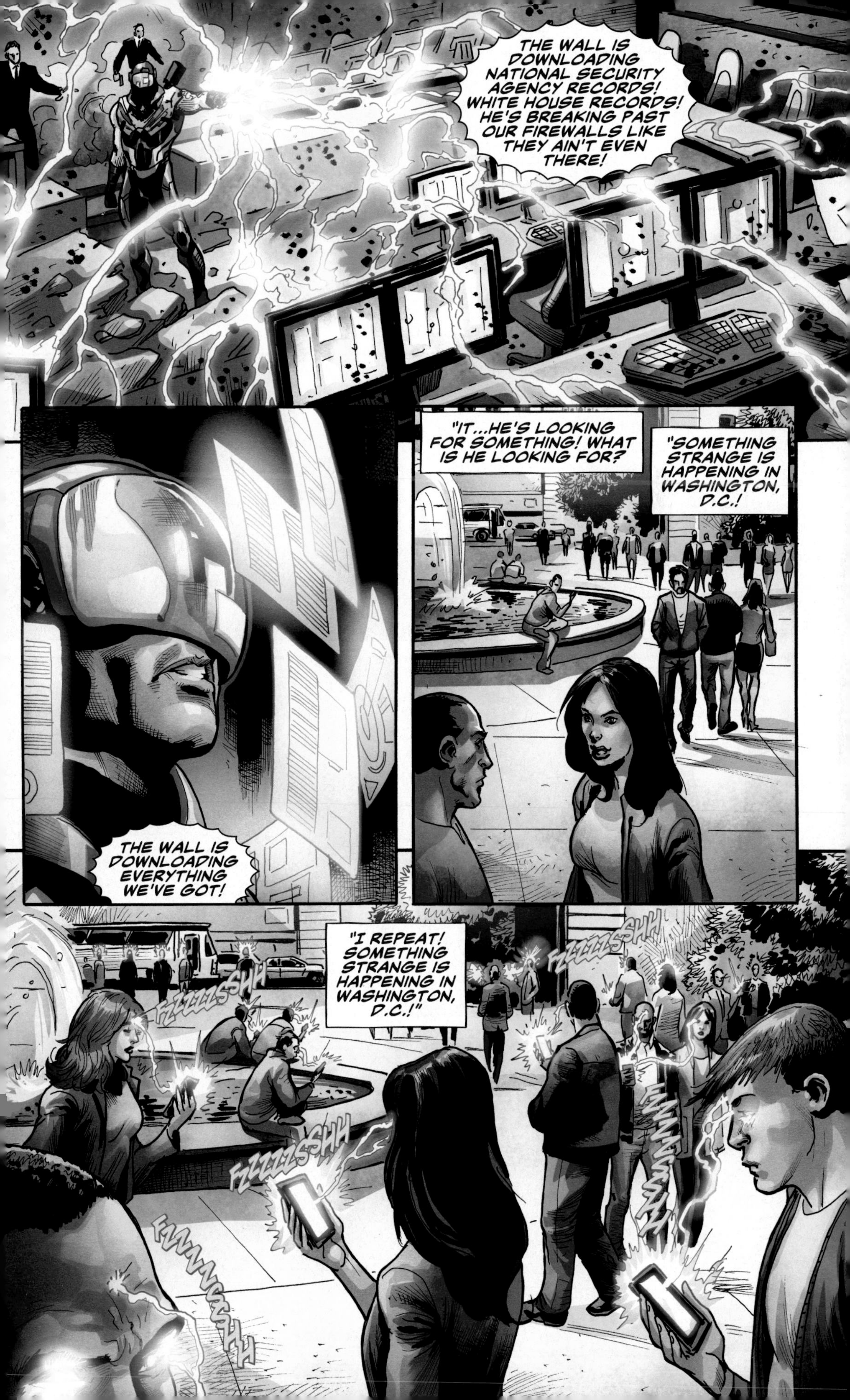
THE WALL IS DOWNLOADING NATIONAL SECURITY AGENCY RECORDS! WHITE HOUSE RECORDS! HE'S BREAKING PAST OUR FIREWALLS LIKE THEY AIN'T EVEN THERE!
THE WALL IS DOWNLOADING EVERYTHING WE'VE GOT!
"IT...HE'S LOOKING FOR SOMETHING! WHAT IS HE LOOKING FOR?
"SOMETHING STRANGE IS HAPPENING IN WASHINGTON, D.C.!
"I REPEAT! SOMETHING STRANGE IS HAPPENING IN WASHINGTON, D.C.!"
FZZZZSSHH
FZZZZSSHH
FZZZZSSHH
FZZZZSSHH
FZZZSSSHH
FZZZZSSHH

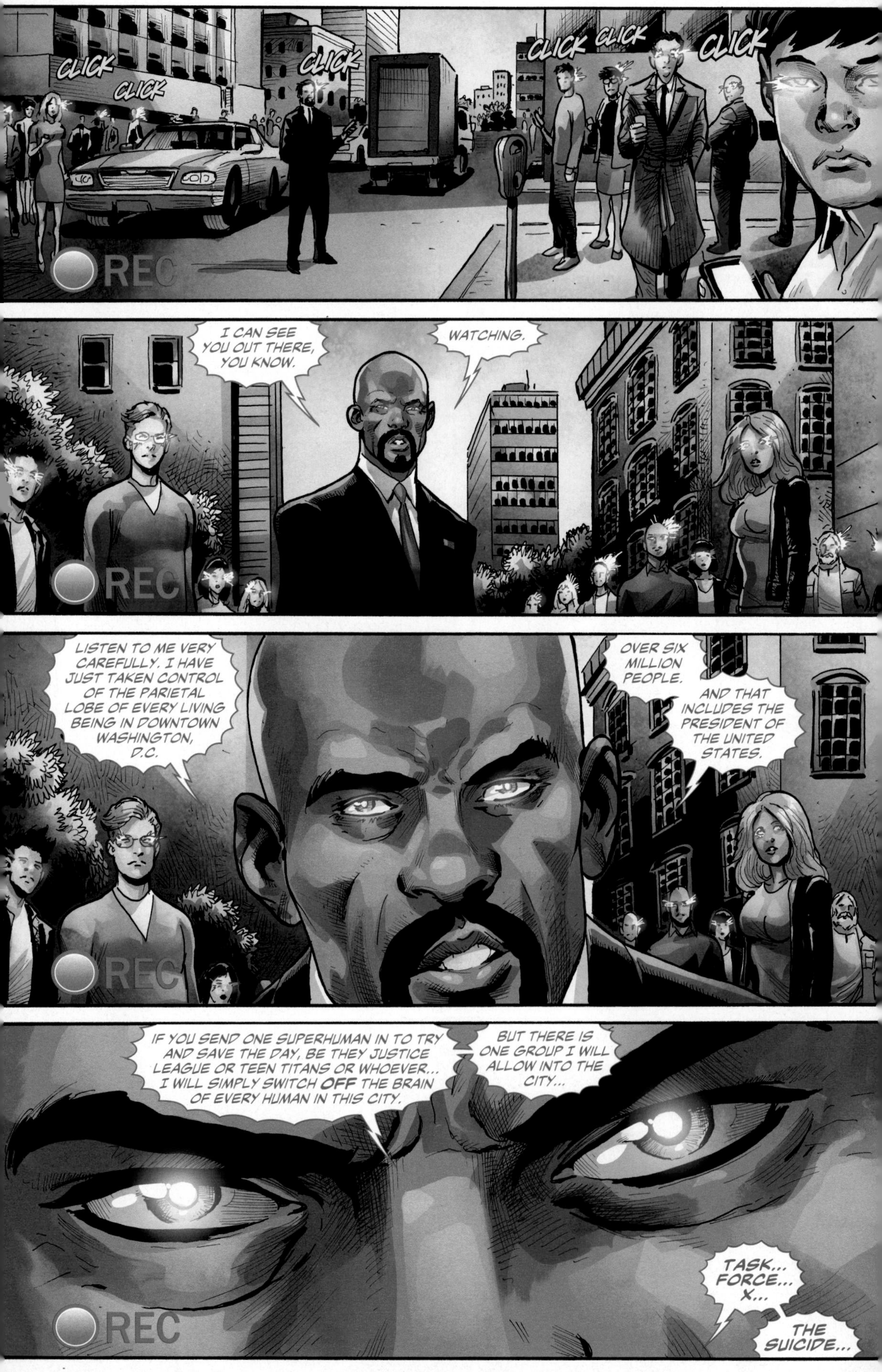
CLICK
CLICK
CLICK
CLICK
CLICK
CLICK
REC
I CAN SEE YOU OUT THERE, YOU KNOW.
WATCHING.
REC
LISTEN TO ME VERY CAREFULLY. I HAVE JUST TAKEN CONTROL OF THE PARIETAL LOBE OF EVERY LIVING BEING IN DOWNTOWN WASHINGTON, D.C.
OVER SIX MILLION PEOPLE.
AND THAT INCLUDES THE PRESIDENT OF THE UNITED STATES.
REC
IF YOU SEND ONE SUPERHUMAN IN TO TRY AND SAVE THE DAY, BE THEY JUSTICE LEAGUE OR TEEN TITANS OR WHOEVER... I WILL SIMPLY SWITCH OFF THE BRAIN OF EVERY HUMAN IN THIS CITY.
BUT THERE IS ONE GROUP I WILL ALLOW INTO THE CITY...
TASK... FORCE... X...
THE SUICIDE...
REC

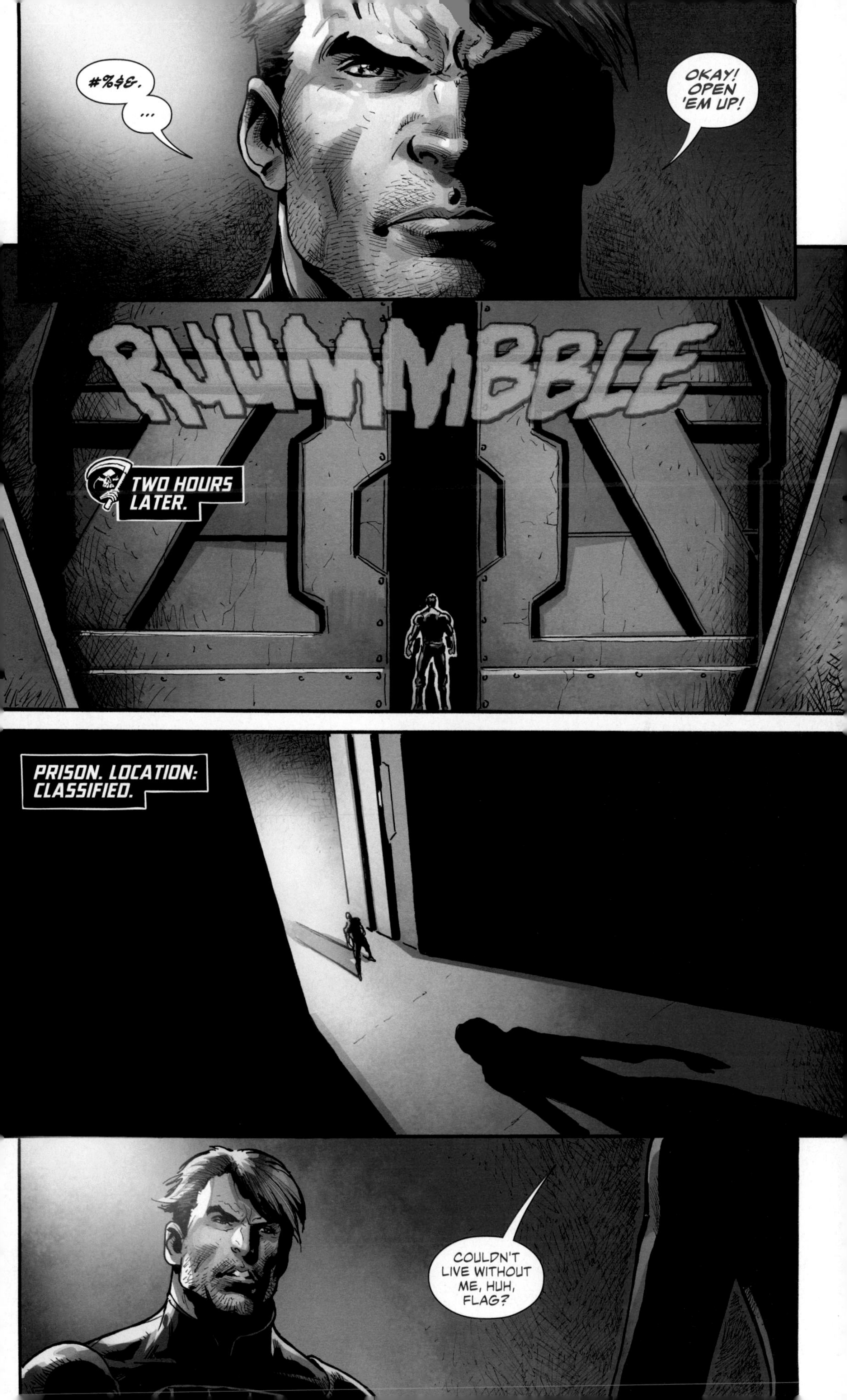
#%$&.
...
OKAY! OPEN 'EM UP!
RHUMMBBLE
TWO HOURS LATER.
PRISON. LOCATION: CLASSIFIED.
COULDN'T LIVE WITHOUT ME, HUH, FLAG?

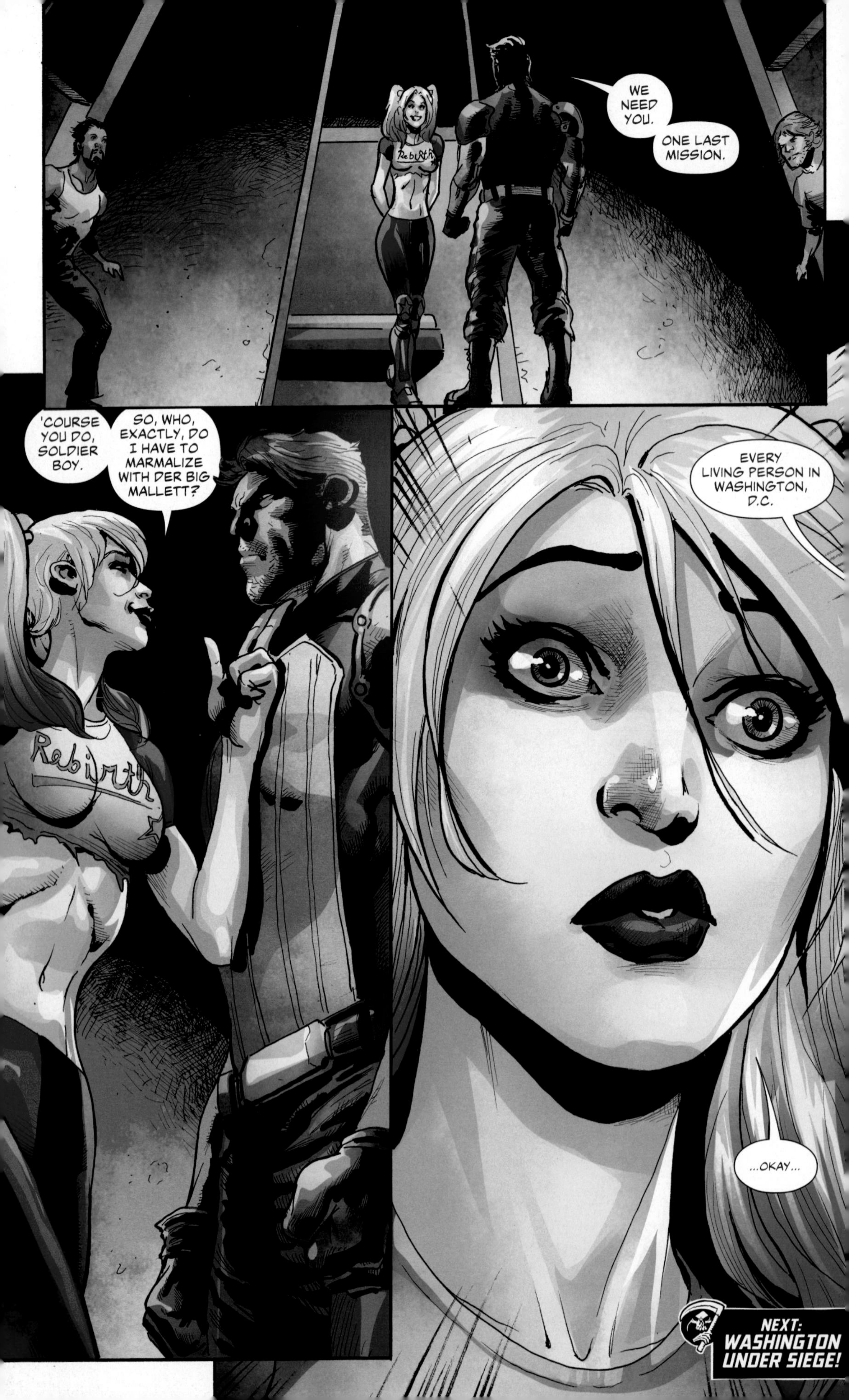
WE NEED YOU.
ONE LAST MISSION.
'COURSE YOU DO, SOLDIER BOY.
SO, WHO, EXACTLY, DO I HAVE TO MARMALIZE WITH DER BIG MALLETT?
EVERY LIVING PERSON IN WASHINGTON, D.C.
...OKAY...
NEXT: WASHINGTON UNDER SIEGE!

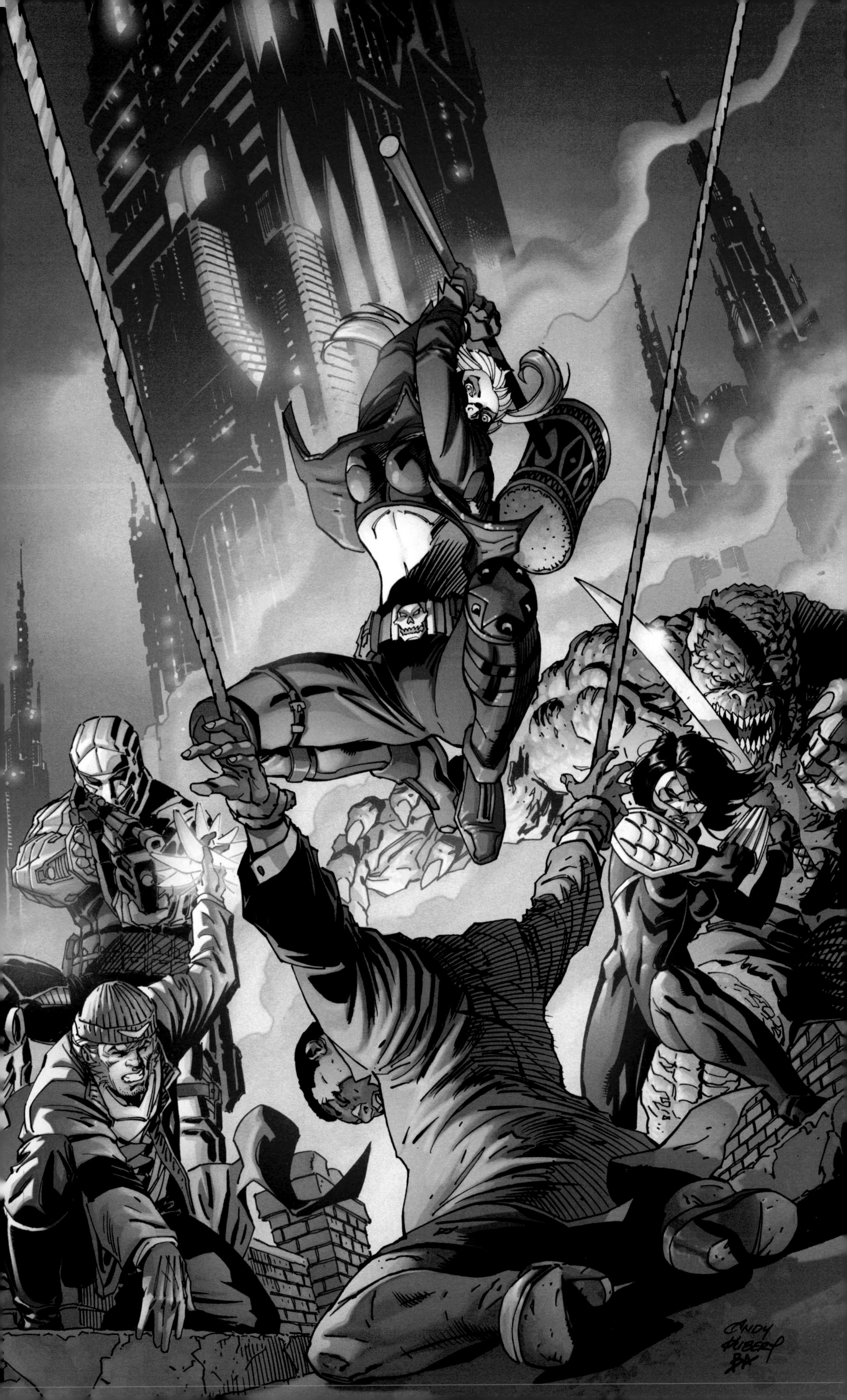
ANDY KUBERT BA

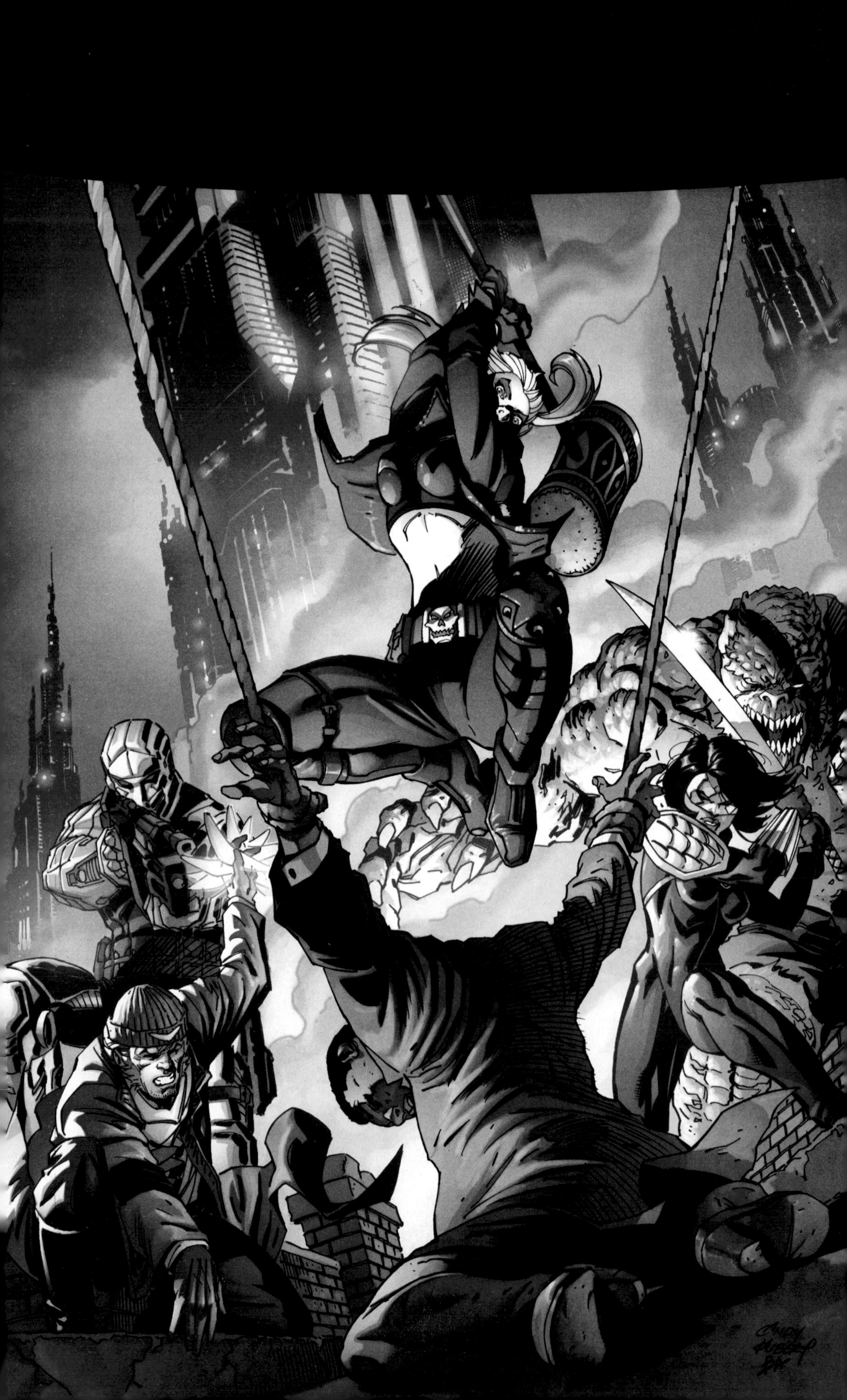

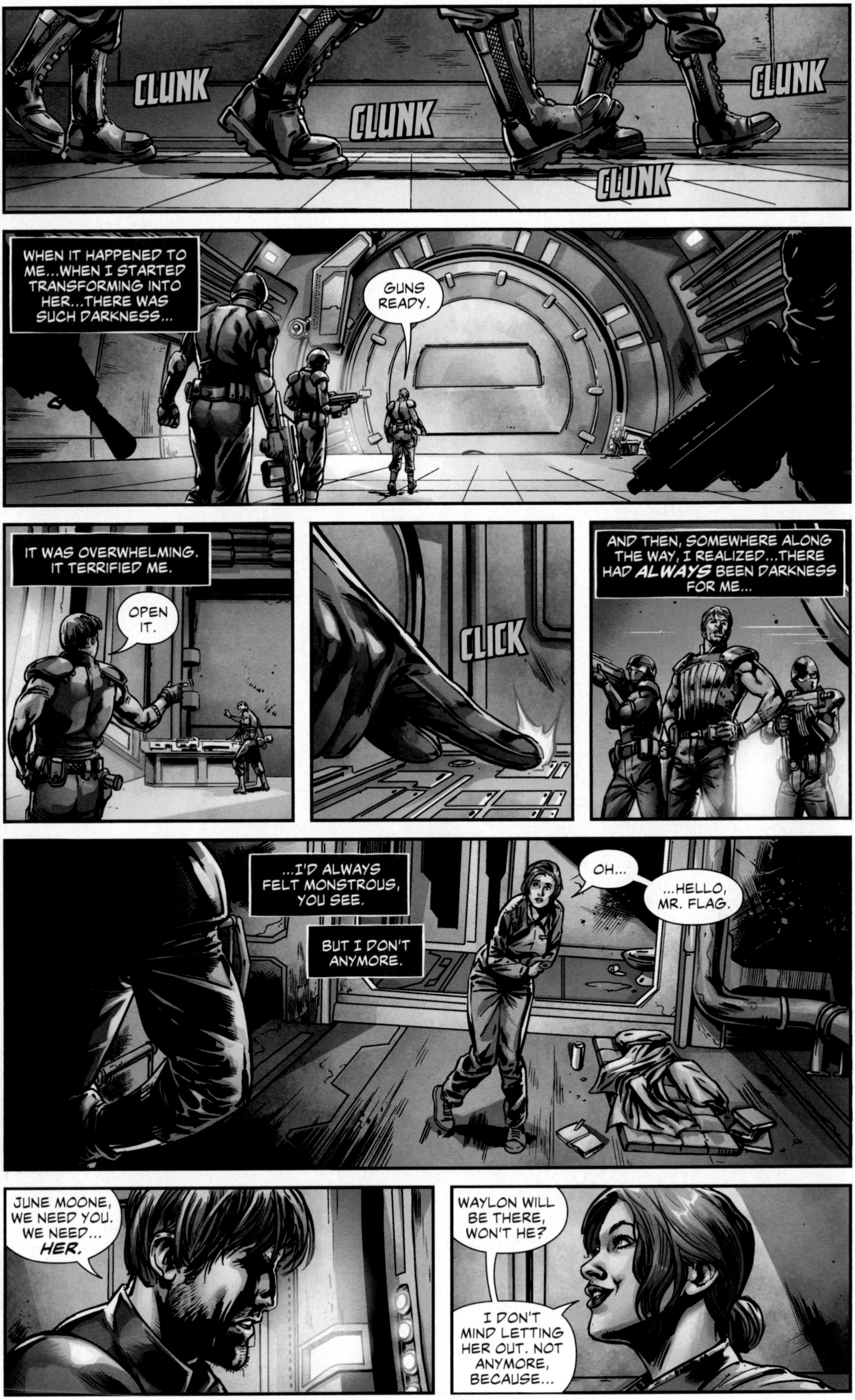
CLUNK
CLUNK
CLUNK
CLUNK
WHEN IT HAPPENED TO ME...WHEN I STARTED TRANSFORMING INTO HER...THERE WAS SUCH DARKNESS...
GUNS READY.
IT WAS OVERWHELMING. IT TERRIFIED ME.
OPEN IT.
CLICK
AND THEN, SOMEWHERE ALONG THE WAY, I REALIZED...THERE HAD ALWAYS BEEN DARKNESS FOR ME...
...I'D ALWAYS FELT MONSTROUS, YOU SEE.
BUT I DON'T ANYMORE.
OH...
...HELLO, MR. FLAG.
JUNE MOONE, WE NEED YOU. WE NEED... HER.
WAYLON WILL BE THERE, WON'T HE?
I DON'T MIND LETTING HER OUT. NOT ANYMORE, BECAUSE...

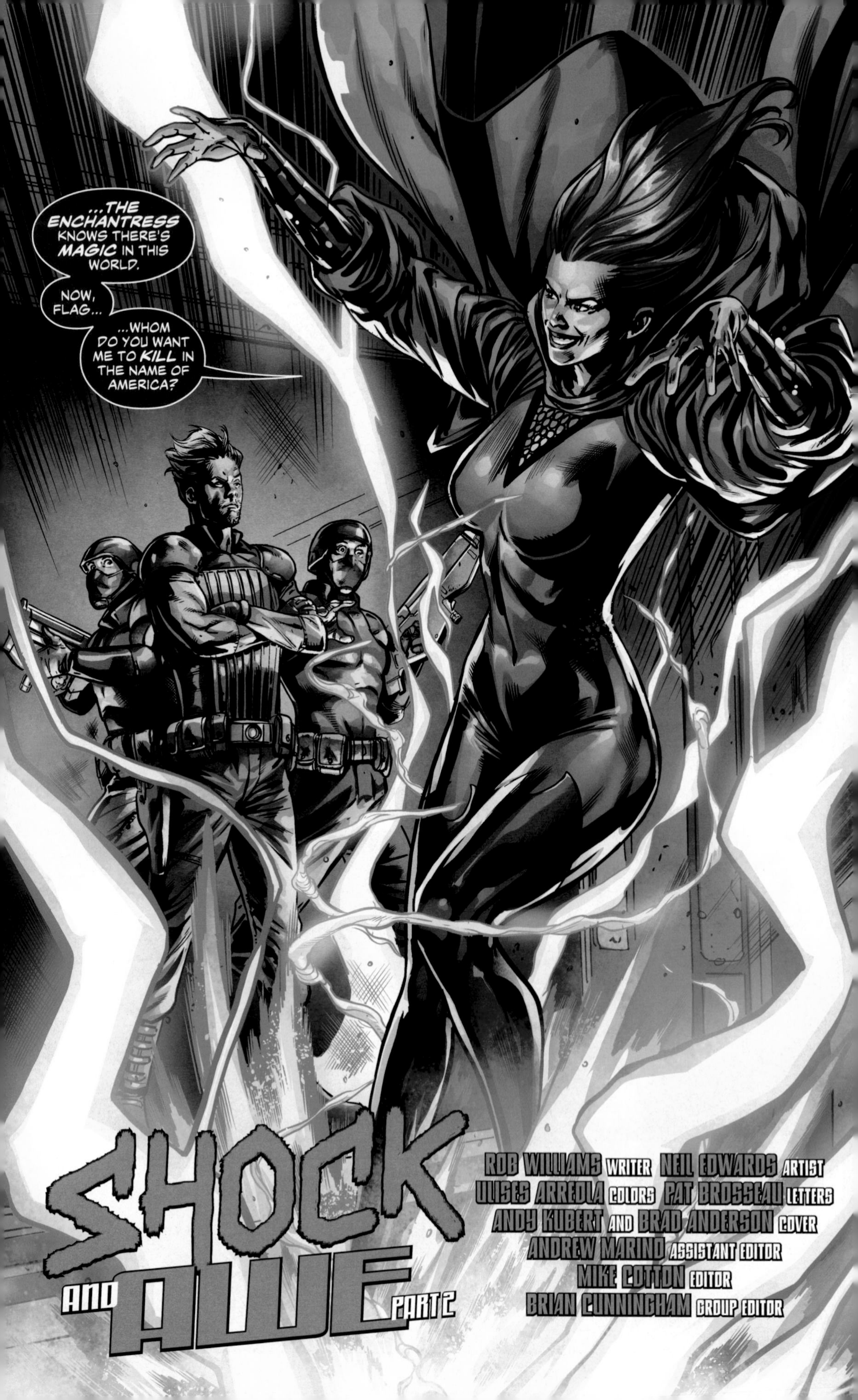
...THE ENCHANTRESS KNOWS THERE'S MAGIC IN THIS WORLD.
NOW, FLAG...
...WHOM DO YOU WANT ME TO KILL IN THE NAME OF AMERICA?
SHOCK AND AWE PART 2
ROB WILLIAMS WRITER NEIL EDWARDS ARTIST
ULISES ARREOLA COLORS PAT BROSSEAU LETTERS
ANDY KUBERT AND BRAD ANDERSON COVER
ANDREW MARINO ASSISTANT EDITOR
MIKE COTTON EDITOR
BRIAN CUNNINGHAM GROUP EDITOR

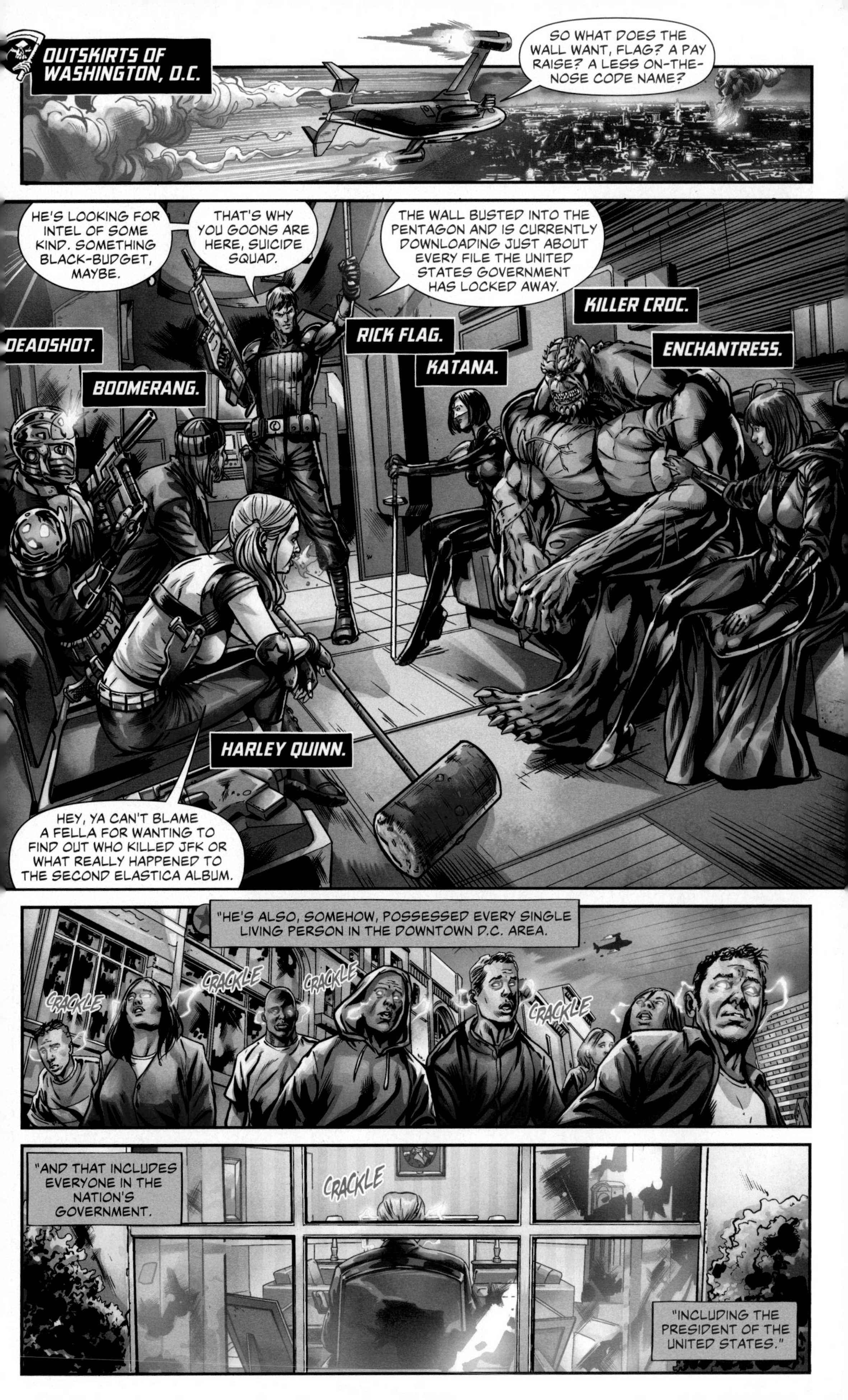
OUTSKIRTS OF WASHINGTON, D.C.
SO WHAT DOES THE WALL WANT, FLAG? A PAY RAISE? A LESS ON-THE-NOSE CODE NAME?
HE'S LOOKING FOR INTEL OF SOME KIND. SOMETHING BLACK-BUDGET, MAYBE.
THAT'S WHY YOU GOONS ARE HERE, SUICIDE SQUAD.
THE WALL BUSTED INTO THE PENTAGON AND IS CURRENTLY DOWNLOADING JUST ABOUT EVERY FILE THE UNITED STATES GOVERNMENT HAS LOCKED AWAY.
DEADSHOT.
BOOMERANG.
RICK FLAG.
KATANA.
KILLER CROC.
ENCHANTRESS.
HARLEY QUINN.
HEY, YA CAN'T BLAME A FELLA FOR WANTING TO FIND OUT WHO KILLED JFK OR WHAT REALLY HAPPENED TO THE SECOND ELASTICA ALBUM.
"HE'S ALSO, SOMEHOW, POSSESSED EVERY SINGLE LIVING PERSON IN THE DOWNTOWN D.C. AREA.
CRACKLE
CRACKLE
CRACKLE
CRACKLE
"AND THAT INCLUDES EVERYONE IN THE NATION'S GOVERNMENT.
CRACKLE
"INCLUDING THE PRESIDENT OF THE UNITED STATES."

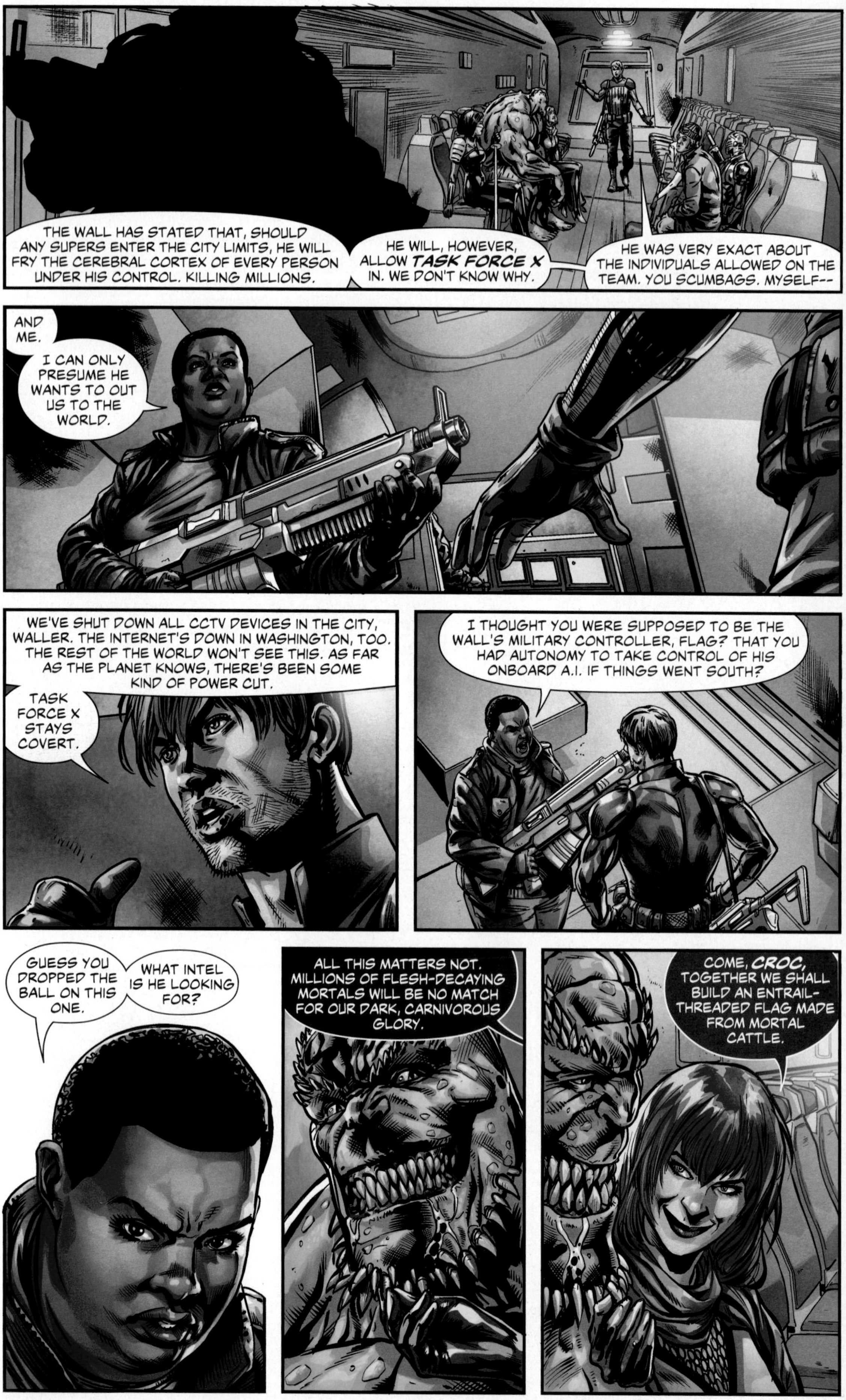
THE WALL HAS STATED THAT, SHOULD ANY SUPERS ENTER THE CITY LIMITS, HE WILL FRY THE CEREBRAL CORTEX OF EVERY PERSON UNDER HIS CONTROL. KILLING MILLIONS.
HE WILL, HOWEVER, ALLOW TASK FORCE X IN. WE DON'T KNOW WHY.
HE WAS VERY EXACT ABOUT THE INDIVIDUALS ALLOWED ON THE TEAM. YOU SCUMBAGS. MYSELF--
AND ME.
I CAN ONLY PRESUME HE WANTS TO OUT US TO THE WORLD.
WE'VE SHUT DOWN ALL CCTV DEVICES IN THE CITY, WALLER. THE INTERNET'S DOWN IN WASHINGTON, TOO. THE REST OF THE WORLD WON'T SEE THIS. AS FAR AS THE PLANET KNOWS, THERE'S BEEN SOME KIND OF POWER CUT.
TASK FORCE X STAYS COVERT.
I THOUGHT YOU WERE SUPPOSED TO BE THE WALL'S MILITARY CONTROLLER, FLAG? THAT YOU HAD AUTONOMY TO TAKE CONTROL OF HIS ONBOARD A.I. IF THINGS WENT SOUTH?
GUESS YOU DROPPED THE BALL ON THIS ONE.
WHAT INTEL IS HE LOOKING FOR?
ALL THIS MATTERS NOT. MILLIONS OF FLESH-DECAYING MORTALS WILL BE NO MATCH FOR OUR DARK, CARNIVOROUS GLORY.
COME, CROC, TOGETHER WE SHALL BUILD AN ENTRAIL-THREADED FLAG MADE FROM MORTAL CATTLE.

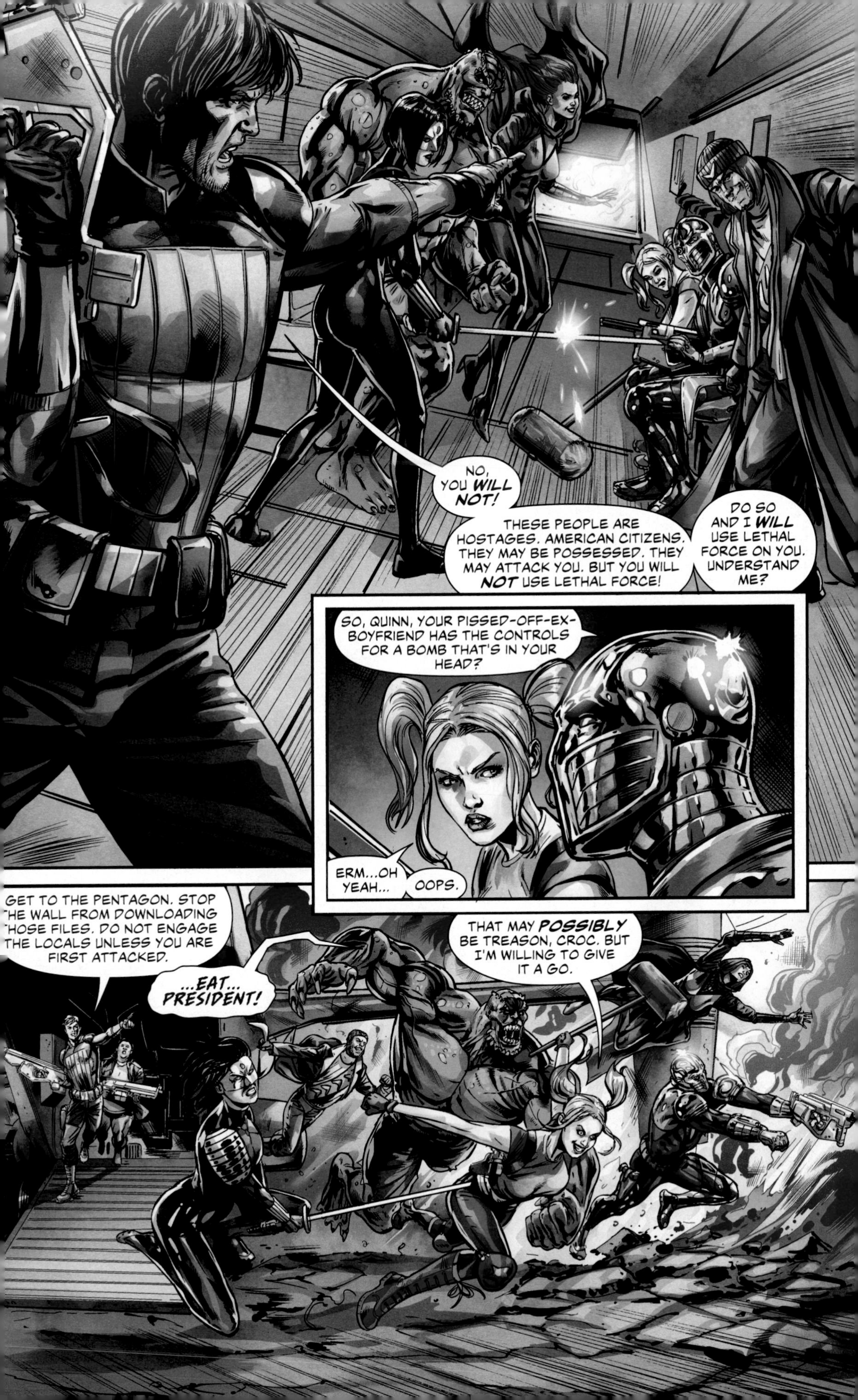
NO, YOU WILL NOT!
THESE PEOPLE ARE HOSTAGES. AMERICAN CITIZENS. THEY MAY BE POSSESSED. THEY MAY ATTACK YOU. BUT YOU WILL NOT USE LETHAL FORCE!
DO SO AND I WILL USE LETHAL FORCE ON YOU. UNDERSTAND ME?
SO, QUINN, YOUR PISSED-OFF-EX-BOYFRIEND HAS THE CONTROLS FOR A BOMB THAT'S IN YOUR HEAD?
ERM...OH YEAH...
OOPS.
GET TO THE PENTAGON. STOP THE WALL FROM DOWNLOADING THOSE FILES. DO NOT ENGAGE THE LOCALS UNLESS YOU ARE FIRST ATTACKED.
...EAT... PRESIDENT!
THAT MAY POSSIBLY BE TREASON, CROC. BUT I'M WILLING TO GIVE IT A GO.

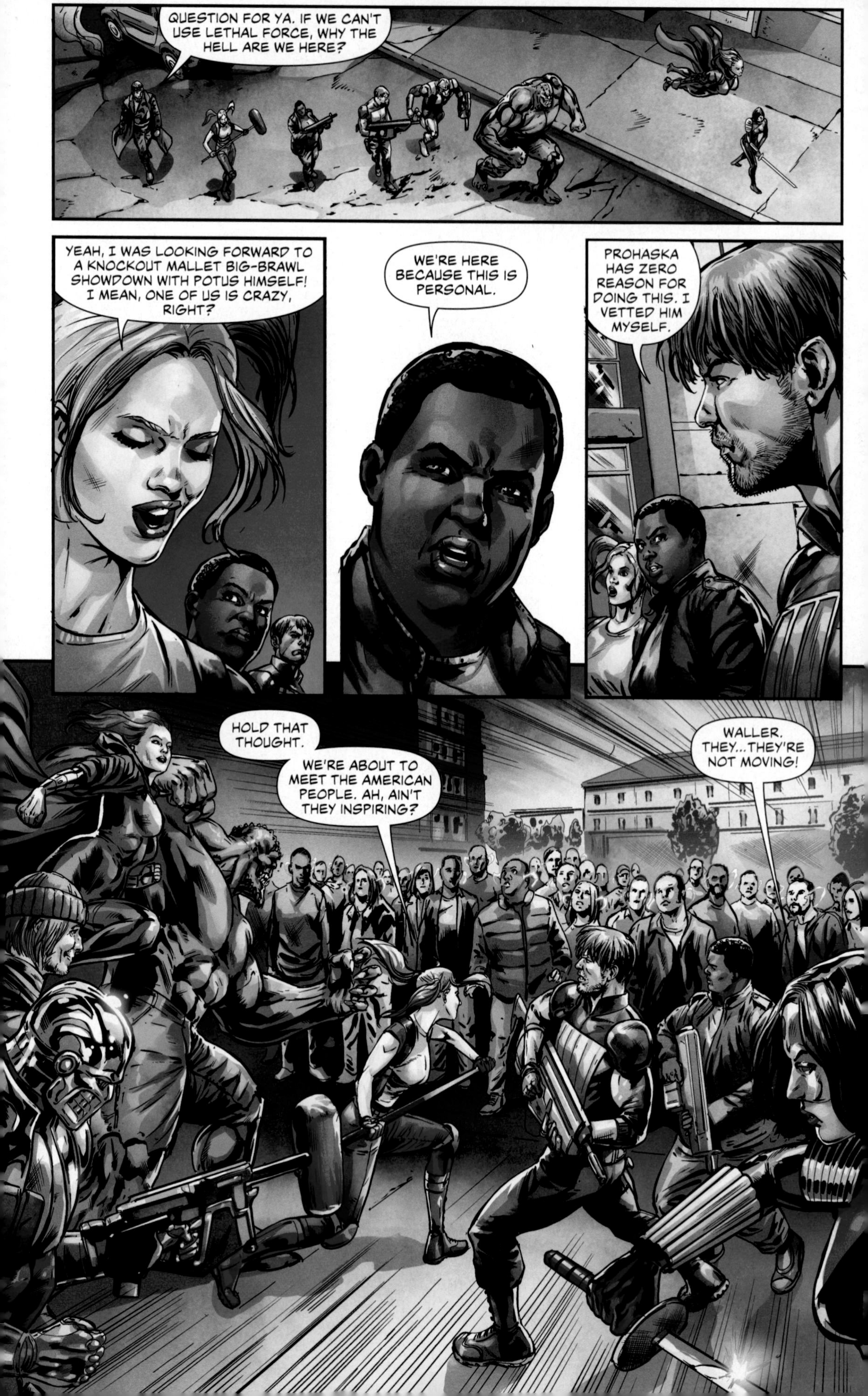
QUESTION FOR YA. IF WE CAN'T USE LETHAL FORCE, WHY THE HELL ARE WE HERE?
YEAH, I WAS LOOKING FORWARD TO A KNOCKOUT MALLET BIG-BRAWL SHOWDOWN WITH POTUS HIMSELF! I MEAN, ONE OF US IS CRAZY, RIGHT?
WE'RE HERE BECAUSE THIS IS PERSONAL.
PROHASKA HAS ZERO REASON FOR DOING THIS. I VETTED HIM MYSELF.
HOLD THAT THOUGHT.
WE'RE ABOUT TO MEET THE AMERICAN PEOPLE. AH, AIN'T THEY INSPIRING?
WALLER. THEY...THEY'RE NOT MOVING!

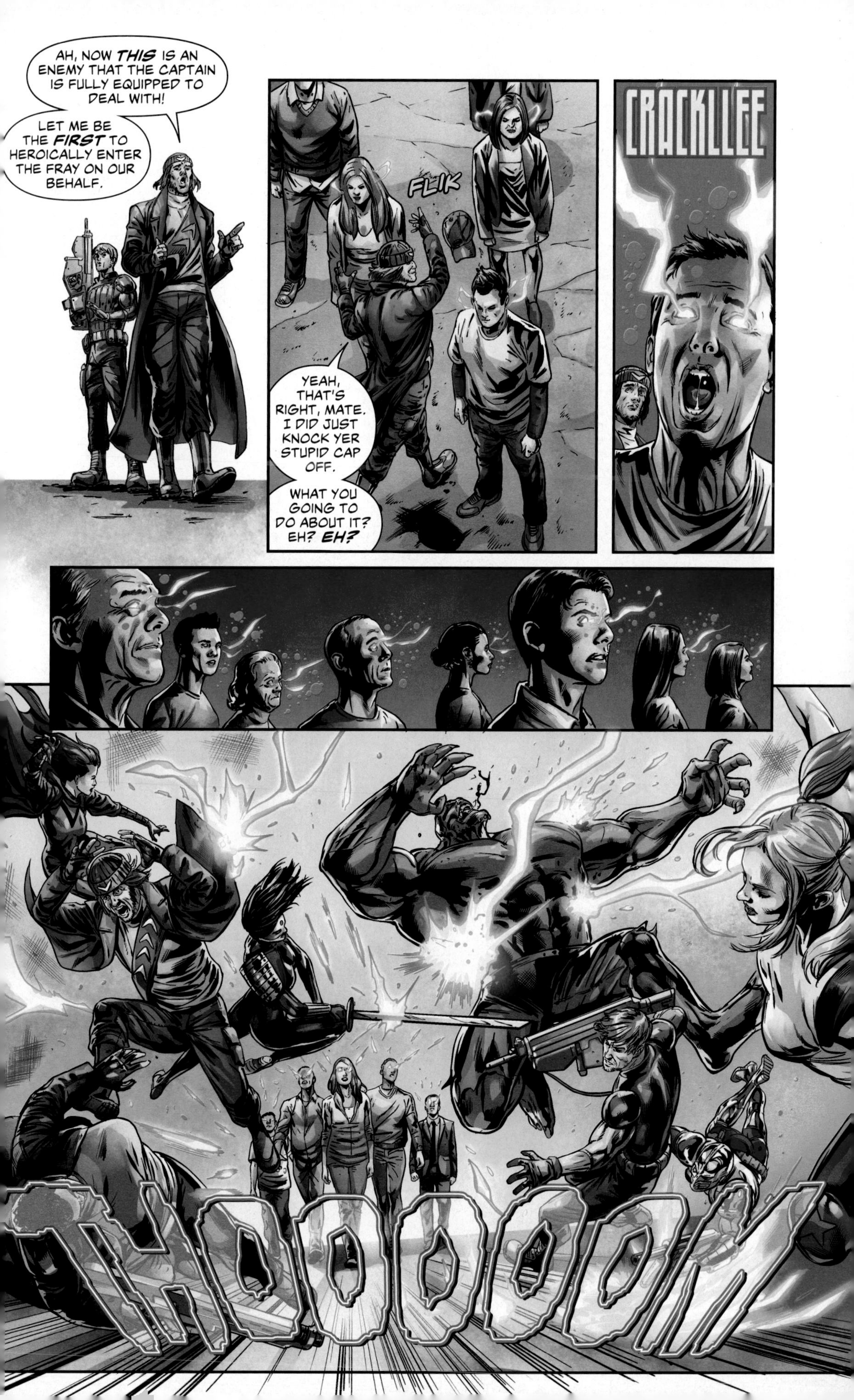
AH, NOW THIS IS AN ENEMY THAT THE CAPTAIN IS FULLY EQUIPPED TO DEAL WITH!
LET ME BE THE FIRST TO HEROICALLY ENTER THE FRAY ON OUR BEHALF.
FLIK
YEAH, THAT'S RIGHT, MATE. I DID JUST KNOCK YER STUPID CAP OFF.
WHAT YOU GOING TO DO ABOUT IT? EH? EH?
CRACKLLEE
THOOOOM

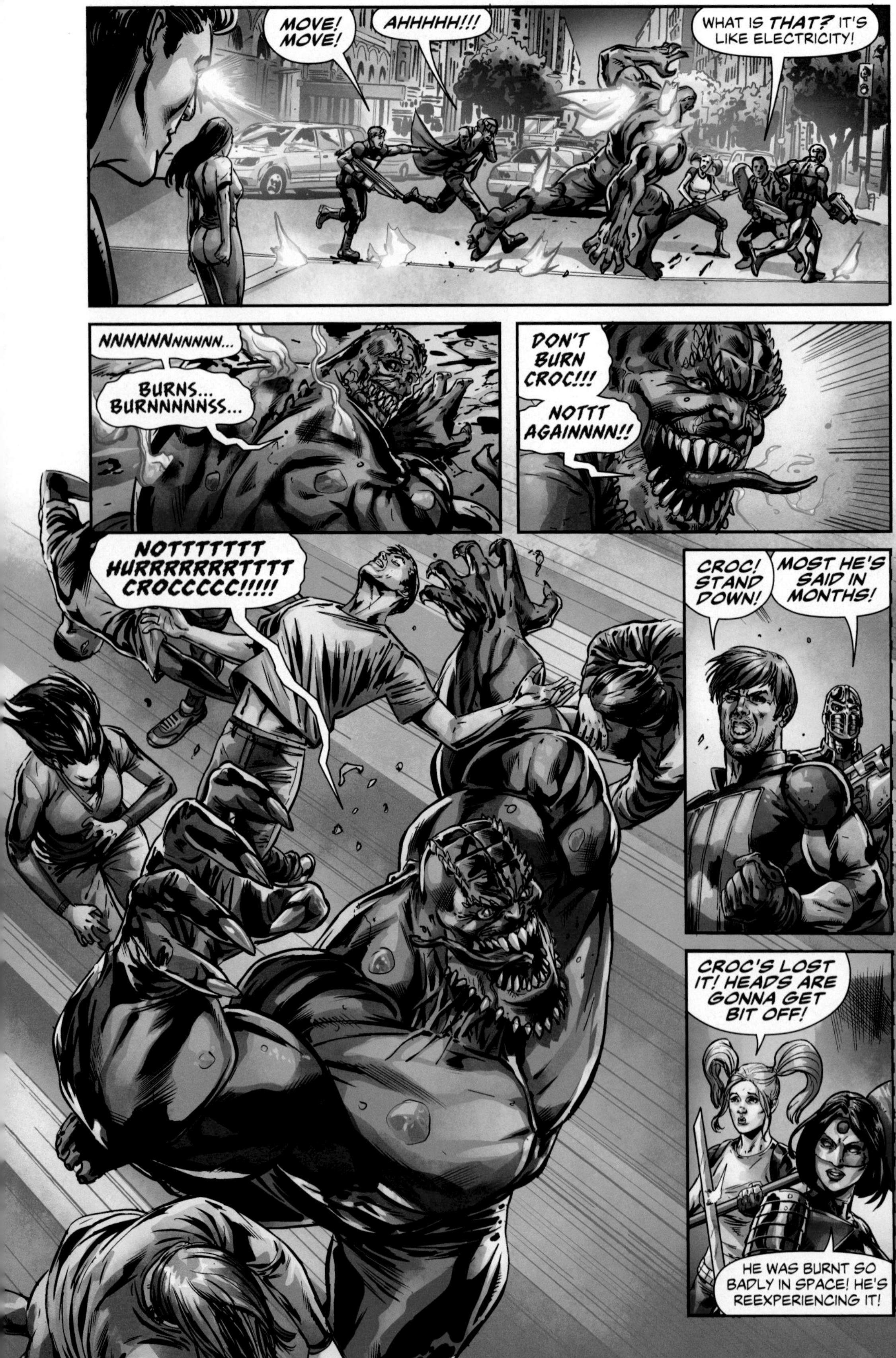

MOVE! MOVE!
AHHHHH!!!
WHAT IS THAT? IT'S LIKE ELECTRICITY!
NNNNNNnnnnn...
BURNS... BURNNNNNSS...
DON'T BURN CROC!!!
NOTTT AGAINNNN!!
NOTTTTTTT HURRRRRRRTTTT CROCCCCC!!!!!
CROC! STAND DOWN!
MOST HE'S SAID IN MONTHS!
CROC'S LOST IT! HEADS ARE GONNA GET BIT OFF!
HE WAS BURNT SO BADLY IN SPACE! HE'S REEXPERIENCING IT!

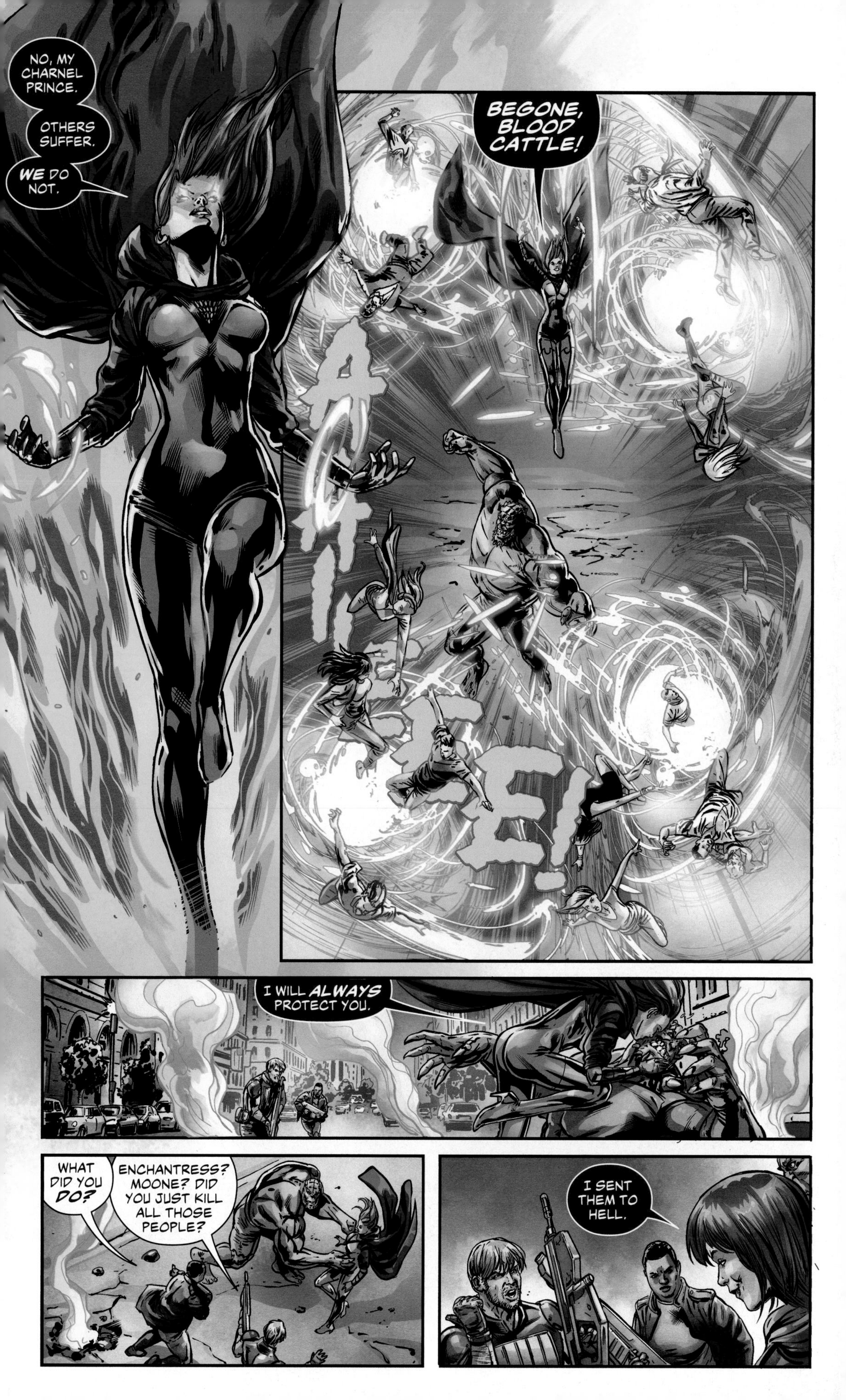
NO, MY CHARNEL PRINCE.
OTHERS SUFFER.
WE DO NOT.
BEGONE, BLOOD CATTLE!
I WILL ALWAYS PROTECT YOU.
WHAT DID YOU DO?
ENCHANTRESS? MOONE? DID YOU JUST KILL ALL THOSE PEOPLE?
I SENT THEM TO HELL.

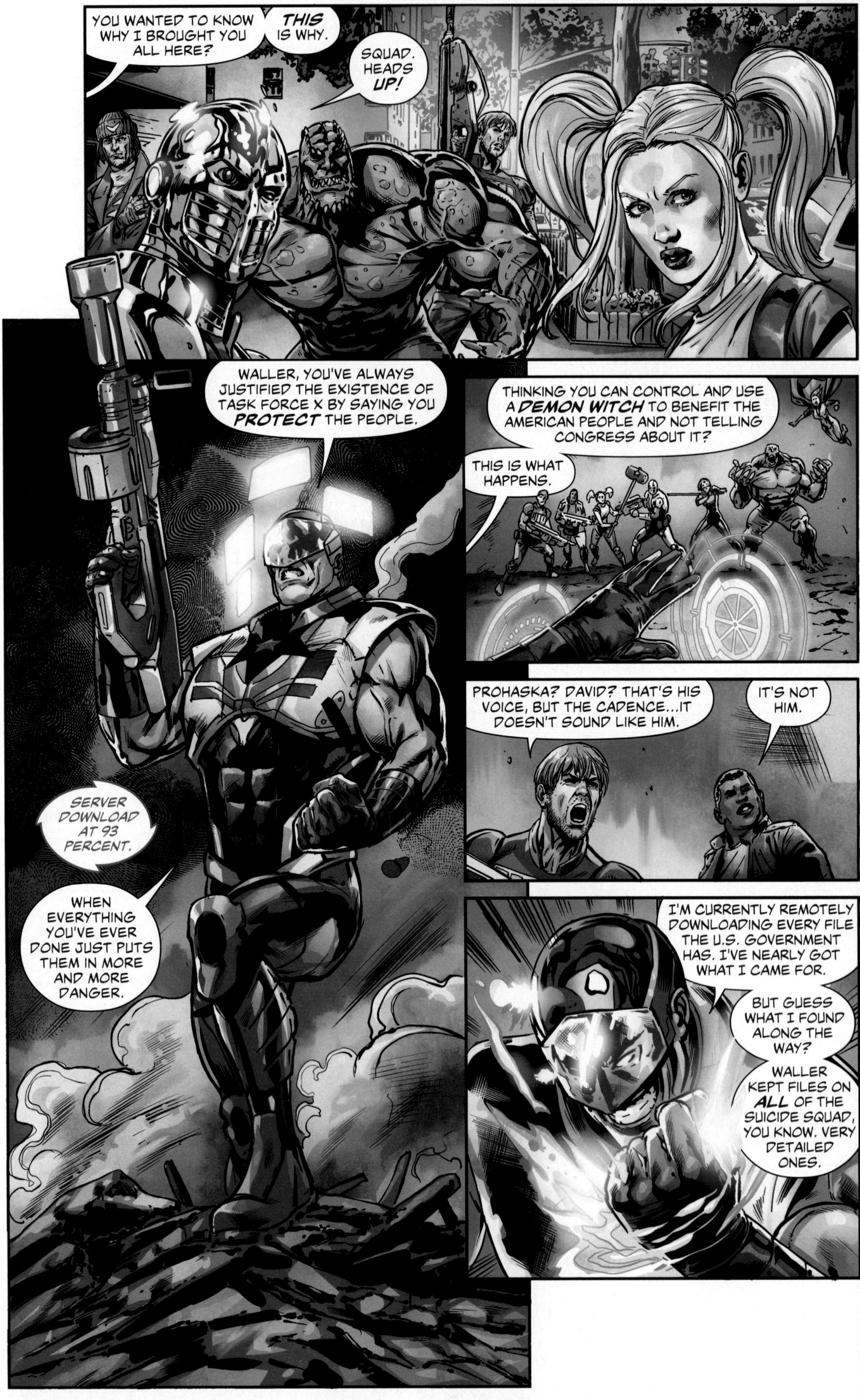
YOU WANTED TO KNOW WHY I BROUGHT YOU ALL HERE?
THIS IS WHY.
SQUAD. HEADS UP!
WALLER, YOU'VE ALWAYS JUSTIFIED THE EXISTENCE OF TASK FORCE X BY SAYING YOU PROTECT THE PEOPLE.
THINKING YOU CAN CONTROL AND USE A DEMON WITCH TO BENEFIT THE AMERICAN PEOPLE AND NOT TELLING CONGRESS ABOUT IT?
THIS IS WHAT HAPPENS.
SERVER DOWNLOAD AT 93 PERCENT.
WHEN EVERYTHING YOU'VE EVER DONE JUST PUTS THEM IN MORE AND MORE DANGER.
PROHASKA? DAVID? THAT'S HIS VOICE, BUT THE CADENCE...IT DOESN'T SOUND LIKE HIM.
IT'S NOT HIM.
I'M CURRENTLY REMOTELY DOWNLOADING EVERY FILE THE U.S. GOVERNMENT HAS. I'VE NEARLY GOT WHAT I CAME FOR.
BUT GUESS WHAT I FOUND ALONG THE WAY?
WALLER KEPT FILES ON ALL OF THE SUICIDE SQUAD, YOU KNOW. VERY DETAILED ONES.

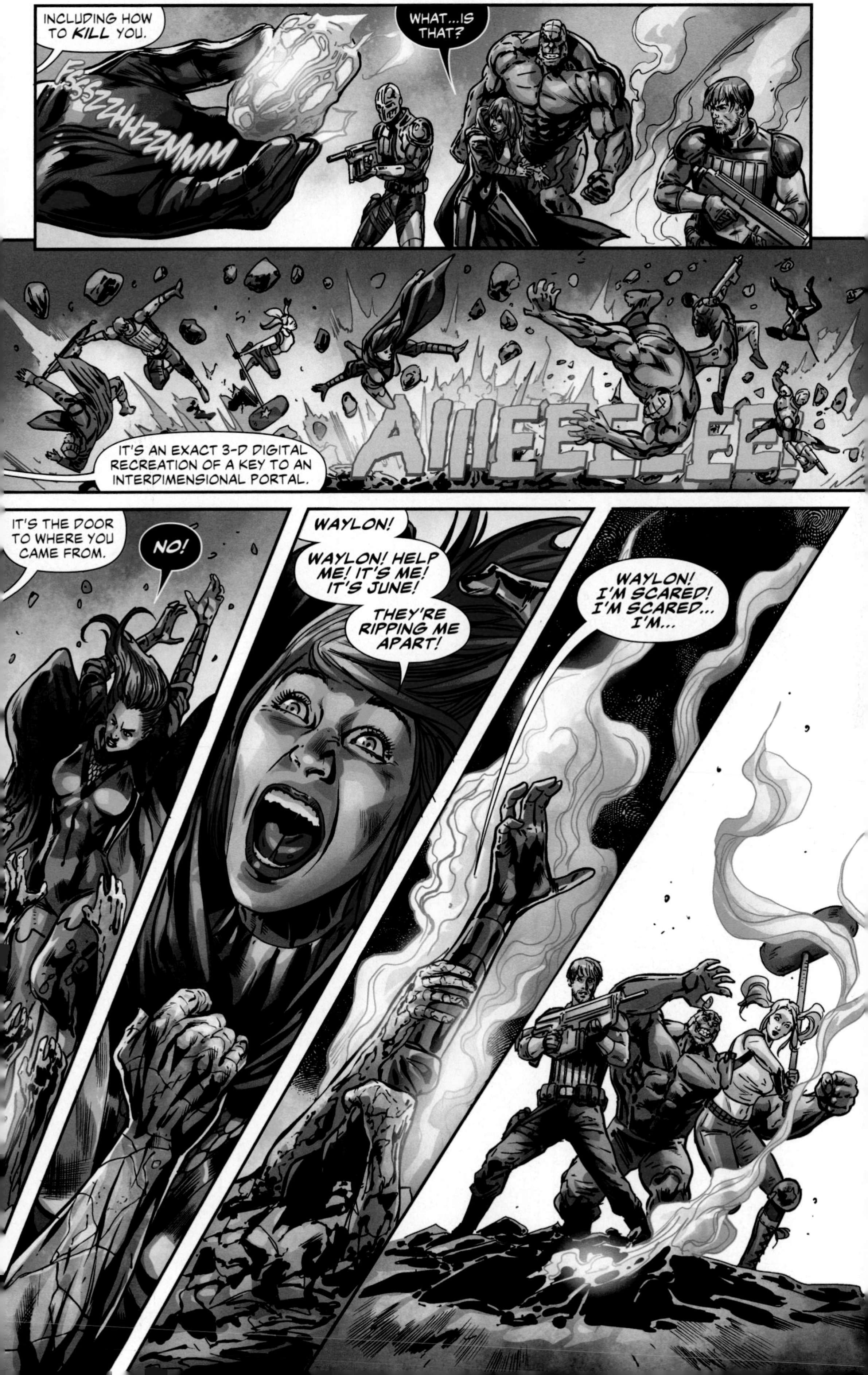

INCLUDING HOW TO KILL YOU.
FSSSZZHHZZMMMM
WHAT...IS THAT?
IT'S AN EXACT 3-D DIGITAL RECREATION OF A KEY TO AN INTERDIMENSIONAL PORTAL.
AIIIEEEEEE!
IT'S THE DOOR TO WHERE YOU CAME FROM.
NO!
WAYLON!
WAYLON! HELP ME! IT'S ME! IT'S JUNE!
THEY'RE RIPPING ME APART!
WAYLON! I'M SCARED! I'M SCARED... I'M...

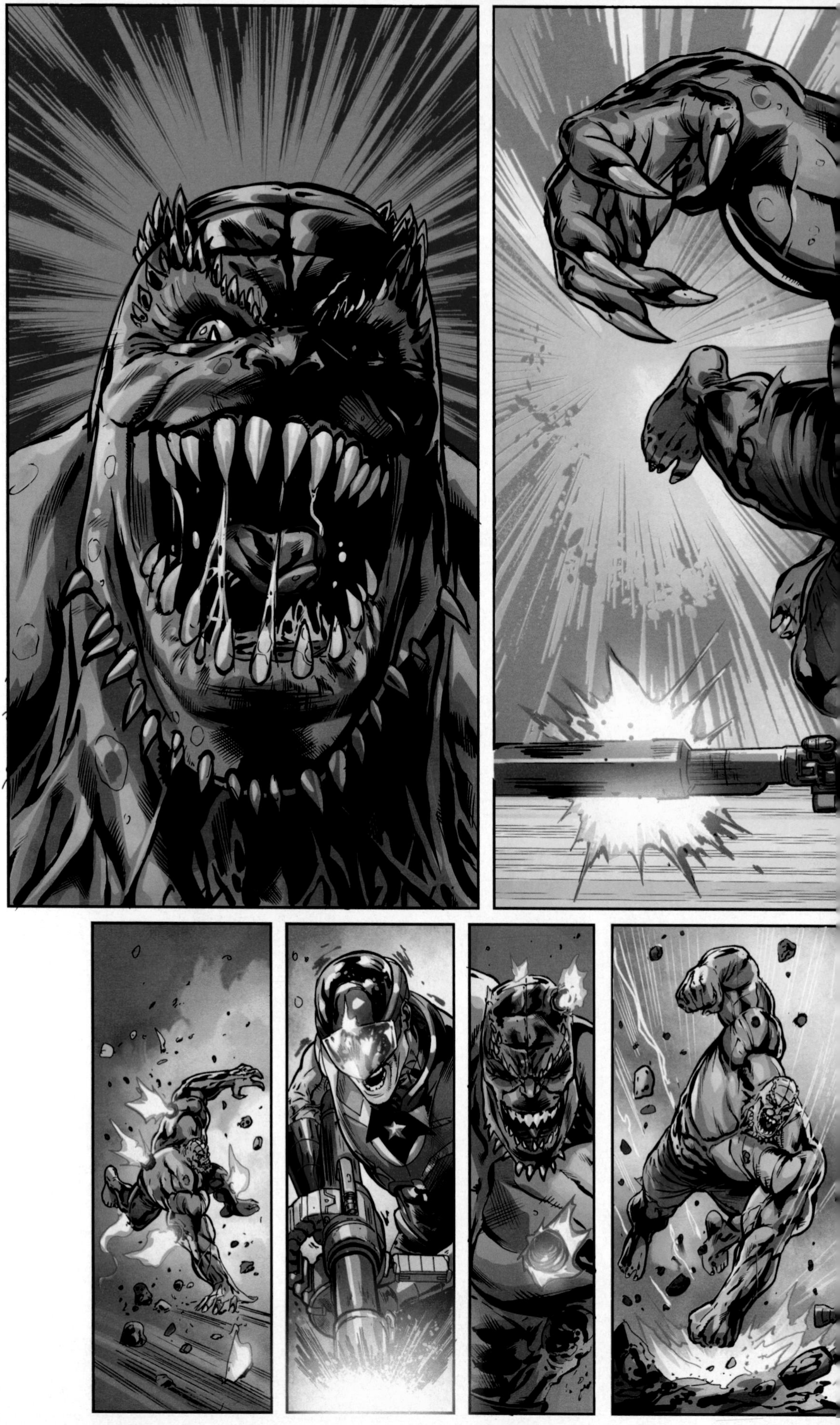

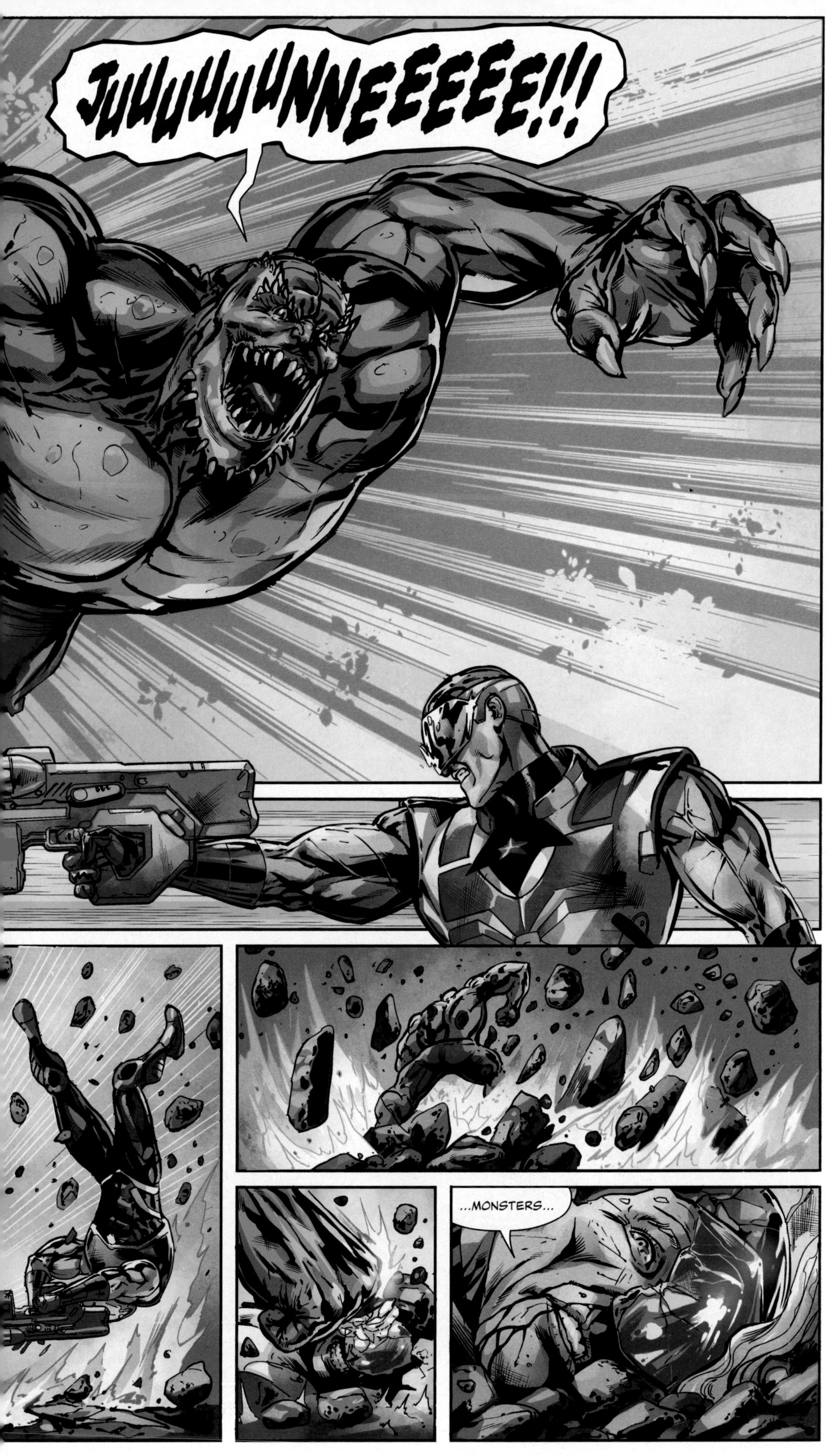
JUUUUUUUNNEEEEEE!!!
...MONSTERS...

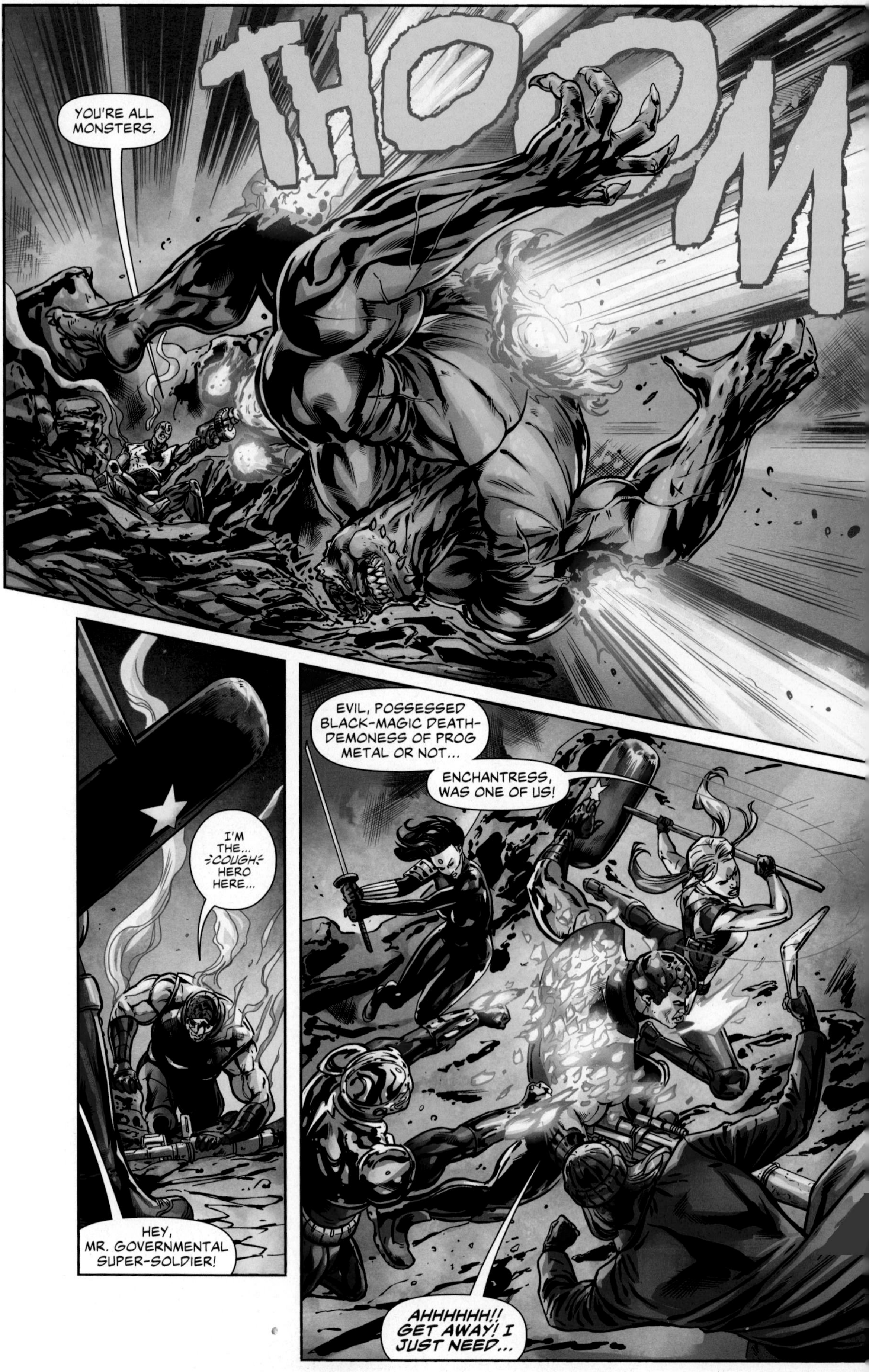
THOOM
YOU'RE ALL MONSTERS.
I'M THE... *COUGH* HERO HERE...
HEY, MR. GOVERNMENTAL SUPER-SOLDIER!
EVIL, POSSESSED BLACK-MAGIC DEATH-DEMONESS OF PROG METAL OR NOT...
ENCHANTRESS, WAS ONE OF US!
AHHHHHH!! GET AWAY! I JUST NEED...

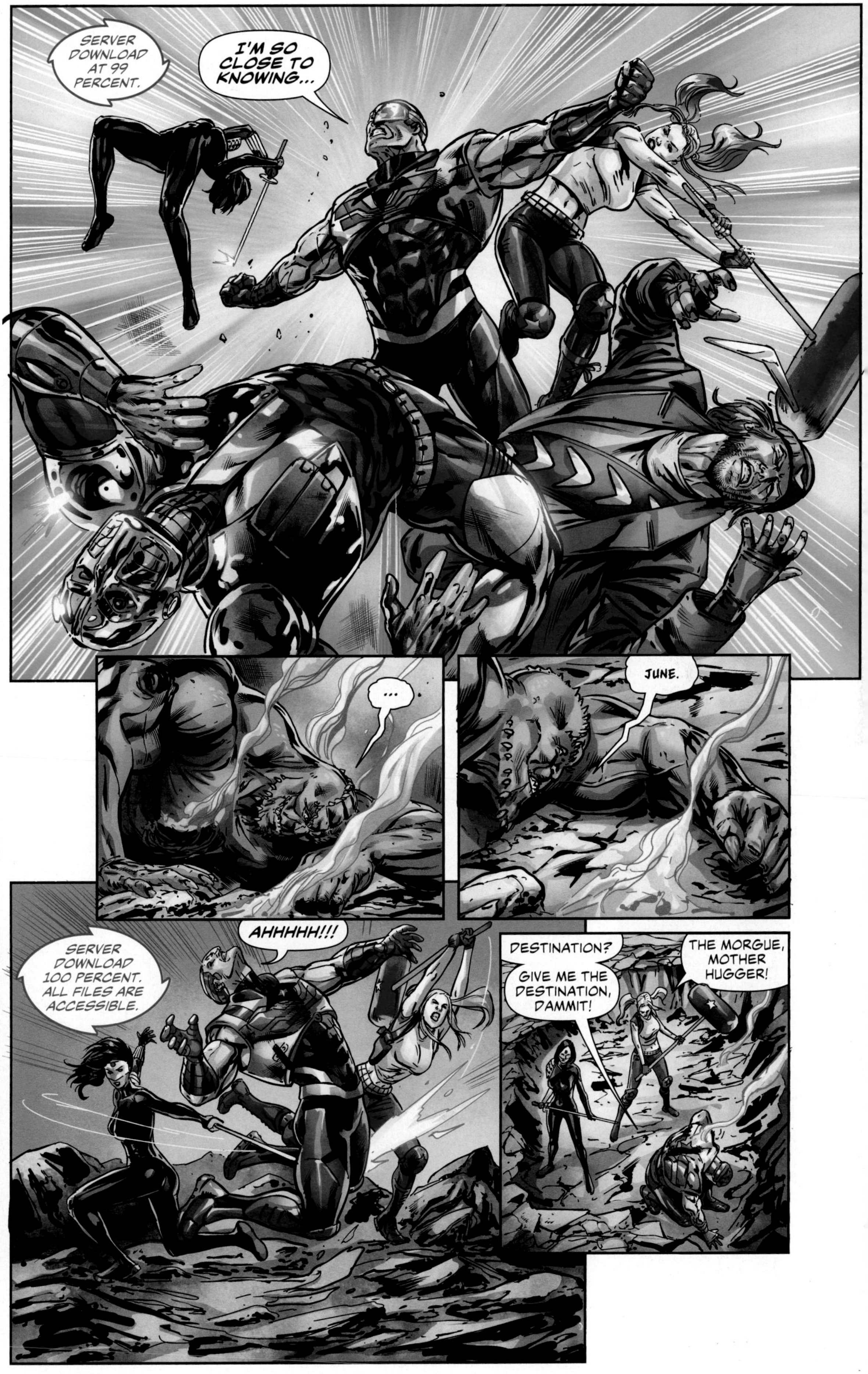
SERVER DOWNLOAD AT 99 PERCENT.
I'M SO CLOSE TO KNOWING...
...
JUNE.
SERVER DOWNLOAD 100 PERCENT. ALL FILES ARE ACCESSIBLE.
AHHHHH!!!
DESTINATION?
GIVE ME THE DESTINATION, DAMMIT!
THE MORGUE, MOTHER HUGGER!

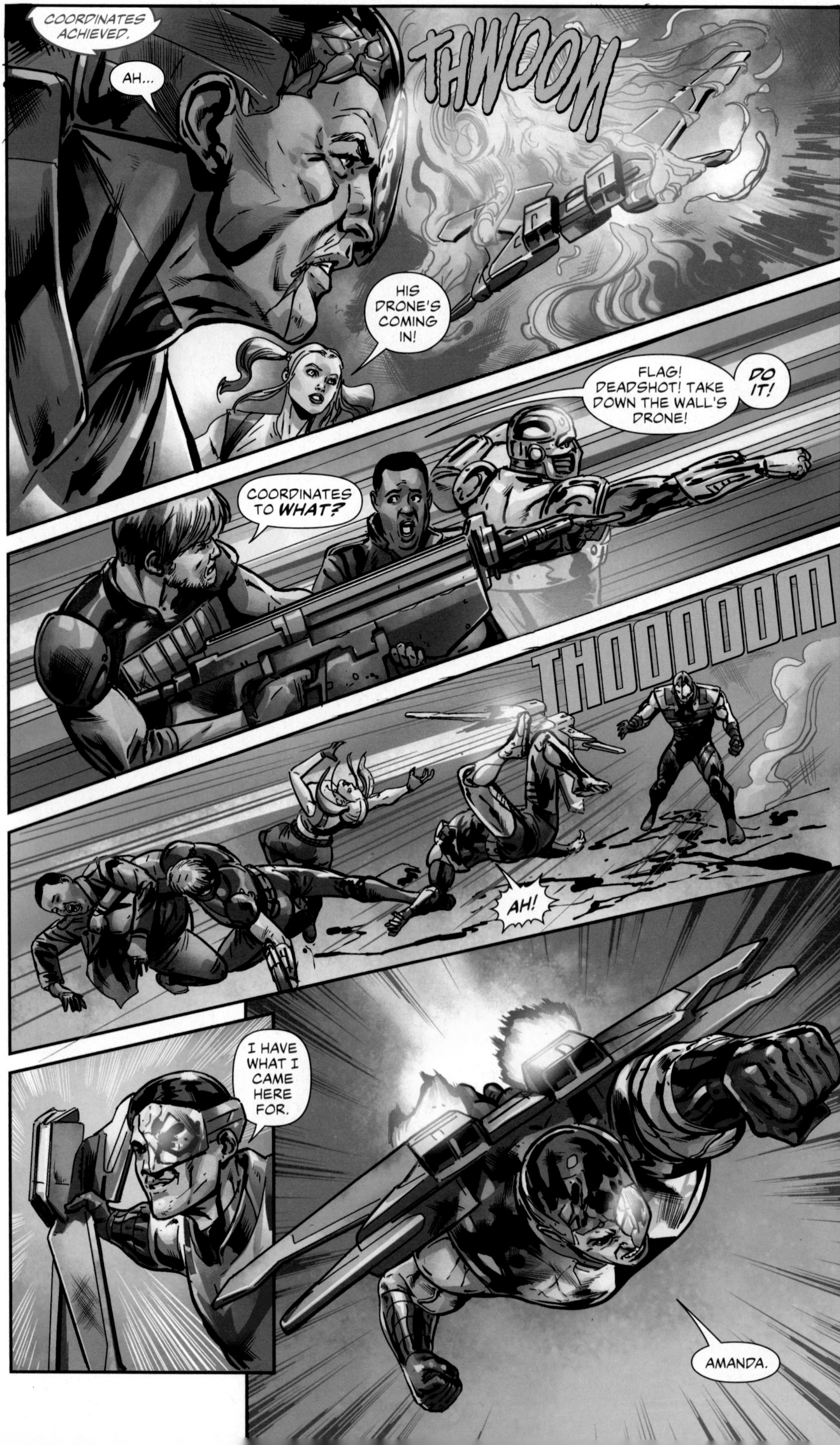
COORDINATES ACHIEVED.
AH...
THWOOM
HIS DRONE'S COMING IN!
FLAG! DEADSHOT! TAKE DOWN THE WALL'S DRONE!
DO IT!
COORDINATES TO WHAT?
THOOOOOM
AH!
I HAVE WHAT I CAME HERE FOR.
AMANDA.

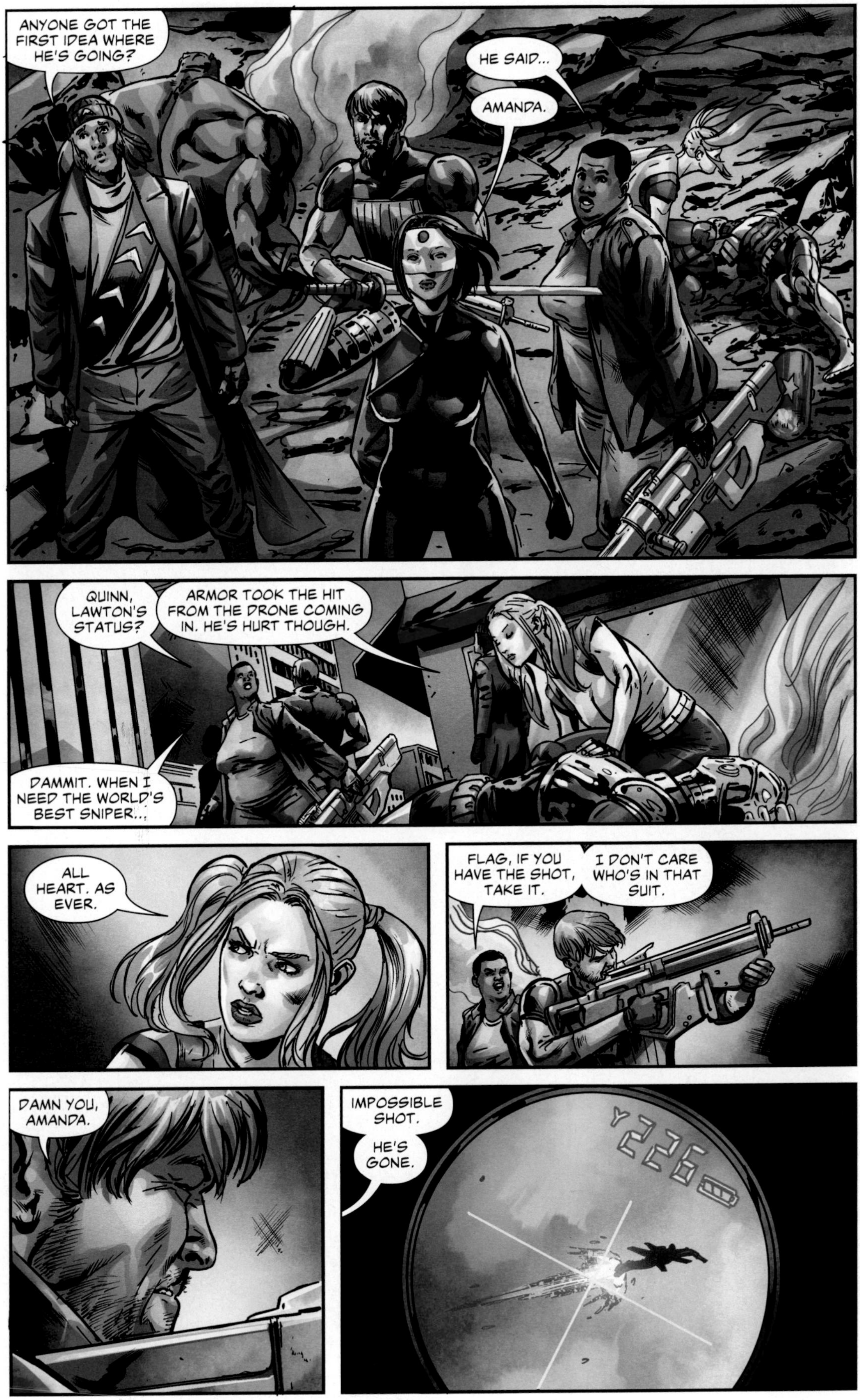
ANYONE GOT THE FIRST IDEA WHERE HE'S GOING?
HE SAID...
AMANDA.
QUINN, LAWTON'S STATUS?
ARMOR TOOK THE HIT FROM THE DRONE COMING IN. HE'S HURT THOUGH.
DAMMIT. WHEN I NEED THE WORLD'S BEST SNIPER...
ALL HEART. AS EVER.
FLAG, IF YOU HAVE THE SHOT, TAKE IT.
I DON'T CARE WHO'S IN THAT SUIT.
DAMN YOU, AMANDA.
IMPOSSIBLE SHOT.
HE'S GONE.
Y226

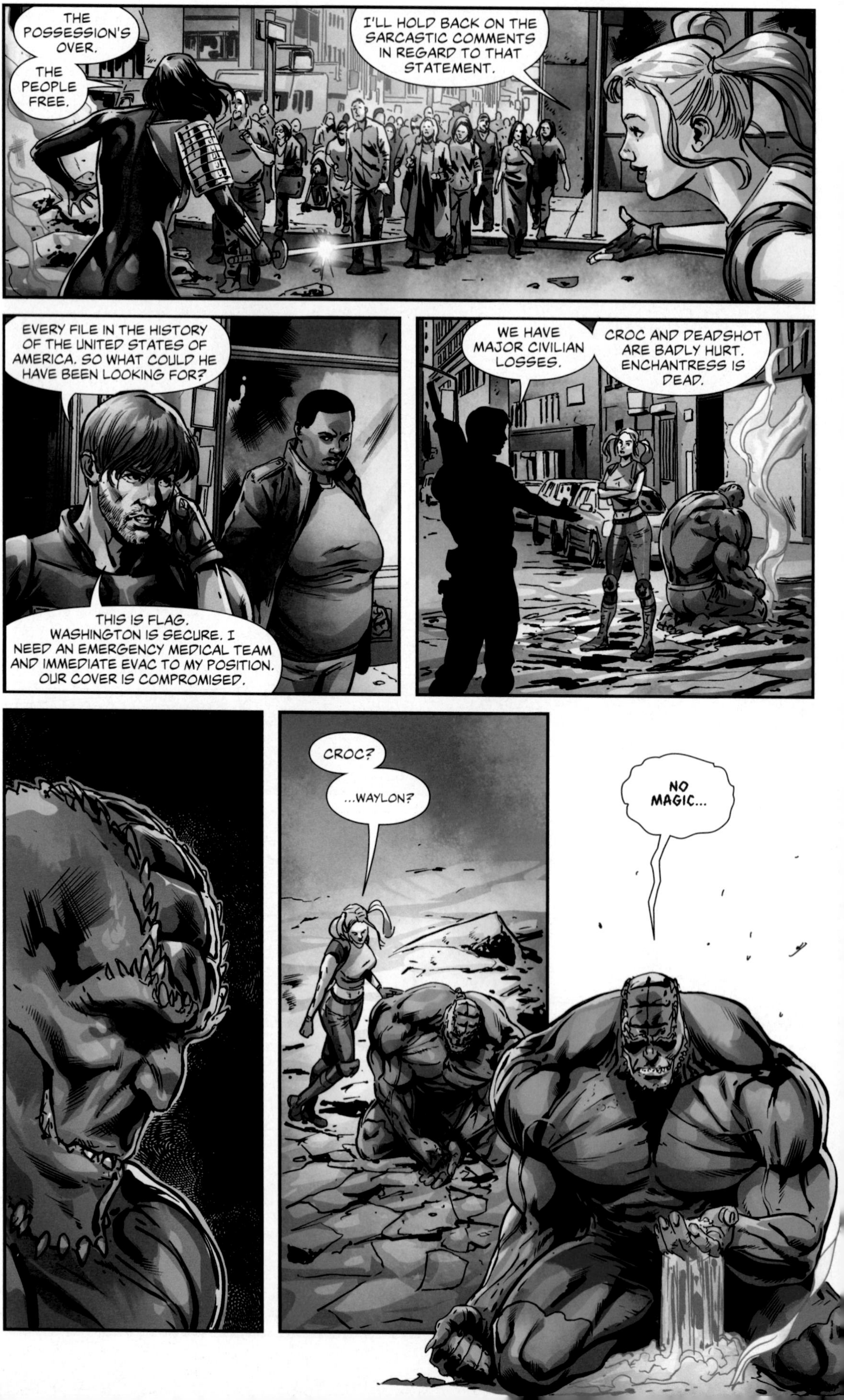
THE POSSESSION'S OVER.
THE PEOPLE FREE.
I'LL HOLD BACK ON THE SARCASTIC COMMENTS IN REGARD TO THAT STATEMENT.
EVERY FILE IN THE HISTORY OF THE UNITED STATES OF AMERICA. SO WHAT COULD HE HAVE BEEN LOOKING FOR?
THIS IS FLAG. WASHINGTON IS SECURE. I NEED AN EMERGENCY MEDICAL TEAM AND IMMEDIATE EVAC TO MY POSITION. OUR COVER IS COMPROMISED.
WE HAVE MAJOR CIVILIAN LOSSES.
CROC AND DEADSHOT ARE BADLY HURT. ENCHANTRESS IS DEAD.
CROC?
...WAYLON?
NO MAGIC...

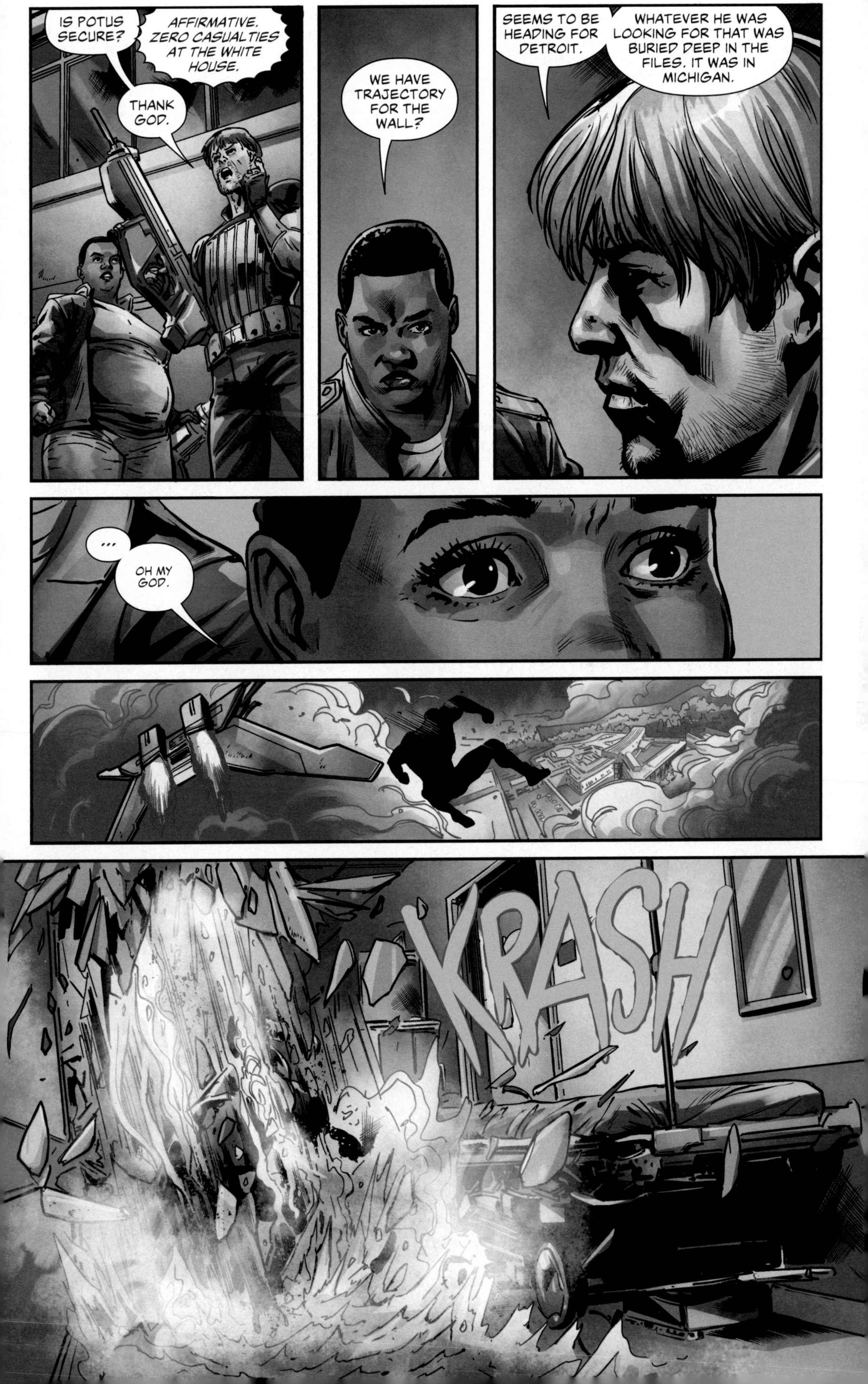
IS POTUS SECURE?
AFFIRMATIVE. ZERO CASUALTIES AT THE WHITE HOUSE.
THANK GOD.
WE HAVE TRAJECTORY FOR THE WALL?
SEEMS TO BE HEADING FOR DETROIT.
WHATEVER HE WAS LOOKING FOR THAT WAS BURIED DEEP IN THE FILES. IT WAS IN MICHIGAN.
...
OH MY GOD.
KRASH

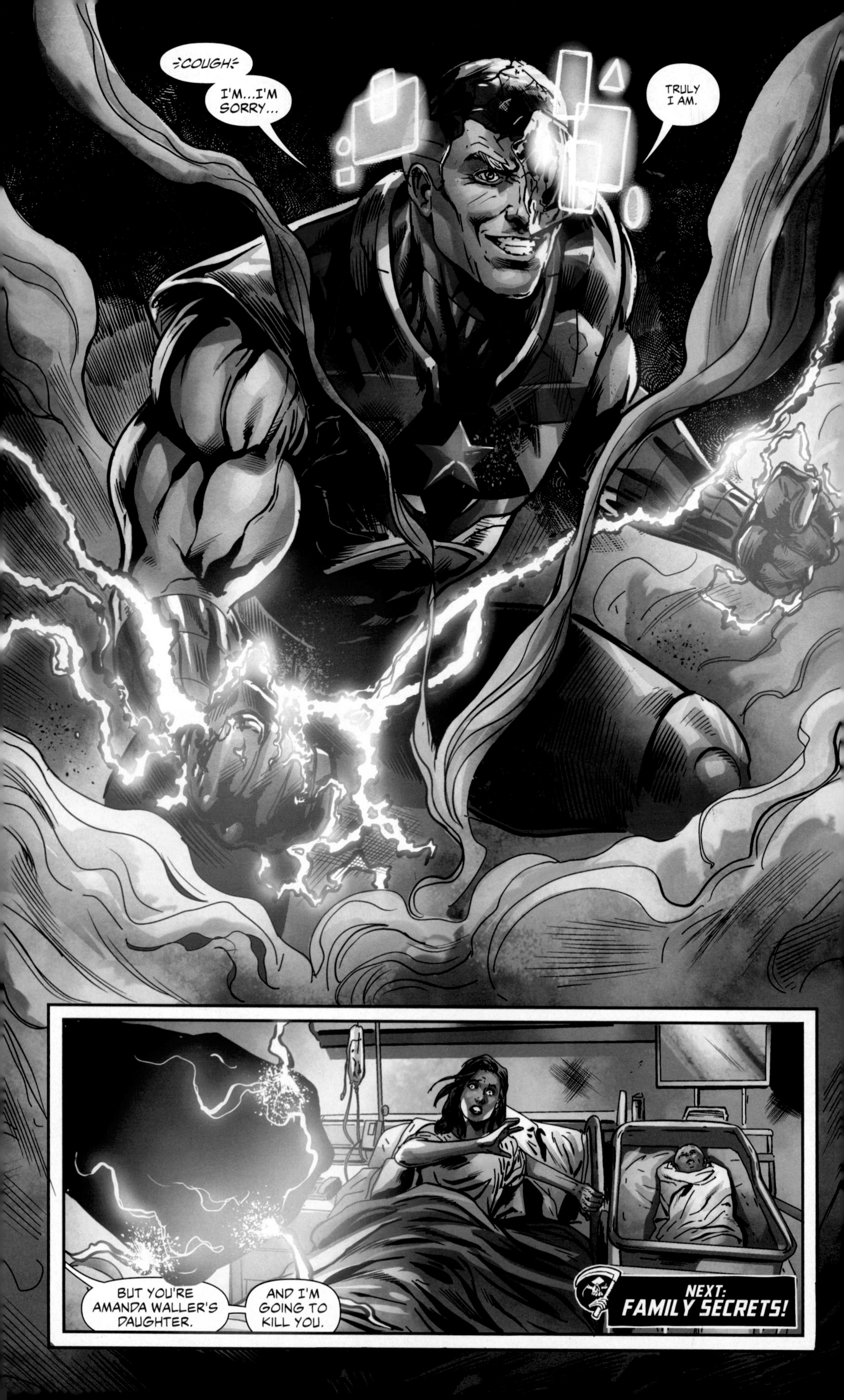
COUGH
I'M...I'M SORRY...
TRULY I AM.
BUT YOU'RE AMANDA WALLER'S DAUGHTER.
AND I'M GOING TO KILL YOU.
NEXT: FAMILY SECRETS!

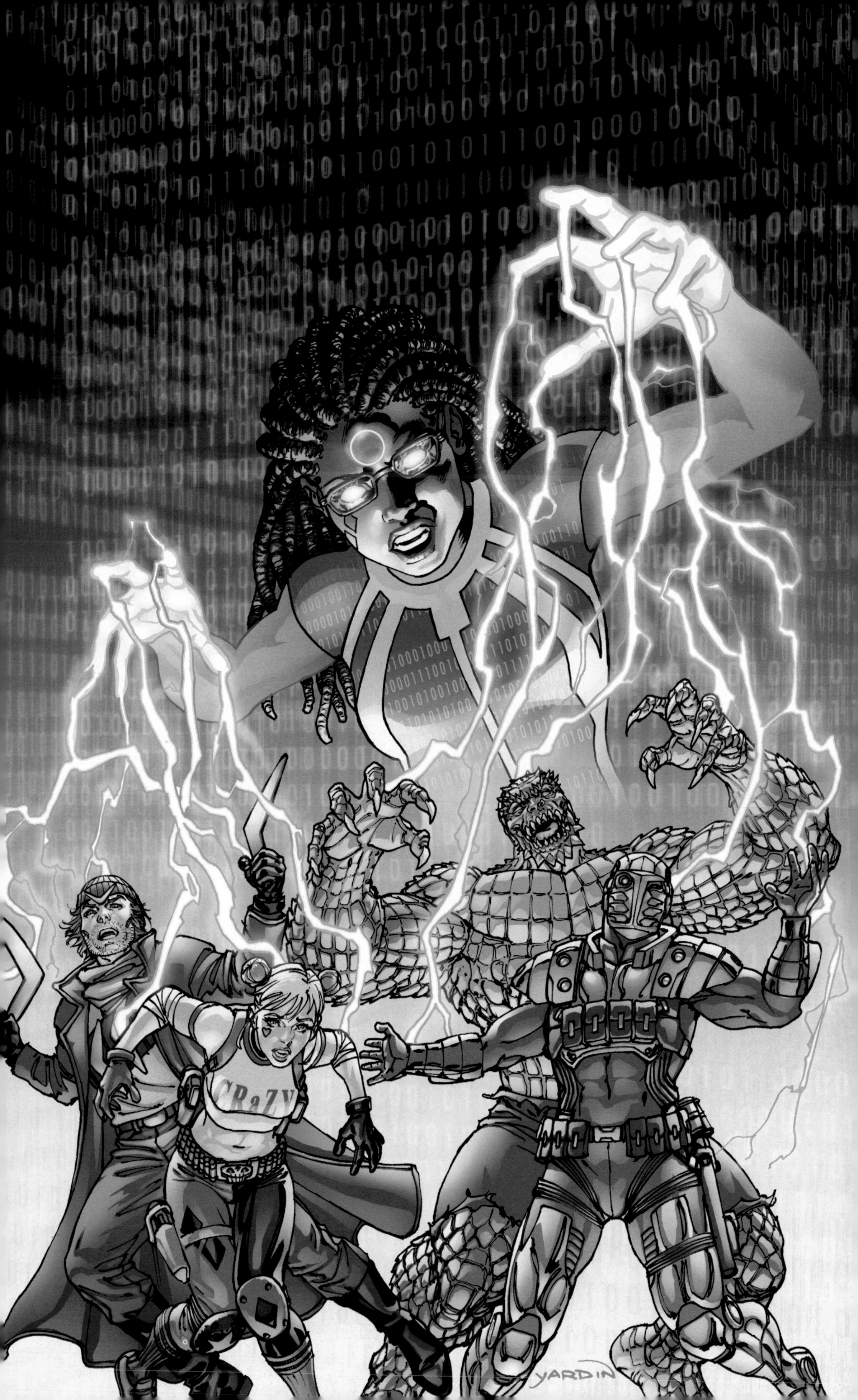
CRaZY
YARDIN

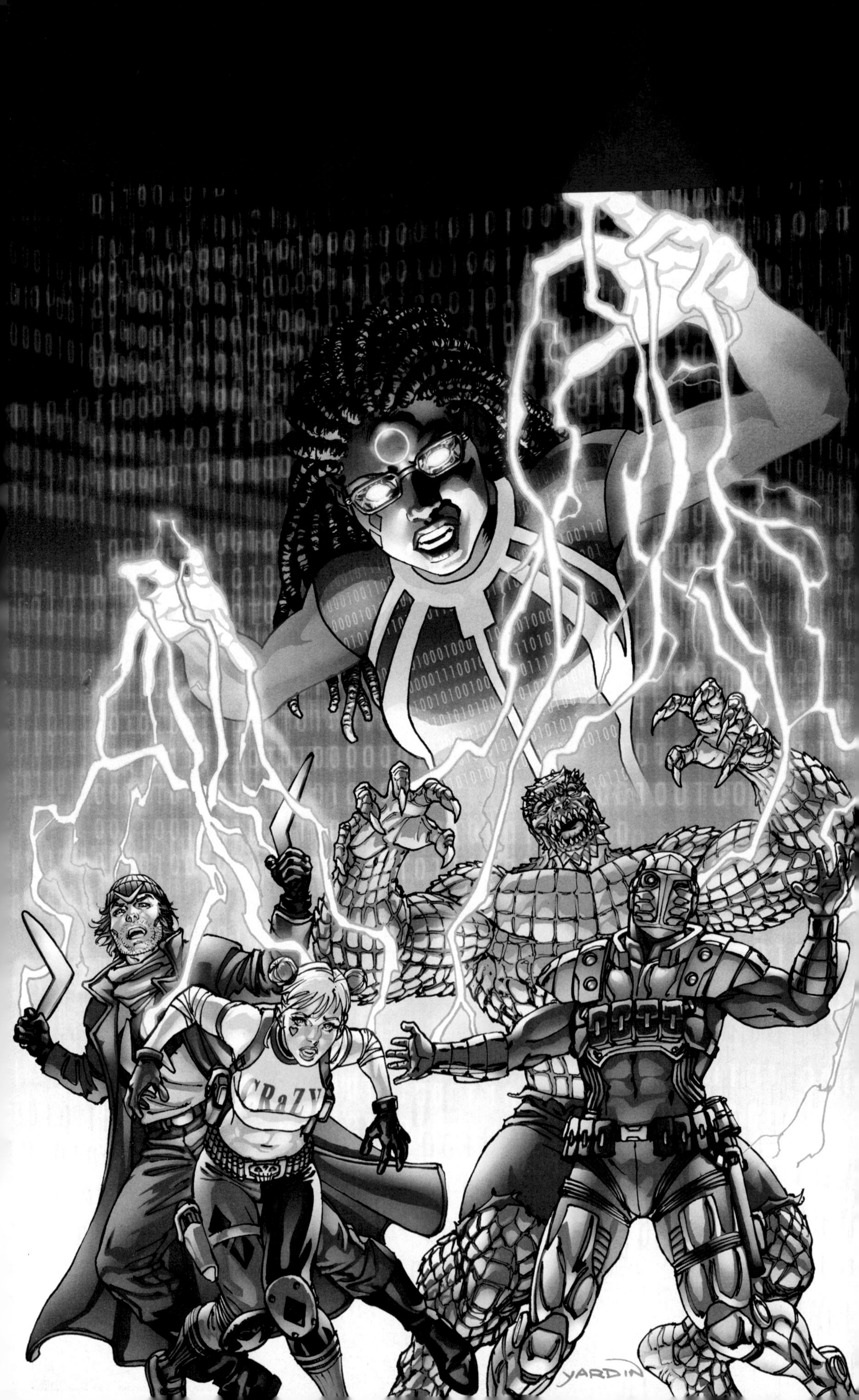
CRaZY
YARDIN

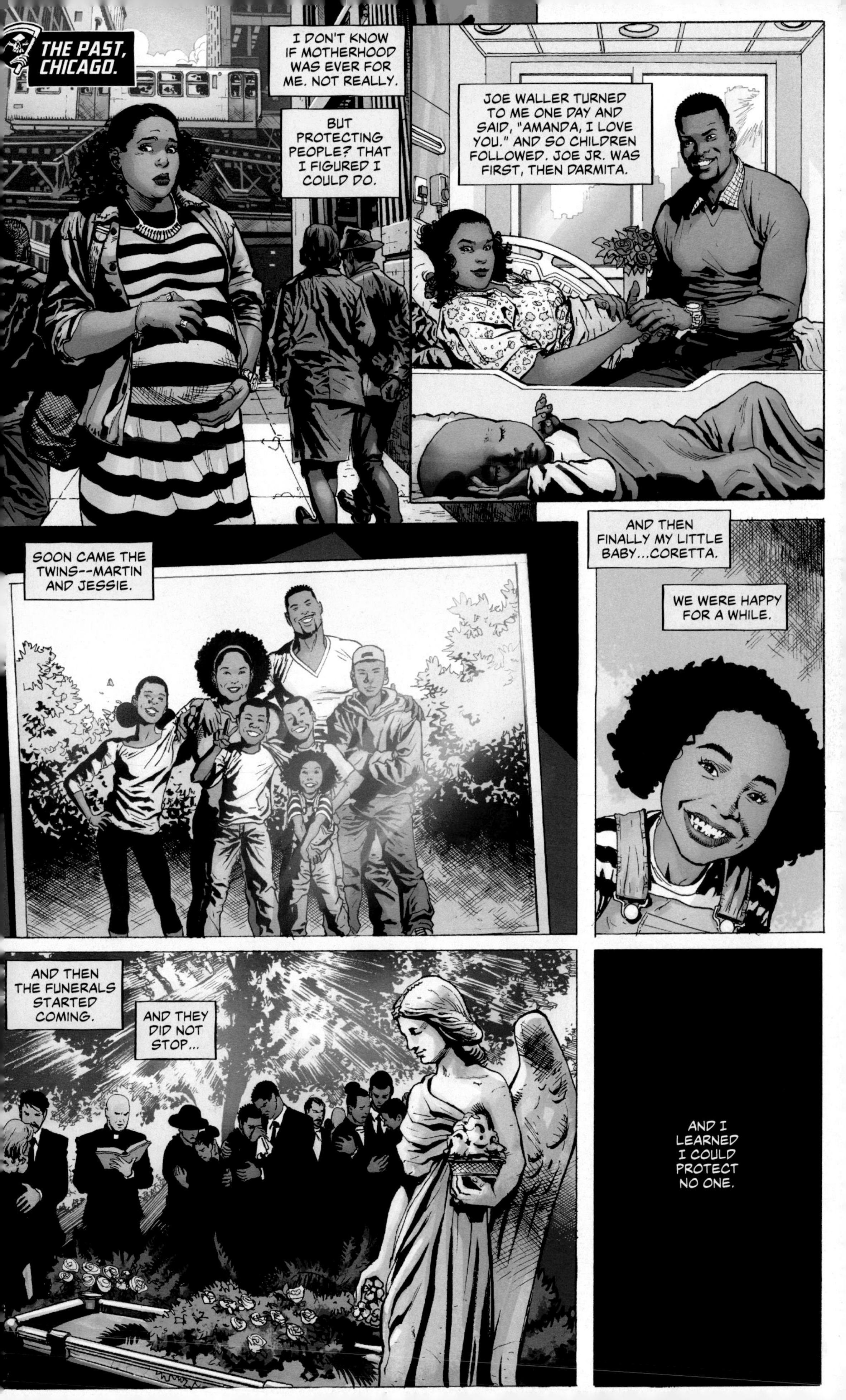
THE PAST, CHICAGO.
I DON'T KNOW IF MOTHERHOOD WAS EVER FOR ME. NOT REALLY.
BUT PROTECTING PEOPLE? THAT I FIGURED I COULD DO.
JOE WALLER TURNED TO ME ONE DAY AND SAID, "AMANDA, I LOVE YOU." AND SO CHILDREN FOLLOWED. JOE JR. WAS FIRST, THEN DARMITA.
SOON CAME THE TWINS--MARTIN AND JESSIE.
AND THEN FINALLY MY LITTLE BABY...CORETTA.
WE WERE HAPPY FOR A WHILE.
AND THEN THE FUNERALS STARTED COMING.
AND THEY DID NOT STOP...
AND I LEARNED I COULD PROTECT NO ONE.

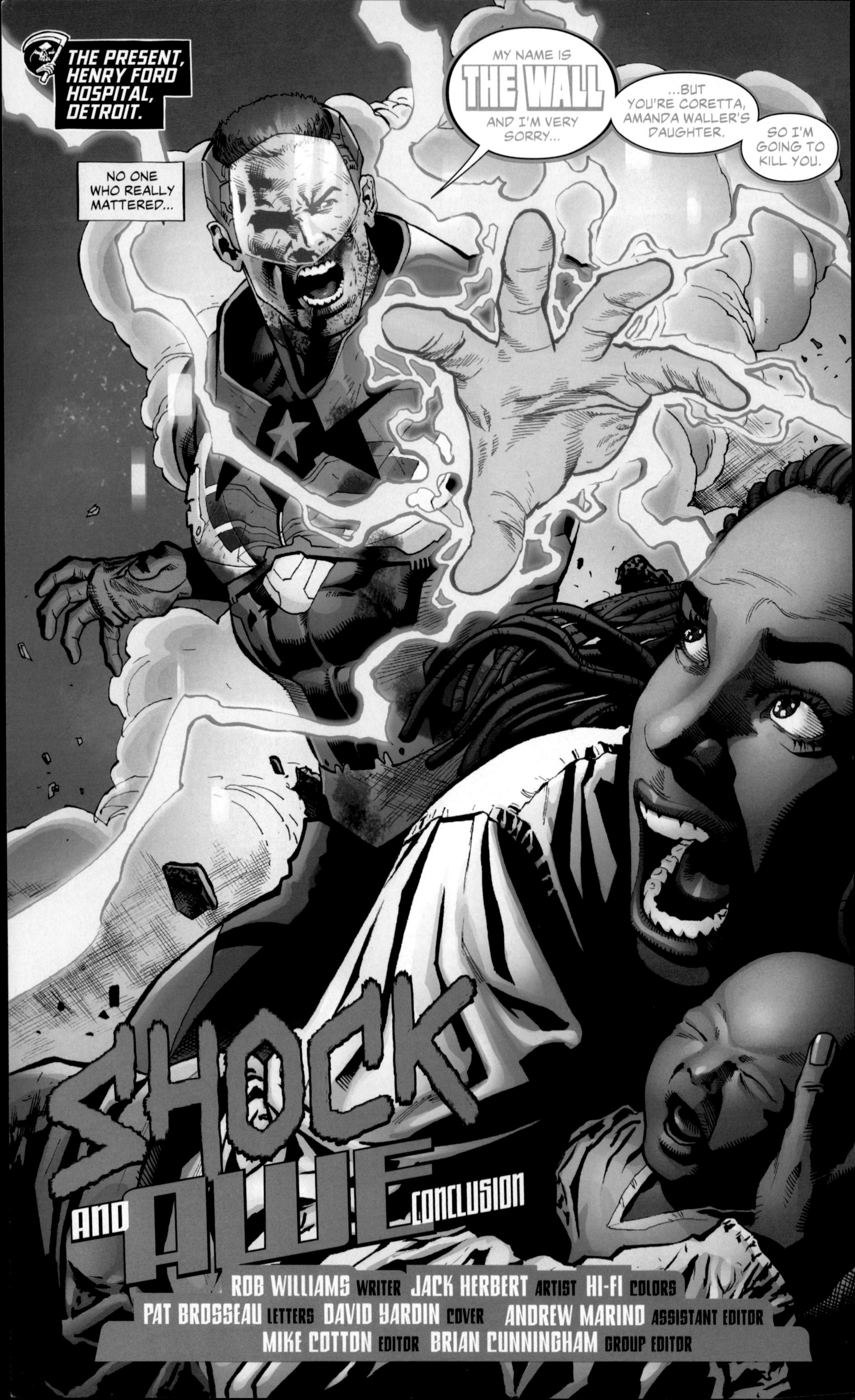
THE PRESENT, HENRY FORD HOSPITAL, DETROIT.
NO ONE WHO REALLY MATTERED...
MY NAME IS THE WALL AND I'M VERY SORRY...
...BUT YOU'RE CORETTA, AMANDA WALLER'S DAUGHTER.
SO I'M GOING TO KILL YOU.
SHOCK AND AWE CONCLUSION
ROB WILLIAMS WRITER JACK HERBERT ARTIST HI-FI COLORS
PAT BROSSEAU LETTERS DAVID YARDIN COVER ANDREW MARINO ASSISTANT EDITOR
MIKE COTTON EDITOR BRIAN CUNNINGHAM GROUP EDITOR

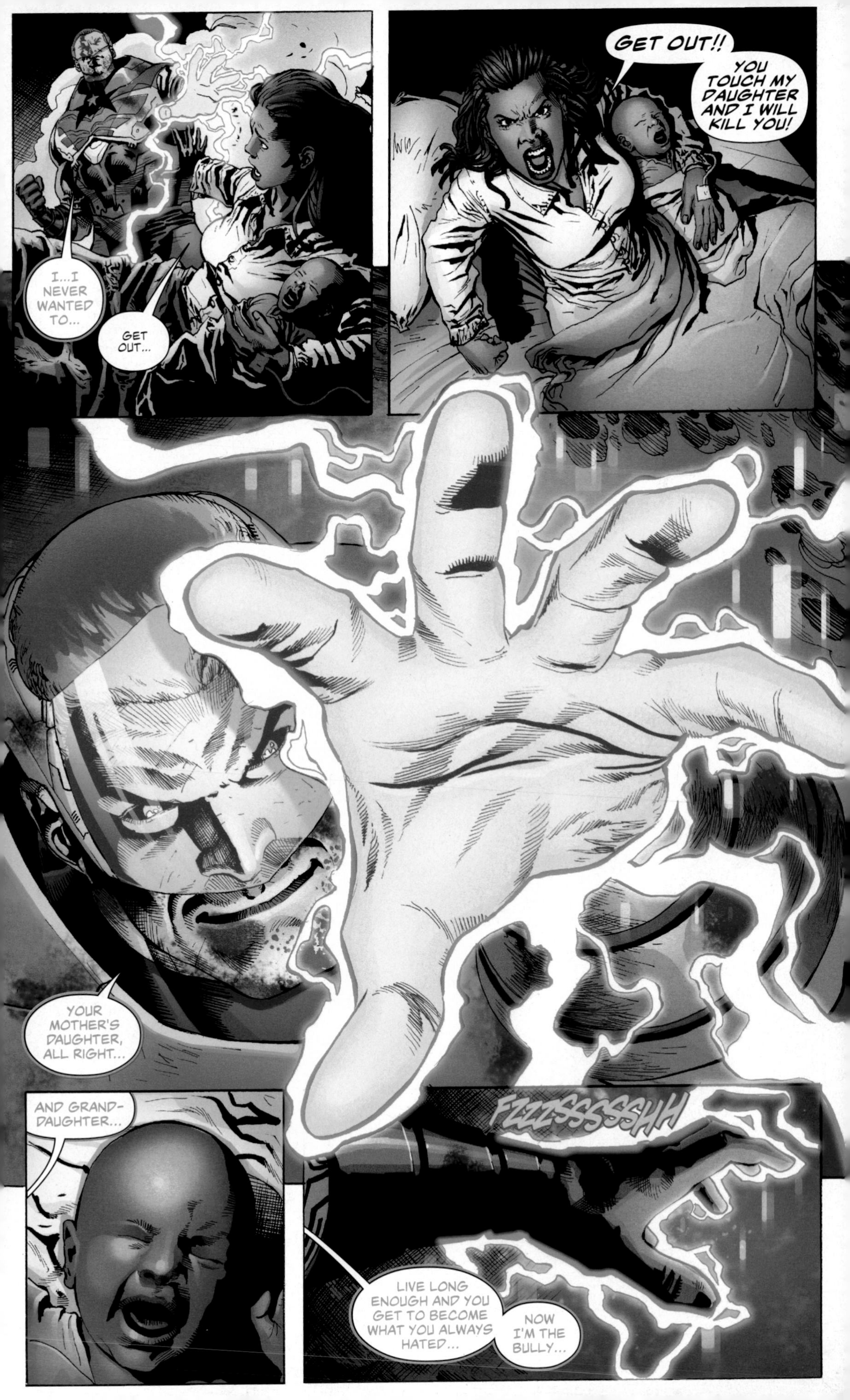
I...I NEVER WANTED TO...
GET OUT...
GET OUT!!
YOU TOUCH MY DAUGHTER AND I WILL KILL YOU!
YOUR MOTHER'S DAUGHTER, ALL RIGHT...
AND GRAND-DAUGHTER...
FZZZSSSSSHH
LIVE LONG ENOUGH AND YOU GET TO BECOME WHAT YOU ALWAYS HATED...
NOW I'M THE BULLY...

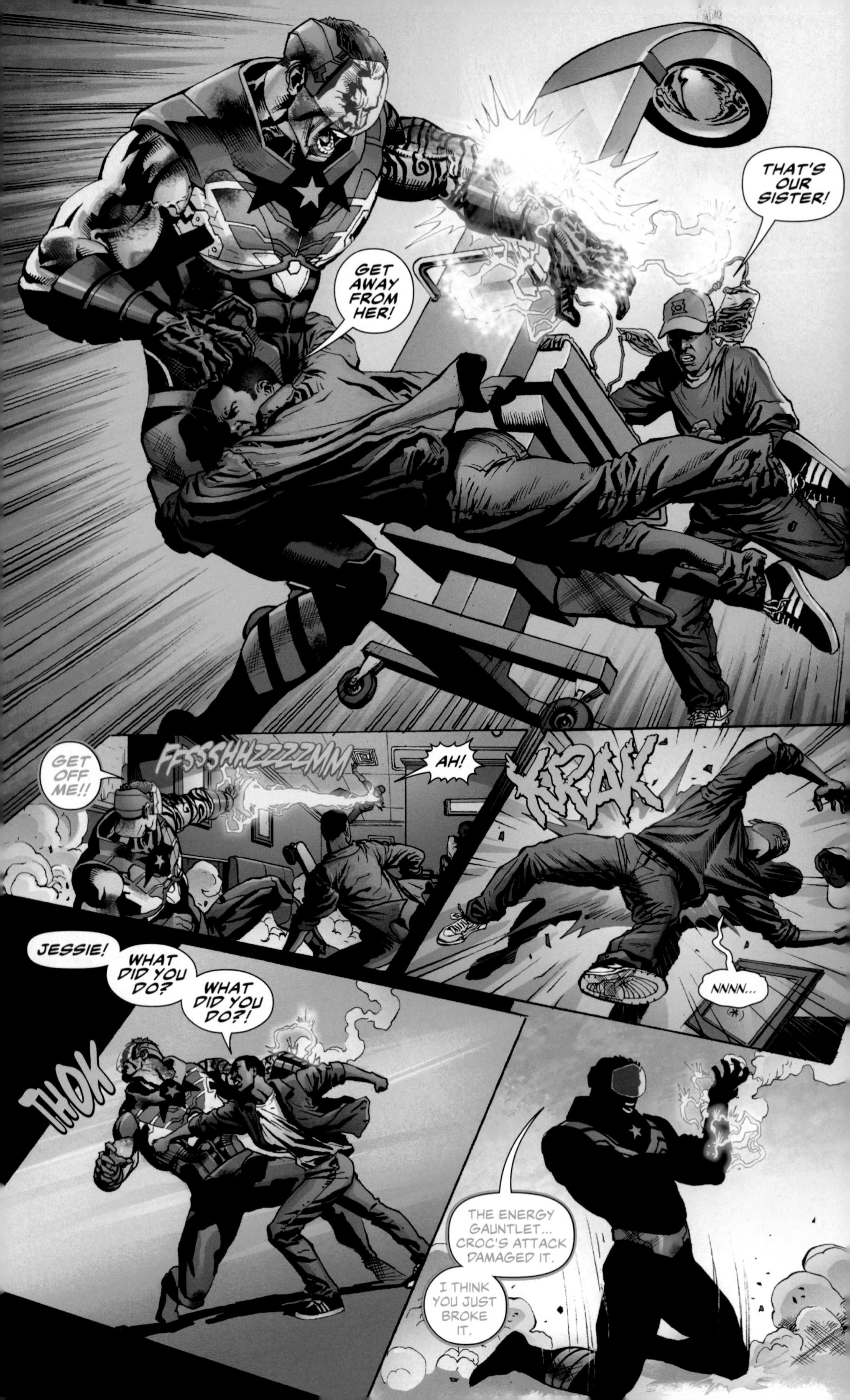

GET AWAY FROM HER!
THAT'S OUR SISTER!
GET OFF ME!!
FFSSSHHZZZZZMM
AH!
KRAK
NNNN...
JESSIE!
WHAT DID YOU DO?
WHAT DID YOU DO?!
THOK
THE ENERGY GAUNTLET... CROC'S ATTACK DAMAGED IT.
I THINK YOU JUST BROKE IT.

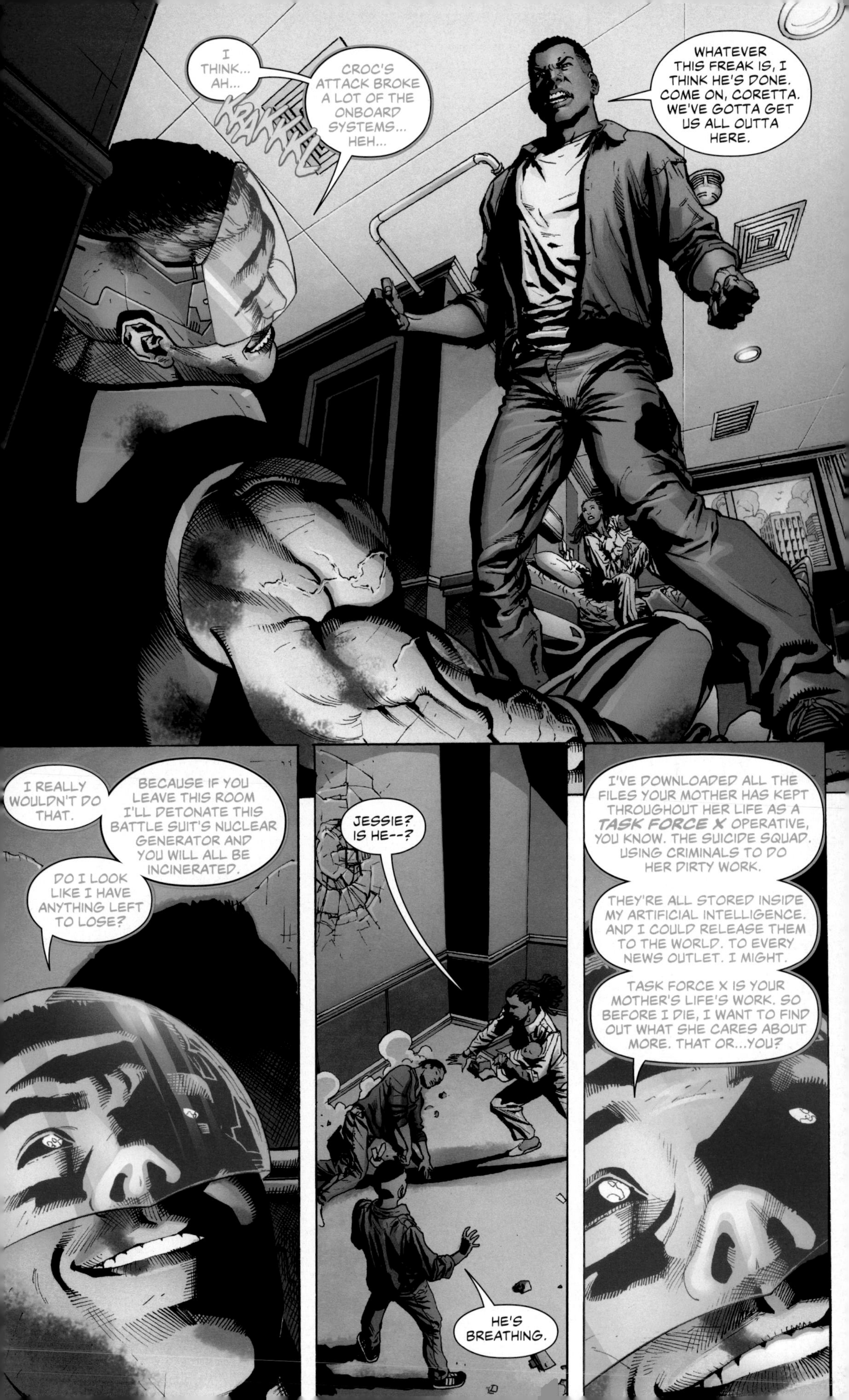
I THINK... AH...
KRAKKL
CROC'S ATTACK BROKE A LOT OF THE ONBOARD SYSTEMS... HEH...
WHATEVER THIS FREAK IS, I THINK HE'S DONE. COME ON, CORETTA. WE'VE GOTTA GET US ALL OUTTA HERE.
I REALLY WOULDN'T DO THAT.
BECAUSE IF YOU LEAVE THIS ROOM I'LL DETONATE THIS BATTLE SUIT'S NUCLEAR GENERATOR AND YOU WILL ALL BE INCINERATED.
DO I LOOK LIKE I HAVE ANYTHING LEFT TO LOSE?
JESSIE? IS HE--?
HE'S BREATHING.
I'VE DOWNLOADED ALL THE FILES YOUR MOTHER HAS KEPT THROUGHOUT HER LIFE AS A *TASK FORCE X* OPERATIVE, YOU KNOW. THE SUICIDE SQUAD. USING CRIMINALS TO DO HER DIRTY WORK.
THEY'RE ALL STORED INSIDE MY ARTIFICIAL INTELLIGENCE. AND I COULD RELEASE THEM TO THE WORLD. TO EVERY NEWS OUTLET. I MIGHT.
TASK FORCE X IS YOUR MOTHER'S LIFE'S WORK. SO BEFORE I DIE, I WANT TO FIND OUT WHAT SHE CARES ABOUT MORE. THAT OR...YOU?

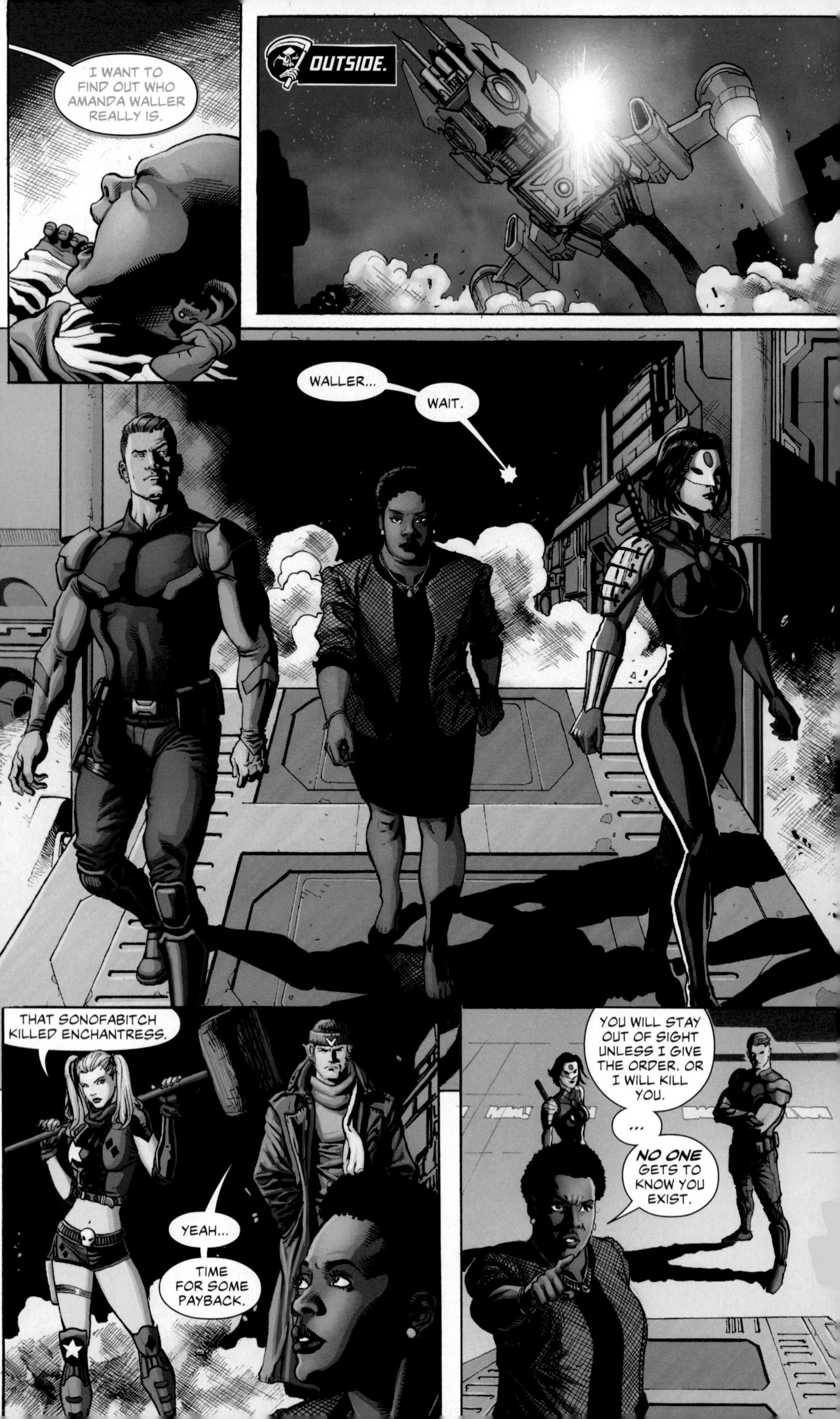
I WANT TO FIND OUT WHO AMANDA WALLER REALLY IS.
OUTSIDE.
WALLER...
WAIT.
THAT SONOFABITCH KILLED ENCHANTRESS.
YEAH...
TIME FOR SOME PAYBACK.
YOU WILL STAY OUT OF SIGHT UNLESS I GIVE THE ORDER. OR I WILL KILL YOU.
...
NO ONE GETS TO KNOW YOU EXIST.

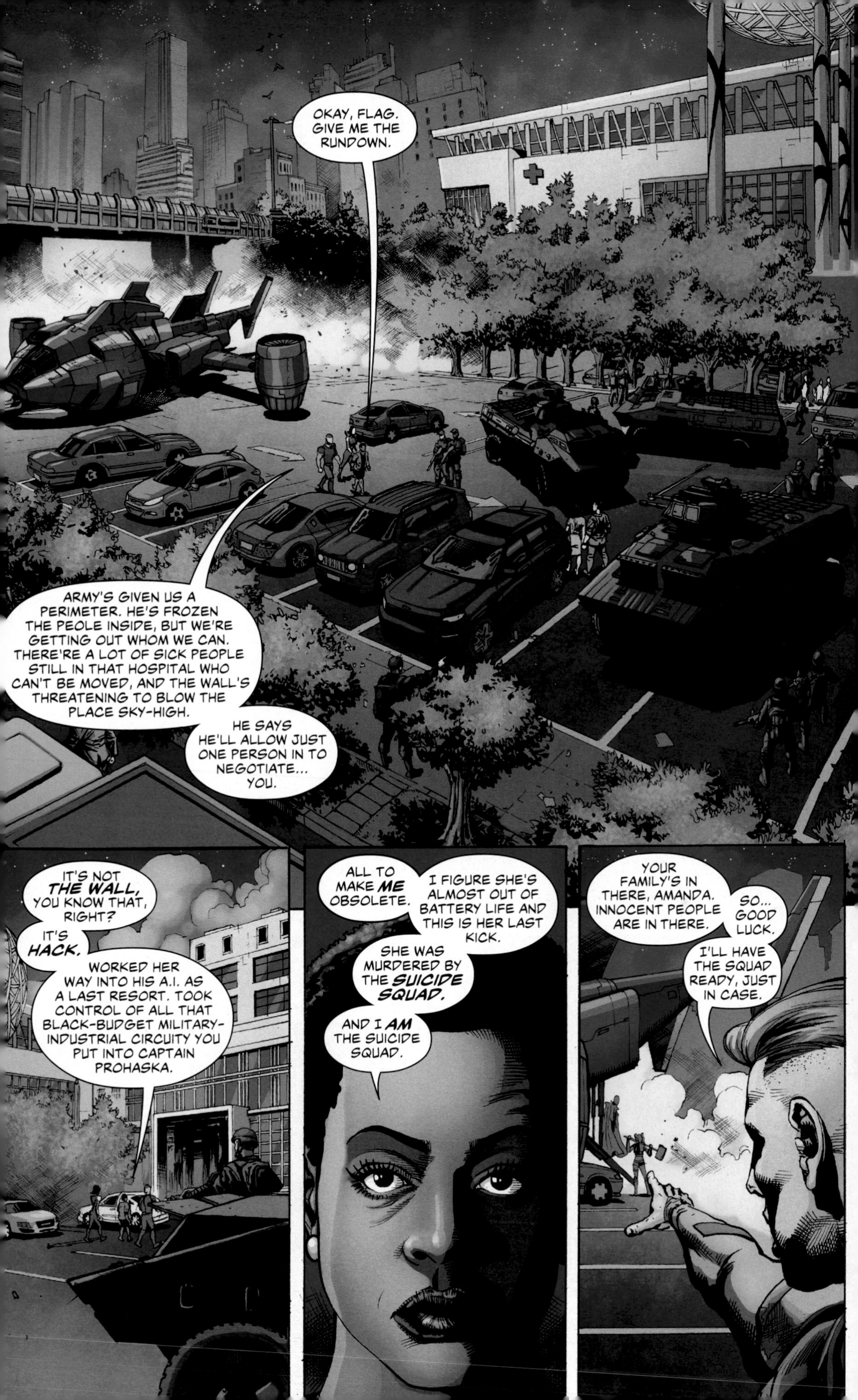
OKAY, FLAG. GIVE ME THE RUNDOWN.
ARMY'S GIVEN US A PERIMETER. HE'S FROZEN THE PEOLE INSIDE, BUT WE'RE GETTING OUT WHOM WE CAN. THERE'RE A LOT OF SICK PEOPLE STILL IN THAT HOSPITAL WHO CAN'T BE MOVED, AND THE WALL'S THREATENING TO BLOW THE PLACE SKY-HIGH.
HE SAYS HE'LL ALLOW JUST ONE PERSON IN TO NEGOTIATE... YOU.
IT'S NOT ***THE WALL,*** YOU KNOW THAT, RIGHT?
IT'S ***HACK.***
WORKED HER WAY INTO HIS A.I. AS A LAST RESORT. TOOK CONTROL OF ALL THAT BLACK-BUDGET MILITARY-INDUSTRIAL CIRCUITY YOU PUT INTO CAPTAIN PROHASKA.
ALL TO MAKE ***ME*** OBSOLETE.
I FIGURE SHE'S ALMOST OUT OF BATTERY LIFE AND THIS IS HER LAST KICK.
SHE WAS MURDERED BY THE ***SUICIDE SQUAD.***
AND I ***AM*** THE SUICIDE SQUAD.
YOUR FAMILY'S IN THERE, AMANDA. INNOCENT PEOPLE ARE IN THERE.
SO... GOOD LUCK.
I'LL HAVE THE SQUAD READY, JUST IN CASE.

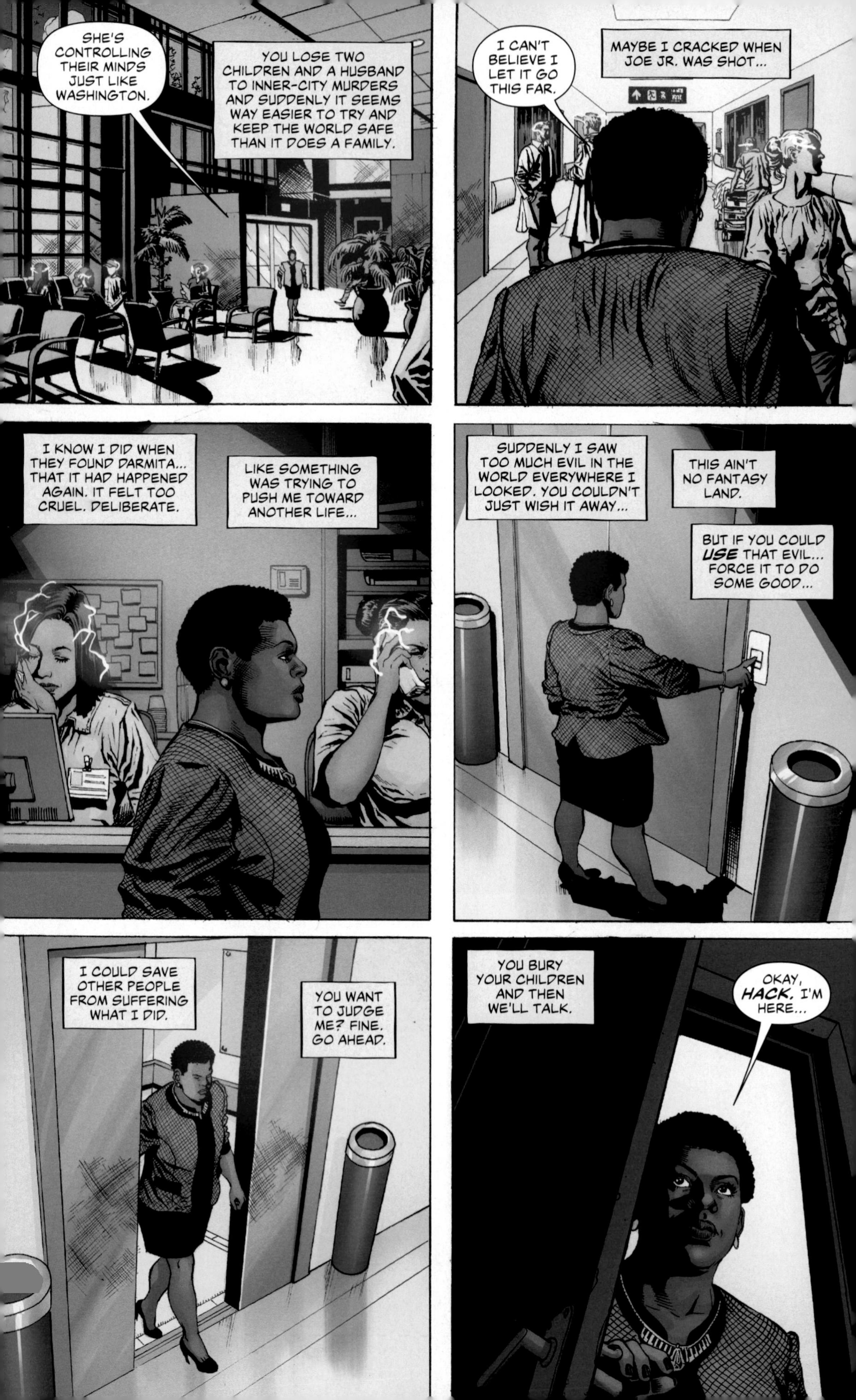
SHE'S CONTROLLING THEIR MINDS JUST LIKE WASHINGTON.
YOU LOSE TWO CHILDREN AND A HUSBAND TO INNER-CITY MURDERS AND SUDDENLY IT SEEMS WAY EASIER TO TRY AND KEEP THE WORLD SAFE THAN IT DOES A FAMILY.
I CAN'T BELIEVE I LET IT GO THIS FAR.
MAYBE I CRACKED WHEN JOE JR. WAS SHOT...
I KNOW I DID WHEN THEY FOUND DARMITA... THAT IT HAD HAPPENED AGAIN. IT FELT TOO CRUEL. DELIBERATE.
LIKE SOMETHING WAS TRYING TO PUSH ME TOWARD ANOTHER LIFE...
SUDDENLY I SAW TOO MUCH EVIL IN THE WORLD EVERYWHERE I LOOKED. YOU COULDN'T JUST WISH IT AWAY...
THIS AIN'T NO FANTASY LAND.
BUT IF YOU COULD USE THAT EVIL... FORCE IT TO DO SOME GOOD...
I COULD SAVE OTHER PEOPLE FROM SUFFERING WHAT I DID.
YOU WANT TO JUDGE ME? FINE. GO AHEAD.
YOU BURY YOUR CHILDREN AND THEN WE'LL TALK.
OKAY, HACK, I'M HERE...

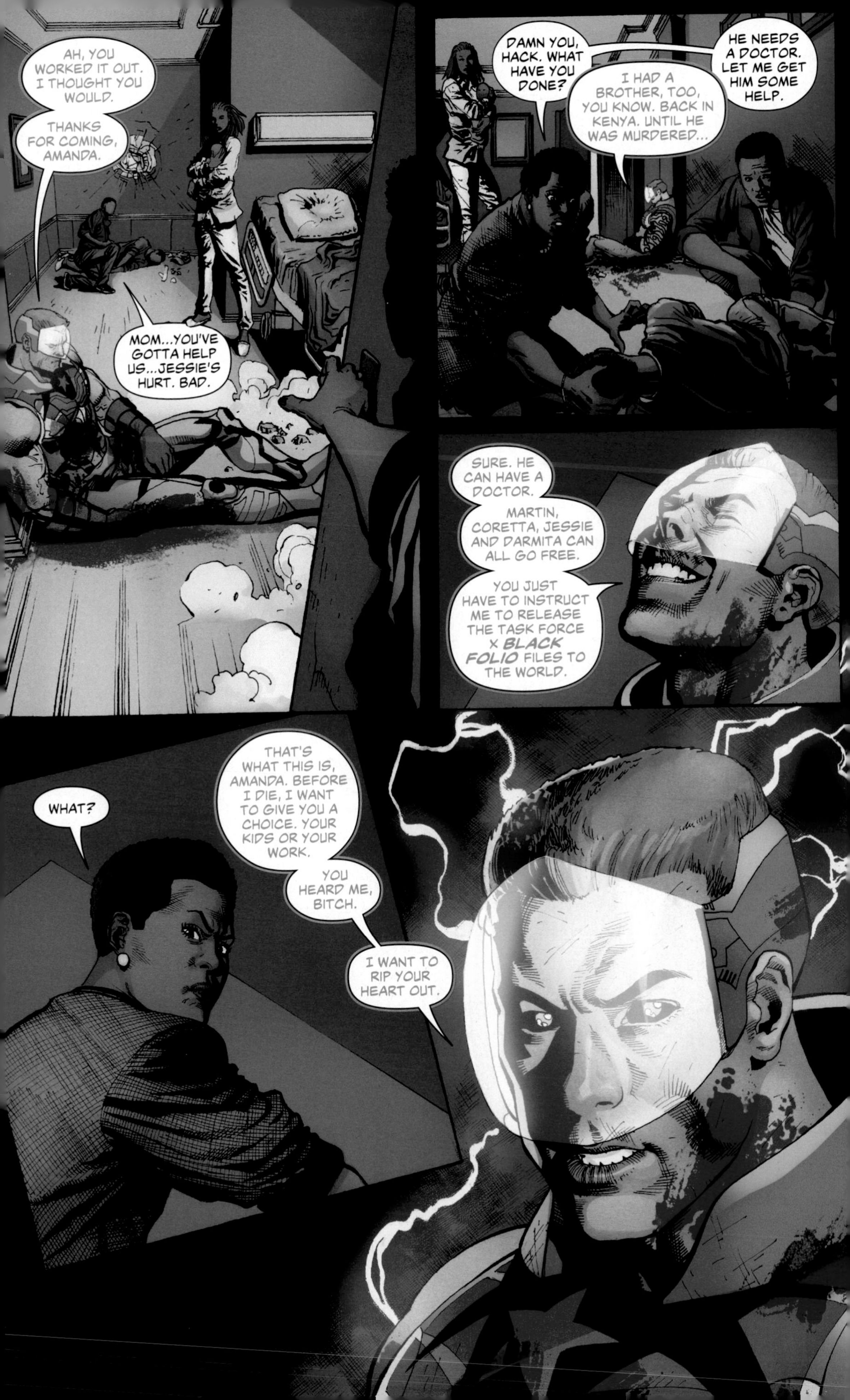
AH, YOU WORKED IT OUT. I THOUGHT YOU WOULD.
THANKS FOR COMING, AMANDA.
MOM...YOU'VE GOTTA HELP US...JESSIE'S HURT. BAD.
DAMN YOU, HACK. WHAT HAVE YOU DONE?
HE NEEDS A DOCTOR. LET ME GET HIM SOME HELP.
I HAD A BROTHER, TOO, YOU KNOW. BACK IN KENYA. UNTIL HE WAS MURDERED...
SURE. HE CAN HAVE A DOCTOR.
MARTIN, CORETTA, JESSIE AND DARMITA CAN ALL GO FREE.
YOU JUST HAVE TO INSTRUCT ME TO RELEASE THE TASK FORCE X BLACK FOLIO FILES TO THE WORLD.
WHAT?
THAT'S WHAT THIS IS, AMANDA. BEFORE I DIE, I WANT TO GIVE YOU A CHOICE. YOUR KIDS OR YOUR WORK.
YOU HEARD ME, BITCH.
I WANT TO RIP YOUR HEART OUT.

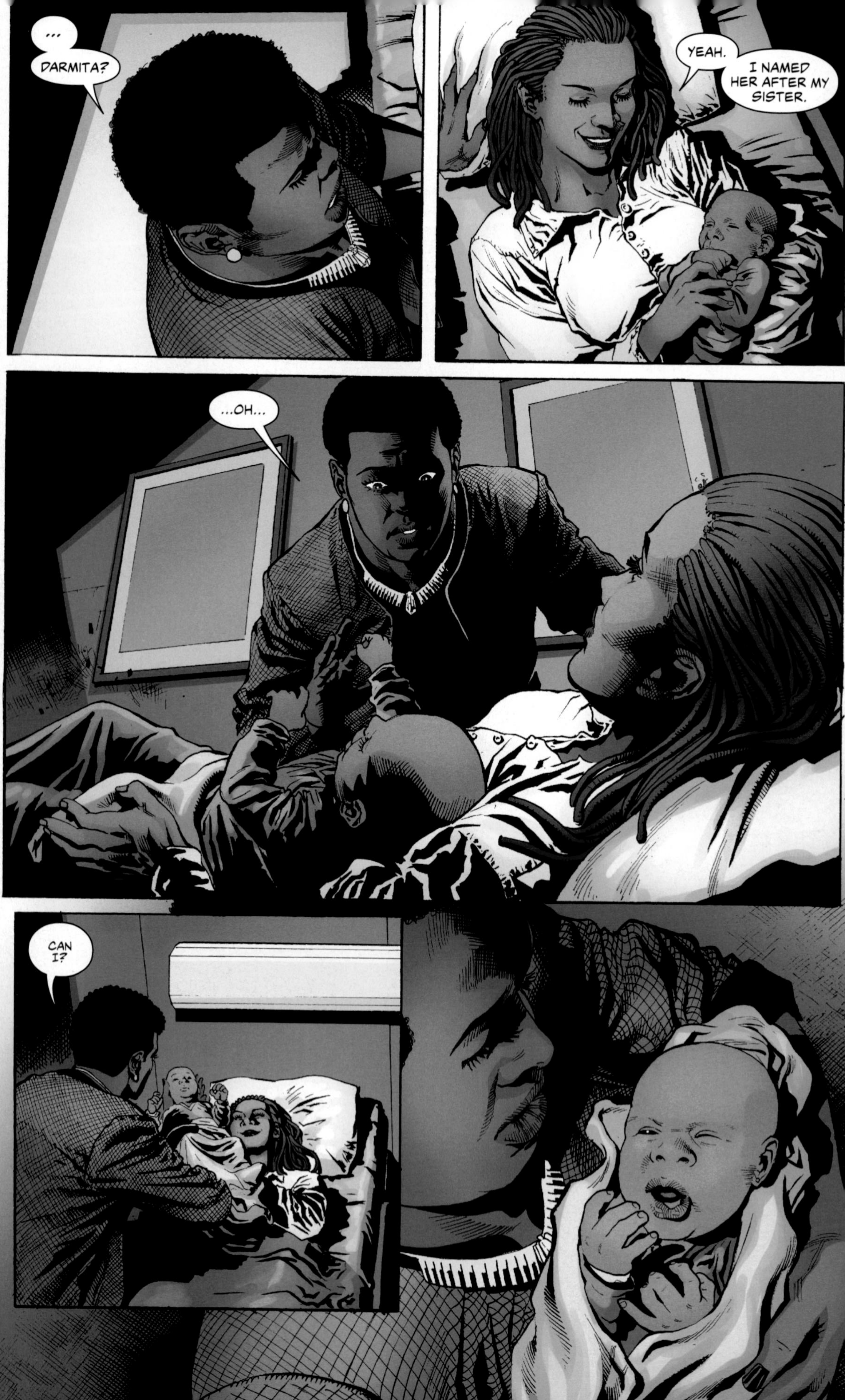
...
DARMITA?
YEAH.
I NAMED HER AFTER MY SISTER.
...OH...
CAN I?

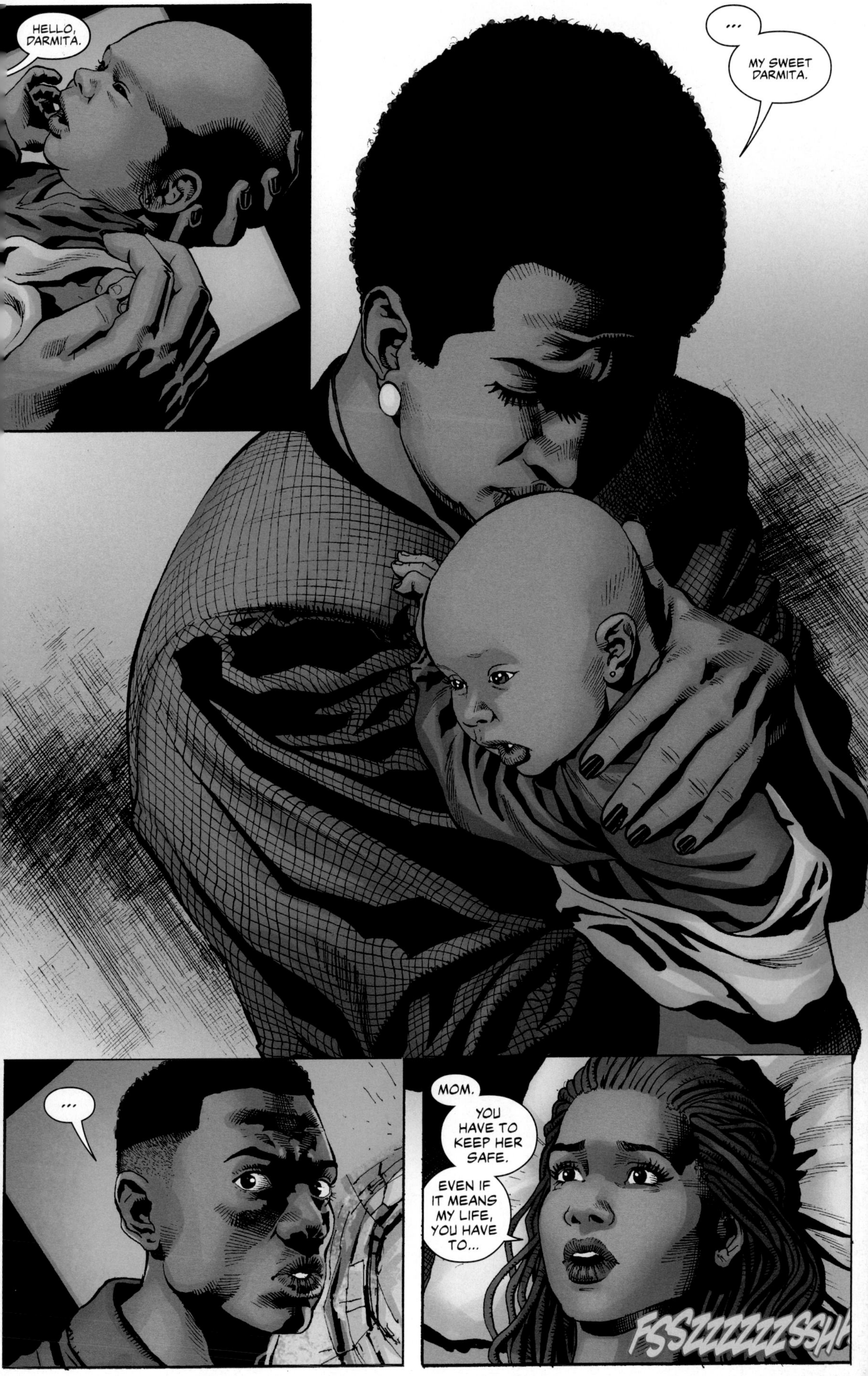
HELLO, DARMITA.
...
MY SWEET DARMITA.
...
MOM.
YOU HAVE TO KEEP HER SAFE.
EVEN IF IT MEANS MY LIFE, YOU HAVE TO...
FSSZZZZZZZSSH!

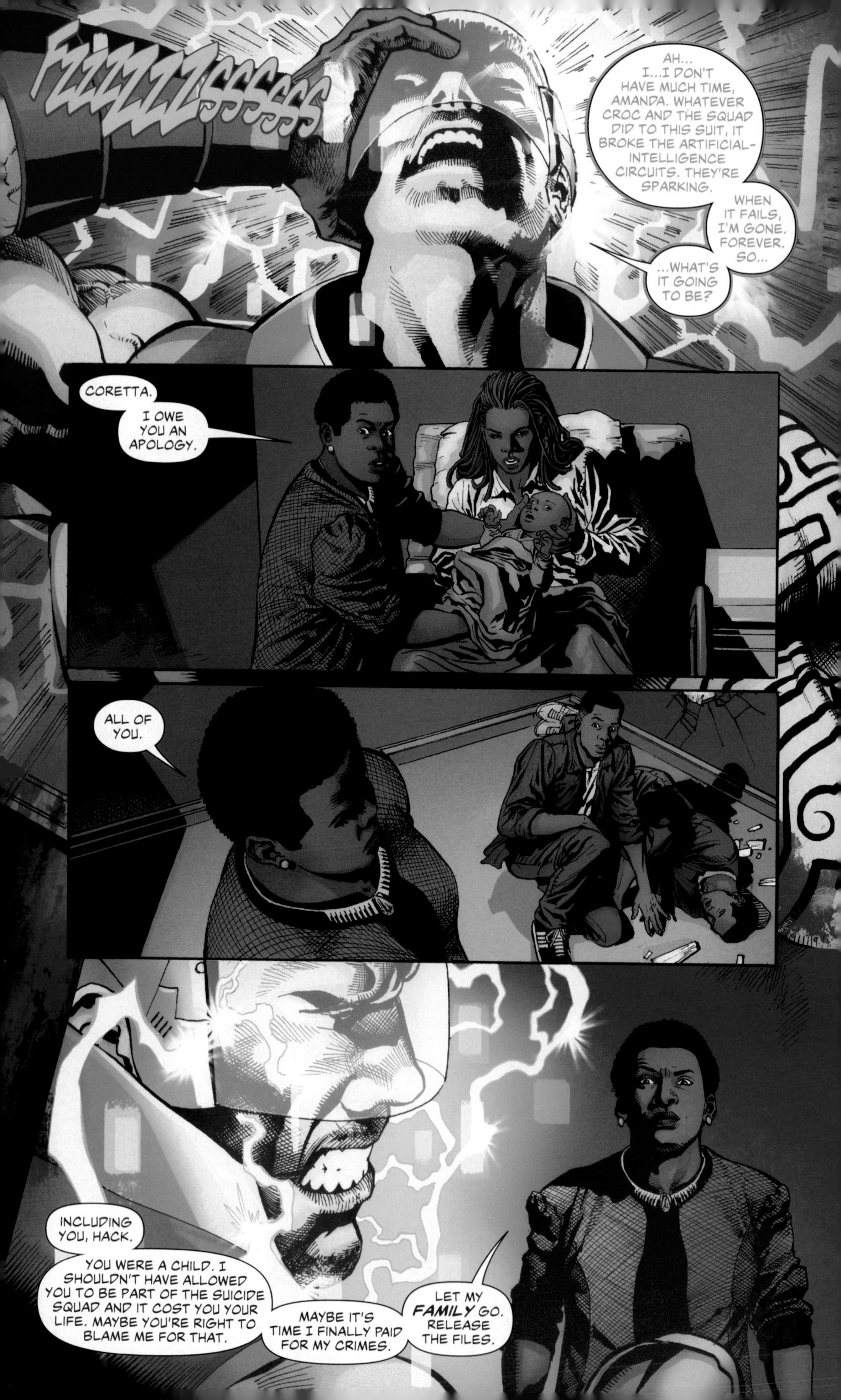
FZZZZZZSSSSSS
AH... I...I DON'T HAVE MUCH TIME, AMANDA. WHATEVER CROC AND THE SQUAD DID TO THIS SUIT, IT BROKE THE ARTIFICIAL-INTELLIGENCE CIRCUITS. THEY'RE SPARKING.
WHEN IT FAILS, I'M GONE. FOREVER. SO...
...WHAT'S IT GOING TO BE?
CORETTA.
I OWE YOU AN APOLOGY.
ALL OF YOU.
INCLUDING YOU, HACK.
YOU WERE A CHILD. I SHOULDN'T HAVE ALLOWED YOU TO BE PART OF THE SUICIDE SQUAD AND IT COST YOU YOUR LIFE. MAYBE YOU'RE RIGHT TO BLAME ME FOR THAT.
MAYBE IT'S TIME I FINALLY PAID FOR MY CRIMES.
LET MY *FAMILY* GO. RELEASE THE FILES.

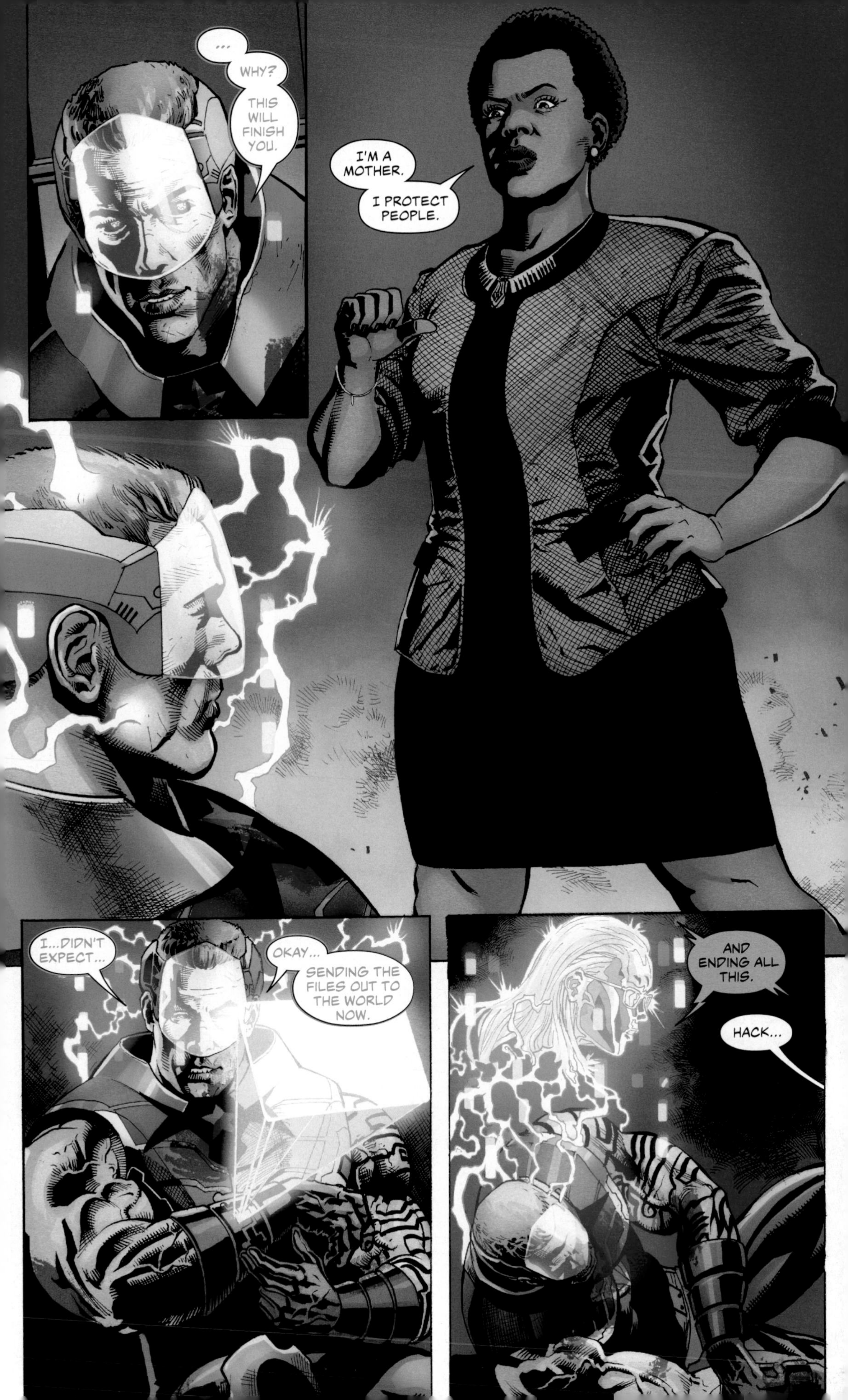
...
WHY?
THIS WILL FINISH YOU.
I'M A MOTHER.
I PROTECT PEOPLE.
I...DIDN'T EXPECT...
OKAY...
SENDING THE FILES OUT TO THE WORLD NOW.
AND ENDING ALL THIS.
HACK...

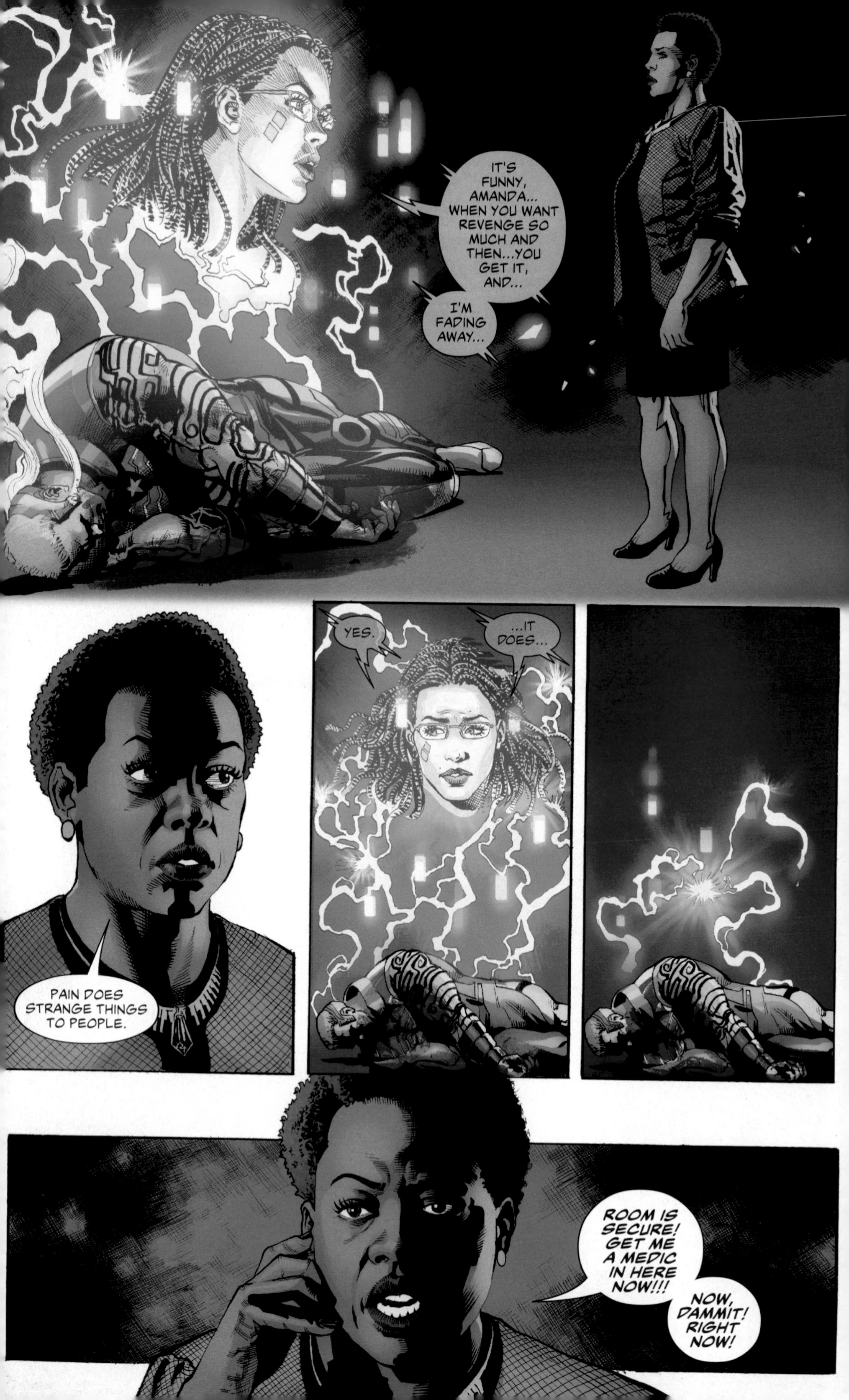
IT'S FUNNY, AMANDA... WHEN YOU WANT REVENGE SO MUCH AND THEN...YOU GET IT, AND...
I'M FADING AWAY...
PAIN DOES STRANGE THINGS TO PEOPLE.
YES.
...IT DOES...
ROOM IS SECURE! GET ME A MEDIC IN HERE NOW!!!
NOW, DAMMIT! RIGHT NOW!

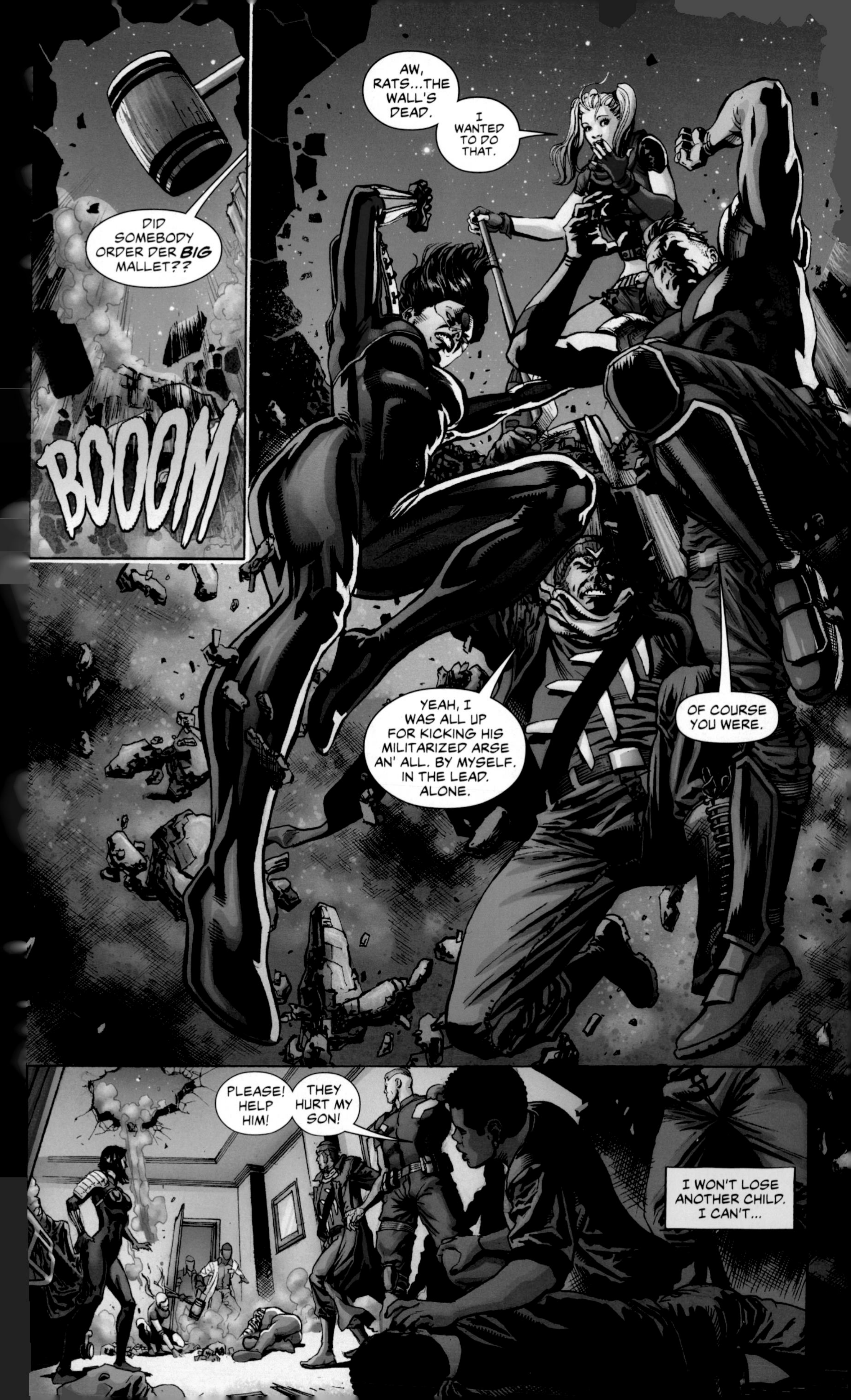
DID SOMEBODY ORDER DER BIG MALLET??
BOOOM
AW, RATS...THE WALL'S DEAD.
I WANTED TO DO THAT.
YEAH, I WAS ALL UP FOR KICKING HIS MILITARIZED ARSE AN' ALL. BY MYSELF. IN THE LEAD. ALONE.
OF COURSE YOU WERE.
PLEASE! HELP HIM!
THEY HURT MY SON!
I WON'T LOSE ANOTHER CHILD. I CAN'T...

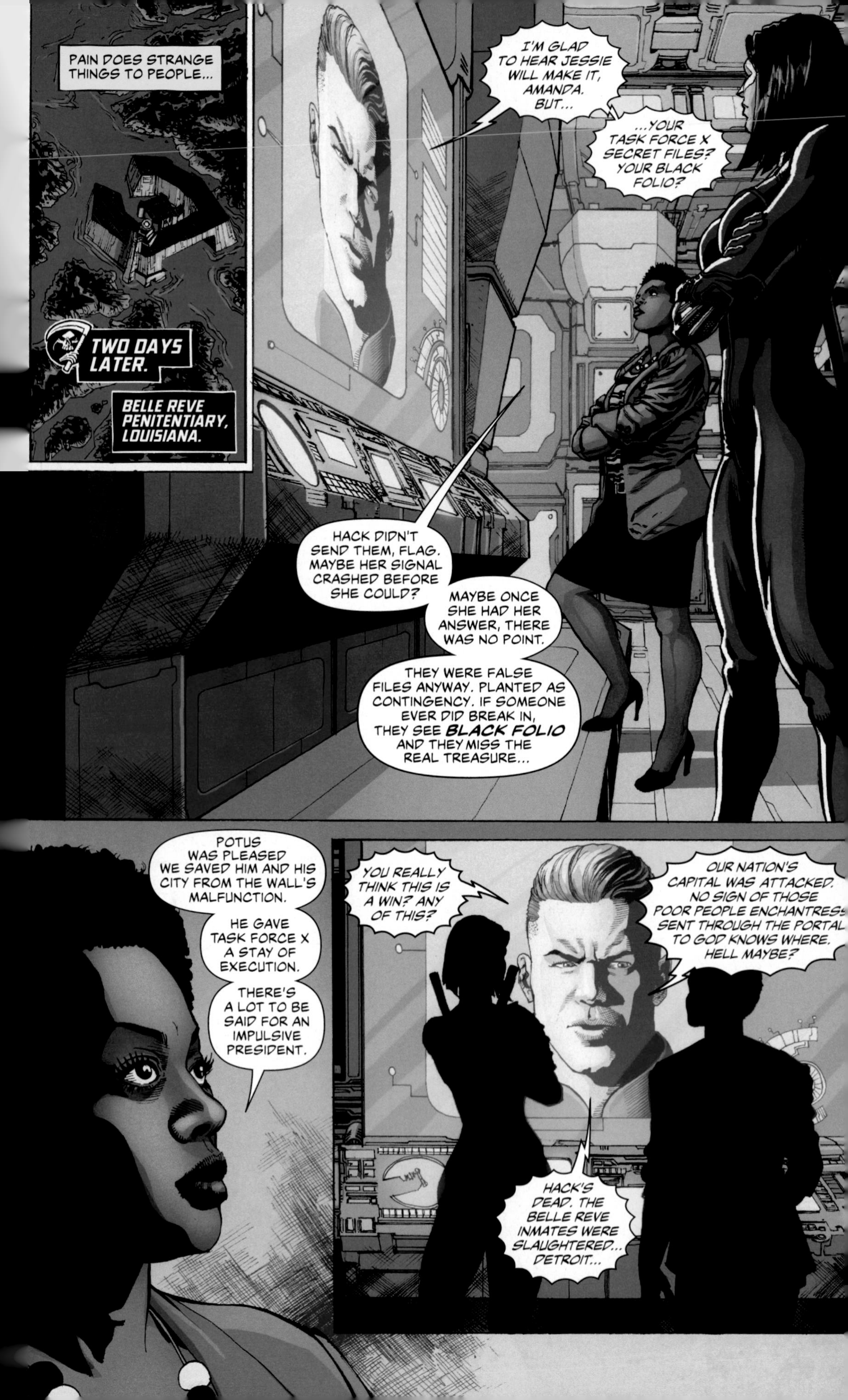
PAIN DOES STRANGE THINGS TO PEOPLE...
TWO DAYS LATER.
BELLE REVE PENITENTIARY, LOUISIANA.
I'M GLAD TO HEAR JESSIE WILL MAKE IT, AMANDA. BUT...
...YOUR TASK FORCE X SECRET FILES? YOUR BLACK FOLIO?
HACK DIDN'T SEND THEM, FLAG. MAYBE HER SIGNAL CRASHED BEFORE SHE COULD?
MAYBE ONCE SHE HAD HER ANSWER, THERE WAS NO POINT.
THEY WERE FALSE FILES ANYWAY. PLANTED AS CONTINGENCY. IF SOMEONE EVER DID BREAK IN, THEY SEE BLACK FOLIO AND THEY MISS THE REAL TREASURE...
POTUS WAS PLEASED WE SAVED HIM AND HIS CITY FROM THE WALL'S MALFUNCTION.
HE GAVE TASK FORCE X A STAY OF EXECUTION.
THERE'S A LOT TO BE SAID FOR AN IMPULSIVE PRESIDENT.
YOU REALLY THINK THIS IS A WIN? ANY OF THIS?
OUR NATION'S CAPITAL WAS ATTACKED. NO SIGN OF THOSE POOR PEOPLE ENCHANTRESS SENT THROUGH THE PORTAL TO GOD KNOWS WHERE. HELL MAYBE?
HACK'S DEAD. THE BELLE REVE INMATES WERE SLAUGHTERED... DETROIT...

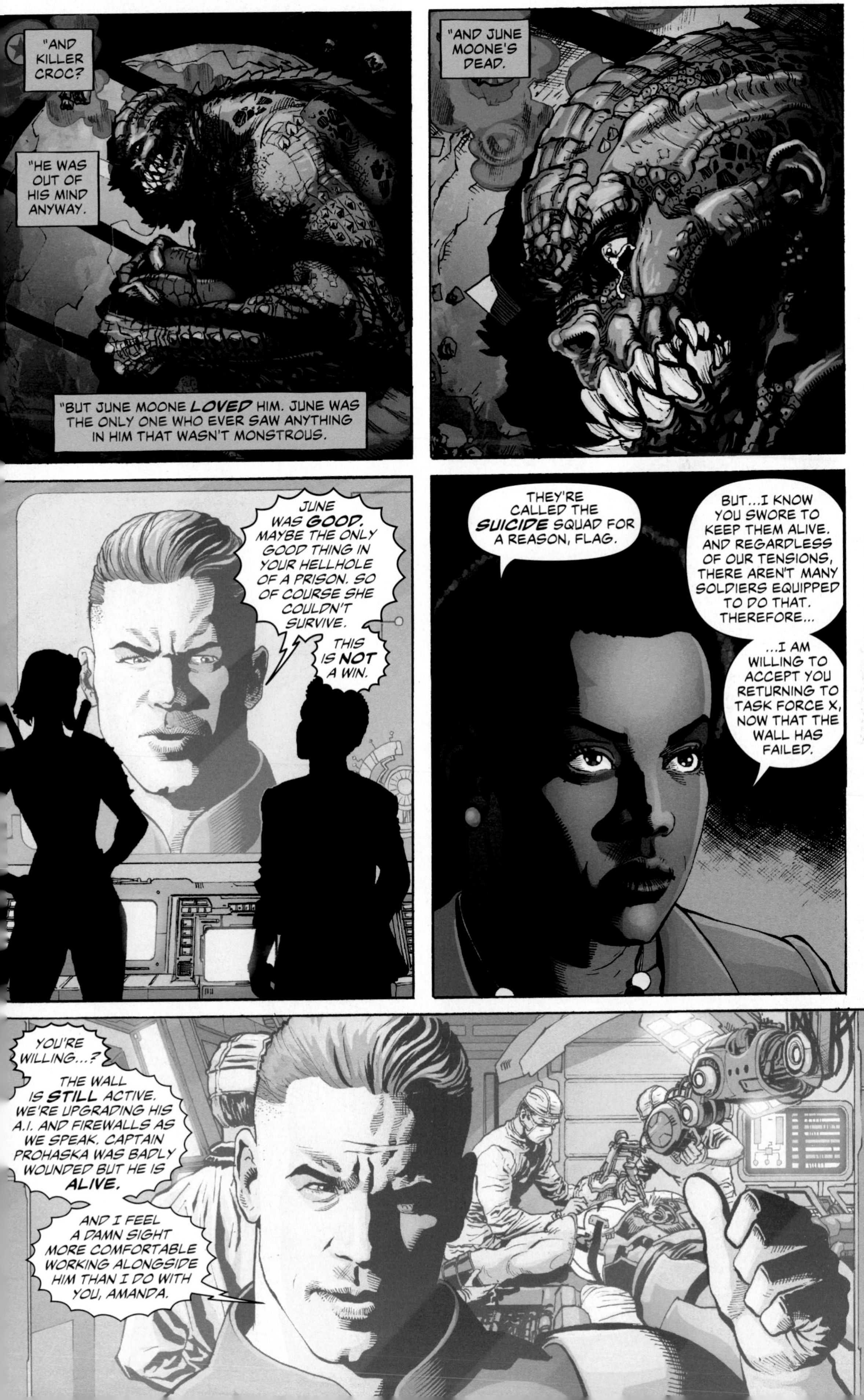
"AND KILLER CROC?
"HE WAS OUT OF HIS MIND ANYWAY.
"BUT JUNE MOONE LOVED HIM. JUNE WAS THE ONLY ONE WHO EVER SAW ANYTHING IN HIM THAT WASN'T MONSTROUS.
"AND JUNE MOONE'S DEAD.
JUNE WAS GOOD. MAYBE THE ONLY GOOD THING IN YOUR HELLHOLE OF A PRISON. SO OF COURSE SHE COULDN'T SURVIVE.
THIS IS NOT A WIN.
THEY'RE CALLED THE SUICIDE SQUAD FOR A REASON, FLAG.
BUT...I KNOW YOU SWORE TO KEEP THEM ALIVE. AND REGARDLESS OF OUR TENSIONS, THERE AREN'T MANY SOLDIERS EQUIPPED TO DO THAT. THEREFORE...
...I AM WILLING TO ACCEPT YOU RETURNING TO TASK FORCE X, NOW THAT THE WALL HAS FAILED.
YOU'RE WILLING...?
THE WALL IS STILL ACTIVE. WE'RE UPGRADING HIS A.I. AND FIREWALLS AS WE SPEAK. CAPTAIN PROHASKA WAS BADLY WOUNDED BUT HE IS ALIVE.
AND I FEEL A DAMN SIGHT MORE COMFORTABLE WORKING ALONGSIDE HIM THAN I DO WITH YOU, AMANDA.

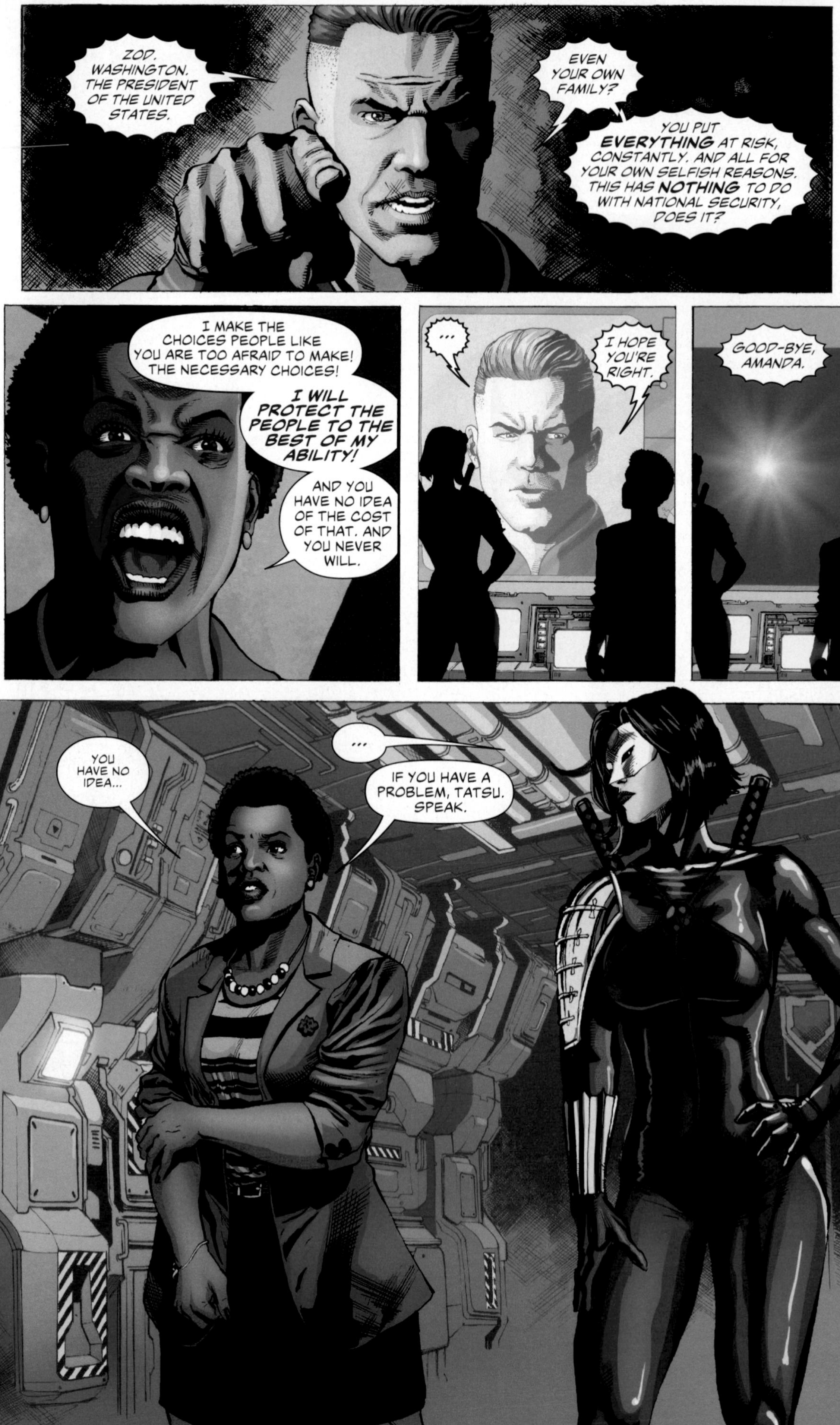
ZOD. WASHINGTON. THE PRESIDENT OF THE UNITED STATES.
EVEN YOUR OWN FAMILY?
YOU PUT **EVERYTHING** AT RISK, CONSTANTLY. AND ALL FOR YOUR OWN SELFISH REASONS. THIS HAS **NOTHING** TO DO WITH NATIONAL SECURITY, DOES IT?
I MAKE THE CHOICES PEOPLE LIKE YOU ARE TOO AFRAID TO MAKE! THE NECESSARY CHOICES!
I WILL PROTECT THE PEOPLE TO THE BEST OF MY ABILITY!
AND YOU HAVE NO IDEA OF THE COST OF THAT. AND YOU NEVER WILL.
...
I HOPE YOU'RE RIGHT.
GOOD-BYE, AMANDA.
YOU HAVE NO IDEA...
...
IF YOU HAVE A PROBLEM, TATSU. SPEAK.

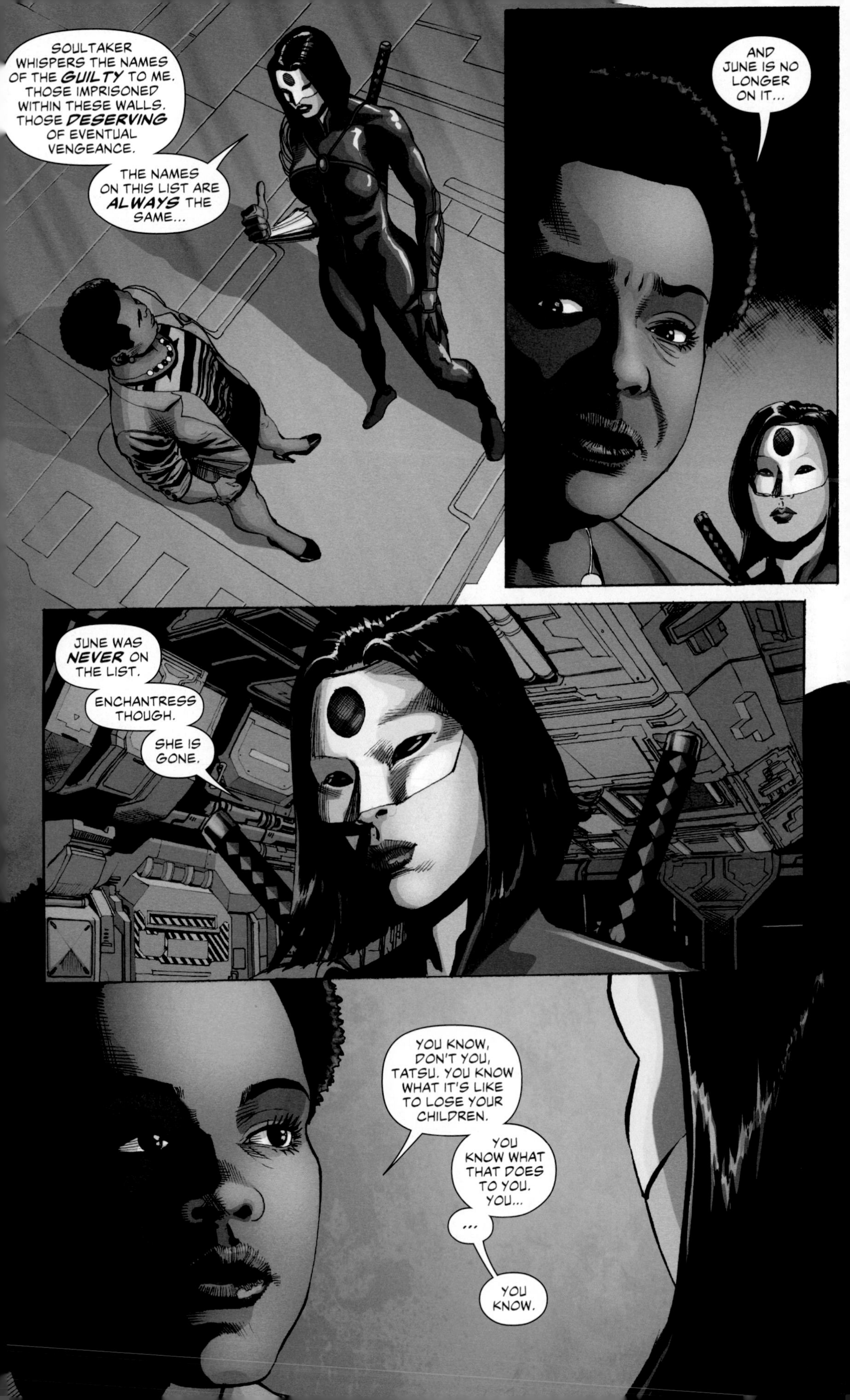
SOULTAKER WHISPERS THE NAMES OF THE GUILTY TO ME. THOSE IMPRISONED WITHIN THESE WALLS. THOSE DESERVING OF EVENTUAL VENGEANCE.
THE NAMES ON THIS LIST ARE ALWAYS THE SAME...
AND JUNE IS NO LONGER ON IT...
JUNE WAS NEVER ON THE LIST.
ENCHANTRESS THOUGH.
SHE IS GONE.
YOU KNOW, DON'T YOU, TATSU. YOU KNOW WHAT IT'S LIKE TO LOSE YOUR CHILDREN.
YOU KNOW WHAT THAT DOES TO YOU. YOU...
...
YOU KNOW.

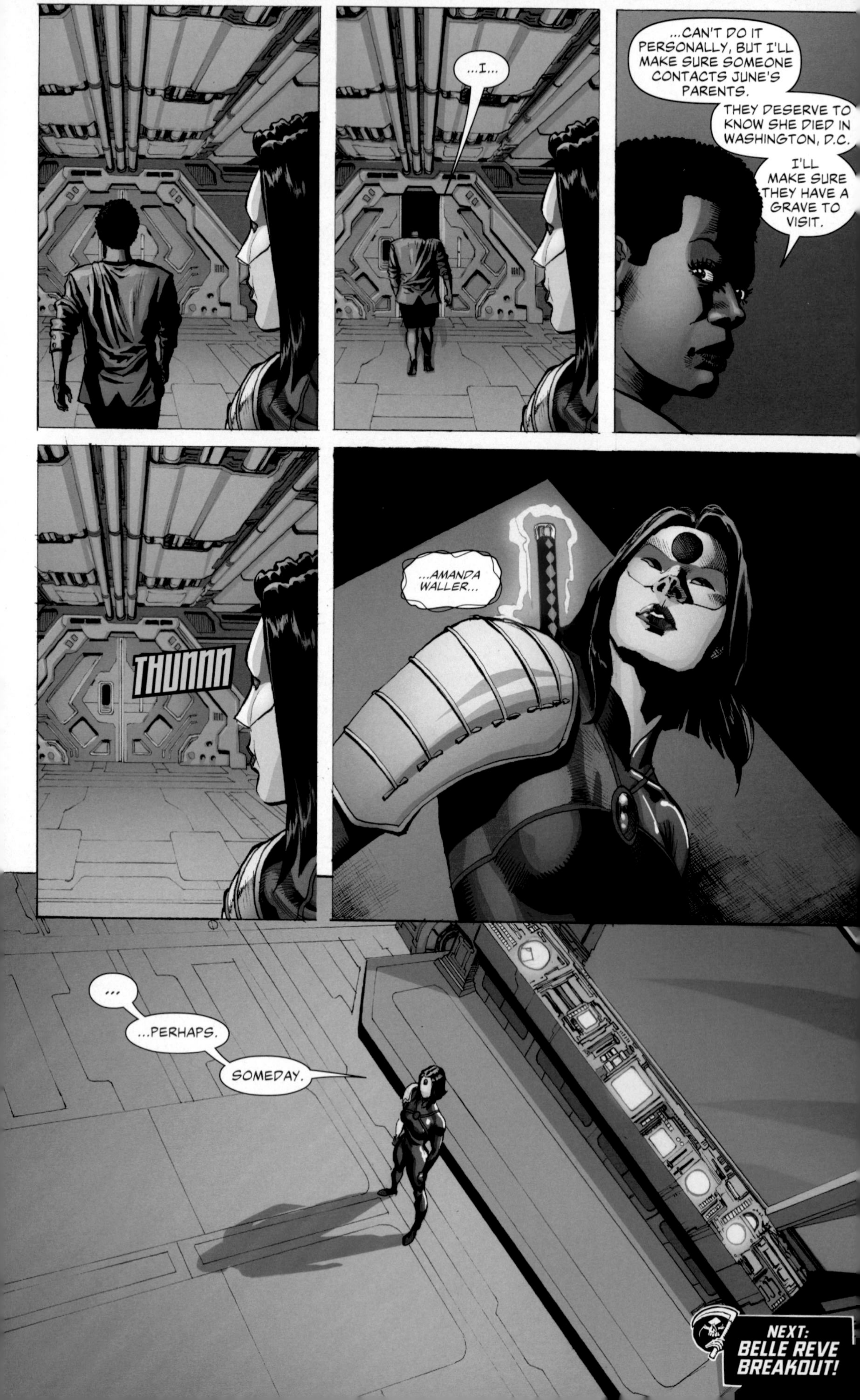
...I...
...CAN'T DO IT PERSONALLY, BUT I'LL MAKE SURE SOMEONE CONTACTS JUNE'S PARENTS.
THEY DESERVE TO KNOW SHE DIED IN WASHINGTON, D.C.
I'LL MAKE SURE THEY HAVE A GRAVE TO VISIT.
THUNNN
...AMANDA WALLER...
...
...PERHAPS.
SOMEDAY.
NEXT: BELLE REVE BREAKOUT!

Variant cover art for SUICIDE SQUAD #33
by WHILCE PORTACIO and ALEX SINCLAIR

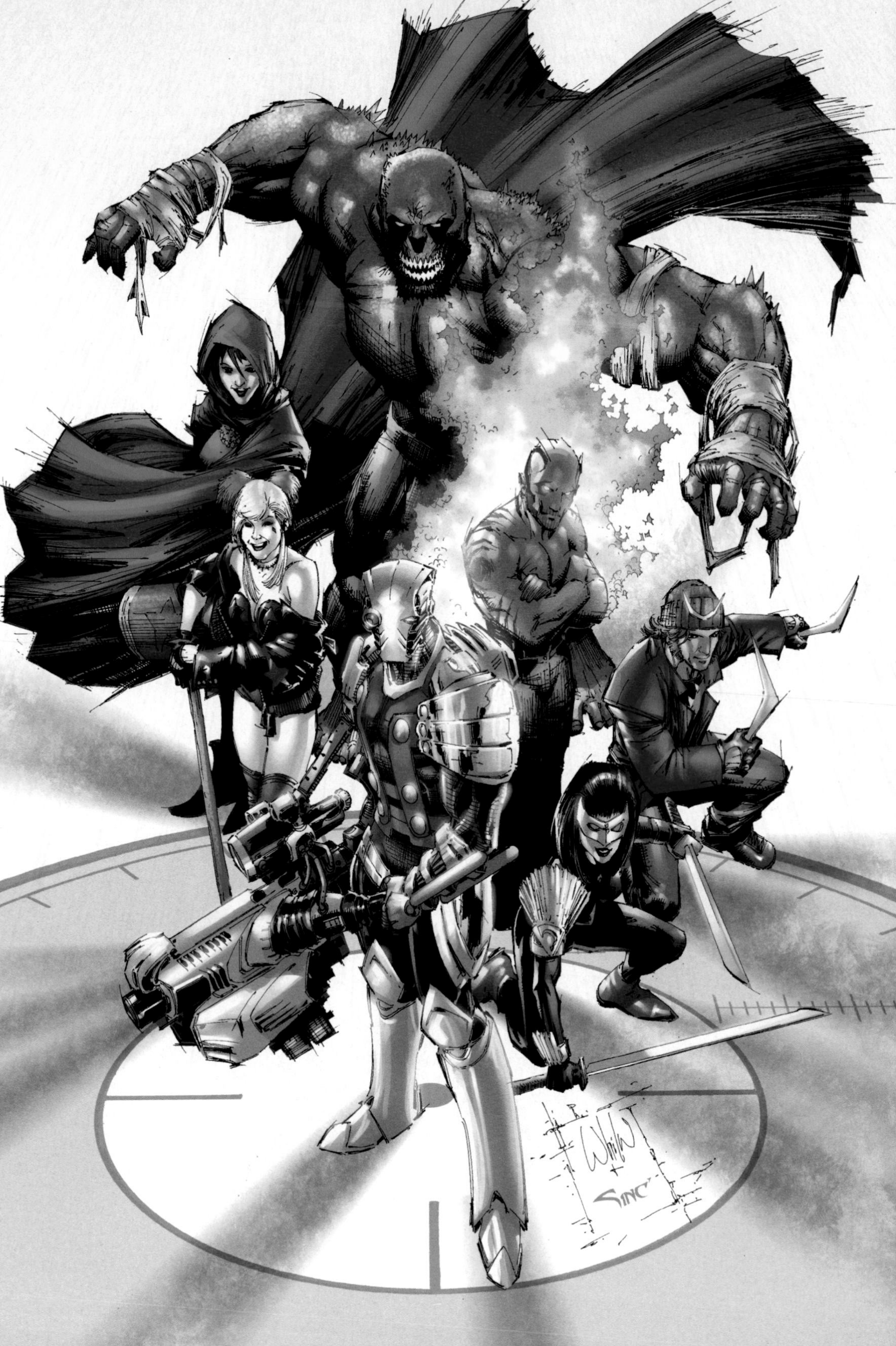

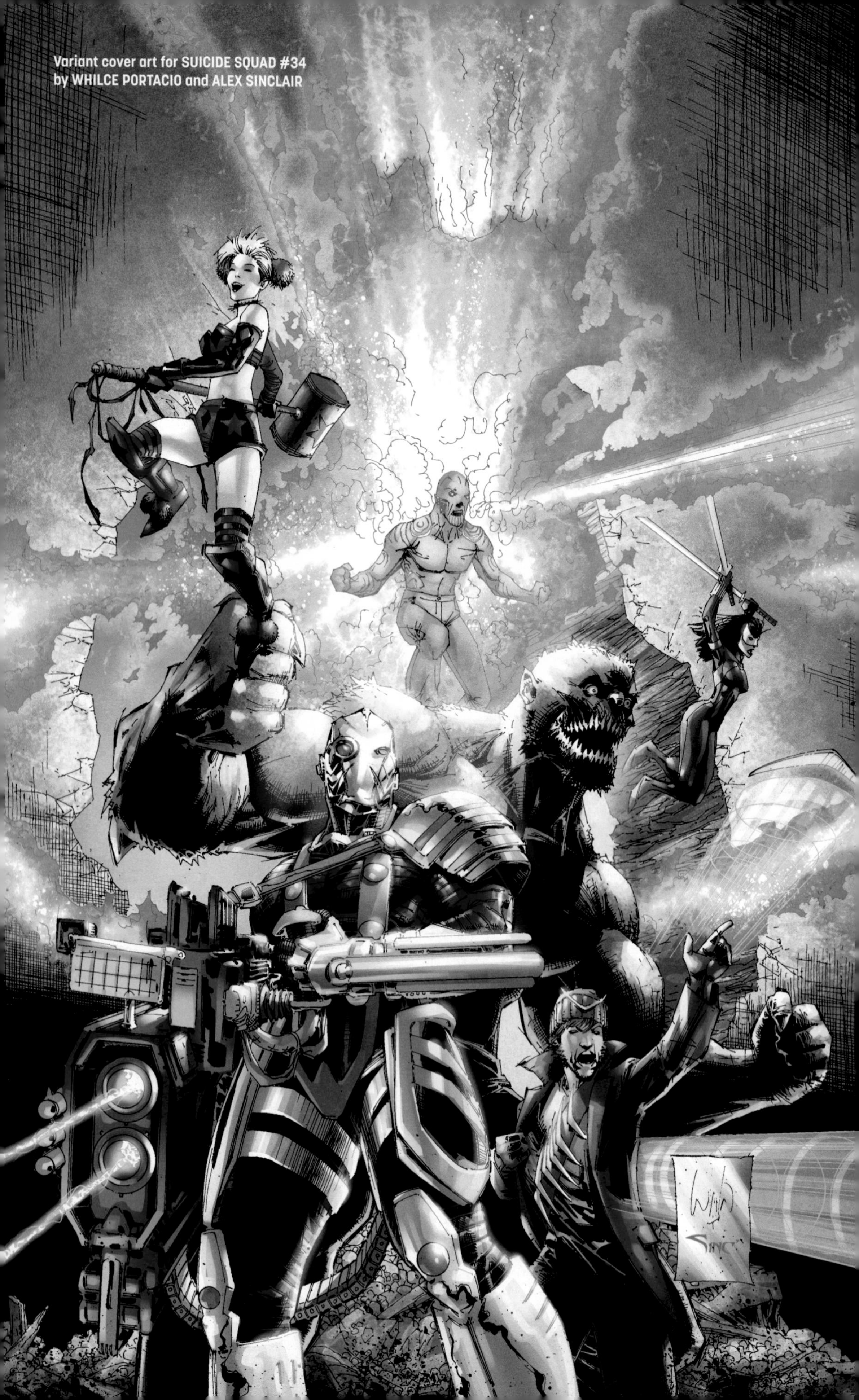

Variant cover art for SUICIDE SQUAD #34
by WHILCE PORTACIO and ALEX SINCLAIR

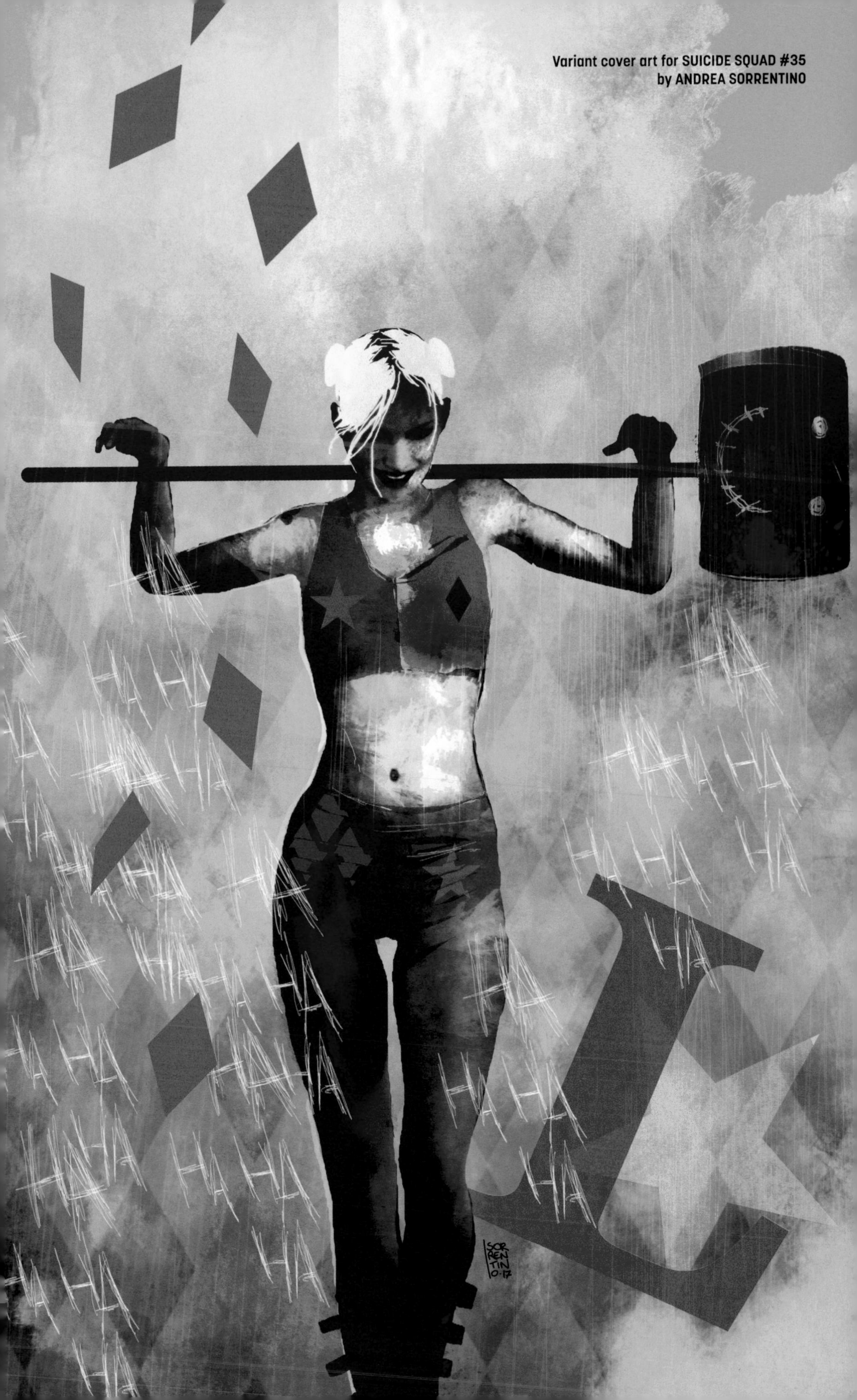

Variant cover art for SUICIDE SQUAD #35
by ANDREA SORRENTINO

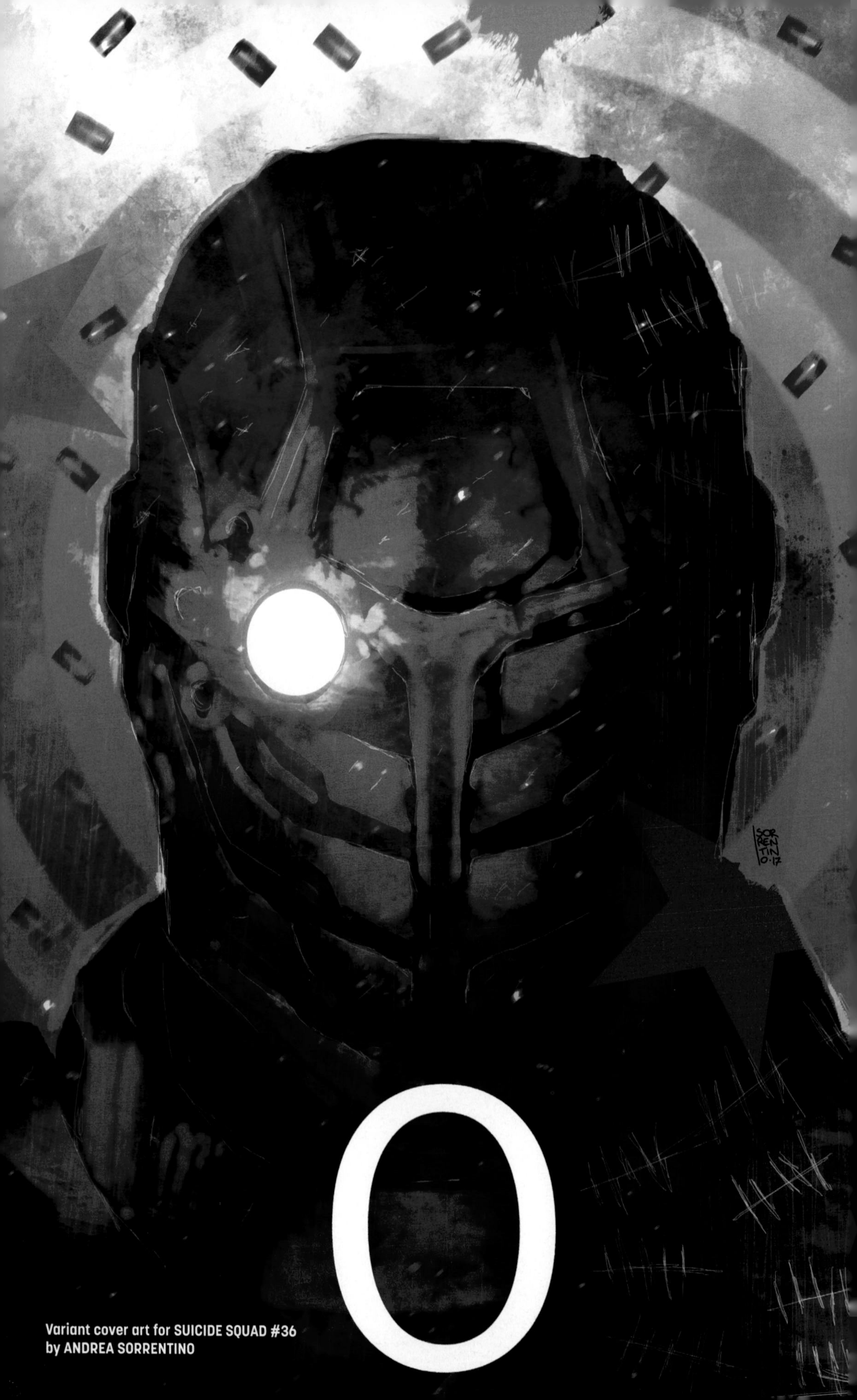
0

Variant cover art for SUICIDE SQUAD #36
by ANDREA SORRENTINO

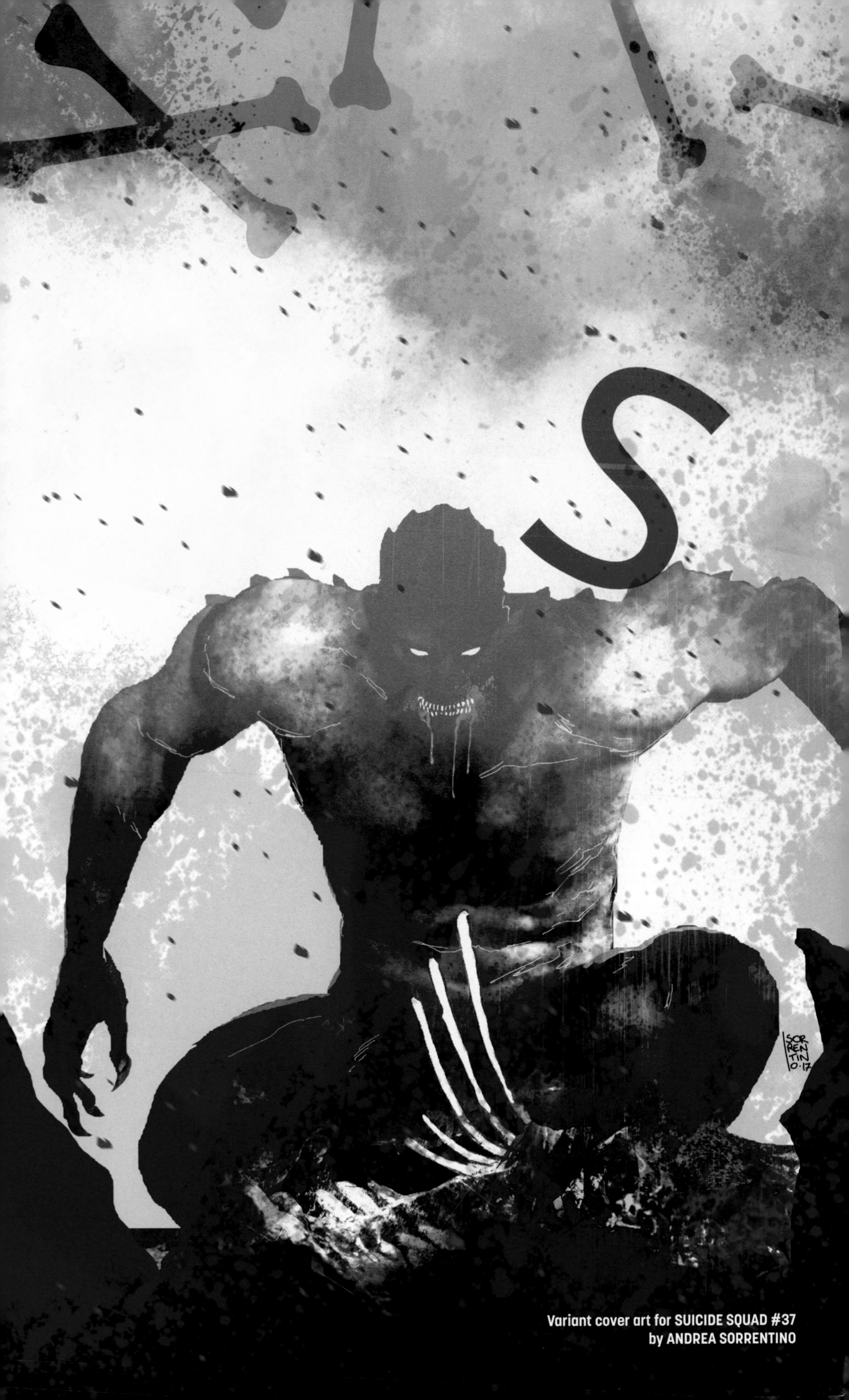
S

Variant cover art for SUICIDE SQUAD #37
by ANDREA SORRENTINO

Variant cover art for SUICIDE SQUAD #38
by ANDREA SORRENTINO

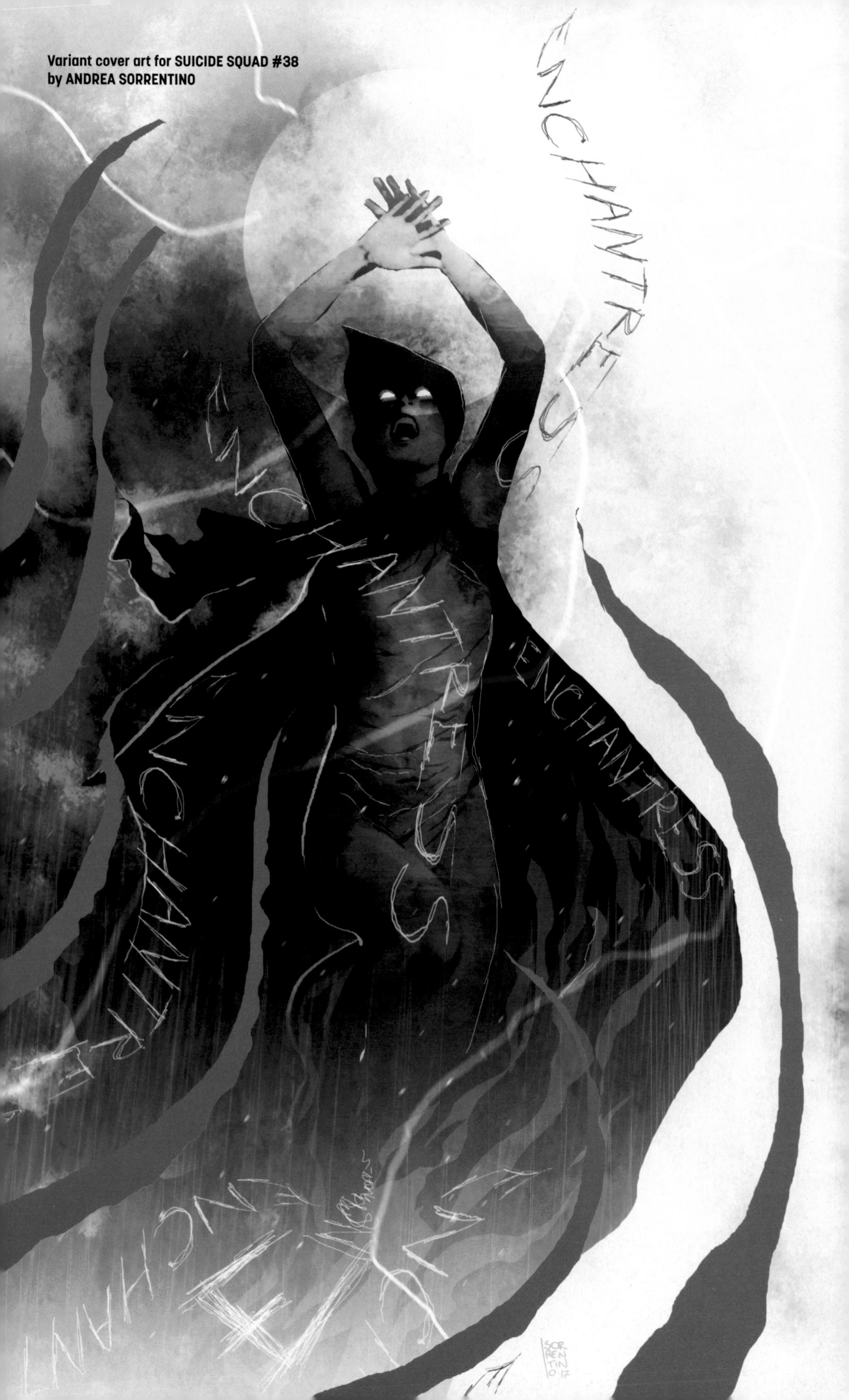
ENCHANTRESS
ENCHANTRESS
SORRENTINO 017

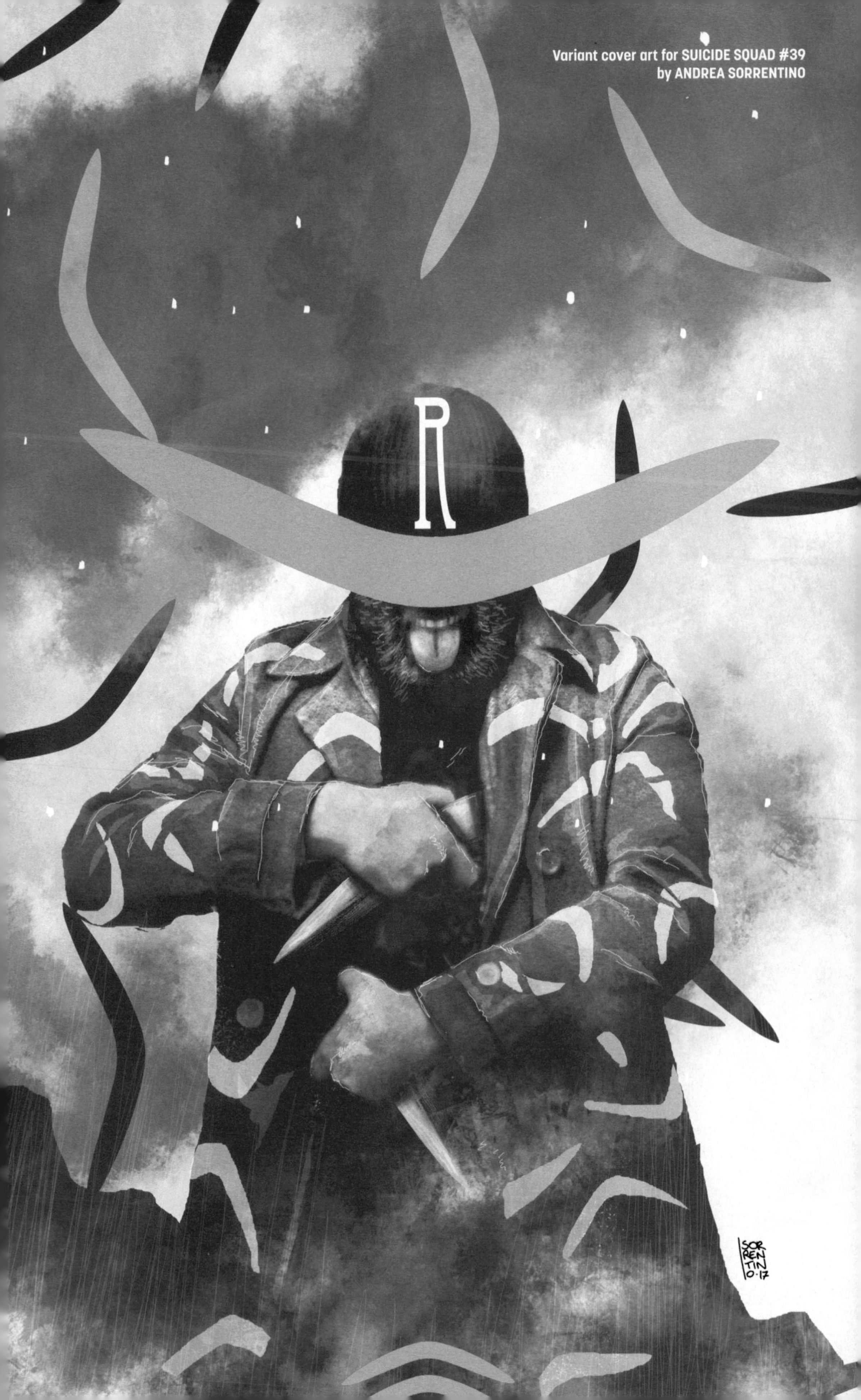
SOR
REN
TIN
O·17

Variant cover art for SUICIDE SQUAD #39
by ANDREA SORRENTINO

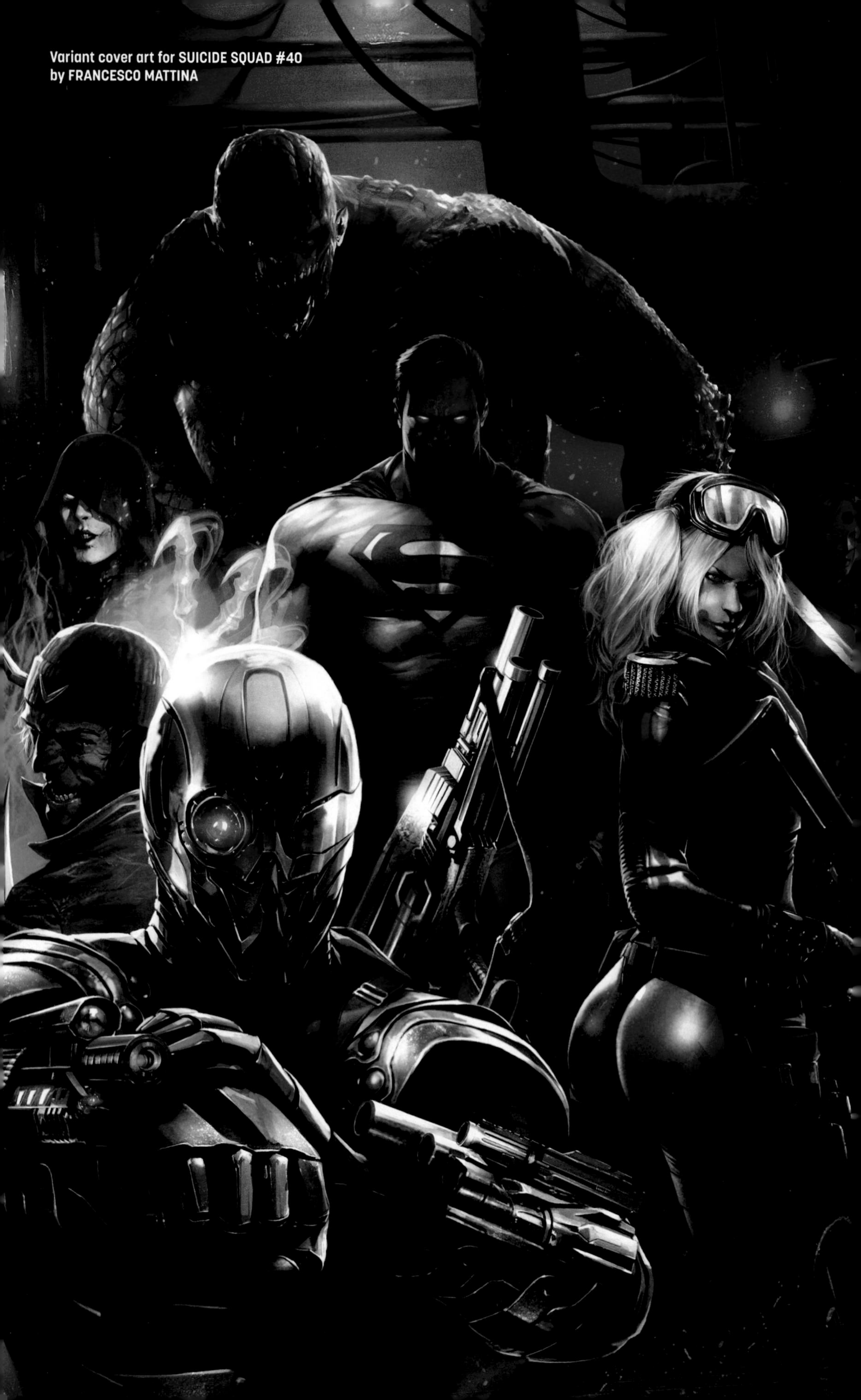

Variant cover art for SUICIDE SQUAD #40
by FRANCESCO MATTINA

THE WALL character design by JORGE JIMENEZ

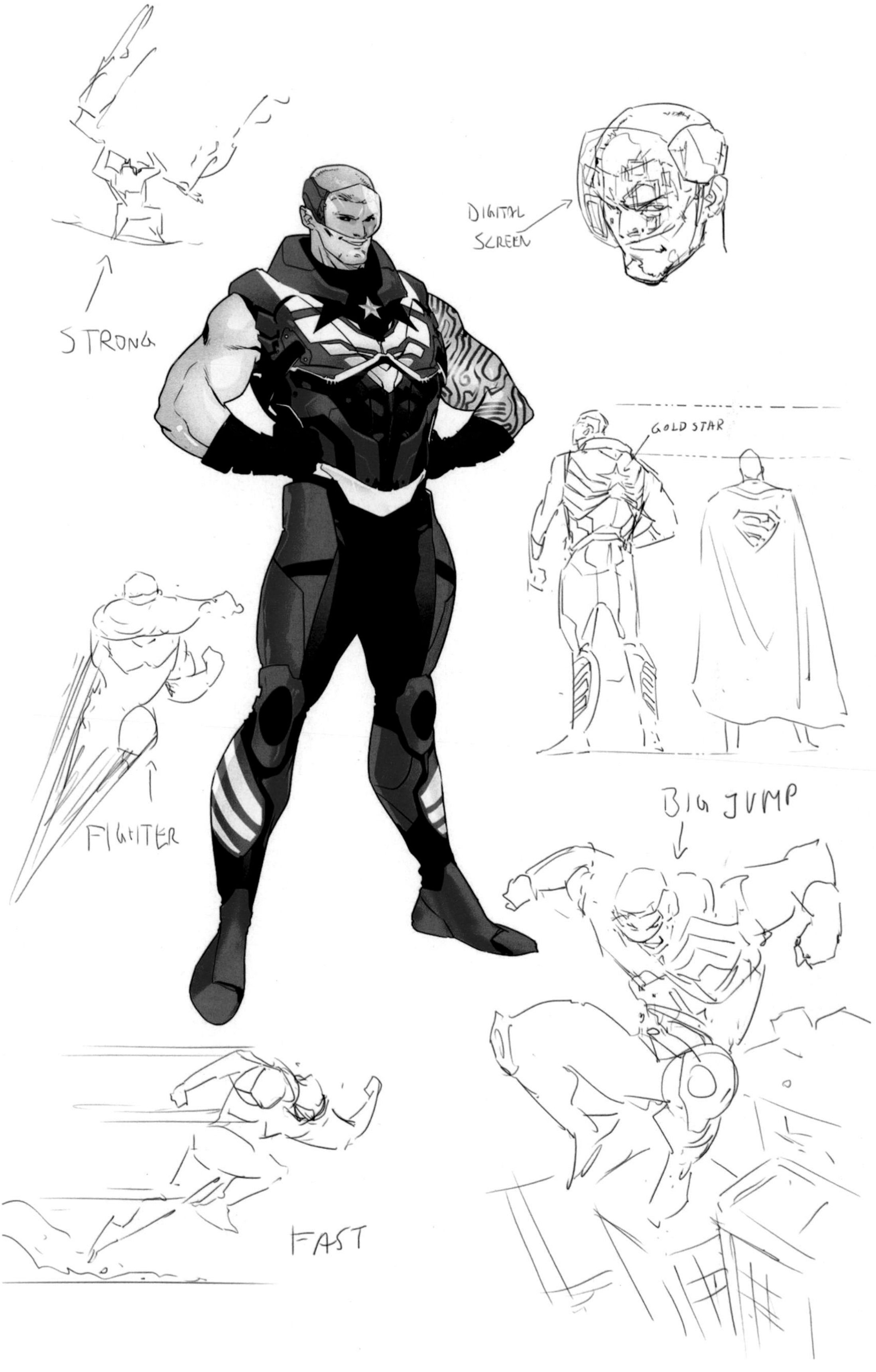
STRONG
DIGITAL SCREEN
GOLD STAR
FIGHTER
BIG JUMP
FAST

SUICIDE SQUAD #35 layouts by EDUARDO PANSICA

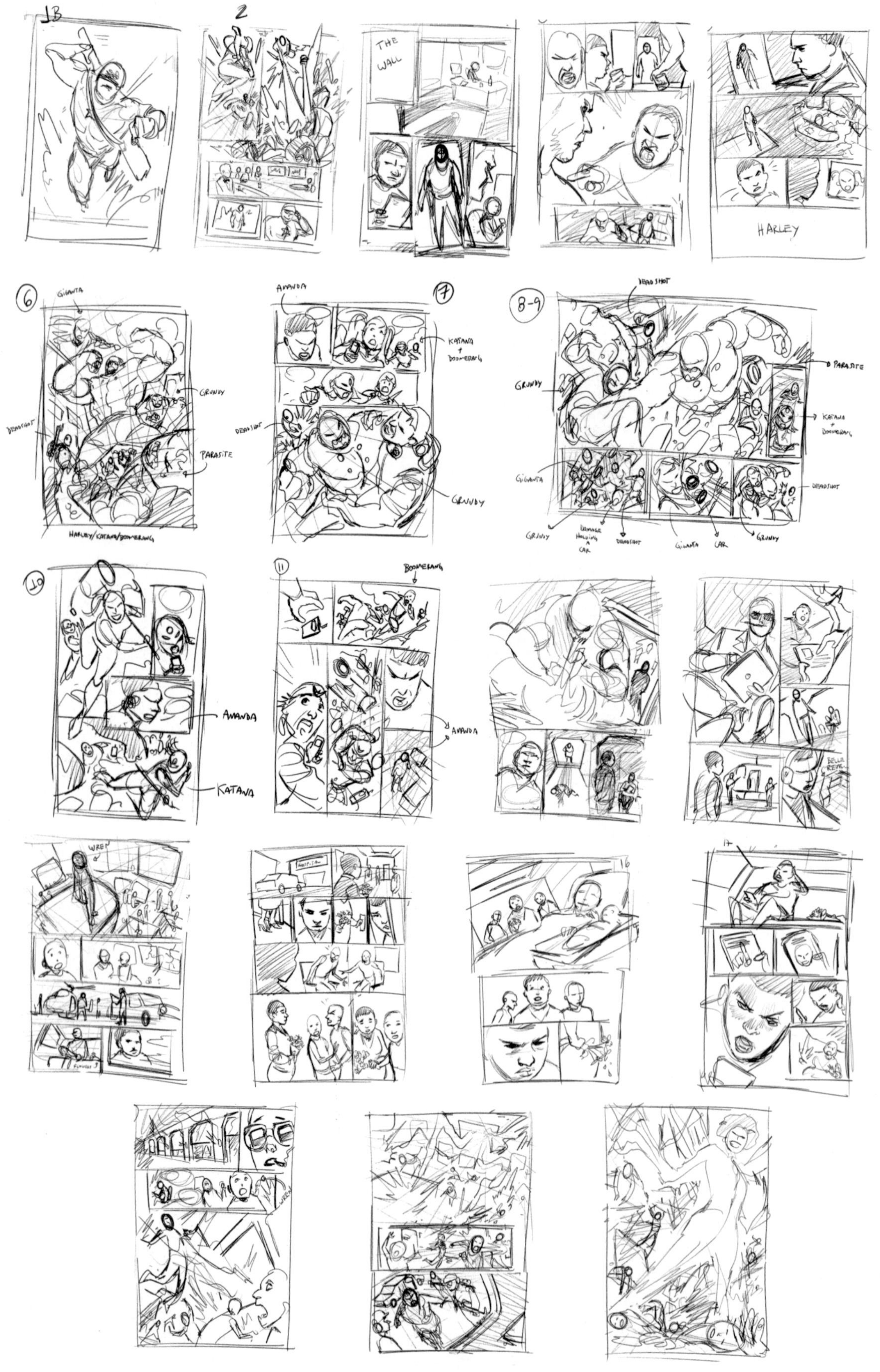
THE WALL
HARLEY
GIGANTA
GRUNDY
DEADSHOT
PARASITE
HARLEY/KATANA/BOOMERANG
AMANDA
KATANA + BOOMERANG
DEADSHOT
GRUNDY
PARASITE
KATANA + BOOMERANG
GIGANTA
DEADSHOT
GRUNDY
DAMAGE HOLDING A CAR
DEADSHOT
GIGANTA
CAR
GRUNDY
AMANDA
KATANA
BOOMERANG
AMANDA
WREN

SUICIDE SQUAD #36 layouts by EDUARDO PANSICA

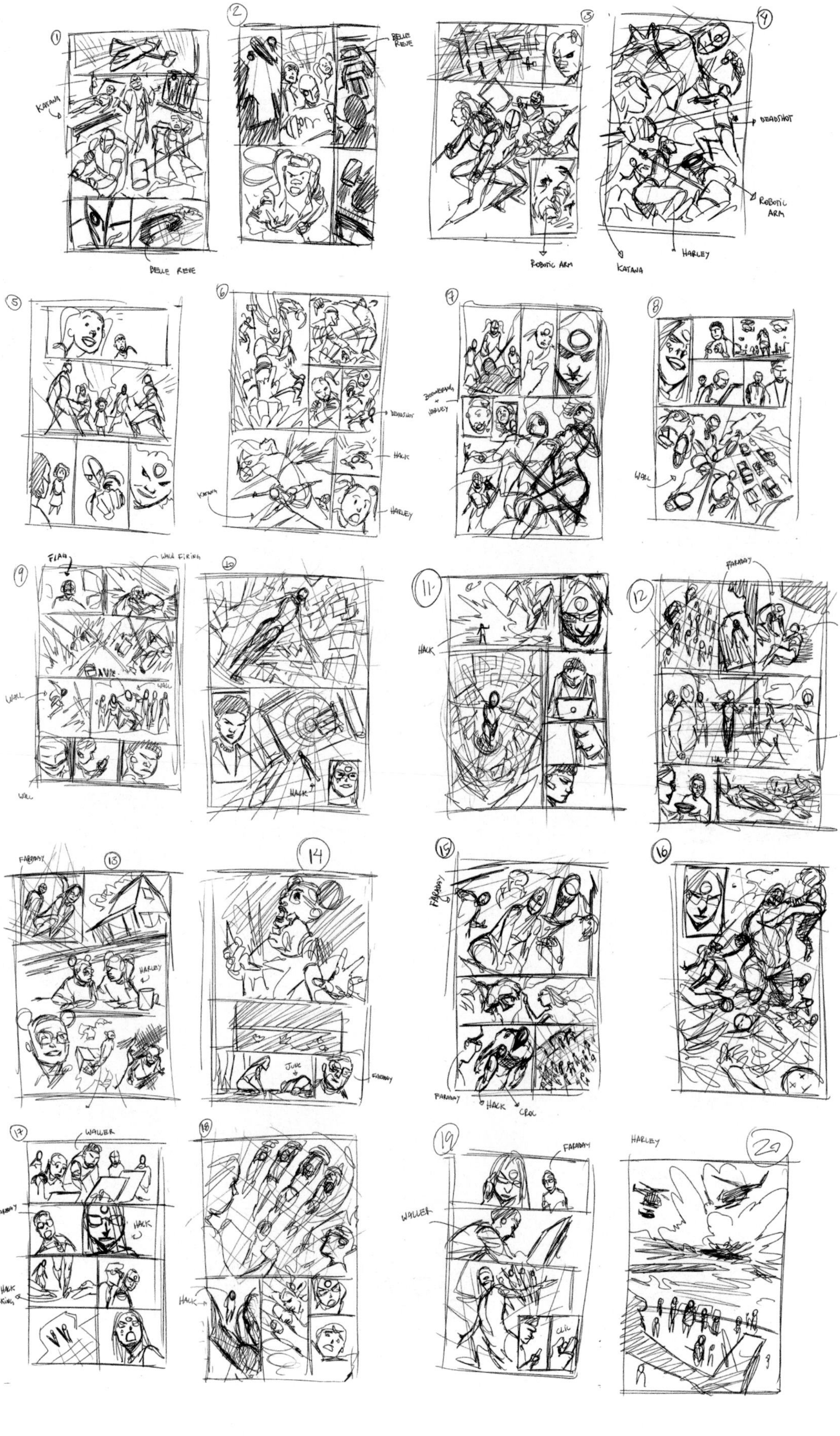
1
KATANA
BELLE REVE
2
BELLE REVE
3
ROBOTIC ARM
4
DEADSHOT
ROBOTIC ARM
KATANA
HARLEY
5
6
DEADSHOT
HACK
KATANA
HARLEY
7
BOOMERANG + HARLEY
8
WALL
9
FLAG
WALL FIRING
WALL
WALL
WALL
10
HACK
11
HACK
12
FARADAY
MOONE
FARADAY
HACK
13
FARADAY
HARLEY
14
JUNE
FARADAY
15
FARADAY
FARADAY
HACK
CROC
16
17
WALLER
FARADAY
HACK
HACK WALKING
18
HACK
19
FARADAY
WALLER
CLIC
HARLEY
20

SUICIDE SQUAD #36 cover sketch by David Yardin

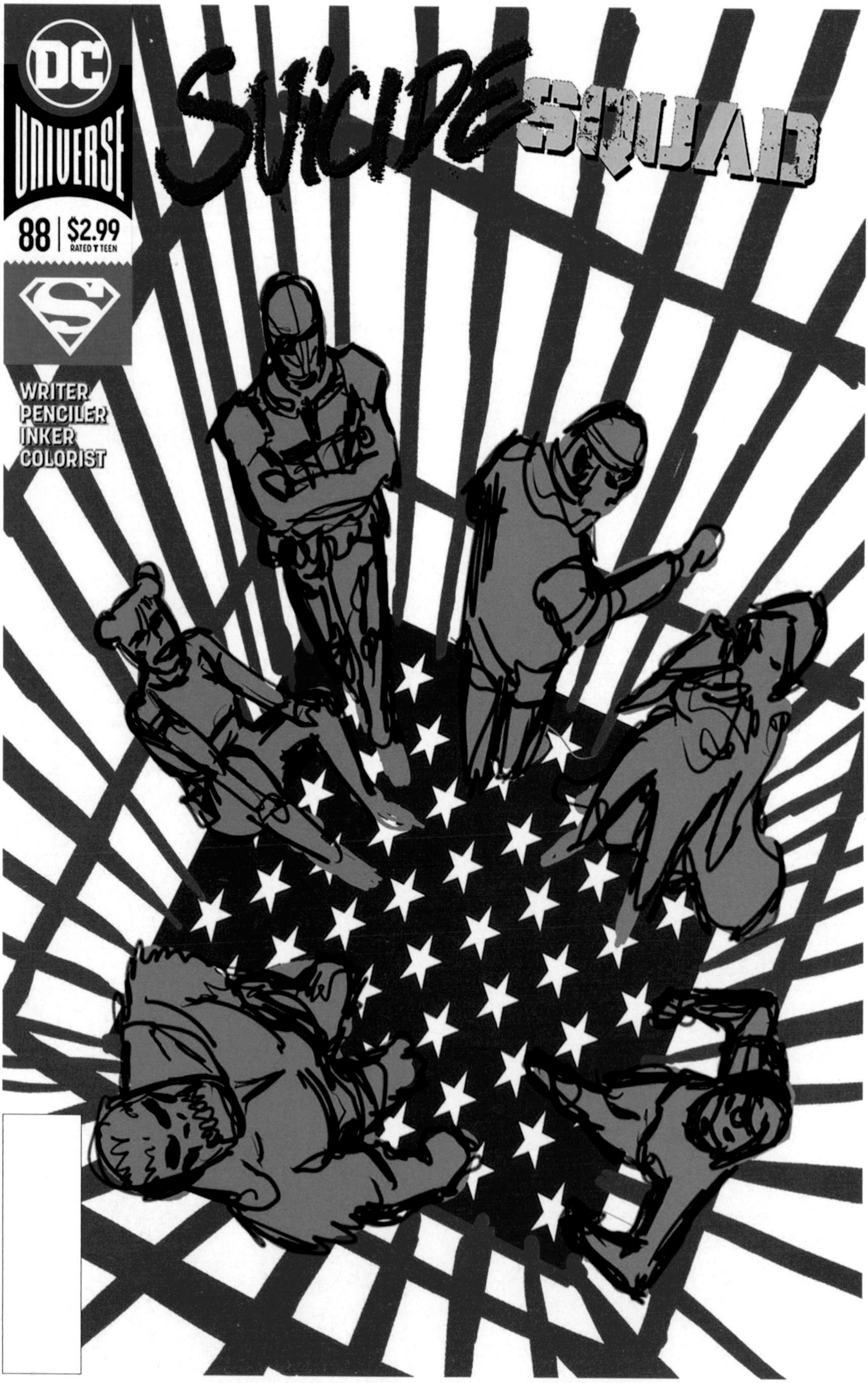
DC
UNIVERSE
88 | $2.99
RATED T TEEN
SUICIDE SQUAD
WRITER
PENCILER
INKER
COLORIST